Dawn on the crest of the
Warner Mountains

HIKING NORTHERN CALIFORNIA

A GUIDE TO THE REGION'S GREATEST HIKING ADVENTURES

REVISED EDITION

Bubba Suess

FALCONGUIDES

GUILFORD, CONNECTICUT

For my brother, Matthew Suess.
He has always been my hero and has been my role model for a life of honor, integrity,
and wisdom. His spirit of adventure and love of the outdoors inspired my own.

FALCONGUIDES®

An imprint of Globe Pequot

Falcon and FalconGuides are registered trademarks and Make Adventure Your Story is a trademark of Rowman & Littlefield.

Distributed by NATIONAL BOOK NETWORK

Copyright © 2017 by Rowman & Littlefield

TOPO! Maps copyright © 2017 National Geographic Partners, LLC. All Rights Reserved.

Photos by Bubba Suess

Copyright © 2017 National Geographic Partners, LLC. All Rights Reserved.

British Library Cataloguing in Publication Information Available

Library of Congress Cataloging-in-Publication Data

ISBN 978-1-4930-0271-9 (paperback)

ISBN 978-1-4930-3145-0 (e-book)

Printed in the United States of America

∞™ The paper used in this publication meets the minimum requirements of American National Standard for Information Sciences—Permanence of Paper for Printed Library Materials, ANSI/ NISO Z39.48-1992.

The author and Rowman & Littlefield assume no liability for accidents happening to, or injuries sustained by, readers who engage in the activities described in this book.

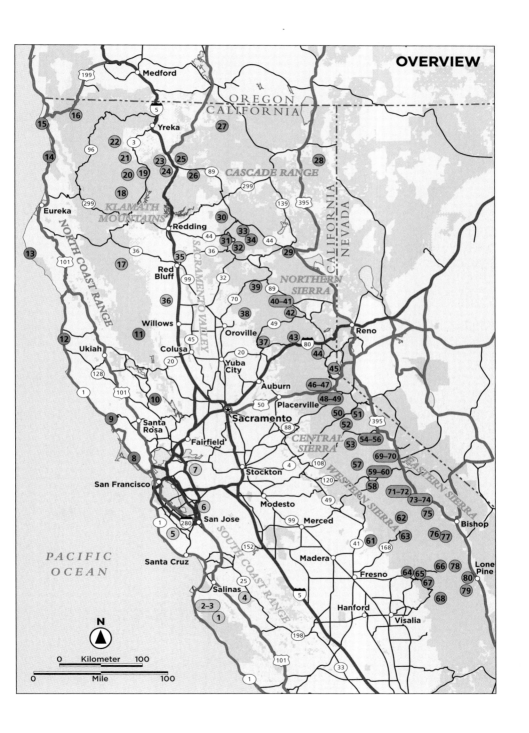

OVERVIEW

A hiker contemplates the majesty of Mount Ritter and Banner Peak.

CONTENTS

Cascades

Sacramento Valley

Northern Sierra

Central Sierra

MEET YOUR GUIDE

A native of Sonoma County in California's wine country, Christopher "Bubba" Suess grew up hiking the trails on his home turf as well as those in the famed Sierra Nevada. His first backpacking trip at age 5 sparked a love affair with granite and rushing water. Deeply influenced by his parents to appreciate the outdoors and by his older brother to always strive and persevere, Bubba was further moved to value the conservation of wilderness during his time in the Boy Scouts. A four-year sojourn in Texas for graduate school forced Bubba to find beauty in more subtle places and areas that are generally overlooked. Now a resident of Mount Shasta in far northern California, he loves living a rural life, centered on time spent with his wife, Harmony, and three children.

ACKNOWLEDGMENTS

Writing this book was an enormous undertaking, and it would not have been possible without the contributions from several people. First and most important is my wife, Harmony. Without her encouragement, patience, hard work, and love, the book would not have even been a possibility. She made this endeavor a reality, and she forever has my love and gratitude.

Not enough thanks can be given to my parents, Ron and Jane Suess. Their logistical support in taking care of my children while I was on the trail, as well as while I was sequestered working on the manuscript, was instrumental in bringing this project to completion. Their sacrificial contribution cannot be overstated. I owe them far more than I can ever repay, for this and a great many other things. It is my hope that I have been a good son, worthy of what they have given.

My mother-in-law, Gretchen McPherson, also lovingly spent time with my children. Her time invested with them is greatly appreciated.

Several people joined me on the trail during the journey through the wilds of Northern California. My wife, Harmony, and our three children, Carson, Laramie, and Jed, were most welcome companions on several hikes, including our family favorites Heart Lake and South Gate Meadow. In pursuit of this book, Carson, at the age of 6, also joined my wife and me for his first trip on the Panorama Trail.

My father, Ron, a lifelong Yosemite devotee, got his first taste of Sequoia National Park while joining me on the hike through Tokopah Valley.

My brother, Matt, spent a great weekend with me in the Eastern Sierra, where we tackled the epic hike to Thousand Island and Garnet Lakes. For a chaser we headed up to the Gaylor Lakes the next morning. That weekend was the highlight of the summer.

Two of his children, Nathan and Rachel, joined me for hikes in Big Sur. Old Uncle Bubba can learn a thing or two about speed from them!

Magnificent Lake Aloha is one of the most spectacular destinations in the Northern Sierra.

My brother-in-law, Peter McPherson, spent three days with me in Sequoia and Kings Canyon. I don't get to spend enough time with him, and it was an excellent weekend.

My cousin, Mark Gattey, hit the trail with me on the James Irvine Trail and the rainy hike to the Devil's Punchbowl. His enthusiasm and energy are infectious. His sons, Sebastian, Matthias, and Andreas, were also welcome company.

Last, but not least, my nephew, Barry Lawlor, put up with me on the hot hike around the summit of Mount Diablo. He was great company and very patient with his old uncle.

I was also graciously welcomed into a few homes while on the road. My brother and his wife, Dana, my aunt, Karry Brillsour, my wife's aunt and uncle, Dave and Nancy Tomlinson, and longtime friends John and Betty Phillips were all gracious enough to let me stay with them. It was a great respite to a weary traveler.

I would also like to express my immense gratitude to Katie Benoit Cardoso of Falcon Guides for entrusting this project to me.

Lastly, I would like to acknowledge Ron Adkison and his family. Anything I have accomplished with this book is only building on Ron's excellence and vision.

Map and Icon Legends

ICON LEGEND

 BEST PHOTOS

 FAMILY FRIENDLY

 WATER FEATURES

 DOG FRIENDLY

 FINDING SOLITUDE

NOTES ON MAPS

Topographic maps are an essential companion to the activities in this guide. Falcon has partnered with National Geographic to provide the best mapping resources. Each activity is accompanied by a detailed map and the name of the National Geographic TOPO! map (USGS), which can be downloaded for free from natgeomaps.com.

If the activity takes place on an area covered on a National Geographic Trails Illustrated map, it will be noted. Continually setting the standard for accuracy, each Trails Illustrated topographic map is crafted in conjunction with local land managers and undergoes rigorous review and enhancement before being printed on waterproof, tear-resistant material. Trails Illustrated maps and information about their digital versions, which can be used on mobile GPS applications, can be found at natgeomaps.com.

MAP LEGEND

Symbol	Description	Symbol	Description
⑤	Interstate Highway		Marsh/Swamp
50	US Highway		National/State Park
①	State Road	Ⓟ	Parking
21	County/Forest/Local Road	≻	Pass/Gap
– – – –	Unpaved Road	▲	Peak
⊢——⊣	Railroad	⊼	Picnic Area
▪▪▪▪▪▪	Featured Route on Trail	□	Point of Interest
▬▬▬▬	Featured Route on Road	▲	Primitive Campsite
------	Trail		Restroom/Latrine
⌣	Bridge	⬅	Scenic View
	Boat Ramp		Spring
▲	Campground		Tower
∩	Cave	①	Trailhead
•–•	Gate	?	Visitor Center/Information
	Headquarters		Waterfall
	Inn/Lodging		

Wildflowers enhance the view of Red Lake Peak.

	BEST PHOTOS	FAMILY FRIENDLY	WATER FEATURES	DOG FRIENDLY	FINDING SOLITUDE
SOUTH COAST RANGE					
1. Ewoldsen Trail/McWay Falls	•	•	•		
2. Pfeiffer Falls		•	•		
3. Andrew Molera State Park	•				•
4. Pinnacles	•				
5. Big Basin	•		•		
6. Sunol Regional Wilderness		•	•	•	•
7. Mount Diablo Grand Loop	•				•
NORTH COAST RANGE					
8. Alamere Falls	•	•	•		
9. Sonoma Coast	•	•	•		•
10. Palisades (Napa Valley)	•				•
11. Snow Mountain				•	•
12. Russian Gulch			•		
13. Lost Coast		•	•	•	
14. James Irvine Trail/Fern Canyon	•		•		
15. Boy Scout Tree		•	•		
KLAMATH MOUNTAINS					
16. Devil's Punchbowl	•		•	•	•
17. North Yolla Bolly Mountains			•	•	•
18. Canyon Creek	•		•	•	
19. Bear Lakes	•		•	•	•
20. Gulch Lakes Loop			•	•	•
21. Taylor and Hogan Lakes		•	•	•	

	BEST PHOTOS	FAMILY FRIENDLY	WATER FEATURES	DOG FRIENDLY	FINDING SOLITUDE
KLAMATH MOUNTAINS–CONTINUED					
22. Shackleford Basin	•		•	•	•
23. Mount Eddy	•		•	•	
24. Heart Lake	•	•	•	•	
CASCADE RANGE					
25. South Gate Meadow	•	•	•		
26. McCloud River Falls	•	•	•	•	
27. Lava Beds		•			•
28. Pine Creek Basin/ Patterson Lake	•		•	•	•
29. Susan River		•	•	•	
30. Thousand Lakes Wilderness	•		•	•	•
31. Lassen Peak	•	•			
32. Warner Valley		•	•		
33. Butte Lake-Snag Lake Loop	•		•		•
34. Caribou Wilderness		•	•	•	
SACRAMENTO VALLEY					
35. Iron Canyon	•	•	•	•	•
36. Orland Buttes		•		•	•
NORTHERN SIERRA					
37. Independence Trail/Jones Hole Loop		•	•		
38. Feather Falls			•	•	
39. Bucks Lake Wilderness	•	•	•	•	•
40. Frazier Falls		•	•	•	
41. Lakes Basin	•		•		

	BEST PHOTOS	FAMILY FRIENDLY	WATER FEATURES	DOG FRIENDLY	FINDING SOLITUDE
NORTHERN SIERRA–CONTINUED					
42. Sierra Buttes	•			•	
43. Glacier Lake	•		•	•	•
44. Five Lakes Basin			•	•	
45. Rubicon Trail		•	•		
46. Twin Lakes (Desolation Wilderness)	•	•	•	•	
47. Desolation Valley	•		•	•	
CENTRAL SIERRA					
48. Meiss Meadow/Showers Lake	•		•	•	•
49. Round Top Loop	•		•	•	
50. Wheeler Lake		•	•	•	•
51. Noble Lake	•		•	•	•
52. Sword Lake			•	•	•
53. Burst Rock and Lake Valley	•		•	•	
54. Blue Canyon	•		•	•	•
55. Sardine Falls		•	•	•	
56. Leavitt Meadow Loop	•		•	•	•
WESTERN SIERRA					
57. Hetch Hetchy	•	•	•		
58. Panorama Trail	•		•		
59. Tuolumne River to Glen Aulin	•		•		
60. Gaylor Lakes	•		•		•
61. San Joaquin River Gorge			•	•	•
62. Twin Lakes (Kaiser Wilderness)	•	•	•	•	•

	BEST PHOTOS	FAMILY FRIENDLY	WATER FEATURES	DOG FRIENDLY	FINDING SOLITUDE
WESTERN SIERRA–CONTINUED					
63. Dinkey Lakes	•		•	•	
64. Redwood Mountain Loop					•
65. Weaver Lake		•	•	•	
66. Mist Falls	•		•		
67. Tokopah Valley	•	•	•		
68. White Chief Basin	•				•
EASTERN SIERRA					
69. Green Creek Basin	•		•	•	•
70. Lundy Canyon	•	•	•	•	
71. Devils Postpile/ Rainbow Falls		•	•	•	
72. Thousand Island Lake	•		•	•	
73. Duck Lake Pass	•		•	•	
74. Convict Canyon	•		•	•	•
75. Little Lakes Valley	•	•	•	•	
76. Sabrina Basin	•		•	•	•
77. Cloudripper Loop	•		•	•	•
78. Kearsarge Pass	•		•	•	
79. Cottonwood Lakes	•		•	•	
80. Alabama Hills	•	•		•	•

McWay Creek runs through a redwood-lined canyon.

BEFORE YOU HIT THE TRAIL

California! For more than 150 years, it has been one of the most evocative names in all of America. For many generations, California has symbolized prosperity, opportunity, freedom, and exceptional natural beauty. While most of these attributes pertained to the economic abundance produced by the state, it also promises amazing abundance for hikers. California as a whole, and in particular the northern two-thirds of the state, features some of the most spectacular, iconic, and unforgettable landscapes to be found anywhere in the world. For people looking to hit the trail, Northern California is likely to end up being paradise. Whether you long to hike remote, rugged coastlines, massive volcanoes, towering redwoods, thundering waterfalls, glacier-clad mountains, or along surging rivers, Northern California offers all of these sights and more. Indeed, for lovers of the natural world, all roads eventually lead to Northern California.

In no other place in the world can you find as much diversity in the land as you can in Northern California. This is not simply because the area is so vast, but because there is an unusual degree of geologic complexity coupled with a unique position on the continent that ensures temperate weather and ideal growing conditions. Consider for a moment the extremes that exist within California. Mount Whitney, the highest point in the lower forty-eight states, is less than 100 miles away from Furnace Creek in Death Valley, the lowest point in North America.

The Sierra Nevada, the monumental spine of the state, is among the longest single mountain ranges in the country. In this mountain range, you find Yosemite Falls, the tallest waterfall in North America; Lake Tahoe, the largest alpine lake in North America; and giant sequoias, the most massive living things on the planet. On the east side of the Sierra is the Owens Valley, the deepest valley on the continent. On the valley's east side are the White Mountains, which contain the bristlecone pines, the oldest living thing on Earth.

The coastline of Northern California is the most rugged in the coterminous states, and just inland rise the coast redwoods, the tallest trees in the world. A little farther inland from the coast are the Klamath Mountains, which have some of the greatest biodiversity in the world, including forests with more conifers than any other place on the planet. Even farther inland you find prominent, glacier-clad Mount Shasta, the second-highest peak in the long Cascade Range and the largest mountain by volume in the contiguous states. Nearby is Lassen Peak, one of only two volcanoes in the lower forty-eight states to erupt in the twentieth century and still surrounded by active geothermal features. Lying in the middle of all these superlatives is the great Central Valley, watered by a host of mountain rivers, the most agriculturally productive region in the world.

All these superb attributes may perhaps begin to give an idea of the grandeur of Northern California's natural world, but they do not even begin to scratch the surface of stunning destinations that await hikers. Despite being the most populous state in the

Union, California also has one of the highest concentrations of federally protected wilderness in the country. Moreover, most of Northern California actually has a very low population density, since most of the people are gathered around the San Francisco Bay Area, Sacramento, and the Central Valley. Outside these large urban areas, Northern California is very rural, with much of it quite isolated and remote.

Hikers looking to explore the beautiful natural landscapes of the state or escape the trappings of daily life cannot do better than to hit the trail in Northern California. Spectacular vistas and lifetime experiences await.

ABOUT THE BOOK

This book is not intended to be an exhaustive account of all the hiking opportunities in Northern California. With a land as vast and packed with as much awesome scenery as California is, it is nearly impossible to even approach anything like a comprehensive collection of all the state's best hikes. To attempt to bring them all together in one volume would not do them justice in terms of narrative, descriptions, accuracy, and quality images.

What this book attempts to do is select a collection of trails from each region of Northern California and give a sampling of some of the best trails in each area. It is meant to be a primer, a jumping-off point, to direct you toward trails that distill each part of the state to its best attributes. Its intent is to expose you to the beauty of each area and entice you to explore further. The desire is to instill a passion for this blessed land and a thirst to see more of it.

The Lathe Arch in the Alabama Hills frames Mount Whitney and the peerless Sierra Nevada.

The trail selection process was not limited to the best scenery. With so many options, even picking the best would still leave too many. In order to narrow it down further, and also to increase the value of the guide to its users, a number of other criteria were employed. Each of the nine regions of Northern California needed to be well represented. As much as possible, the hikes needed to travel wild, undeveloped land. Each trail needed to be accessible to all kinds of vehicles, not just high-clearance vehicles. There needed to be a sampling from a variety of difficulty levels, or trails needed to have multiple worthy destinations with differing degrees of challenge so that hikers can choose how hard and how far they want to go. Whenever possible, shuttle trips were avoided to make hikes more feasible logistically. Also, since this is a hiking guide, not a backpacking guide, each hike needed to be able to be completed in a single day. Though there are a few long trails listed here, they were hiked as reasonable, though challenging, day hikes. In spite of this, a large number of the trails in the guide make great backpacking trips, and a certain amount of flexibility on that account was built into the selection of trails. Of course there is an exception or two to some of these attributes, but for the most part, the intent is to make the most recommendations useful to as many people as possible.

GEOGRAPHY

The landscape of Northern California is, in fact, a smaller part of larger geographic provinces. The mountains in the state are part of the American Cordillera, which is a long band of mountains that stretch from Alaska down the length of North America and down the entire western side of South America. Northern California is a critical segment in this massive chain of mountains and is located at the meeting place of numerous geographic regions.

To the north, in what is generally referred to as the Pacific Northwest, the dominant mountain areas are the Coast Ranges and the Cascade Range. While the former is famous for its rugged coastline, the latter is well known for its towering volcanoes and enormous glaciers. Both mountain ranges extend southward into Northern California. While the coastal mountain ranges cover the length of the entire state, they are breached near the center of the state by the great Sacramento–San Joaquin River network. Though not unheard of, it is unusual for a mountain range to be bisected by a sea-level pass. The Cascades, on the other hand, do not push too deep into California. From the Oregon state line, they only penetrate about 130 miles into the state. They occupy the northeastern-most corner of California, which happens to be one of the least-populated regions. Consequently, the Cascades in California do not often enter the public imagination.

At the southern end of the Cascades, the geology of the mountains abruptly changes. Rather than the volcanism that defines the Cascade Range, these new mountains, the mighty Sierra Nevada, are composed of plutons of hard, dense granite. In some areas significant bands of sedimentary, metavolcanic or ultramafic rock are interspersed between the plutons, but it is the granite that defines these mountains. The Sierra extends 400 miles to the south, an unbroken line of tall, rugged mountains. The longest, tallest, and largest mountain region in California, the range is the state's dominant and most important

At 14,179 feet, massive Mount Shasta is among the tallest mountains in the United States.

physical feature. Without the Sierra, the rest of the state would be much thirstier than it already is, and would likely not have nearly as many people living in it. Without the water that these mountains provide, there would not be the ability to meet the demand for water made by the state's cities and vast agricultural industry.

Most of the state's water needs lie west of the Sierra Nevada, on the coast around San Francisco Bay and in the interior of the state, in the giant basin of the Central Valley. The majority of California's major rivers flow out of the mountains into the great bowl of the valley. Those rivers north of San Francisco Bay are collected into the Sacramento River, while those south of the bay all join the San Joaquin. The two rivers meet just as they reach the edge of the bay. This huge but compact hydrologic system is the lifeblood of California, sustaining its unequalled agricultural output as well as its cities.

To the east of the Sierra Nevada and the California section of the Cascades is the Great Basin. This endorheic basin, one of the four major deserts in the United States, is a large bowl that has no outlet to the sea. All the water that falls or flows into the basin from the mountains has no outlet and evaporates or dissipates into the desert. This huge region covers parts of California, Oregon, Idaho, Utah, and almost all of Nevada.

South of both the Sierra Nevada and the Coast Ranges, both sets of mountains merge into the Transverse Range, a large group of mountains that begin along the coast and cut inland to the east before encountering the Peninsular Range. These mountains begin east of Los Angeles and extend far into Mexico.

For the purposes of this book, Northern California has been divided into nine regions. The integrity of the larger geographic blocks—the Coast Ranges, the Central Valley, the Cascades, and the Sierra Nevada—has been maintained as much as possible. The further breakdown helps isolate the specific character of each region as well as group the trails by proximity and similar access lines. The Coast Ranges have been broken into three sections: the South Coast Range, the North Coast Range, and the Klamath Mountains. Both the Central Valley and the Cascades have sections of their own (though the Central Valley is only represented by its northern half, known as the Sacramento Valley, and even then only two trails are included). The Sierra Nevada is divided into four regions. These are determined by their position within the range, geologic composition, and manner of access.

CONSERVATION

At the beginning of his Western epic *Lonesome Dove*, author Larry McMurtry quoted T. K. Whipple's assessment of the role of wilderness in the life of the American people. Whipple states:

> All America lies at the end of the wilderness road, and our past is not a dead past, but still lives in us. Our forefathers had civilization inside themselves, the wild outside. We live in the civilization they created, but within us the wilderness still lingers. What they dreamed, we live, and what they lived, we dream.

This is truer today than it ever has been. Americans have always been a people with a frontier, a place where civilization came to an end and the natural, wild world was dominant. The perpetual push past the frontier, the journey through the wilderness, shaped the national character. As urban areas continue to grow and encroach on that which is undeveloped, as life for more and more people is centered on city life, the need for a frontier is pressing. One of the joys of hiking in Northern California is the opportunity to immerse yourself in the natural world, to shed the trappings of normal life and revel in the purity and beauty of creation. Whether to escape or discover, the wilds of Northern California are a refuge for people as much as they are for the natural world they preserve.

It is not surprising that the fantastic and unique landscapes of Northern California have been at the epicenter of the development of wildlands conservation. This history reaches deep into the nineteenth century. In 1864, at the height of the Civil War, Abraham Lincoln had the foresight to preserve Yosemite Valley and the nearby Mariposa Grove of giant sequoias in their natural state. The Yosemite Grant gave the lands to California to be administered as a state park. This was the first time the federal government had set land aside for the specific purpose of the preservation of its natural character, and it set an important precedent for the establishment of Yellowstone, the first national park, eight years later.

By the time Yellowstone was created, John Muir had already arrived in Yosemite. Over the next forty years, Muir was instrumental in informing and motivating the public to move public policy toward conserving the natural landscape. It is not a coincidence that the second and third national parks, Sequoia and Yosemite, were created in the Sierra Nevada in 1890. John Muir wrote prodigiously, and his writings played an important role in influencing the next generation of conservationists. Again, it is not a coincidence that leaders like Theodore Roosevelt sought Muir out and joined him in Yosemite. Under Roosevelt's direction, great swaths of the western United States were protected through the creation of national parks, national monuments, and forest reserves, the predecessors of today's national forests.

While the federal government was busy preserving significant tracts of the public domain in California and elsewhere around the country, California's state government got into the action and established the California State Parks System. Big Basin Redwoods in the Santa Cruz Mountains was the first park, established in 1902, but by 1928 efforts were in full swing to add more parks around the state. Particularly important was the successful push to preserve as much of the coastline and old-growth redwoods as possible.

By the mid-twentieth century, conservation efforts had expanded beyond simply establishing preserves for nature that were free from development. The focus shifted to enshrining wild, primeval land with protections that would maintain that condition in perpetuity. This began in 1924 when the Gila Wilderness in southwestern New Mexico became the world's first preserve specifically created to keep land in its wild state. This was accomplished through the foresight and leadership of Aldo Leopold. Throughout the 1930s, other primitive areas were established in national forests, again to maintain a region's wild character. In 1964 this became national policy when President Lyndon B. Johnson signed the National Wilderness Act. Many of the first primitive areas became the initial class of wilderness areas at that time. The wilderness act states:

> A wilderness, in contrast with those areas where man and his own works dominate the landscape, is hereby recognized as an area where the earth and its community of life are untrammeled by man, where man himself is a visitor who does not remain.

Several areas in California, including the Marble Mountains, Yolla Bolly–Middle Eel, South Warner, Caribou, Mokelumne, Hoover, Minarets (later renamed for Ansel Adams), and John Muir Wilderness Areas were part of this first phase of wilderness designation. Twenty years later, the California Wilderness Act established a sweeping number of new wilderness areas and enlarged several old ones, bringing the map of wilderness areas in California close to what it looks like today.

A significant majority of the trails in this book pass through national parks, national forests, federal wilderness areas, and California state parks. The opportunity to shed the modern world and return to the wild, natural one is the legacy of more than 150 years of work to preserve the wilderness. It is a distinctly American accomplishment, one that transcends generational and political boundaries. As society coarsens, as urbanization accelerates, as sacrifice becomes obsolete, and as gratification becomes paramount, it is imperative that the legacy is carried over to the next generation and not lost. John Muir said:

> [T]housands of tired, nerve-shaken, over-civilized people are beginning to find out that going to the mountains is going home, that wilderness is a

Berry Creek Falls is framed by massive old-growth redwoods.

necessity; and that mountain parks and reservations are useful not only as fountains of timber and irrigating rivers, but as fountains of life.

Peoples' need for wilderness is greater now than it ever has been.

WATER

Although the 100th meridian does not divide the United States in any physical or political sense, it does fall very close to the line that marks the westernmost reach of the moist air that pushes up from the Gulf of Mexico. This in turn is the functional demarcation between the humid climates of the eastern United States and the semiarid environment that dominates most of the western part of the country. Though water is important throughout the nation, it is critically important in the West, where water resources are much scarcer. Water must be managed carefully in order to ensure that there is enough to meet demand.

Most of Northern California is not desert or high desert like much of the West. Despite this, water remains scarce and does not fall abundantly as rain, as it does in the East. Fortunately for the state, the Sierra Nevada, Cascades, and the Klamath Mountains are tall enough to catch significant snowfall. This snow functions like a frozen reservoir, melting over the course of the summer and feeding the rivers, which in turn flow down into the valley, where it is distributed to farmers and cities. A complex network of canals and reservoirs transport and contain the water, delivering it to where it is needed and saving it for drier times.

As droughts take their toll on society, the increasing importance of water in Northern California is made evident. Although not its specific purpose, this guide is, in part at least, intended to be a grand tour not just of the state's great physical monuments but also of its most precious resource. Several of the state's most important rivers are explored in some fashion on many of the hikes. These rivers include the Trinity, McCloud, Sacramento, Feather, Yuba, Mokelumne, Stanislaus, Tuolumne, Merced, San Joaquin, Kings, and Kaweah. The headwaters or significant tributaries of other major rivers, including the Pit, Klamath, Salmon, and American Rivers, are also present here. In short, the vast majority of the water resources in the state of California are explored by the hikes in this guide. As you hit the trail, consider the profound impact these regions have on the rest of the state and the crucial need to protect them and maintain their integrity.

CLIMATE

Northern California has cold, wet winters with significant precipitation and warm, dry summers. The climate in this part of the state is justly lauded for its excellent, temperate weather. It is not unusual to be able to explore the high country of the mountains from June through October; for nearly half a year the mountains are available for hiking. Some years there may be a smaller window due to unusually heavy winters. When the high mountains are blanketed in snow, other parts of Northern California are in their prime seasons. The Pacific coast, the redwoods, the Central Valley, and the foothills of the Sierra Nevada are all great options for hiking during the fall, winter, and spring months. Northern California is truly a year-round outdoor playground.

HAZARDS

Hiking the trails of Northern California is not without its dangers. The four most common are bears, mountain lions, rattlesnakes, and poison oak. The last is only found on trails at the lower elevations in this book. In most cases the trails pass through stands of the bush, and careful walking will allow you to avoid touching it.

Bears: There are plenty of bears throughout Northern California, though it is uncommon to encounter one on the trails. The best thing to do is to be alert and, if possible, travel in groups. Make noise to make your presence known to any bears in the area. Clapping and speaking loudly are effective ways to do this. If you do encounter a bear, do not run. Stay still until the bear has left. If the bear continues approaching you, fall to your stomach and lie still until the bear departs. If you are actually attacked by a bear, fight back. Bears generally do not expect prey to hit and kick them, and this can deter them from continuing to attack.

Mountain Lions: Mountain lions are present in most of the areas covered in this book, but they are rarely seen. It is unlikely that you will encounter one on the trail. As always, hiking in groups is safer than hiking alone. If you do encounter a mountain lion, pick up any small children. The cats consider smaller animals easier to catch. Do not run. Mountain lions expect their prey to flee, and running will cause them to pursue. Try to look as large as you can, and do not crouch, kneel, or sit. People do not resemble the cats' normal prey when they are standing. Lastly, as with bears, if you are attacked, fight back. They can be made to flee.

Rattlesnakes: Rattlesnakes are found throughout Northern California. Be alert to what is on the trail. If you see one, do not try to handle it. Stay at least 6 feet away—the farther away the better. Be especially careful when climbing up rock piles and similar places where snakes may be hiding.

Other hazards include disorientation, exposure, lightning, and flash floods. Some of these can often occur together, as when a storm soaks a hiker and causes him or her to get lost. Stay alert to your surroundings and the changes in weather patterns. Weather can change swiftly in the mountains, and clear weather can quickly become a powerful thunderstorm. Come prepared, and be on guard.

PERMITS AND REGULATIONS

Although the trails in this guide are all intended to be hiked in a day, several of them also make great backpacking trips. Various restrictions apply, depending on the destination and trailhead. In many places it is necessary to get a wilderness permit in order to camp overnight. In lightly traveled areas like the backcountry trails in the Klamath Mountains, these can be self-issued at the trailhead. In more heavily traveled regions like much of the Sierra Nevada, you must get one from a ranger station, either in person or via reservation. In most places a fire permit is necessary if you plan to have a campfire. Fires are completely prohibited in higher elevation or high-impact areas. If you plan to spend the night in the backcountry, it is important to check with the administrative authorities to see what measures and restrictions are in place.

If you are hiking with a dog, remember that dogs are not allowed on the trails in California state parks. This rules out most of the coastal and redwood trails. National parks also generally prohibit dogs on the trails. On the other hand, national forests and lands administered by the Bureau of Land Management (BLM) usually allow dogs. Be sure to check the regulations before bringing your canine pal on the trail with you.

CAMPING

Campgrounds are common throughout the public lands in Northern California. National parks, national forests, the BLM, and California state parks all operate a multitude of campgrounds. Local governments such as county and city administrations also offer campgrounds in some areas. These are particularly useful in Inyo County, in the Eastern Sierra. It is also permissible to camp at most national forest and BLM trailheads, although overnight camping may be prohibited at some trailheads in highly trafficked areas. Dispersed camping—spending the night in a spot that is not maintained as a campground—is prohibited in national and state parks. The national forests and BLM do allow dispersed camping, unless otherwise posted.

Hiking at Andrew Molera State Park means excellent views of the Big Sur coast.

SOUTH COAST RANGE

CALIFORNIA'S SOUTH COAST RANGE is a major mountain region that lies between the Pacific Ocean on the west and the Central Valley to the east. The long block of mountains stretches from the Carquinez Strait in San Francisco Bay down to Santa Barbara County, where it merges into the rugged Transverse Range. The southern part of this range falls into Southern California's sphere, but the northern part of the range is geographically and historically linked to Northern California.

When California was still a part of Mexico, the capital was established at the city of Monterey, on the south end of Monterey Bay. This area, near San Francisco Bay, was part of the stage upon which California's independence unfolded. These events, along with the subsequent gold rush and growth of San Francisco, tied Monterey to Northern California. Despite these ties, the region retains a distinct flair and culture of its own.

The South Coast Range is broken up into several smaller, distinct mountain ranges. This is especially true at its northern half, where San Francisco Bay, Monterey Bay, the Santa Clara Valley, and the Salinas River Valley all separate the mountains of the South Coast Range into specific groups. Along the coast, the Santa Cruz Mountains occupy the San Francisco Peninsula and extend south to the northern end of Monterey Bay. Farther south are the great Santa Lucia Mountains, the home of the magnificent Big Sur coast. The meeting of the Santa Lucias and the Pacific Ocean is the most rugged collision of land and sea in the lower forty-eight states.

These coastal areas are separated from the interior of the South Coast Range by San Francisco Bay, the Santa Clara Valley, and the Salinas River Valley. The largest of the interior ranges is the Diablo Range, which stretches from the Carquinez Strait, the point where the water drained from the majority of Northern California's mountains reaches the sea, far to the south, where the range subsides and merges with the Temblor Range. The northern Diablo Range forms the line of hills east of San Francisco Bay and is crowned by the solitary cone of Mount Diablo. Forming a high wall between the southern Diablo Range and the Santa Lucias is the Gabilan Range. These mountains are home to Pinnacles National Park, which protects an awesome set of volcanic crags as well as the aeries of the endangered California condor.

The trails in the South Coast Range cover a variety of different landscapes, from towering, sunbaked peaks to deep, rain forest–like canyons. Many of the trails in this area pass through groves of coast redwoods, which reach the southern limit of their range in the Santa Lucia Mountains. Other trails in this part of Northern California explore vast oak savannas, rugged interior mountains, and the caves and crags of the Pinnacles. The diverse landscape is protected by a diverse patchwork of land administration. Nearly every level of preservation, including national parks and national forests, a host of state parks, and even county preserves, keeps the wildlands and trails of the South Coast Range open to those in search of the region's unique beauty.

1. EWOLDSEN TRAIL/ MCWAY FALLS

WHY GO?

This awesome hike showcases many of the best features of the Big Sur region in grand fashion. Abundant redwoods and waterfalls, epic coastal vistas, and a rugged meeting of sea and land are all part of this memorable trip.

THE RUNDOWN

Start: Trailhead at main parking area, just past park entrance station
Total distance: 0.5 mile out and back (McWay Falls); 4.75-mile lollipop (Ewoldsen Trail)
Hiking time: 2–3 hours
Difficulty: Moderate
Elevation gain: None (McWay Falls); 1,360 feet (Ewoldsen Trail)
Season: Year-round

Trail surface: Wood plank, packed dirt, rocky
Canine compatibility: Dogs not permitted
Fees and permits: Entrance fee
Land status: Julia Pfeiffer Burns State Park
Trail contact: www.parks.ca.gov/ ?page_id=578
Other: Water is available at the trailhead and from creeks.

FINDING THE TRAILHEAD

From Monterey, drive south on CA 1 for 41.5 miles. Turn left at the signed entrance to Julia Pfeiffer Burns State Park. The trailhead parking area is just past the entrance station. Both the Ewoldsen Trail and the walkway to McWay Falls begin here. **Trailhead GPS:** 36°15'1.86"N / 121°46'56.81"W

WHAT TO SEE

When California was still part of Mexico, the capital was located in Monterey. To the south rose the great escarpment of the Santa Lucia Mountains, dropping precipitously into the sea in a breathtaking collision. The residents of Monterey referred to this incredible landscape as *el país grande del sur*, "the big land to the south." Over the years this name has been modified to Big Sur, but the land remains as it was: spectacular and overwhelmingly beautiful.

Hikers looking to experience the essence of Big Sur would do well to venture to Julia Pfeiffer Burns State Park and hike the Ewoldsen Trail. This path collects many of the best features Big Sur has to offer and lines them up in delightful fashion for your enjoyment. Deep, wild canyons are filled with redwoods, windswept vistas offer incredible views of the magnificent coastline, and rushing creeks spring from cliffs, creating lovely waterfalls. This hike has two sections. The first is the short, easy walk out to the overlook above famed

McWay Falls is one of the most scenic waterfalls in California.

McWay Falls. The second part is the climb up into the Santa Lucia Mountains. This second part is much longer, and the ascent requires a lot of effort, but the payoff is well worth it.

Your first destination should be world-famous McWay Falls. Located in a picture-perfect cove, the waterfall pours through a narrow slot in the cliffs and falls 80 feet into the surf below. The small waterfall is an unforgettable sight. To get there, follow the path along the creek and pass through a tunnel beneath CA 1. On the far side a wooden plank trail leads 0.25 mile along the cliff edge to a wonderful vista of the cove and the falls. After taking in the scene, return to the main parking area.

For the Ewoldsen Trail, head east from the trailhead, closely following McWay Creek. Redwoods immediately close in on the path as you enter a place of quiet beauty. The route soon crosses over the creek and continues upstream. After 0.2 mile a trail branches off to the left and follows the creek upstream a short distance to Canyon Falls. This 30-foot waterfall is not nearly as pretty as McWay Falls, but it is surrounded by redwoods and has a charm all its own. After checking the small cataract, continue on the main trail, which now begins a long, arcing climb up the side of the canyon. It cuts into a side canyon, crosses a stream, and then continues traversing the side of the main canyon. Some sections of the path are narrow, and the trail is slung onto the steep hillside. There are good views down into the canyon where McWay Creek flows through redwood snags and over small cataracts. After climbing 1.0 mile from the trailhead, you arrive at a bridge over the creek, where a fork in the trail marks the beginning of the loop.

The Ewoldsen loop can be hiked in either direction, but hiking it counterclockwise allows you to enjoy ocean views while you walk, rather than having to look back over your shoulder on some sections. To hike the loop in this direction, do not cross the bridge but continue following McWay Creek on a steady grade up the canyon through the redwoods. After hiking 0.5 mile from the beginning of the loop, cross McWay Creek on a small bridge and start the ascent out of the canyon. As you round the corner of a ridge, the forest recedes and good views of McWay Creek's deep canyon open up. All too soon, however, the forest swallows the trail back up. Note that the redwoods have given way; the woods are now dominated by oaks and other trees better suited to the drier environment.

From the open spot, the trail continues to wind around the head of the canyon. Watch for a signed spur trail to the right, leading to the overlook above the coast. Proceed along the path as it leads upward; stay left at the junction, following the ridgetop to the south. There are great views all along the grassy ridge, and numerous wildflowers can be found lining the slopes in springtime. A bench with more exceptional views marks the end of the trail. Press on a little farther on a use trail to some rock outcroppings. Here the best panoramas are revealed and you can see far to the south. Trace the narrow band of white created by the collision of the green-and-gold earth and the blue sea. The waves hammer away at the coastline interminably, creating a magnificent spectacle as you gaze down from more than 1,400 feet above the sea.

When you eventually pull yourself away from this incredible spot, head back down the spur and turn right, back on the Ewoldsen Trail. It is all downhill from this point. The path descends to McWay Creek's main canyon and continues along its slopes. The trees clear here, and the views get better as you lose elevation. The path soon arrives at the very edge of the mountains, where you can look down directly on CA 1 and the coast, which lie more than 1,000 feet below. You soon turn inland again and reenter the redwoods as the route drops the final distance to the beginning of the loop. Cross the bridge and pick up the main trail coming from the parking area. From here, follow the path back to the trailhead.

The rugged mountains of Big Sur plunge into the Pacific Ocean.

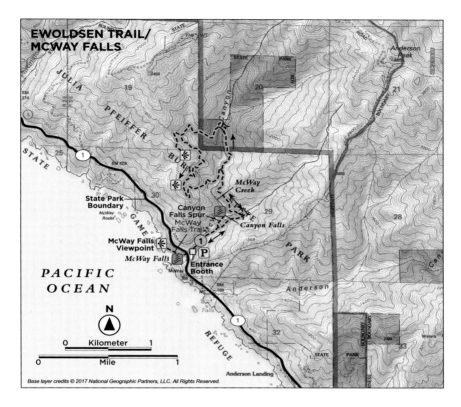

MILES AND DIRECTIONS

0.0 Start toward the south and west for an easy walk to McWay Falls and the McWay Falls Viewpoint. Retrace the route back to the trailhead. Follow the trail inland, ascending McWay Creek's canyon.

0.2 Follow the short spur trail to Canyon Falls then continue on the main path.

1.0 Arrive at the beginning of the Ewoldsen loop. Stay to the right, continuing up the canyon.

2.0 Turn right onto the spur that leads to the overlook.

2.25 Enjoy the amazing views of the Big Sur coast.

2.5 Return to main loop trail and turn right, beginning the descent back to the trailhead.

3.75 Reach the end of the loop. Cross the bridge over McWay Creek and turn right onto the main trail.

4.75 Arrive back at the trailhead.

2. PFEIFFER FALLS

WHY GO?

The short hike to Pfeiffer Falls features many of the best features of the Big Sur area in one small and easy package. A walk through beautiful redwoods and a detour to an overlook high above the Big Sur Valley lead to the pretty waterfall set in a rocky canyon.

THE RUNDOWN

Start: Southwest corner of large parking area
Distance: 2.6 miles out and back
Hiking time: 1–2 hours
Difficulty: Easy
Elevation gain: 750 feet
Season: Year-round
Trail surface: Packed dirt, duff
Canine compatibility: Dogs not permitted

Fees and permits: Entrance fee
Land status: Pfeiffer Big Sur State Park
Trail contact: 47225 Highway 1, Big Sur 93920; (831) 667-2315; www .parks.ca.gov/?page_id=570
Other: Water is available at the trailhead.

FINDING THE TRAILHEAD

 From Monterey, drive south on CA 1 for 29 miles to the community of Big Sur. Turn left at the signed entrance to Pfeiffer Big Sur State Park. Follow the park road past the store and the entrance station. Park in the large parking area on the right. **Trailhead GPS:** 36°15'1.86"N / 121°46'56.81"W

WHAT TO SEE

Big Sur is a land of contrasts: tall mountains, vast ocean, towering redwoods, small creeks, intimate canyons, and big views. No other trail in the region condenses all of these features down to one nice little package as well as that to Pfeiffer Falls. This waterfall may not be the most spectacular along the Big Sur coast, but it is the most accessible and is worth the trip.

Start the hike in the southwest corner of the large parking area. Cross the bridge and follow the wide path along the Big Sur River. The largest watershed on this part of the California coast, the Big Sur River starts deep in the adjacent Ventana Wilderness and flows 15 miles to its outlet near Point Sur. Though it can appear small later in the year, in spring it has a powerful flow. A second bridge brings the path back over the river to reach the Big Sur Lodge. Cross the park road and begin climbing gently through redwoods before arriving at the official trailhead for Pfeiffer Falls.

Past the trailhead you will immediately cross Pfeiffer Creek. This charming stream meanders through a gully surrounded by redwoods. The route then leaves the redwoods

Pfeiffer Falls

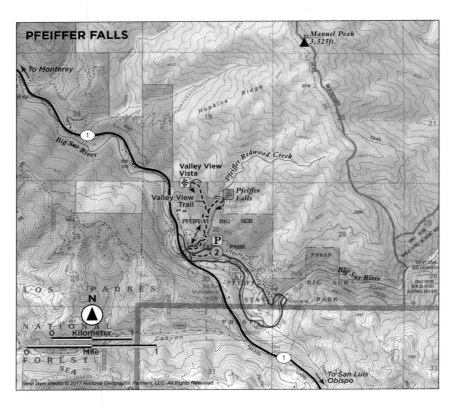

and enters typical coastal forest. A few switchbacks are followed by a steady climb up the hill. There are a few breaks in the trees that provide glimpses of the valley. After 0.9 mile from the Big Sur Lodge, you arrive at a fork in the trail. Staying right leads to Pfeiffer Falls, while the Valley View Trail branches off to the left. This latter option climbs gently for 0.3 mile to a vista point overlooking the Big Sur Valley. The heavily forested west side of the canyon is a surprising contrast to the chaparral that blankets the walls on the east side. In the distance you can see the blue Pacific Ocean and the rocky prominence of Point Sur.

Returning to the main trail, you now make a quick descent and reenter the redwood forest. Cross Pfeiffer Creek and wind around some large redwoods to a point where you can observe graceful Pfeiffer Falls. The 60-foot waterfall flows down the dark rock like a slender white ribbon. During wetter times of the year, two or three other strands of falling water complement the main channel. It is possible to climb a little higher into the small amphitheater and reach the base of the falls. From here you can gaze upward and see additional waterfalls as Pfeiffer Creek tumbles down the steep canyon above Pfeiffer Falls. Retrace your steps back to the trailhead.

The Valley View Vista is a good place to spot Point Sur and the Pacific Ocean.

MILES AND DIRECTIONS

0.0 Start at the trailhead and follow the trail west along the Big Sur River.

0.25 Pass the Big Sur Lodge and begin climbing along Pfeiffer Creek through the redwood-filled canyon.

0.85 Turn left onto the Valley View Trail.

1.15 Reach the Valley View vista point.

1.45 Return to the main trail and turn left to head toward Pfeiffer Falls.

1.65 Arrive at Pfeiffer Falls. Follow the trail back to the trailhead.

2.6 Arrive back at the trailhead.

3. ANDREW MOLERA STATE PARK

WHY GO?

Andrew Molera State Park presents a fantastic coastal adventure. The trail climbs over high hills with exceptional views of the Big Sur coastline and the mountains of the Ventana Wilderness and before following low seaside bluffs past a hidden, hikers-only beach on the way back to the trailhead.

THE RUNDOWN

Start: Trailhead in large parking lot by the entrance station.
Distance: 8.4-mile lollipop
Hiking time: 4-5 hours
Difficulty: Moderate
Elevation gain: 1,100 feet
Season: Year-round
Trail surface: Packed dirt, sandy
Canine compatibility: Dogs not permitted
Fees and permits: Entrance fee

Land status: Andrew Molera State Park
Trail contact: www.parks.ca.gov/?page_id=582
Special considerations: This trail requires a ford of the Big Sur River that may be impassable certain times of the year. Poison oak is found in abundance along parts of this hike.
Other: Water is available from the Big Sur River at the trailhead.

FINDING THE TRAILHEAD

From Monterey, drive south on CA 1 for 24.4 miles. Turn left at the entrance to Andrew Molera State Park. The driveway quickly forks. Stay right and then immediately turn right into the large parking lot after paying the parking fee.
Trailhead GPS: 36°17'14.62"N / 121°50'38.67"W

WHAT TO SEE

The coastal terrain around Andrew Molera State Park is gentler than most of the rest of the Big Sur region. Rather than steep mountainsides thrusting upward out of the Pacific Ocean, the land has low rolling hills and a broad, grassy plain. This distinct geography results in part from the presence of the Big Sur River, which meets the sea at the nexus of the rolling hills and the open plain. Lacking the rugged mountains that typify much of the Santa Lucia Range, the trails in this area shift the focus onto the sea. Since this hike is mostly through grassy terrain, there are nearly constant views over the course of the whole hike.

To begin the hike, head west from the trailhead and pass through a tunnel of dense brush. In short order you arrive at the edge of the Big Sur River. In spring or after a good rain, the river will be high and is either impassable or requires a ford through the water. Later in the spring through fall, the river's size is reduced significantly, and boards are put

Pico Blanco peeks over the steep ridge above the Big Sur Valley.

out to bridge the river. Cross over the river and continue west on the Beach Trail. This wide path follows the Big Sur River, though the water is almost entirely out of sight. After 0.9 mile look for an unsigned trail branching off to the left, toward the south. This path is a wide old road that passes along some tall hedges. In 0.1 mile veer right to begin hiking on the Ridge Trail.

Ascending steadily, the Ridge Trail climbs up onto the tall grassy hills that lie at the mouth of the Big Sur Valley. The first 1.0 mile is the steepest part of the hike, rising almost 700 feet to a prominent point on the summit ridge. Shortly after the climb begins, there are great views to the north toward Point Sur. Persevere up the hill until the wide path rounds the top of a bald hill and descends briefly back onto the ridge. Though the trail is wide, be careful to avoid patches of poison oak found all along the path. This part of the hike affords great views toward the Santa Lucia Mountains, rising more than 3,000 feet to the east. The most notable sight is the stark white cone of Pico Blanco, one of the most beautiful and interesting peaks in this part of Big Sur. Though the mountain lies just outside the vast Ventana Wilderness, it remains a wild and lonely peak.

Continue down from the bald hill along the crest of the hills until you arrive at a junction with the Hidden Trail, an alternative route from the trailhead. Stay straight and begin climbing along the crest of the ridge again. Fortunately the grade is less severe here. In 0.9 mile from the junction with the Hidden Trail, you pass another junction, this time with the South Boundary Trail. Stay straight and enter into a large, hilltop grove of redwoods. These trees are not as large or attractive as other groves nearby, but they are a welcome sight on the trail and the first shade since crossing the Big Sur River. On the far side of the redwoods, the trail crosses one last grassy slope before reaching the highest point on the hike.

Although the views are good from this spot, it is better to press on a little farther to Panorama Point if you plan on taking a break with a view. To get there, follow the Panorama Trail downhill for 0.25 mile. Brushy terrain dominates this area, and the views are good. The route along this section hugs the southern boundary of Andrew Molera State Park, and private residences can be seen past the fence line. In short order you arrive at a clearing in the brush where Panorama Point's unforgettable vista unfolds. Looking south, the low hills lead the eye toward the mouth of the Big Sur River and the rocky prominence of Point Sur beyond. Bluffs, sea stacks, coastal plains, beaches, and brush-covered mountains all combine to form the awesome panorama.

To complete the loop from here, continue hiking on the Panorama Trail as it turns and heads north. The path winds through canyons as it descends through dense patches of coastal chaparral. At 1.4 miles past the vista point, the path crosses a small creek. After it climbs out of the creek's small gully, a spur branches off to the left and follows the stream down to a beautiful hidden beach. About 50 yards from the sand, the trail fades away and you must pick your way over large driftwood logs. This beautiful beach can only be accessed via this trail or by boat, and it is likely that you will have the whole area to yourself. After enjoying the beach, follow the path back to the Panorama Trail.

Looking north to Point Sur from Panorama Point.

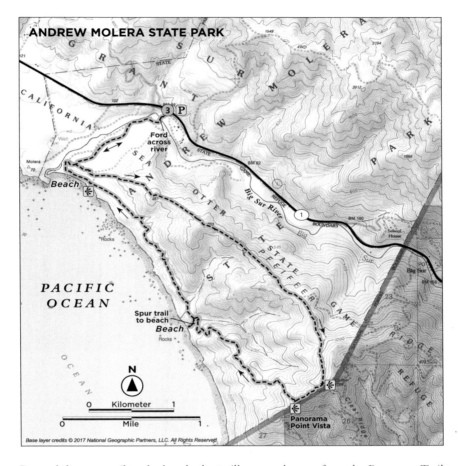

Beyond the spur trail to the beach, the trail's name changes from the Panorama Trail to the Bluff Trail. As the name implies, the route follows along a succession of low bluffs that rise about 100 feet above the crashing waves. Views of the hills to the east and the ocean to the west improve as you progress northward. The trail has an easy grade as it weaves in and out of a few gullies and crosses some small streams. Watch for use trails branching off to the west and leading to a trail that hugs the edge of the bluffs, providing an option that stays closer to the water. This optional route ultimately rejoins the Bluff Trail just as it pulls closer to the edge of the bluffs itself. Here there are fantastic views south down the length of the bluffs back toward Panorama Point. Just a little farther a short trail branches off toward the beach when the Bluff Trail turns inland. It then passes through forest a short distance before rejoining the Beach Trail at the junction with the Ridge Trail, completing the loop. Follow the Beach Trail back to the trailhead.

The hidden beach on the Bluff Trail can only be accessed by hikers.

MILES AND DIRECTIONS

0.0 Start at the trailhead and immediately cross the Big Sur River. At times this may be impassable; other times it may be necessary to ford the river. Later in the year, when water levels are lower, planks are put out to bridge the water. Proceed down the Beach Trail.

0.9 At an unsigned junction, turn left onto an old dirt road.

1.0 Turn right again onto the Ridge Trail.

2.1 Pass the junction with the Hidden Trail.

3.0 Pass the junction with the South Boundary Trail.

3.75 Reach the highest point on the trail and head south on the Panorama Trail.

4.0 Arrive at Panorama Point and enjoy the spectacular vista.

5.5 A short spur trail leads to a hidden beach.

5.6 The spur ends at the beach. Return to the main trail.

5.7 Return to the main trail and turn left onto the Bluff Trail.

7.4 Turn right onto the Beach Trail.

8.4 Arrive back at the trailhead.

4. PINNACLES

WHY GO?

The exciting hike through Pinnacles National Park is an action-packed journey through incredible rock formations that features unique trail engineering, caves, and the chance to see the endangered California condor.

THE RUNDOWN

Start: Chaparral Trailhead
Distance: 8.6-mile loop
Hiking time: 4–5 hours
Difficulty: Moderate
Elevation gain: 1,300 feet
Season: Year-round, though spring is best; summers can be brutally hot.
Trail surface: Packed dirt, rocky, rock hand and foot holds, rock scrambling
Canine compatibility: Dogs not permitted

Fees and permits: Entrance fee
Land status: Pinnacles Wilderness, Pinnacles National Park
Trail contact: 5000 Highway 146, Paicines 95043; (831) 389-4486; www.nps.gov/pinn
Special considerations: Route passes through caves so bring a flashlight.
Other: Water is available at the trailhead.

FINDING THE TRAILHEAD

From CA 101 in Soledad, take exit 302 for CA 146. Turn onto Front Street, drive toward the downtown area, and turn right onto East Street. After 0.3 mile turn right onto CA 146, which is also signed as Metz Road. Proceed for 2.7 miles then turn left to continue on CA 146. Follow this road 9.3 miles to the trailhead in Pinnacles National Park. **Trailhead GPS:** 36°29'30.06"N / 121°12'33.51"W

WHAT TO SEE

Rising suddenly from the chaparral-covered hills of the Gabilan Range, the Pinnacles are a striking collection of volcanic domes and towers. The red, pink, and purple hues of the rock make a stark contrast against the green and gold of the surrounding hills. In some ways, the Pinnacles seem out of place compared to the rest of the landscape. Geologically, this is certainly the case. The strange rocks are the remnants of an old volcano that geologists believe to have been broken in half by the infamous San Andreas Fault. The other half of the old volcano lies a couple hundred miles to the south. As the fault shifted, it broke the volcano apart, and the two portions were ultimately separated. The geologic and scenic importance of the Pinnacles was recognized early on. In 1908 they were designated a national monument, and in 2013 their status was upgraded to a national park. The area is also protected in the 15,985-acre Hain Wilderness. The geology of the Pinnacles and their preservation has produced some of the best trails in the South Coast Range.

It is fortunate for hikers that this geologic stranger has made its home in the Gabilan Range, an interior subrange of the South Coast Range. Trails through the park do not just travel around the base of the spectacular rocks; they climb up onto, into, over, and through the crags. You are able to experience the Pinnacles in an intimate, hands-on fashion, but the trails also yield spectacular vistas of the crags and much of the Gabilan and Santa Lucia Ranges. There is also the chance of catching a glimpse of the incredible California condor, the largest bird in North America and one that has taken significant steps away from the brink of extinction.

This hike combines several trails to make a loop through the Pinnacles. Near the end of the hike, the route passes through talus caves, so be sure to bring flashlights or head-lamps. The trip begins at the Chaparral Trailhead on the west side of the Pinnacles. Start on the Juniper Canyon Trail; the namesake tree is found in abundance along this section of the trail. In short order the path begins to pass through large boulders. Like the rest of the Pinnacles, these are composed of andesite and rhyolite, dense volcanic rocks. Like granite, these igneous rocks are popular with rock climbers, and the Pinnacles have become a significant rock climbing destination.

At 0.6 mile from the trailhead, the path turns and begins to climb into the Pinnacles themselves. The purple and pink rocks loom overhead on all sides of the trail. The trail soon begins a long series of switchbacks as it ascends into the heart of the crags. At 1.1 miles the trail intersects the Tunnel Trail. Stay to the right and continue climbing higher into the Pinnacles. The views of the surrounding area get better as you get higher. The path straightens out and makes a long traverse across the flanks of the crags before

California Condors may be seen while hiking in the Pinnacles.

The High Peaks Trail has great views of the Balconies area formations.

climbing a second set of switchbacks. Finally, 1.7 miles from the trailhead, you reach the crest of the Pinnacles, where there is a junction with the High Peaks Trail.

Turn left onto the High Peaks Trail and begin one of the most exciting sections of the hike. For the next mile the trail winds, weaves, and climbs along the crest of the Pinnacles. The trail has been engineered to make the route as exciting as possible. In some places steps have been cut into the rock and rails have been installed to help get over difficult sections where no normal trail can be established. It moves over rocks, along ledges, and over overhangs, all the while exposing hikers to far-reaching vistas. The journey is both expansive, as you can observe much of the Gabilan Range, and intimate, since you must crawl over the rock and use your hands to negotiate the crags. Be alert for California condors along this section of the hike. The majestic birds like to roost in the secluded towers and can be seen flying in this area.

As you near the end of the High Peaks section, stay straight when the Tunnel Trail rejoins the High Peaks Trail. Watch for the large pink dome of the Balconies to the north. After a mile on the High Peaks Trail, you finally leave the towers of the Pinnacles behind and descend one of the formation's high shoulders. This unique section of the hike finally comes to an end when you arrive at the junction with the Condor Gulch Trail, where you will stay straight, continuing on the High Peaks Trail. As you descend, watch for the tall Chalone Peaks to the south. These are the highest peaks in Pinnacles National Park.

Once you pass the Condor Gulch Trail, you make a 2.0-mile descent through chaparral and oak savanna to reach the bottom of the Pinnacles at Chalone Creek. Turn left onto the Old Pinnacles Trail, which runs parallel to Chalone Creek. In spring the creek has good flow, and wildflowers are abundant along this section of the hike. Much of the park's support infrastructure can be seen on the far side of the creek, as well as a shaded

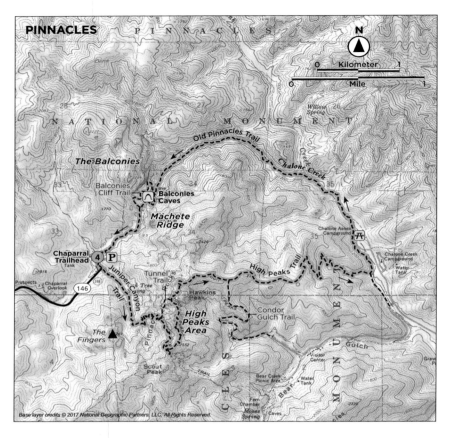

picnic area. About 0.5 mile after turning onto the Old Pinnacles Trail, you cross a bridge over the creek. The trail crosses back over after another 0.4 mile and then makes a very gentle ascent along the creek for another 1.6 miles before intersecting the Balconies Cliff Trail. This path bypasses the awesome Balconies Caves. If you do not like confined spaces or do not have a flashlight or headlamp, take this trail to complete the loop.

For the Balconies Caves, continue on the Old Pinnacles Trail 0.1 mile farther to reach the entrance. A gate has been installed to prevent entry when conditions are dangerous. These caves are not typical passages through the earth. These are talus caves, which are essentially gaps between enormous boulders that collapsed into this area in a large rock-slide. In spring Chalone Creek flows through the first section of the caves, emanating from somewhere within the large talus pile. There is a rudimentary path through the rocky caves, but some sections do require using your hands to climb or balance. The route is obvious, and markers have been painted onto the rocks in some places to indicate the way. After working your way through the darkness, you emerge back into the light but not yet out of the rocks. Here the trail travels through a long crack in a truly colossal

rock for several yards. It is necessary to duck under large boulders that have been chocked into the crack.

When you finally emerge out of the cave complex, the trail resumes in a shady grotto. The path soon leaves the rocks behind and follows a small seasonal stream through a grassy valley. Be sure to look back at sharp-edged Machete Ridge and the high crags of the Pinnacles. The gently climbing trail continues for another 0.6 mile before it arrives back at the Chaparral Trailhead, where the Pinnacles loom in awesome fashion above the parking area.

MILES AND DIRECTIONS

0.0   Start from the Chaparral Trailhead on the Juniper Canyon Trail.

0.75 Begin a long climb up a series of switchbacks.

1.1   Stay right at Tunnel Trail.

1.7   Turn left onto the High Peaks Trail.

2.3   Continue straight when the Tunnel Trail joins the High Peaks Trail.

3.0   Stay straight at the intersection with the Condor Gulch Trail.

4.9   Turn left onto the Old Pinnacles Trail.

7.4   Intersect the Balconies Cliff Trail. (**Option:** Take this trail to complete the loop without visiting the caves.)

7.5   Enter the Balconies Caves.

7.8   Exit the caves and continue hiking on the Balconies Trail.

8.6   Arrive back at the trailhead.

5. BIG BASIN

WHY GO?

Cutting deep into the heart of the Santa Cruz Mountains, this long hike features giant old-growth redwoods and a trio of awesome waterfalls in a wild setting.

THE RUNDOWN

Start: Trailhead west of the visitor center and park headquarters
Distance: 10.2-mile loop (*Option:* moderate 6.2-mile loop bypassing the three waterfalls)
Hiking time: About 6 hours or overnight
Difficulty: Moderately strenuous
Elevation gain: 2,000 feet (waterfall loop)
Season: Year-round; waterfalls are at their best in spring.
Trail surface: Packed dirt, duff, rocky
Canine compatibility: Dogs not permitted

Fees and permits: Entrance fee
Land status: West Waddell Creek State Wilderness, Big Basin Redwoods State Park
Trail contact: 21600 Big Basin Way, Boulder Creek 95006; (831) 338-8860; www.parks.ca.gov/?page_id=540
Special considerations: Route passes through caves, so bring a flashlight.
Other: Water is available at the trailhead.

FINDING THE TRAILHEAD

 From Santa Cruz, drive north on CA 9 for 13 miles to CA 236. Turn left and follow CA 236 to the park headquarters. The trailhead is west of the visitor center and headquarters.

The park can also be reached via a windy route from the San Francisco Bay Area. Drive south from San Francisco about 20 miles on I-280. Turn south on CA 35 and continue for another 25 miles. Turn west on CA 9 and after 6 miles turn west again onto CA 236. Stay on this windy road for 8 miles to the park headquarters and visitor center. **Trailhead GPS:** 37°10'23.22"N / 122°13'22.94"W

WHAT TO SEE

Of all the redwood groves south of San Francisco, the most magnificent groves and the greatest redwood wilderness is found in Big Basin Redwoods State Park, deep in the Santa Cruz Mountains. The park, California's oldest state park, preserves 18,000 acres, more than half of which is old-growth forest. The rest of the park is made of second-growth redwoods and mixed forests of oaks and firs and coastal chaparral. While the ancient redwoods are a chief attraction, the park also boasts numerous beautiful waterfalls. The combination of the unique trees and falling water is magical and gives the forests here an enchanted feeling.

The Golden Cascade is aptly named for its vivid color.

Big Basin Redwoods offers hikers more than 80 miles of trail. However, it is the loop that combines the famed Skyline-to-the-Sea Trail with the Sunset Trail that is the premier adventure. This hike has two options. A shorter 6.2-mile loop features excellent redwoods. The longer loop has the redwoods but also passes three great waterfalls, including iconic Berry Creek Falls, one of the most photographed waterfalls in California. This longer hike is demanding but worth the effort, not just for the redwoods and beautiful falls but also the exciting trail engineering and the sense of deep immersion in this unique wilderness.

The hike begins on the west side of the large parking area near the Big Basin visitor center. The trail immediately crosses a bridge over large Opal Creek and then splits. Turn right onto the Dool Trail. Massive redwoods line the large creek as the trail meanders through the forest. After 0.2 mile turn left onto the Sunset Trail and begin climbing steeply up a wooded sloop. In short order you will cross a wide dirt fire road. The road, which provides access to firefighters in the event of a fire, also functions as the east boundary of the West Waddell Creek State Wilderness. Pick up the Sunset Trail on the far side of the road and begin a long gradual descent down into the Kelly Creek drainage. Roughly 0.3 mile from the fire road you will pass the Sunset Connector Trail on your left. This short path cuts down to the Skyline-to-the-Sea Trail, which is the return portion of the loop. As the trail descends through the redwoods, it rounds the shoulder of a ridge and enters the West Waddell Creek drainage. The trail continues to lose elevation, crossing little Timms Creek as it drops, until it finally arrives at the creek, 2.75 miles from the trailhead.

Cross the pretty creek on a wooden bridge and begin climbing up the far side of the canyon. You will quickly arrive at a junction with the Timms Creek Trail. (*Option: If you* want to bypass the waterfalls for the shorter, 6.2-mile loop, turn left here. The trail follows West Waddell Creek for 0.9 mile to the confluence with Kelly Creek, where you join the Skyline-to-the-Sea Trail. Take this route back to the trailhead.) To continue on to the waterfalls, stay left on the Sunset Trail and climb out of the West Waddell Creek drainage. Once at the top of a forested ridge, the trail then descends down into the canyon drained by Berry Creek. Cross over the creek and climb out of the shallow canyon.

Above Berry Creek, the forest recedes for the only time on this hike as the trail crosses over some exposed sandstone formations. The trees are noticeably smaller here, as the hard rock provides poor conditions. Views of the heavily forested ridges of the Waddell Creek watershed give this slice of the Santa Cruz Mountains a deep sense of isolation. All too soon the trail plunges back into the deep forest. Pass a signed spur trail on the right that leads to Sunset Camp, where backpackers are afforded the rare opportunity to camp in the redwoods. Just beyond the spur, the trail veers left as it reaches West Berry Creek and the commencement of an exquisite stretch of trail.

Proceed a short distance along the creek before arriving at the upper portion of the Golden Cascades. Here the waterfall cascades in sheets over bright orange sandstone. The trail follows the creek closely and descends wooden steps before arriving at the lower section of the Golden Cascades. Here the creek tumbles down an orange sandstone staircase. The two halves of the waterfall are quite different, but both are beautiful. Just a few feet past the base of the lower cascade the trail comes to an abrupt end at a large sandstone slab where West Berry Creek pours over the precipice as 60-foot Silver Falls. The route crosses the rock slab, with the water flowing over the cliff just inches away from the trail. A steel-cable fence provides safety as well as defining the direction you should follow. The fence leads to the left, down a stone staircase tucked up against the edge of the cliff. It is very reminiscent of Yosemite's famous Mist Trail. The stone steps transition to a well-built wooden staircase, which leads to the base of free-falling Silver Falls.

The beauty continues as the trail continues downstream from the waterfalls. It hugs the bank of the creek and travels through one of the most magnificent moss-covered redwood groves on the trail. After crossing over the creek, the path leads across a ledge where a wooden fence makes the passage safe. Below the cliff crashes fantastic Berry Creek Falls. This memorable waterfall pours more than 70 feet into a rocky bowl surrounded by ferns and redwoods. Descend a few steps to a spur trail that leads to an observation platform below the falls. After enjoying the view of the falls, return to the main trail and continue a short distance to the junction with the Skyline-to-the-Sea Trail. Turn left and follow the trail to a crossing over Berry Creek. A short climb leads to a switchback, where there is one last view of the falls through the dense redwood forest. From there the trail leads to West Waddell Creek, where it crosses the water on some large planks. The planks may be removed when water levels are high.

Once on the south side of the creek, you begin the long, lovely climb out of the West Waddell Creek Wilderness. Most hikers visiting Berry Creek Falls use this route, so the traffic here is considerably higher than on the Sunset Trail. The path winds through the magical redwood canyon, where the water spills over rocks, moss and ferns cover large

Berry Creek Falls

Large redwoods line the Skyline-to-the-Sea Trail.

boulders, and huge redwoods tower above the canyon bottom. After 1.0 mile, pass the Timms Creek Trail. As you do, you leave West Waddell Creek but keep climbing alongside Kelly Creek. The canyon remains as attractive as it has been, but the creek is noticeably smaller. In another mile the trail crosses the small stream and climbs up the north side of the canyon.

As you gain elevation, the redwoods remain large, and many grow right along the trail. A little more than 0.5 mile after crossing Kelly Creek, you reach the Sunset Connector Trail. This leads back to the Sunset Trail in 0.1 mile. Climbing up to the Sunset Trail and returning to the trailhead by that route cuts 0.5 mile off the hike. If you choose to stay on the Skyline-to-the-Sea Trail, it climbs for another 0.6 mile before crossing the dirt fire road. It then winds through more old-growth redwoods before reaching Opal Creek. Turn left on the trail and follow the creek back to the bridge, completing the loop.

MILES AND DIRECTIONS

0.0 Start at the trailhead, crossing over Opal Creek and turning right onto the Dool Trail.

0.2 Turn left onto the Sunset Trail.

0.5 Pass the Sunset Connector Trail.

2.9 Cross West Waddell Creek and then stay right at the junction with the Timms Creek Trail to continue on the Sunset Trail. (**Option:** Turn left onto the Timms Creek Trail for the 6.2-mile loop.)

4.9 Arrive at the Golden Cascades and Silver Falls.

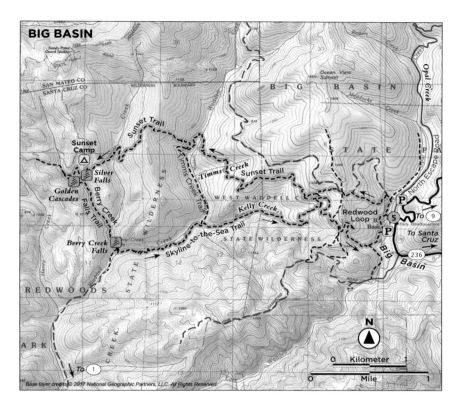

6.0 Reach the observation deck below Berry Creek Falls.

6.1 Head east on the Skyline-to-the-Sea Trail.

7.25 Pass the Timms Creek Trail and continue climbing on the Skyline-to-the-Sea Trail.

8.8 Pass the Sunset Connector Trail.

10.0 Reach Opal Creek and turn left to return to the trailhead.

10.2 Arrive back at the trailhead.

6. SUNOL REGIONAL WILDERNESS

WHY GO?
This surprisingly wild hike leads through oak savannas and grassy hillsides to scenic panoramas and rugged rock scrambles set in beautiful creeks.

THE RUNDOWN
Start: Footbridge over Alameda Creek, just upstream from the visitor center
Distance: 7.3-mile lollipop
Hiking time: 4–5 hours or overnight
Difficulty: Moderate
Elevation gain: 1,575 feet
Season: Year-round; creeks and wildflowers are at their best in spring.
Trail surface: Packed dirt, dirt roads, rock scrambling

Canine compatibility: Dogs permitted
Fees and permits: Entrance fee; fee per dog
Land status: Sunol Regional Wilderness, East Bay Regional Park District
Trail contact: 1895 Geary Rd., Sunol 94586; (510) 544-3249; www.ebparks.org/parks/sunol
Other: Water is only available in creeks.

FINDING THE TRAILHEAD

From I-680 in Sunol, take exit 21A for Calaveras Road. Drive south on Calaveras Road for 4.3 miles. Turn left onto Geary Road and drive 1.8 miles to Sunol Regional Wilderness. Park in the large parking area near the visitor center.
Trailhead GPS: 37°30'56.25"N / 121°49'50.45"W

WHAT TO SEE
The San Francisco Bay Area is blessed with an overabundance of public land within easy striking distance of urban areas. A surprising number of these parks have retained much of their wild characteristics and offer hikers great options for getting outdoors and enjoying beautiful scenery. Few of the Bay Area parks can rival the Sunol Regional Wilderness for both its wild nature and the rugged, diverse, and scenic landscape. Managed as a wilderness area, the majority of the park beyond the visitor center is untamed and untrammeled. The variety of the preserve is impressive. Oak-covered hills and grassy ridges are typical here, but there are some rugged peaks and craggy rock outcroppings. One of the highlights is the rocky gorge of Little Yosemite, which manages to live up to its bold name and does not fail to impress. Other rocky veins offer intrepid hikers scrambling opportunities not found elsewhere in the Bay Area. A well-developed trail network accesses remote corners of the preserve, providing hikers with numerous loop options. The presence of backcountry campsites means that overnight trips are an option on this

Flag Hill is prominently visible while hiking through the Sunol Wilderness.

hike. This journey connects several interesting features from around the park into one impressively scenic loop.

The hike begins in the Sunol Valley, at the footbridge over Alameda Creek, just upstream from the visitor center. Cross over the large creek and turn right onto the Indian Joe Nature Trail. This wide path parallels the water almost 0.4 mile before it splits into several trails. Take the Indian Joe Creek Trail north, following the small namesake creek. The creek and the trail maintain the same course for 1.25 miles of steady climbing. After passing the Hayfield Trail on the left, the trail climbs above the creek and follows a ridge to the junction with Cave Rocks Road. This wide dirt road comes from the High Valley Camp, one of the two backcountry backpacker campgrounds.

Turn right on Cave Rocks Road, an old dirt ranch road, and hike up the trail through grassy fields with scattered oak trees. Stay straight when you pass the Eagle View Road and, a short distance later, the Eagle View Trail. As you climb, the panorama above Alameda Creek's canyon continues to improve. Watch for the large barn that marks the High Valley Camp backpacker campsite. The old ranch road makes a few switchbacks past a small stock tank, where cattle may congregate at times. Above the tank, you climb above the trees onto a grassy ridgeline and finally reach the high point of the climb at the Cerro Este Overlook, 2.65 miles from the trailhead. The overlook is located at the junction with Cerro Este Road. A rocky monument marks this spot and offers a great vantage point more than 1,300 feet above the creek. In addition to numerous peaks and ridges visible from this spot, the Calaveras Reservoir is a prominent feature to the south.

From the overlook, proceed downhill on Cerro Este Road. After 0.3 mile, leave Cerro Este Road at a small stock pond and head east on the McCorkle Trail. This path makes a lazy descent over rolling hills that in springtime are filled with poppies and other wildflowers. The path reaches the "W" Tree Rock Scramble after 0.8 mile. This unusual route travels through a creek channel that is filled with boulders. Hidden waterfalls and splendid isolation are found deep in the rocky gully. Completing the scramble means hopping and climbing on rocks the entire distance rather than hiking on a trail. If you want to attempt the rock scramble, turn right at the creek and begin following the rocks downstream to Camp Ohlone Road, where you will indeed find a tree shaped like a "W." From here turn right onto Camp Ohlone Road. If you choose to continue the hike, cross over the creek; in moments you will arrive at a signed fork that leads to the Sunol backpacker camp. Instead of going to the camp, head downhill on the Backpack Trail. This path crosses more grassy hillsides, but these are now complemented by a striking rock tower rising abruptly from the hillside. In a little a little more than 0.5 mile you reach Camp Ohlone Road, where you will turn right.

Alameda Creek crashes over large boulders in the narrow gorge of Little Yosemite.

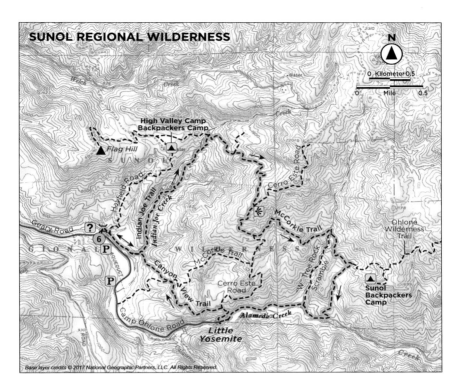

Base layer credits © 2017 National Geographic Partners, LLC. All Rights Reserved.

Camp Ohlone Road is a wide gravel road, but no vehicular traffic is permitted. Alameda Creek, the main watershed of the Sunol Wilderness, lies just below the road and makes this an especially beautiful section of the hike. Later in the year this creek dries up, but in spring it is a lovely torrent. In 0.25 mile you pass the "W" Tree and the entrance to the rock scramble. Continue heading west on Camp Ohlone Road, passing the Canyon View Trail, until you arrive at Little Yosemite, 0.7 mile from the Backpack Trail. Here the creek pours through a narrow rocky gorge and then spreads out into numerous channels that flow between very large boulders. The name Little Yosemite falls short if you anticipate this little area looking like the great valley itself. However, it is quite reminiscent of the Happy Isles area in Yosemite Valley.

At Little Yosemite, leave Camp Ohlone Road and climb briefly up Cerro Este Road. After 0.2 mile turn left onto the Canyon View Trail and head west, back toward the trailhead. This beautiful trail traverses open, grassy hillsides where views of the Sunol Valley get better as you near the end of the loop. Particularly interesting is the perspective on Flag Hill, which does indeed vaguely resemble the American flag with its large rock outcropping and stratified hillside. Finally, after 1.0 mile on the Canyon View Trail, you rejoin the Indian Joe Nature Trail, closing the loop. Follow this path back to the trailhead to complete the hike.

MILES AND DIRECTIONS

0.0 Start by crossing the bridge over Alameda Creek and walking on the Indian Joe Nature Trail.

0.4 Turn left on the Indian Joe Creek Trail and climb alongside the small creek.

1.6 Turn right on Cave Rocks Road.

2.6 Arrive at the Cerro Este Overlook and begin hiking on Cerro Este Road.

3.0 Veer left onto the McCorkle Trail.

3.8 Cross the "W" Tree Rock Scramble.

4.25 At the entrance to the Sunol backpacker camp, head downhill on the Backpack Trail.

4.8 Turn right onto Camp Ohlone Road.

5.75 Reach Little Yosemite. From here, climb uphill on Cerro Este Road.

6.0 Turn left on the Canyon View Trail.

6.9 Turn left onto the Indian Joe Nature Trail.

7.3 Cross the bridge over Alameda Creek and arrive back at the trailhead.

7. MOUNT DIABLO GRAND LOOP

WHY GO?

The Grand Loop on Mount Diablo is a strenuous but rewarding hike on one of the iconic landmarks of the Bay Area. This view-packed hike leads through remote forests and chaparral up to the summit, where one of the most staggering vistas in the world awaits.

THE RUNDOWN

Start: Diablo Valley Overlook, adjacent to the Juniper Campground entrance
Distance: 7.2-mile loop
Hiking time: 4–5 hours
Difficulty: Strenuous
Elevation gain: 2,000 feet
Season: Year-round, though summers can be very hot.
Trail surface: Dirt road, packed dirt, rocky

Canine compatibility: Dogs not permitted
Fees and permits: Entrance fee
Land status: Mount Diablo State Park
Trail contact: 96 Mitchell Canyon Rd., Clayton 94517; (925) 837-2525; www.parks.ca.gov/?page_id=517
Other: Water is available at the Juniper Campground and at the summit museum.

FINDING THE TRAILHEAD

From I-690 in Danville, take exit 39 for Diablo Road. Drive east on Diablo Road, turning right to stay on Diablo Road after 0.7 mile. Continue on Diablo Road for 2.1 miles and then turn left onto Mount Diablo Scenic Boulevard. Proceed 1.1 miles then turn right where the road merges with South Gate Road. Drive 5.8 miles on this windy road then turn right onto Summit Road at the Junction Ranger Station. Continue for 2.3 miles to the large parking area at the Diablo Valley Overlook, which is adjacent to the entrance to the Juniper Campground. **Trailhead GPS:** 37°52'36.31"N / 121°55'52.23"W

WHAT TO SEE

Mount Diablo is one of the highest mountains in the Bay Area and probably the most prominently visible. Situated to the east of San Francisco Bay and rising out of the flatlands just south of the delta of the Sacramento and San Joaquin Rivers, Mount Diablo can be seen from all over the Bay Area. It can also be observed from distant counties in the Central Valley and even from the great Sierra Nevada to the east. The converse of this incredible visibility is that the panorama from the top is one of the most staggering you will find anywhere.

The mountain is preserved within Mount Diablo State Park, which has a large network of trails. Perhaps the best way to experience the best of Mount Diablo is to hike the Grand Loop. This route circumnavigates the upper flanks of the main summit by

Eagle Peak is a prominent landmark while traversing the north side of Mount Diablo.

combining numerous fire roads and foot trails. It reveals several of Mount Diablo's sub-sidiary peaks, its creeks, perspectives on the mountain itself, as well as the communities that are clustered at its feet. The loop also leads to the observation tower at the summit, where you can enjoy the superlative vantage point.

The Grand Loop starts at the Diablo Valley Overlook, which is adjacent to the Juniper Campground entrance. Enter the campground and follow the paved road to the far end, where a gate blocks vehicular access to a dirt road. Follow the road, which is named the Deer Flat Road. Very soon after leaving the campground, you have panoramic views to the west and south. Grassy slopes fall steeply away from the trail to oak groves and chaparral-covered ridges. Parts of Danville, Alamo, and Walnut Creek are visible in the distance. The old road descends gently for 0.7 mile before intersecting Meridian Ridge Road. Turn right onto Meridian Ridge Road and commence a descent down a series of wide switchbacks. As you descend, the perspective shifts and you are now able to see rugged Eagle Peak, one of Mount Diablo's major subpeaks, as well as look down on the delta, Suisun Bay, and many of the mountains in Napa and Sonoma Counties.

Much of this section of Meridian Ridge Road passes through grass-covered slopes punctuated with oaks and gray pines. At 1.85 miles stay right at the junction with the Mitchell Canyon Road. Continue downhill a little farther and cross over Deer Flat Creek, one of the few sources of water on this hike. In summer this creek is usually very small or completely dry. Climb out of the creek's drainage and around a ridge, passing the long spur trail that leads to Eagle Peak, before reaching the Prospectors Gap Road 3 miles from the trailhead.

Stay straight on the Prospectors Gap Road and pass through extremely dense chapar-ral. To the east the inaccessible northern face of North Peak, the secondary summit of Mount Diablo, looms high overhead. Rock outcroppings push through the dense vegeta-tion, giving the mountain a weathered visage. After 0.8 mile of hiking on the Prospectors Gap Road you cross a small creek, the last potential water on the trail. Once across the creek, the dirt road winds onto a ridge and begins a long, steady, and brutal climb up to Prospectors Gap. This is the steepest part of the loop, and there is not much shade. As you persevere up the grade, you can make out the observation tower on the summit of Mount Diablo. When you finally reach the top of the grade, 4.3 miles from the begin-ning of the hike, there is a four-way junction. Turn right here onto the North Peak Trail.

The singletrack path is a welcome change from the fire roads that have made up the loop thus far. Though it climbs steadily, the grade is not as steep as the ascent to Prospec-tors Gap. Plus the scenery gets progressively better the higher you get. North Peak looms large to the east, and much of the Central Valley to the southeast can be seen from the trail. Much of the vegetation below this point was burned in a fire, and snags still cling to the steep slopes. As the path bends around the shoulder of a ridge onto the south side of Mount Diablo, you feel like you are on the edge of the world. The slopes drop away rap-idly, and you get a sense of just how high above everything you are. The trail keeps climb-ing as it traverses the south face of the mountain. The observation tower now seems so close that you can just scramble up to it. Stick to the trail and arrive at the main park road.

Summit view of North Peak, the Delta, and the Sierra Nevada.

Signs direct you to turn right onto the Summit Trail. This route climbs through thick brush before emerging on the park road a second time. Follow the pavement to the right a short distance until the road forks. Ignore the Fire Interpretive Trail, which makes a loop just below the summit. Instead cross the road at the fork and continue climbing up the trail through shady forest. Skirt the edge of radio tower installation before dropping down to the observation tower and museum's parking area. Don't be bothered by the fact that you have suffered while others have made the easy drive to get here. Hiking up to the summit of Mount Diablo is the only way to truly earn the astonishing panorama.

Walk across the parking lot and head into the tower. From the second-story observation deck you can enjoy one of the most spectacular views imaginable. In the east, most of the Sierra Nevada's length is evident; to the far north, Lassen Peak is visible on clear days. Individual subranges of the Sierra, like the Desolation Wilderness, can be made out. To the south, the Diablo Range extends out toward the horizon; to the north, the North Coast Range rises on the far side of the delta and Suisun Bay. Mount Tamalpais and several other North Bay mountains line the horizon. Parts of San Francisco Bay, including most of its bridges, as well as the city of San Francisco all gleam in the distance. It is a truly astounding panorama.

Eventually it will be necessary to finish the hike. Retrace your steps from the tower back down to the road at the top of the Summit Trail. Pass the trail and walk down the road toward a picnic area. Continue beyond the picnic area to a large parking lot. The Juniper Trail begins on the west side of the lot. Head down this path. It crosses a paved road and then makes a steady 1.0-mile descent back down to the Diablo Valley Overlook. Arrive at the trailhead and complete the Grand Loop.

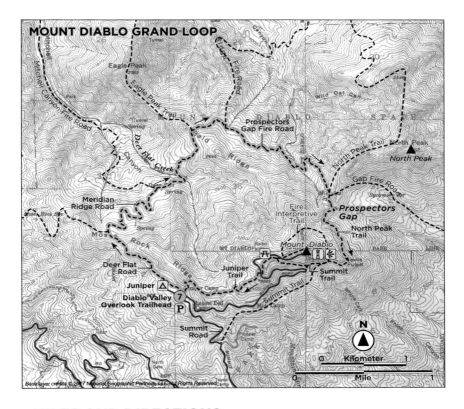

MILES AND DIRECTIONS

0.0 Start from the Diablo Valley Overlook and walk through the Juniper Campground. Pass a gate and continue on Deer Flat Road.

0.7 Turn right onto Meridian Ridge Road. Stay right at the next two trail junctions.

3.0 Stay straight to continue onto Prospectors Gap Road.

4.3 Reach Prospectors Gap. Turn right onto the North Peak Trail.

5.3 Once you get to the park road, turn right onto the Summit Trail.

5.5 At the second road crossing, turn right and follow the road to where it forks. Take the path that leads through trees between the two roads.

5.75 Arrive at the museum and observation tower at the summit of Mount Diablo. Retrace your steps to the second road crossing.

6.0 At the second road crossing, stay on the road and continue past the summit picnic area to a large parking lot.

6.2 Look for the Juniper Trail at the west end of the large parking lot.

7.2 Arrive back at the overlook.

NORTH COAST RANGE

LIKE ITS SIBLING COASTAL RANGE TO THE SOUTH, the North Coast Range is a vast mountain region that lies between the Pacific Ocean and the Central Valley. Extending from San Francisco Bay to the Oregon border, this is generally a very remote mountain range that occupies one of the most lightly populated parts of California. Only the southern end of the range, nearest San Francisco Bay, is near significant population centers.

This large mountain province can be divided up into three regions. The southernmost section of the range lies between Clear Lake, the largest freshwater lake entirely within California, and San Francisco Bay. This area is best known for its world-famous grape-growing areas and its wine production. The mountains here are the only part of the Coast Ranges where extensive volcanic forces created the terrain. A few recognizable volcanoes, such as prominent Mount Konocti, can be observed in this area.

The rest of the North Coast Range, which is the majority of the range, is composed of sedimentary rock and can be divided into two parts along a longitudinal axis. The two halves of the range are roughly separated by the north-flowing Eel River and the south-flowing Russian River. This is an imprecise boundary and not entirely accurate in terms of the geography, but as a rule of thumb, or when just looking at a map, these are helpful lines to distinguish that areas.

The western side of the range is a long band of lower, heavily forested mountains. Peaks in this area rarely exceed 4,000 feet. The area is cut by innumerable steep-sided canyons. Though not tall, there are areas that are exceedingly rugged. It is in these mountains, close to the coast and with very temperate conditions, that you find the great expanses of the fabled coast redwood. The tallest living things on Earth, these magnificent trees once blanketed the entire region, but nineteenth- and early twentieth-century lumber harvesting considerably reduced the amount of old-growth redwoods. Fortunately, much of what remains is protected in a patchwork of state parks and Redwood National Park.

The east side of the range is much higher than its western counterpart. Several peaks rise above 7,000 feet, and its highest point, on Mount Linn in the South Yolla Bolly Mountains, exceeds 8,000 feet. Despite their height, there are only a handful of natural lakes in this high country, and most of them are not large. Most of this area is contained in Mendocino National Forest. A few wildlands, notably the Yuki, Yolla Bolly–Middle Eel, and Snow Mountain Wilderness Areas, protect large swaths of this mountain terrain.

Hiking in this area is largely focused on the dramatic coastline and in the redwoods. While there are a few great trails in the high country, commercial activity still outweighs recreational use considerably.

8. ALAMERE FALLS

WHY GO?

The highlight of this trip is an excellent waterfall plunging off a cliff directly into the Pacific Ocean. Along the way you enjoy wonderful ocean vistas and pass rare seaside freshwater lakes.

THE RUNDOWN

Start: Palomarin Trailhead
Distance: 8.2 miles out and back
Hiking time: About 4 hours
Difficulty: Moderate
Elevation gain: 1,050 feet
Season: Year-round; waterfall best in winter to spring
Trail surface: Packed dirt, rocky, bare rock
Canine compatibility: Dogs not permitted
Fees and permits: None

Land status: Phillip Burton Wilderness
Trail contact: Point Reyes National Seashore, 1 Bear Valley Rd., Point Reyes Station 94956; (415) 464-5100; www.nps.gov/pore
Special considerations: The final leg of the hike features abundant poison oak. A difficult scramble through a narrow, rocky chute is needed to reach the beach. Exercise caution.

FINDING THE TRAILHEAD

From the small village of Olema, located at the intersection of CA 1 and Sir Francis Drake Boulevard, drive south on CA 1 for 9.1 miles. Turn right onto Olema Bolinas Road; after 1.5 miles turn left to stay on Olema Bolinas Road. Continue for 0.5 mile then turn right onto Mesa Road. Follow this road, paved at first and then gravel, for 4.5 miles to the Palomarin Trailhead. There is room for about 40 cars at the trailhead but on busy days, cars can line up quite a ways down the road. **Trailhead GPS:** 37°56'3.43"N / 122°44'49.65"W

WHAT TO SEE

The Point Reyes Peninsula is one of the most striking features on the Northern California coast. The presence of the peninsula is a testimony to the powerful forces that created most of California and continue to shape the landscape. Though the peninsula looks to be wholly connected to the mainland, it is separated by the San Andreas Fault. This seemingly invisible divider runs through the Bolinas Lagoon, along the length of the Olema Valley, and onward through Tomales Bay toward Bodega Bay on the Sonoma Coast. These powerful geologic forces have rendered the Point Reyes area a land apart from the rest of California, cast on a divergent course from the rest of the state. One result of this is that the rugged coastline is left without roads. The intrusion of the sea along the fault at the Bolinas Lagoon and Tomales Bay meant that CA 1 was routed inland, through the

Olema Valley. Consequently, Point Reyes boasts one of only three wilderness coastlines in the coterminous United States.

This wildland is preserved within the borders of Point Reyes National Seashore. A national park in all but name, the scenery here is equal to this lofty designation. The primeval character of the land is enshrined in the Phillip Burton Wilderness, which protects the more remote corners of the park, including the terrain you must hike through to reach Alamere Falls. Most of the hike follows the Coast Trail as it journeys along this beautiful meeting of land and sea, leading to one of the most unusual and attractive waterfalls in Northern California. It must be noted that this hike has gotten significantly more popular in the age of social media, and its proximity to the Bay Area means it can be crowded. The National Park Service works to mitigate the impact of this popularity, but tread lightly to preserve this amazing land.

The Coast Trail begins in an attractive grove of eucalyptus trees. It initially travels inland, on the south side of Arroyo Hondo, which will usually have some water flowing in it. The trail eventually crosses the creek and turns west back toward the coast. The sound of the surf soon becomes audible and the trail leaves the eucalyptus behind, exposing excellent views of the Pacific Ocean. From here the path turns northwest and begins to traverse the cliffs above the sea. The route is generally about 300 feet above Palomarin Beach, and a few routes are visible leading down to the sand. As the Coast Trail heads northwest, it travels in and out of a few drainages but generally maintains a northerly course above the sea.

After 1.2 miles the trail turns northeast, entering a large gulch. It crosses over the small creek flowing through the gulch and swings back to the west, climbing the north

Pelican Lake is the largest of the lakes passed en route to Alamere Falls.

Alamere Falls crashes onto the beach.

side. After another switchback, the trail climbs out of the gulch. After leaving the ravine, the route enters a narrow slot, where it tops out on a low pass at about 580 feet. The trail descends a little then levels off and begins the inland section of the hike, where it encounters a handful of lakes. The Mud Lakes are the first of these bodies of water the Coast Trail encounters. The pools are small and uninviting. Continue to the northwest, passing a few meadows but mostly staying beneath a very heavy forest canopy. Eventually Bass Lake comes into view. This lake is large and clear, and people can be seen swimming in it at times. Although the route only skirts the north end of the lake, a spur trail breaks away to the left and descends to the water.

After leaving Bass Lake, the Coast Trail climbs another low pass. Sections along this part of the hike cross over seeps and small streams that leave the path very muddy. As you hike west, you will eventually leave the forest behind and enter a large coastal prairie. Double Point, a prominent cone rising out of the sea, comes into view for the first time, rising attractively from the shore of Pelican Lake. This is the prettiest of the seaside lakes. Set in a large bowl beneath Double Point, the lake is surrounded by brushy slopes on all sides. Seabirds can often be seen floating in the water. At the north end of the lake, the Coast Trail comes to a three-way junction. The first, faint path leads up to the top of Double Point, a worthy trip in itself, though it is at times closed to protect nesting birds. The second trail has a sign indicating the way to Alamere Falls and noting that the route is unmaintained. The Coast Trail continues north to numerous destinations, among them Wildcat Camp. If you are able to get a reservation at this backcountry camp, you can enjoy a great overnight trip right on the ocean.

From the junction with the Coast Trail, the spur to Alamere Falls descends to the west, following the gulch drained by Alamere Creek. The trail swings north, passing through an

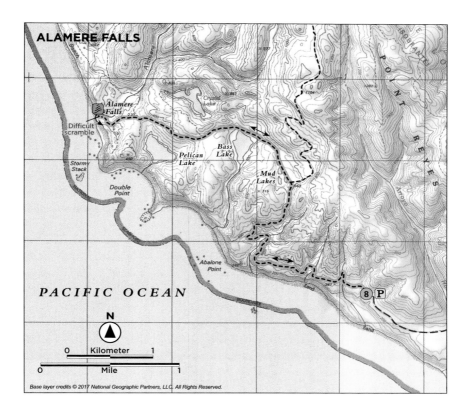

area of extremely dense brush. Poison oak is present in abundance here. It is easy to avoid, but be sure not to brush up against the hedges along the path. The route then descends a badly eroded series of ditches. It requires use of hands and some nimble maneuvering but is not too difficult. At the bottom you are deposited between two large cataracts on Alamere Creek. The one upstream to the right is the taller and prettier. Cross the creek and approach the cliffs to see Alamere Falls spilling onto the beach below. It is a spectacular sight. Extending north from the falls is beautiful Wildcat Beach. Coastal bluffs fall away steeply to the sandy ribbon. To get to the beach, there is a gully north of the falls through which you can descend. The route through the gully is badly eroded and requires climbing. If you are unsure about the descent or return ascent, stay on top and enjoy the view from the precipice. For those climbing down, note the interesting strata exposed in the walls of the gully. Once you hit the beach, the falls and the base of Double Point are to the left. To the right, the long sandy strand of Wildcat Beach extends north. Stand on the beach and look at the towering face of Double Point while the constant roar of the tidefall on the left and the receding and returning thunder of the surf to your right. It is an exceptional experience. In addition to the falls, Wildcat Beach offers excellent beach

Dramatic Wildcat Beach stretches north from Alamere Falls.

walking. When you can tear yourself away, scramble back up to the trail and follow it back to the trailhead.

MILES AND DIRECTIONS

0.0 Start at the Palomarin Trailhead.

1.2 The trail enters a large gulch, veering away from the ocean as it climbs up to a low pass.

2.25 Pass the shallow Mud Lakes on your left.

2.75 Large Bass Lake appears below the trail to the left.

3.25 Pelican Lake, the prettiest of the lakes on the trail, appears in a grassy bowl.

3.6 Turn left onto the spur trail leading to Alamere Falls.

4.0 Arrive at the top of Alamere Falls.

4.1 Reach the beach and the base of the falls after a difficult scramble through the cliffs. Climb back up to the trail and return the way you came.

8.2 Arrive back at the trailhead.

9. SONOMA COAST

WHY GO?

Traveling along gorgeous seaside bluffs and through high coastal hills, this trip along the Sonoma Coast offers the best of ocean hiking.

THE RUNDOWN

Start: Pullout along Goat Rock Road
Distance: 8.5-mile lollipop (*Option:* easy 3.0 miles out and back to Shell Beach on the Kortum Trail)
Hiking time: About 5 hours
Difficulty: Moderate
Elevation gain: 950 feet
Season: Year-round
Trail surface: Dirt, paved

Canine compatibility: Dogs not permitted
Fees and permits: None
Land status: Sonoma Coast State Park
Trail contact: 3095 Highway 1, Bodega Bay 94923; (707) 875-3483; www.parks.ca.gov/?page_id=451
Special considerations: This hike requires crossing CA 1.

FINDING THE TRAILHEAD

From US 101 in Santa Rosa, take the River Road exit and drive west on River Road and CA 116 for 27.4 miles to the intersection with CA 1. River Road becomes CA 116 in the town of Guerneville. Turn left onto CA 1 and drive south for 1 mile. Turn right onto Goat Rock Road. Drive on this paved road for 0.5 mile to a pullout where the road turns to the north. If this small parking area is full, there is one back up the road a couple hundred feet. Trails from both parking areas connect to the Kortum Trail. **Trailhead GPS:** 38°25'56.33"N / 123°7'1.42"W

WHAT TO SEE

The Sonoma Coast is one of the prettiest stretches of coast in Northern California. It is blessed with numerous sea stacks, tall cliffs rising out of the surf, numerous beaches, and grass-covered hills climbing high just beyond the immediate coastal areas. Small groves of redwoods are hidden among the folds of the hills, and the Russian River, one of the largest rivers in the North Coast Range, reaches the sea amid this beautiful scene. Much of the Sonoma Coast is preserved in excellent Sonoma Coast State Park. This large preserve includes a significant amount of the coast itself, as well as substantial tracts in the hills just beyond the sea. This hike combines the best trails that explore each section of the park into one magnificent oceanfront journey. In one trip you can enjoy dramatic cliffs above the surf, scenic rock formations, redwood trees, and spectacular vistas overlooking the mouth of the Russian River as well as reaching 30 miles inland. (*Option:* For a shorter hike, take the coast section or the loop through the hills to the top of Red Hill. If you're

Beautiful views of the Sonoma Coast are a highlight of the Kortum Trail.

planning to do the shorter options, consider parking at the Shell Beach parking area, 0.9 mile past Goat Rock Road on CA 1.)

Start the hike at one of the pullouts along Goat Rock Road. These all descend a grassy hillside and converge on the Kortum Trail at a large cluster of rocks called the Sunset Boulders. Though there is some poison oak around the rocks, they are fun to scramble on. As you hike south from the boulders, the Kortum Trail swings close to the precipice high above the sea, affording great views of the Pacific Ocean. Numerous sea stacks of various sizes populate the water just off the beaches. The waves crashing into the rocky towers are some of nature's high drama. As you continue south, you pass another large tower rising out of the grassy plain. The trail then crosses a bridge over a small creek and swings inland, where it soon crosses a second bridge. After the second bridge, watch for use trails leading closer to the edge of the cliffs, affording more opportunities to look down at the ocean. A larger spur also leads to a great vista a little farther on.

Soon the trail arrives at the Shell Beach parking area. A well-built path provides access to the beach. (**Options:** If you do not plan to hike into the hills, this is a good place to turn around, though you might want to continue south along the Kortum Trail. More beach access and ocean vistas await.) To hike the loop through the hills, walk east, along the parking lot driveway, all the way to CA 1. Carefully cross the highway and walk to the gated road on the other side. This is the beginning of the loop hike up to the summit of Red Hill.

From the gate, hike east on the Pomo Canyon Trail. You immediately begin to climb as you traverse the slope of a grassy hill. After climbing for 0.5 mile you arrive at a trail junction. The Red Hill Trail branches off to the right here. You will return by this route. Stay left, continuing on the Pomo Canyon Trail. Fortunately, the terrain levels off and you can enjoy the open scenery. In 0.35 mile you will arrive at a spur leading to the north. Following this leads quickly to a great overlook above the Russian River. The water here is slow moving as it makes its final push to the sea, a striking contrast to the vigorous river that flows through Mendocino and northern Sonoma Counties. The open, level terrain continues a little farther before the path plunges into dense brush and heavy forest. This continues with sporadic openings for 1.0 mile until the trail reaches the junction with the Red Hill Trail. The Pomo Canyon Trail continues beyond the junction, leading through a second-generation redwood grove before ending at the Pomo Canyon Campground. This hike can be done from this trailhead as well, but the route from Shell Beach coupled with the Kortum Trail is a better option.

At the intersection of the Pomo Canyon and Red Hill Trails, turn right onto the Red Hill Trail and begin climbing across the grassy slopes of Red Hill. In spring a small creek runs through this area and wildflowers line the trail. In 0.4 mile you reach the spur leading to the summit of Red Hill. Turn left here and continue climbing. The broad, grassy summit lies another 0.4 mile ahead. Along the way, the path weaves through a hilltop redwood grove. Once on top of Red Hill, an awesome 360-degree panorama unfolds. To the west, 30 miles distant, the high peaks of the Mayacamas Mountains, the backbone of the Wine Country, is crowned by the high peaks of Mount Saint Helena and Cobb Mountain. To the north, the Russian River reaches the ocean. The small village of Jenner can be observed huddling on a steep hillside above the river. To the south you can see the peninsulas that are the handiwork of the San Andreas Fault. Bodega Head and the Point Reyes Peninsula are both on the opposite side of the fault from the rest of the land and are moving in a different direction than the rest of California.

Red Hill boasts an excellent view of the Russian River as it reaches the Pacific Ocean.

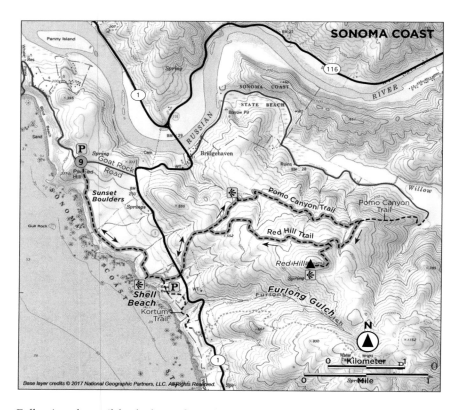

Following the trail back down from the top of Red Hill, turn left to continue the loop on the Red Hill Trail. The path skirts the edge of the redwood grove as it begins the descent back toward Shell Beach. Beyond the redwoods, the trail crosses open, wind-swept hillsides where views of the Pacific continue to be good. After crossing a small stream, the path passes between two large rock outcroppings. The northern one makes a fine scramble with a good perch at the top. From the rocks it is a short walk down to the junction with the Pomo Canyon Trail. Follow that back down to CA 1 and carefully cross the highway. Retrace your steps back along the Kortum Trail to the trailhead at Goat Rock Road.

MILES AND DIRECTIONS

0.0 Start from one of the pullouts on Goat Rock Road and head downhill to the Sunset Boulders, where the various paths converge on the Kortum Trail.

1.5 Arrive at the Shell Beach parking area. Walk east and cross over CA 1 to begin the Red Hill loop. (**Option:** Turn around here for a 3.0-mile out-and-back hike.)

Hiking to Red Hill includes inland panoramas such as Cobb Mountain and Mount Saint Helena.

2.1 Stay left to continue on the Pomo Canyon Trail at its intersection with the Red Hill Trail. You'll return on Red Hill Trail as you complete the loop.

2.5 Turn left on a short spur to reach an overlook above the Russian River.

3.8 At the second intersection with the Red Hill Trail, turn right and begin climbing toward the summit.

4.3 Turn left on the spur leading to the summit.

5.1 After returning from the top of Red Hill, turn left to continue on the Red Hill Trail.

6.4 At the junction with the Pomo Canyon Trail, turn left and descend to CA 1 and the Shell Beach parking lot.

7.0 From the Shell Beach parking area, head north on the Kortum Trail back toward the Sunset Boulders and the trailhead.

8.5 Arrive back at the trailhead on Goat Rock Road.

10. PALISADES (NAPA VALLEY)

WHY GO?

Journeying into some of the Wine Country's most spectacular terrain, the hike through the Palisades is an adventure into a wilderness of rock high above the world-famous Napa Valley.

THE RUNDOWN

Start: Mount Saint Helena Trailhead at Robert Louis Stevenson State Park
Distance: 10.5-mile shuttle (along Palisades to Calistoga) (**Options:** easy 4.6 miles out and back to Table Rock)
Hiking time: 5–6 hours
Difficulty: Moderate
Elevation gain: 1,330 feet
Season: Year-round
Trail surface: Packed dirt, rocky, bare rock

Canine compatibility: Dogs not permitted
Fees and permits: None
Land status: State park, county land
Trail contact: Robert Louis Stevenson State Park, 3801 Saint Helena Hwy., Calistoga 94515; (707) 942-4575; www.parks.ca.gov/?page_id=472
Special considerations: Parts of this trail climb steep, unshaded slopes that can be very hot in summer.

FINDING THE TRAILHEAD

Table Rock Trail: Starting at the intersection of CA 29 and Silverado Trail near downtown Calistoga, drive north on CA 29 for 7.5 miles. At the summit of the long grade, turn right into the trailhead parking lot. GPS: N38°38.55567' / W122°34.78033'

Oat Hill Mine Road: The trailhead for the Oat Hill Mine Road is at the intersection of CA 29, Silverado Trail, and Lake Street. At the three-way intersection, drive south on Lake Street and immediately turn left into the dirt parking area. Cross over CA 29 to get to the trailhead. **Trailhead GPS:** 38°39'8.69"N / 122°35'58.68"W

WHAT TO SEE

The Napa Valley is among Northern California's most well-known regions. World-class viticulture has established it as one of the country's premier travel destinations. This is one of the few parts of the North Coast Range that is composed of volcanic rock, which stands in contrast to the rest of the range, which is composed of sedimentary rock. The volcanic soils are a significant reason that high-quality wine grapes grow here. Volcanism has also produced several great hiking destinations. While not what the Wine Country is primarily known for, it remains a great place to get outside and enjoy a peaceful, pastoral, and geologically interesting area. One of the best places to experience this beauty is at the north end of the Napa Valley, hiking among the dramatic Palisades. This band of cliffs extends eastward from Mount Saint Helena, the largest and most dominant peak in the

Mount Saint Helena looms beyond the moonscape of Table Rock.

Wine Country. Together, the peak and the Palisades form a striking skyline above the town of Calistoga and the vineyards of the northern Napa Valley.

Hiking along the Palisades gives you an opportunity to experience these crags up close while also providing magnificent bird's-eye views of the entire length of the Napa Valley. Strange rock formations, spring wildflowers, and waterfalls, as well as plenty of history, keep this trail interesting. Fall color in the vineyards is also a seasonal highlight. However, these features are best enjoyed by hiking the Palisades as a shuttle. This is one of the few such hikes recommended in this book. Doing this hike as a one-way trip means it is mostly downhill, and the full extent of the Palisades can be experienced. Fortunately, the two points on the shuttle are only a convenient 7.5 miles and 15-minute drive apart. If you want to visit the Palisades but don't want to make the whole one-way hike, a great option is to drive to the starting point at the Mount Saint Helena trailhead and hike down to Table Rock. This still provides access to some of the interesting rock formations and great Napa Valley panoramas but does not require a shuttle.

The hike begins at the Robert Louis Stevenson State Park trailhead. Most hikers here are heading to the summit of Mount Saint Helena, which begins on the other side of CA 29. Look for the trailhead marker indicating the route to Table Rock and the Palisades on the south side of the parking lot, and begin climbing through a bay forest. After 0.25 mile the canopy parts briefly and a short spur leads to some rocks overlooking fire-ravaged Collayomi Valley. The forest envelopes the trail again, and after some short switchbacks another spur leads farther off-trail to another vista point. Continue climbing on the main path before breaking out of the forest cover at a jumble of rocks. Scramble on the boulders for a fine overlook above the Napa Valley. This is the highest point on the hike.

To continue to Table Rock, head steeply downhill before passing through a rock garden where hikers have stacked and arranged boulders in unusual formations. Look to the north to spot the rounded mass of 7,055-foot Snow Mountain. After the rock garden, the trail descends yet again, this time passing volcanic outcroppings. To the east is the rugged backcountry of Bear Valley. Though this area is privately owned, it exists in an essentially primeval state. At the bottom of the canyon, cross over Garnett Creek and begin climbing toward Table Rock. Finally, 2.1 miles from the trailhead, you arrive at the junction with the Palisades Trail. Whether you are hiking the whole shuttle or just to Table Rock, it is worth the effort to hike out over the moonscape summit of Table Rock. The volcanic rock appears in oddly stratified layers, and little vegetation has managed to eke out an existence on the barren plateau. To the west rises the impressive bulk of Mount Saint Helena. Spreading out below Table Rock to the south is the northernmost end of the Napa Valley, the squared lines of the vineyards providing a pleasing contrast to the naturally flowing contours of the terrain. If this is your destination, you'll need to climb back out to the trailhead from here. For those continuing on the shuttle hike, return to the junction with the Palisades Trail.

When it is time to depart Table Rock, hike south on the Palisades Trail. The path quickly climbs up some switchbacks to a saddle before beginning a long descent into the heart of the Palisades themselves. This is first moderated by a few more switchbacks, some of which are well constructed with stone steps. The path finally straightens out for about 0.25 mile before rounding a shoulder on a steep ridge. Here a plaque identifies the spot as Lasky Point, for Moses Lasky, whose family has facilitated the trail's right-of-way through this stretch of land. At the point you will enjoy the first really good opportunity to observe the Palisades themselves. Consisting of a band of volcanic rock, the cliffs rise 500 to 600 feet above the trail in some places. The route passes along the base of the cliffs, alternating between open, grassy hillsides and forest of oak, pine, and fir.

From Lasky Point, the trail begins to traverse the first of three amphitheaters formed by the Palisades. The cliffs above the trail get progressively more rugged and the terrain more open as you move from the three bowls. The views of the Napa Valley to the south are good whenever you pass through the treeless, grassy sections of trail. Reach the end of the first amphitheater 1.5 miles from the beginning of the Palisades Trail and the end of the second after another 0.8 mile. At the beginning of the third amphitheater, the trail crosses over an open, rocky section as it moves right up to the base of the Palisades. As the trail rounds the corner and enters the third bowl, look for a small waterfall that flows in spring or after a recent rain. The little cataract, located in a small gully, makes a 30-foot plunge off a cliff. The route crosses the stream just above the falls. There are nice rocks nearby on which to perch, enjoy the sound of falling water, and marvel at the awesome panorama unfolding to the south.

After crossing the stream, the trail begins to climb up close to the base of the cliffs again. It soon passes beneath a dense forest canopy at the base of the cliffs. Here there are a few grottos where tall, seasonal waterfalls rain down on large boulders. One in particular has a large flat-topped rock where you can climb up and enjoy the water's cooling effect. Beyond the grottos, sunlight reclaims the trail as it crosses more grassy slopes and then descends to the junction with the Oat Hill Mine Road. Watch for large rectangular rocks. These were quarried nearby and are among the few remnants of the old Holm's Place homestead. Just past the ruins the Palisades Trail arrives at the Oat Hill Mine Road. Turn right here to begin the descent to Calistoga.

The old Oat Hill Mine Road was originally constructed in the nineteenth century to provide access to mercury mines in the remote hills behind the Palisades. When the mines played out, the road fell into disuse and Napa County took possession of the right-of-way. In the latter part of the twentieth century, the route became popular with hikers and mountain bikers. Though this hike only covers the first 4.5 miles of the road, it actually continues all the way to a trailhead near Aetna Springs in secluded Pope Valley. When hiking on the old road, especially the upper sections, watch for ruts worn into the soft volcanic rock. Also worth noting is the grade of the descent. Since the road was built for wagons, it was engineered to make a very gradual climb up the long ridge from Calistoga. For this hike, that means an easy, enjoyable descent.

From the junction with the Palisades Trail, hike south on Oat Hill Mine Road. The land here is very rocky, and there are great views of the Palisades and Mount Saint Helena. These remain in view for 0.75 mile as the road traverses the west side of the ridge. Oat Hill Mine Road then crosses over a saddle in the ridge; as it does so, awesome views down the entire length of the Napa Valley open up. Keen eyes will spot double-peaked Mount Diablo. Once on the east side of the ridge, the trail continues its gentle descent. After another 0.5 mile, spur trails lead to the top of Bald Hill. The top of this rocky knob marks the final opportunity to look out over the Palisades and Mount Saint Helena. Back

The Palisades Trail closesly follows the rugged cliffs above the Napa Valley.

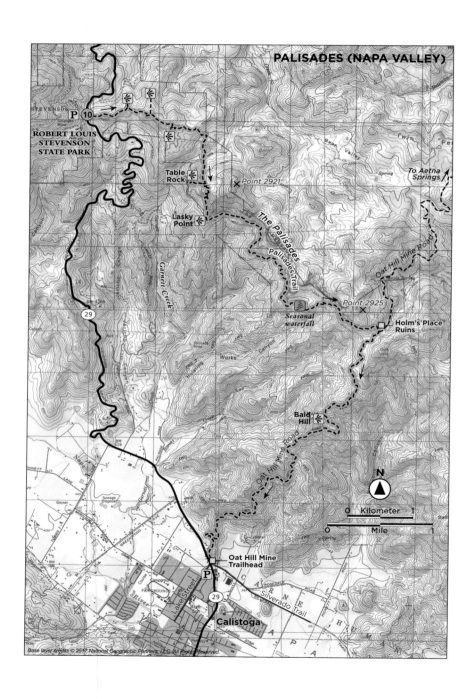

PALISADES (NAPA VALLEY)

ROBERT LOUIS
STEVENSON
STATE PARK

P 10

Table
Rock

Lasky
Point

Point 2921

The Palisades

Palisades Trail

Seasonal
waterfall

Point 2925

Holm's Place
Ruins

Oat Hill Mine Road

To Aetna
Springs

Bean
Valley

Spring

Bald
Hill

Oat Hill Mine Road

Garnett Creek

29

N

0   Kilometer   1

0   Mile   1

Oat Hill Mine
Trailhead

P

29

Silverado Trail

Calistoga

Lake Street

Base layer credits © 2017 National Geographic Partners, LLC. All Rights Reserved

on the road, enjoy the chance to see Napa Valley a little more before being swallowed up into the woods that blanket the lower flanks of the ridge. The trail continues for 3.0 more miles beyond Bald Hill before finally depositing hikers at the trailhead on CA 29, just north of Calistoga. There is a fine pizza place just across the road from the trailhead, perfect for an after-hike meal.

MILES AND DIRECTIONS

0.0 Start at the trailhead on CA 29 and follow the path signed for Table Rock and the Palisades Trail.

1.0 Scramble on some rocky outcroppings for great views at the highest point on the trail.

1.8 Cross over Garnett Creek before making the climb up to Table Rock.

2.1 Arrive at the junction with the Palisades Trail.

2.25 Reach the edge of Table Rock. After enjoying the view, head back to the Palisades Trail and begin following that path. (**Option:** If Table Rock is your destination, retrace your steps from here.)

3.0 After rounding a bend, the first good views of the Palisades open up at Lasky Point. The trail now enters the first amphitheater.

3.9 The Palisades Trail enters the second amphitheater.

4.75 The trail rounds a sharp corner and enters the third amphitheater.

6.1 Arrive at the junction with Oat Hill Mine Road at the ruins of the Holm's Place homestead. Turn right here and hike south on Oat Hill Mine Road.

7.3 Oat Hill Mine Road passes beneath Bald Hill. Scramble up to the top of the hill for the last look at the Palisades.

10.5 Arrive at the Oat Hill Mine Trailhead on CA 29 and pick up your shuttle.

11. SNOW MOUNTAIN

WHY GO?

Venturing into the remote Snow Mountain Wilderness, this hike leads over bare ridges and through high forests and valleys to the bald summit of one of the highest peaks in the North Coast Range, where distant vistas await.

THE RUNDOWN

Start: Summit Springs Trailhead
Distance: 8.2 miles out and back
Hiking time: 4–6 hours
Difficulty: Moderate
Elevation gain: 1,900 feet
Season: Summer, fall
Trail surface: Packed dirt, rocky
Canine compatibility: Dogs permitted
Fees and permits: None

Land status: Snow Mountain Wilderness
Trail contact: Grindstone Ranger District, 825 North Humboldt Ave., Willows 95988; (530) 934-3316; www.fs.usda.gov/main/mendocino
Special considerations: Parts of this trail climb steep, unshaded slopes that can be hot in summer.

FINDING THE TRAILHEAD

From the north on I-5 in Willows, take exit 603 for CA 162/Willows. Turn left on CA 162 and drive west for 20.5 miles. Turn left onto SR 306. Proceed south for 22 miles to the outskirts of the hamlet of Stonyford. Turn right onto Fouts Springs Road. This road is also signed as FR M10/18N01. Stay on this road for 24.5 miles. The road is initially paved as it passes through the Fouts Springs area, where there is a boys' camp and numerous campgrounds. Continue past these facilities as M10 climbs above Stony Creek and traverses the side of the canyon, where the pavement soon gives way to a good dirt road. Eventually you will arrive at a junction where a sign indicates that Summit Springs lies 1 mile ahead. Turn right here and follow the steep road to the trailhead.

Coming from the south on I-5, take exit 586 for Maxwell Colusa Road. Turn left onto Maxwell Colusa Road and drive west for 9.6 miles to the intersection with Sites Lodoga Road. Along the way, Maxwell Colusa Road becomes Oak Street then Sites Maxwell Road and then Maxwell Sites Road. Once at Sites Lodoga Road, turn right. Stay on Sites Lodoga Road for 13.9 miles until you reach the village of Lodoga. Turn right onto Stonyford Lodoga Road and proceed 7.7 miles to the town of Stonyford. Turn left onto Market Street and in 0.3 mile turn left onto Fouts Springs Road. This road is also signed as FR M10/18N01. Stay on this road for 24.5 miles. The road is initially paved as it passes through the Fouts Springs area, where there is a boys' camp and numerous campgrounds. Continue past these facilities as M10 climbs above Stony Creek and traverses the side of the canyon, where the pavement soon gives way to a good dirt road. Eventually you will arrive at a junction where a sign indicates that Summit Springs lies 1 mile ahead. Turn right here and follow the steep road to the trailhead. **Trailhead GPS:** 39°20'45.02"N / 122°45'7.33"W

WHAT TO SEE

Most of the North Coast Range consists of lower elevation mountains and rolling hills that lie in close proximity to the Pacific Ocean. The northern end of the range has an interior area where peaks climb into the 7,000- and 8,000-foot range. This upland area consists primarily of sedimentary rocks and is blanketed by vast conifer forests. At the southern end of this high elevation region lies Snow Mountain, at the epicenter of the 60,076-acre Snow Mountain Wilderness. The highlight of the wilderness is the mountain from which it takes its name, dual-summited Snow Mountain. This high peak climbs to 7,056 feet on its east summit, which is just 18 feet higher than the west summit. The mountain is part of an island of metavolcanic rock that is an outlier in the otherwise sedimentary rock that composes the inner North Coast Range. Interestingly, it is one of the closest mountain wilderness areas to the San Francisco Bay Area. In it hikers will find deep forests, interesting rock formations, meadows, and expansive vistas.

The hike to the top of Snow Mountain begins in a mixed forest of pines and firs and immediately crosses the boundary of the Snow Mountain Wilderness before quickly emerging onto an open, shadeless ridge. It is a steep climb up the ridge through the brush, and at times this climb can get very hot. After 0.6 mile stay straight as a trail from Deafy Glade joins in from the right. The trail soon swings around a shoulder of the ridge and continues to climb upward. Views of the western summit of Snow Mountain are visible from here. The flanks are covered in brush and white snags, ghostly reminders of a fire that burned through here. The highest parts of the mountain are a ruddy color, with lots of exposed stone breaking out of the brush. Finally, after making steady upward progress for 1.8 miles, the trail reaches a saddle and enters the shade of the forest, untouched

The west summit of Snow Mountain rises above the first part of the hike to the summit.

Snow Mountain's east summit is a dramatic backdrop to small meadows.

by the past fire. It soon passes through the small meadow at Cedar Camp, where a vernal pool holds precious water for much of the year. At the south end of the meadow, stay right at a junction with the Milk Ranch Trail.

Continuing past the small meadow, the trail climbs through forest to a sequence of saddles. After the first saddle, the trail turns to the northwest and begins a gradual descent into the valley that lies between the east and west summits of Snow Mountain. Fire has damaged this area too. Of course this results in increased visibility of the surrounding area. The east summit rises above the valley and draws the eye as you continue the hike to the west. Views to the east are good all the way down into the Sacramento Valley and beyond to the Sierra Nevada. Stay left at a junction with a trail coming from Dark Hollow Creek, soon after which forest cover briefly envelops the trail again. The trees fade away before the path enters a gully where unusually colored rock is exposed. On the far side of the gully, you enter a bowl where there is sparse forest cover and a patchwork of small meadows.

After picking your way through the meadows and a little more fire damage, the trail begins climbing steeply up toward the rim of the bowl that lies between the two summits of Snow Mountain. At the top of the rim there is a junction with the trails leading to the two summits and also to the nearby Milk Ranch area. Turn right and begin the climb up toward the east summit, the higher of the two. Climb up the ridge as the trees and brush fade away. Soon all that remains is the bare volcanic soil and colorful rocks. The lack of vegetation leads to dramatic views, which improve until you finally reach the summit. Here an awesome panorama awaits. In the immediate vicinity, the western summit lies to the south and the multihued ridge leading to Point 6,994 draws the eye to the north. To the east, the large bulk of St. John Mountain looms a short distance away. Around all

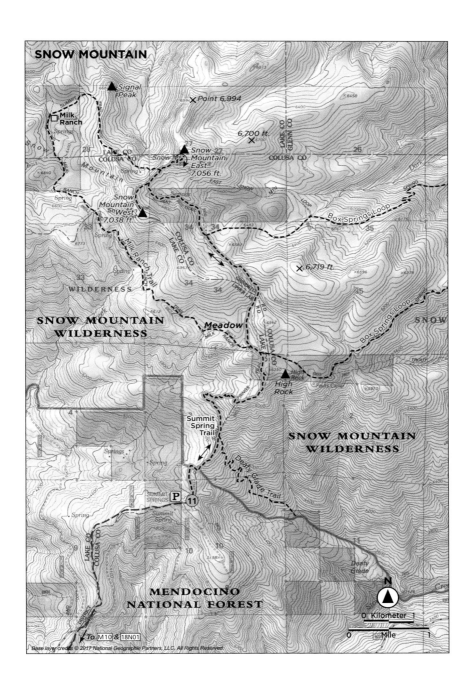

SNOW MOUNTAIN

Signal Peak
Point 6,994
Milk Ranch
Spring
6,700 ft.
LAKE CO
GLENN CO
COLUSA CO
LAKE CO
COLUSA CO
Snow Mountain East
7,056 ft.
Snow
Spring
Snow Mountain West
7,038 ft.
Box Springs Loop
Spring
Milk Ranch Trail
COLUSA CO
LAKE CO
6,719 ft.
SNOW
WILDERNESS
Box Springs Loop
SNOW MOUNTAIN
WILDERNESS
Meadow
Trident
COLUSA CO
LAKE CO
High Rock
High Rock
Faults Camp
Summit
Spring
Trail
SNOW MOUNTAIN
WILDERNESS
Deafy Glade Trail
Springs
Spring
Summit
SPRINGS
P
11
Summit
Spring
LAKE CO
COLUSA CO
Deafy
Glade
N
MENDOCINO
NATIONAL FOREST
0   Kilometer   1
0   Mile   1

To M10 & 18N01

Much of the North Coast Range high country can be observed from the summit of Snow Mountain.

of these sights is the sea of green that makes up the North Coast Range. Beyond this, to the north, lie the two towers of the Cascades, Mount Shasta and Lassen Peak. East of St. John Mountain is the awesome trough of the Sacramento Valley. The small range of the Sutter Buttes is a small island of topography in the sea–flat land. In the distance the great wall of the Sierra Nevada lines the horizon. When done enjoying this vista, follow the trail back to the trailhead.

MILES AND DIRECTIONS

0.0 Start at the Summit Springs Trailhead.

0.6 Stay straight at the intersection with the trail from Deafy Glade.

2.0 Arrive at the small meadow at Cedar Camp. Stay right at the junction with the Milk Ranch Trail.

2.9 Continue left through another trail junction.

3.8 Reach the top of the ridge, where there is a four-way trail intersection. Turn right and continue up the ridge toward the east summit of Snow Mountain.

4.1 Enjoy the vista from the top of Snow Mountain. Return the way you came.

8.2 Arrive back at the trailhead.

12. RUSSIAN GULCH

WHY GO?
Russian Gulch is a narrow canyon cutting into coastal hills filled with redwoods and a rushing creek. The trail leads through this beautiful setting to a lovely waterfall. Nearby is an unusual sinkhole that is also worth visiting.

THE RUNDOWN
Start: Fern Canyon Trailhead
Distance: 5.4-mile lollipop
Hiking time: About 3 hours
Difficulty: Easy
Elevation gain: None
Season: Year-round
Trail surface: Paved, dirt, rock

Canine compatibility: Dogs not permitted
Fees and permits: Entry fee
Land status: Russian Gulch State Park
Trail contact: PO Box 440, Mendocino 95460; (707) 937-5804; www.parks.ca.gov/?page_id=432

FINDING THE TRAILHEAD
From the junction of CA 1 and CA 20, drive south on CA 1 for 6.2 miles. Turn right onto Brest Road at the entrance to Russian Gulch State Park. Immediately turn left onto Point Cabrillo Drive. After paying the entrance fee, follow the main park road toward the campground and trailhead, passing under CA 1 along the way. Continue through the campground to the trailhead. To get to the sinkhole, head back toward the entrance station. After crossing back under CA 1, make the first left and continue to the trailhead parking area. **Trailhead GPS:** 39°19'52.06"N / 123°47'39.12"W

WHAT TO SEE
The coastline of Mendocino County is among the more remote sections of California's coast. Though much of it is traversed by CA 1, it is well removed from US 101, the main artery of transportation on the west side of California. It also falls a long way from major population centers like the Bay Area. This means that much of the Mendocino coast retains a very low-key atmosphere. Of course there are still attractions that draw many visitors, the quaint town of Mendocino being chief among them, but the pace is still slow and the number of people not nearly as high as other coastal destinations. This means that the trails in the numerous state parks are not crowded and retain a very rustic feel. One of the best ways to experience this beautiful area is to hike in Russian Gulch State Park. The park is named in honor of the Russians who frequented this area en route to their outpost at Fort Ross in the first half of the nineteenth century. The main trail travels the length of the gulch, passing redwoods as it follows the creek into the ever-steeper canyon. Near the end there is a beautiful waterfall set amid large redwoods. After hiking the

canyon, it is worth heading to the coastal section of the park and visiting the fascinating sinkhole, one of the more unusual phenomena along this section of the coast.

The Fern Canyon Trail, initially a wide path, departs the trailhead and heads east, into the canyon. Much of the first part of this hike follows an old, paved road. However, the lush vegetation is intent on reclaiming the road and has grown over it to such a degree that the path is hardly larger than a normal singletrack. The creek lies off to the right, and the path soon pulls alongside it, where it will continue to be a presence for most of the hike. Though there are redwoods at the outset of the hike, they do not get particularly large and dense until later in the hike. Still, large trees do pop up in places, despite the creek and steep walls of the canyons drawing most of the attention. Watch out for large trees, often firs, growing out of old stumps of redwoods cut long ago. The roots of the new trees cascade down to the ground, surrounding the old stump in sinuously beautiful designs.

Eventually the old road disappears and the trail enters a truly deep and remote redwood forest. After 1.65 miles you will arrive at two trail junctions. Stay left at the first. This is the Falls Loop Trail, which is the return route for the loop section of the hike. Veer right at the second junction. This is the North Trail, which climbs out of the canyon and heads back to the campground. Continue hiking through the canyon and increasingly large redwoods for another 0.65 mile before you reach beautiful Russian Gulch Falls. When flowing in high vigor, the creek divides into two streams above the falls, creating two separate plunges over the stark, rock cliff. The vegetation around the falls is incredibly dense and is in marked contrast to the parts of the cliff that the water has cleared of any growth. The falls are a little larger than they appear to be. This is because a fallen tree

Russian Gulch Falls is surrounded by beautiful redwoods.

The coastal sinkhole is worth visiting while exploring Russian Gulch.

trunk rests against the cliff. The log seems to make the size of the falls diminish a bit until you realize that it is a redwood log and much larger than a normal tree. To get to the falls, the trail descends steeply down to the pool at its base.

To continue the hike past the waterfall, follow the trail along the base of the falls to a bridge. Once across the creek, the trail climbs up to the top of the waterfall. Here the path is carved into the bedrock and is only a foot or so from the precipice as the water races over. Being able to gaze down to the bottom of the waterfall, as well as enjoy the tall redwoods and unusual trail, makes this is one of the prettier parts of the hike. Just past the top of the falls, stay right at a fork in the path, following signs for the Falls Loop Trail. From there the trail climbs out of the gulch by means of a couple switchbacks. Once over the lip, the trail levels off and begins a winding traverse of a level plateau. Note that the composition of the forest has changed and there are more oaks and firs in this area. After crossing the plateau for 0.75 mile, the trail descends into another deep gulch. Here large redwoods once again dominate the scenery. A gurgling brook flows through the forest, past large ferns. The trail follows this pretty stream back to the main gulch, where you will rejoin the main trail. Turn left and follow the path back to the trailhead.

Having journeyed through Russian Gulch, it is worth the time to make a stop at the state park's large sinkhole. From the trailhead it is an easy 0.1-mile walk to the rim of the sinkhole. The large pit is fenced all the way around its perimeter, but the trail follows the fence line. There are good views all the way around the entire circumference. The sinkhole has extremely steep cliffs down to its sandy bottom. Though it is 150 feet from the sea, the surf has managed to carve out a tunnel beneath the rock. When the waves come in, they shoot through the tunnel and crash onto the sandy beach in the sinkhole. It is a

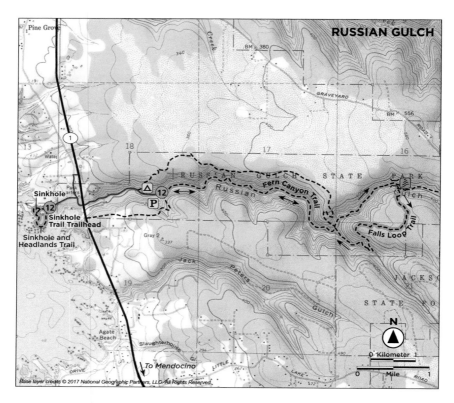

fascinating geologic oddity. The trail to the sinkhole connects to a short network of trails that follow the rim of the dramatic headlands, which are also an easy, worthwhile hike.

MILES AND DIRECTIONS

0.0 Start from the trailhead and follow the old road that serves as a trail into the canyon.

1.65 Arrive at two forks in the trail. Stay left at the first, which is the Falls Loop Trail. You will return by this route. Stay right at the second junction, which is the North Trail.

2.3 The trail leads down to the base of Russian Gulch Falls. Cross the bridge and follow the trail at the top of the falls, where you will veer right onto the Falls Loop Trail.

3.8 The Falls Loop Trail rejoins the Fern Canyon Trail. Turn left and return to the trailhead.

5.4 Arrive back at the trailhead.

13. **LOST COAST**

WHY GO?

This unique trip offers the experience of hiking a remote, rugged, and wild coastline where mountains and ocean meet in dramatic fashion. Grassy prairies give way to sandy beaches and steep cliffs as the trail leads to a historic lighthouse.

THE RUNDOWN

Start: Mattole Beach Trailhead
Distance: 6.5 miles out and back
Hiking time: 3–4 hours
Difficulty: Easy
Elevation gain: None
Season: Year-round
Trail surface: Sandy, dirt, rock scrambling
Canine compatibility: Dogs permitted
Fees and permits: None

Land status: King Range Wilderness, King Range National Conservation Area
Trail contact: 768 Shelter Cove Rd., Whitethorn 95589; (707) 986-5400; www.blm.gov
Special considerations: A short section of this hike is impassable at high tide. It is necessary to either time the hike for when the tide is not high or take the alternative bypass route.

FINDING THE TRAILHEAD

The drive to the trailhead at Mattole Beach is long and windy. Begin on US 101 near Weott. This is 95 miles north of Willits and 45 miles south of Eureka. Take exit 663 and drive west on Bull Creek Flats Road. After 0.5 mile continue onto Lower Bull Creek Flats Road. In 1 mile turn right onto Mattole Road. Stay on Mattole Road for 21 miles, turning right to stay on Mattole Road at 12.8 miles. At Honeydew, turn right to stay on Mattole Road and continue for 13.6 miles. Turn left onto Lighthouse Road and proceed 4.4 miles on this gravel road to the trailhead at Mattole Beach.

Coming from the south, after taking exit 663, turn left on CA 254/Avenue of the Giants and then left onto Bull Creek Flats Road. Continue as above. **Trailhead GPS:** 40°17'20.43"N / 124°21'22.09"W

WHAT TO SEE

Northern California's Lost Coast is a dramatic meeting of sea and mountain. The area's scant population, considerable isolation, and extremely rugged terrain made road building through here an undesirable option. After traveling north for 655 miles from Southern California, CA 1, the Pacific Coast Highway, finally veers inland, turned away from the ocean by the large mountains pushing up against the surf. The highway having abandoned this area and funneling tourists inland, this long section of the coast became "lost." However, having been relegated to the status of traveling backwater has in no way

diminished the district's incredible beauty. Not only is the scenery intact, but the wildness has been maintained as well. The Lost Coast is one of only three wilderness coastlines on the Pacific Coast.

The heart of the Lost Coast is the towering King Range. Within 3 miles of the sea, these mountains attain heights up to King Peak's 4,088 feet. Not quite as high as the Santa Lucia Mountains in Big Sur, but no less rugged than that fabled range. However, the King Range's northern latitude means it gets far more moisture, leaving the mountains here cloaked in deep forest, while much of the Santa Lucias are home to semiarid vegetation and chaparral. The BLM-managed King Range National Conservation Area preserves the region in its primitive beauty. This park has developed a network of trails throughout the mountains, but the premier attraction remains the Lost Coast Trail. This path follows the ribbon of sand and grass that lies between the King Range and the Pacific Ocean for 24.6 miles from Shelter Cove to the Mattole River. The beach hiking in a wild setting is an utterly unique experience and one of the premier backpacking trips in California. Sections of trail also make great day hikes too. One of the best sections to hike is from the trail's northern terminus at the mouth of the Mattole River south to the historic Punta Gorda lighthouse. This hike combines many of the Lost Coast's best features, including beaches, coastal prairie, rocky cliffs, large creeks, and interesting historic sites.

If time permits, it is worth the effort to hike out onto Mattole Beach and see the end of the Mattole River. When it is time to begin the hike, leave the Mattole Trailhead and hike to the south. The trail soon splits before reaching a fenced-off area, only to rejoin past the fencing. Both options lead to the same place, but staying to the right leads to an interpretive display describing the site's archaeological importance. Within the fencing is a series of shell middens, heaps of shells and other debris left by the Mattole people.

These early inhabitants of this region included seafood in their diet and discarded the shells and other refuse in large heaps, called middens. Today the middens are one of the few remaining testimonies of these people.

Past the midden area the sandy trail continues south along the beach. Some hikers opt to bypass the trail altogether and stick to the beach, letting the waves lap their feet as they hike. The trail stays closer to the base of the cliff, crossing small creeks as it continues south. Most of the small streams dissipate once they reach the sandy beaches, rarely flowing all the way to the ocean. At times the trail moves up onto low benches above the sand and then drops back down onto the beach again. After 1.75 miles you arrive at an unsigned junction. Here a wide path begins switchbacking up the steep, grassy hillside while the main trail drops down onto the beach. The trail climbing the hillside is the route that bypasses the section of the hike that travels around Punta Gorda, which is impassable at high tide. This path climbs more than 300 feet before returning back down to the beach. It can be used as part of a lollipop at the end of the hike.

Staying at beach level, proceed down onto the sand and pass some large boulders. About 0.25 mile ahead lies the rocky protrusion of Punta Gorda. This is the first of three sections of the Lost Coast Trail that cannot be passed at high tide, and it is the shortest. When the tide is all the way in, the waves slam against the point's rock and there is no possibility of safe passage. However, when the tide is out, it is very easy to negotiate the rocks here and pick up the trail on the far side of the point. When you arrive here, survey the conditions carefully. If the tide is high, determine whether you want to take the bypass trail over the top of the point or turn around and head back to the trailhead.

Rough seas line the approach to the Punta Gorda lighthouse.

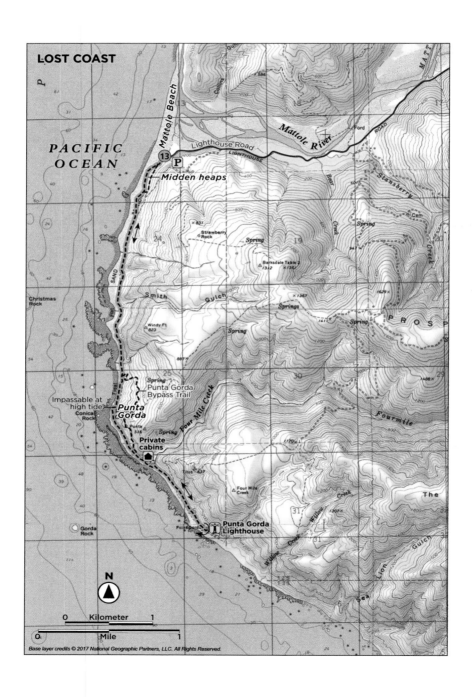

LOST COAST

PACIFIC OCEAN

Mattole Beach

Lighthouse Road

Mattole River

Ford

13

P

Midden heaps

Strawberry Rock

Spring

Spring

Barksdale Table
1312

Christmas Rock

Smith Gulch

Springs

Windy Pt
823

Spring

Spring

Spring

PROSP

Fourmile

Impassable at high tide
Conical Rock

Punta Gorda
Bypass Trail

Punta Gorda

Private cabins

Four Mile Creek

Four Mile Creek

The

Gorda Rock

Punta Gorda Lighthouse

Willow Creek

Sea Lion Gulch

N

0   Kilometer   1

0   Mile   1

If the way is clear, continue through the rocks and pick up the trail on the south side of Punta Gorda.

Once you pick the trail back up, keep heading south on one of the prettiest parts of the hike. The narrow path crosses a low bench above the beach, and views of the cliffs farther south and the sea directly below are wonderful. As you round a curve, the short tower of the abandoned Punta Gorda lighthouse becomes visible. As you approach, note the trail branching off to the left leading to some private cabins. Stay clear of this private property. When the tide is low, this area has some nice tidepools that make a great place to stop and explore. Near the cabins, large Four Mile Creek flows out to the sea. In spring it is large, wide, and formidable. During that time of year, it is necessary to ford the deep, swift creek to reach the lighthouse. Later in the year the flow is much lower and can often be crossed with logs.

Once across Four Mile Creek, you enter the King Range Wilderness for the first time as the trail continues on the grassy bench just above the beach. Nearly 0.2 mile after crossing Four Mile Creek, the path reaches a junction with the Cooskie Creek Trail. This path climbs high into the mountains of the King Range and travels deep into the wilderness. Stay straight, hiking along the beach for another 0.4 mile before finally arriving at the Punta Gorda lighthouse. This unique structure was built in 1912 to help guide ships along this dangerous section of coastline. Just 12 miles north is Cape Mendocino, the westernmost point in California. The lighthouse was decommissioned in 1951. It is now a popular camping spot for backpackers on the Lost Coast Trail, who enjoy the shelter it provides. Be sure to head inside and climb the spiral staircase up to where the light once rotated and warned ships at sea of the dangers in the area. After enjoying the historic setting, head back to Punta Gorda and see whether the tide will allow passage back north. If it is clear, follow the trail back to the trailhead. Otherwise, prepare to wait out the tide, or take the bypass over the grassy ridge in order to return to the trailhead.

MILES AND DIRECTIONS

0.0 Start from the Mattole Beach Trailhead and head south, keeping to the right at a fork in the trail and soon passing an interpretive display giving details about the archaeological site.

1.75 Pass the unsigned Punta Gorda bypass trail. Continue straight along the beach.

2.0 When the tide is not high, pass the rocky prominence of Punta Gorda. At high tide this section is impassable and should not be attempted.

2.6 Cross Four Mile Creek and enter the King Range Wilderness.

2.8 Stay straight at the junction with the Cooskie Creek Trail, continuing along the beach.

3.25 Arrive at the historic Punta Gorda lighthouse. Follow this route back to the trailhead, making sure the tide is low at Punta Gorda before proceeding.

6.5 Arrive back at the trailhead.

14. JAMES IRVINE TRAIL/ FERN CANYON

WHY GO?

This hike features some of best redwoods accessible by trail. In addition to the giant trees, the far end of the trail passes through awesome Fern Canyon and reaches the Pacific Ocean at Gold Bluffs Beach.

THE RUNDOWN

Start: Trailhead at the Prairie Creek Redwoods State Park Visitor Center
Distance: 11.0-mile double-stem lollipop
Hiking time: 5–7 hours
Difficulty: Moderate
Elevation gain: 1,320 feet
Season: Year-round
Trail surface: Packed dirt, rocky, creek bed
Canine compatibility: Dogs not permitted
Fees and permits: Entrance fee

Land status: Murrelet State Wilderness, Prairie Creek Redwoods State Park
Trail contact: 127011 Newton B. Drury Pkwy., Orick 95555; (707) 465-7335; www.parks.ca.gov/?page_id=415
Other: A shorter hike through Fern Canyon can be done by driving to the Fern Canyon Day Use Area and parking there. This hike can also be done as a shuttle. Water is available at the trailhead and from creeks.

FINDING THE TRAILHEAD

 From US 101, 5 miles north of Orick and 36.5 miles south of Crescent City, turn west onto the Newton B. Drury Parkway at the signed entrance to Prairie Creek Redwoods State Park. Drive north 1.1 miles and turn left into the visitor center parking area. **Trailhead GPS:** 41°21'50.84"N / 124°1'22.15"W

WHAT TO SEE

The north coast of California was once covered in vast stands of giant old-growth trees. Due to logging efforts in the nineteenth and early twentieth centuries, most of these grand forests were lost. Today the ancient trees may be fewer, but there are still places where you can lose yourself in the hushed wilderness of the towering redwoods. Perhaps no other trail offers as excellent an opportunity to experience an utterly wild old-growth forest as the James Irvine Trail. Cutting through the heart of Prairie Creek Redwoods' Murrelet State Wilderness, this fantastic hike leads through epic redwood groves. Yet these magnificent trees are not the only highlights of this trip. Beautiful Fern Canyon is a memorable section of trail near where the path ends at the edge of Gold Bluffs Beach on the Pacific Ocean. Rather than being a simple out and back, the middle of the hike

Young hikers enjoy exploring massive redwoods on the James Irvine Trail.

The James Irvine Trail winds through beautiful redwood forests.

follows a different route to the top of a ridge before returning to the trailhead, adding a little variety to the hike. There are still plenty of large trees here, but the increased elevation adds a different perspective on the forest.

The hike begins at the trailhead adjacent to Prairie Creek Redwood State Park's visitor center. The path starts off as a short nature trail loop. You immediately cross a large creek on a sturdy wooden bridge and pass beneath some of the most immense and beautiful trees of the entire hike. Indeed, just walking the nature trail is an excellent option for hikers looking for a shorter option. The nature trail crosses over Prairie Creek and passes two spurs branching off to the right. Follow the signs for the James Irvine Trail, which will be the third trail junction. Turn right here and begin the long journey through the heart of the redwoods.

Once on the James Irvine Trail, the trail makes a gentle ascent through soaring redwoods and an expansive understory of ferns and sorrel. The thick canopy of the tall trees filters out most of the sunlight, but shafts often manage to break through and illuminate the trunks of the trees and other parts of the forest. Though unseen, Godwood Creek flows through the forest. The path used to follow the creek but was rerouted higher up on the slopes of the canyon to prevent the creek from silting up. After hiking on the James Irvine Trail for 0.6 mile, you meet the Miners Ridge Trail. This is the end of the loop on the return part of the hike. Stay right at the junction and continue hiking through the majestic redwoods.

As you continue in a northeasterly direction, the trail leaves Godwood Creek behind and makes an imperceptible crossing over a pass. It now enters the Home Creek watershed and begins a gradual descent toward the Pacific Ocean. At 3.1 miles from the trailhead, just as the path first encounters small Home Creek, you arrive at the Clintonia Trail, which forms part of the loop with the Miners Ridge Trail. Stay right here and continue to the northwest. The nature of the forest changes here, as the dominance of the redwoods gives way to spruce. Follow this small stream for another 1.0 mile before making a traverse through a deeply incised side canyon. When crossing the bridge over the side canyon's creek, be sure to look down into this surprisingly deep, narrow slot. Just beyond the bridge, stay left at the junction with the Friendship Ridge Trail and quickly arrive at the intersection with the Fern Canyon Loop. To the right, this trail travels above the rim of the canyon, which makes a nice loop with the trail through the canyon and also provides a bypass option when water is high and travel is dangerous. Instead, turn left and descend down into awesome Fern Canyon.

With tall, sheer cliffs cloaked in large ferns, Fern Canyon is a beautiful passage to the sea. Home Creek flows along the canyon's rocky bottom and weaves through numerous large tree trunks, remnants of past floods. There is generally no trail in the canyon, but the route is obvious. Wooden planks are put down to allow hikers to crisscross the creek. The walls are unrelentingly vertical, and hardly any part is uncovered by the large ferns. In a few places small waterfalls trickle down the cliffs. The canyon widens at its west end and the trail resumes, bending to the south and leading to the Fern Canyon Trailhead. This day use area is at the point where the Gold Bluffs—steep coastal cliffs—meet Gold Bluffs Beach and the Pacific Ocean. From the day use area, it is a short walk out to the beach, a perfect place to enjoy the view until it is time to make the return trip.

When it is time to head back, hike back through Fern Canyon and rejoin the James Irvine Trail. Upon arrival at the junction with the Clintonia Trail, veer right in order to make a loop through the middle section of the hike. The Clintonia Trail climbs up onto a ridge, where huge redwoods once again dominate the forest. The climb up to the ridge is gentle. About 1.5 miles after leaving the James Irvine Trail, merge onto the Miners Ridge Trail. Follow the Miners Ridge Trail for 1.5 miles through the gorgeous redwoods before rejoining the James Irvine Trail. From there, retrace your steps back to the trailhead.

MILES AND DIRECTIONS

0.0   Start on nature trail near the visitor center.

0.2   Turn right onto the James Irvine Trail and begin passage through the ancient redwoods.

0.8   Pass the Miners Ridge Trail on your left.

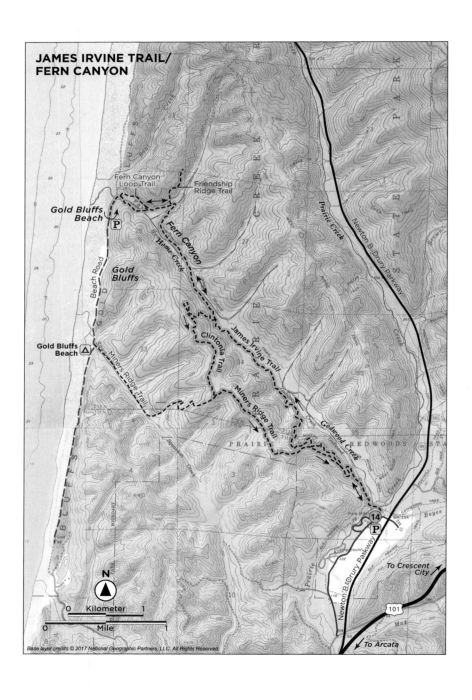

JAMES IRVINE TRAIL/
FERN CANYON

Fern Canyon
Loop Trail

Friendship
Ridge Trail

*Gold Bluffs
Beach*

P

Beach Road

*Gold
Bluffs*

Fern Canyon

Home Creek

James Irvine Trail

Gold Bluffs
Beach

Clintonia Trail

Miners Ridge Trail

Miners Ridge Trail

Godwood Creek

PRAIRIE

REDWOODS

14
P

To Crescent
City

101

To Arcata

N

0   Kilometer   1

0   Mile   1

The Fern Canyon trail crosses Home Creek on numerous wood planks.

3.1 Pass the Clintonia Trail on your left.

4.6 Take the Fern Canyon Trail to the bottom of the canyon, where the route continues along the creek.

5.25 Arrive at the Fern Canyon Trailhead. When it is time to return, head back through Fern Canyon.

5.8 Rejoin the James Irvine Canyon after hiking through Fern Canyon.

7.3 Turn right onto the Clintonia Trail.

8.8 Merge onto the Miners Ridge Trail.

10.3 Turn right to rejoin the James Irvine Trail.

11.0 Arrive back at the trailhead.

15. BOY SCOUT TREE

WHY GO?

This easy hike leads through magnificent old-growth redwoods to the stunning Boy Scout Tree, a mammoth specimen of coast redwood. The path continues past the tree to pretty Fern Falls, a scenic waterfall surrounded by large ferns and more redwoods.

THE RUNDOWN

Start: Trailhead on Howland Hill Road
Distance: 5.2 miles out and back
Hiking time: 5–6 hours
Difficulty: Easy
Elevation gain: 700 feet
Season: Year-round
Trail surface: Packed dirt
Canine compatibility: Dogs not permitted

Fees and permits: None
Land status: Jedediah Smith Redwoods State Park
Trail contact: 1440 Highway 199, Crescent City 95531; (707) 465-7335; www.parks.ca.gov/?page_id=413
Other: Water is available in creeks near Fern Falls.

FINDING THE TRAILHEAD

 Starting at the south end of downtown Crescent City, drive east on US 101 for 0.3 mile. Turn left onto Elk Valley Road and drive 1.1 miles. Turn right onto Howland Hill Road. This road begins to wind up through the forest, becoming a dirt road as it does so. After 1.8 miles stay left to continue on Howland Hill Road. Proceed for 1.9 miles to the trailhead. This section of the road has excellent scenery as it weaves through awesome old-growth redwoods. **Trailhead GPS:** 41°46'7.28"N / 124°6'36.87"W

WHAT TO SEE

Jedediah Smith Redwoods State Park is in the heart of the region that boasts some of the best examples of old-growth coast redwoods. Walking among these monumental trees induces hushed voices and whispers of quiet astonishment. The Boy Scout Tree is a particularly exceptional specimen, but the tree itself is only part of this hike's charm. The trail to the Boy Scout Tree passes through magnificent redwoods that are massive in their own right as it pushes into the wilderness, where a sense of deep isolation prevails. Past the Boy Scout Tree you can hike a little farther before arriving at attractive Fern Falls, making for a great redwood experience.

The trail that leads to the Boy Scout Tree begins in the midst of a magnificent grove of redwoods. Their huge trunks line the path and instantly immerse you in the deep, hushed sense of awe that comes with hiking through these great forest cathedrals. As you pass

A hiker pauses to marvel at
giant fallen redwood

Fern Falls

through the forest, cross a small bridge where a fallen giant has lodged itself against standing redwoods. It is possible to climb up on the trunk and get an elevated perspective on the woods. As you begin an easy climb, watch as the large ferns proliferate on the forest floor. These bright green plants present a vivid contrast to the dark red trees and vivid red of the dried redwood needles that line the forest floor.

The large trees continue to inhabit the areas along the trail as it climbs to the top of a ridge. After crossing the gentle crest 1.0 mile from the trailhead, the path begins to descend, still passing through stands of large trees. About 0.3 mile from the crest, the path encounters small Jordan Creek for the first time. Here the trees begin to get smaller, though many still have significant girth. Other types of trees, absent along the trail prior to this point, now begin to appear. After passing through more large redwoods the route finally drops down to the bottom of the valley and runs parallel to the creek. There are not many redwoods along this stretch of the hike, but after you follow the creek for a little while, they begin to appear again. Many of these are massive and stand in regal isolation from other trees, giving the forest an open feeling.

Finally, after winding along Jordan Creek, a spur branches off to the right, about 2.2 miles from the trailhead. This path makes a short loop around the enormous Boy Scout Tree. Double-trunked, its colossal girth is astonishing. Though it is not unusually tall, the tree is easily the largest one visible on the hike. After pausing here for a while and observing the tree, return to the main trail and turn right. The path follows Jordan Creek a little farther before veering into the gully drained by a small tributary. Around 0.3 mile past the Boy Scout Tree, the trail finally ends at the base of small Fern Falls. Totally surrounded by numerous large ferns, the water cascades over tiers of rocky benches. Neither tall nor large, the waterfall is instead a refreshing complement to the redwoods that line the slopes above the falls. After enjoying this peaceful scene, follow the route back to the trailhead.

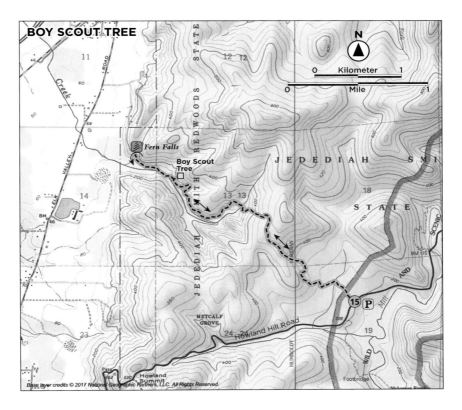

MILES AND DIRECTIONS

0.0 Start the hike in the midst of a grove of monumental redwoods.

1.25 Traverse the top of the ridge and begin descending into a valley.

1.4 Cross small Jordan Creek.

2.2 Turn right onto a short spur and hike a short distance to the giant Boy Scout Tree.

2.6 At the trail's end, arrive at peaceful Fern Falls. This is your turnaround point.

5.2 Arrive back at the trailhead.

Canyon Creek in the Trinity Alps boasts waterfalls and craggy mountains.

KLAMATH MOUNTAINS

THE KLAMATH MOUNTAINS are perhaps California's greatest forgotten mountain range. Located in the sparsely populated northwest corner of the state, these mountains occupy the large space between the Cascade Range in the east and the North Coast Range to the south and west. It is a wild range only lightly touched by the hand of civilization. This is one of the most primitive parts of Northern California, with roughly 1 million acres preserved as wilderness. Hikers can spend a lifetime exploring the unbelievably diverse and spectacular mountains, visiting an incredible array of rivers, waterfalls, lakes, and biodiversity.

The Klamath Mountains are broadly defined by two different metrics that overlap fairly closely. First, the name of the range comes from the presence of the mighty Klamath River. The entire range is part of the Klamath's vast watershed. Rising in central Oregon, the Klamath River flows into California and then cuts through the heart of the Klamath Mountains. Along the way it gathers the water from several large rivers that rise in the high peaks of the range. These rivers include the Shasta, Scott, Salmon, and the powerful Trinity. Several large creeks also flow into the Klamath River that are independent of major rivers, further swelling the river's already impressive size.

While the river watersheds are an important component of defining the boundaries of the Klamath Mountains, the region's geology plays an equally important role. To the east of the Klamaths is the vast volcanic domain of the Cascade Range, while the western and southern borders are bounded by the sedimentary rocks of the North Coast Range. In between these distinct areas is the Klamaths' incredibly complex mélange of different rock types. Metavolcanic and ultramafic rocks, granite, gabbro, and marble are found here in addition to marine sedimentary rocks of different origin and composition than those found in the North Coast Range. The appearance of the Klamaths is often compared to the Sierra—with good reason, since the Northern Sierra is nearly identical geologically. Like the Sierra, the Klamaths have large granite plutons that have been heavily glaciated, resulting in towering granite spires and lakes in stunning glacially carved cirque basins.

The Klamaths are divided into several major mountain regions, some of which have attained name recognition on their own. The major subranges include the Trinity Alps, Marble Mountains, and the Siskiyous. A host of lesser known ranges includes the Trinity Divide, the Russian Wilderness, the Scott Mountains, and the North Yolla Bollies, among others.

In addition to superb mountains and roaring rivers, the Klamath Mountains are best known for their superlative biodiversity. There are several endemic species that only grow in this mountain range, including the Brewer's spruce, Port Orford cedar, and the carnivorous *Darlingtonia californica*. There are also more types of conifers in these mountains than anywhere else in the world. These include unique varieties as well whose main ranges are hundreds of miles away.

16. DEVIL'S PUNCHBOWL

WHY GO?

This beautiful hike explores a spectacular corner of the remote Siskiyou Wilderness. The trail leads through an unusual forest and up into an incredible granite bowl, where towering cliffs and beautiful blue lakes complement vistas of massive Preston Peak.

THE RUNDOWN

Start: Doe Flat Trailhead
Distance: 10.0 miles out and back (*Option:* easy 3.4 miles out and back to Buck Lake)
Hiking time: 5–6 hours
Difficulty: Moderately difficult
Elevation gain: 1,900
Season: Summer, fall
Trail surface: Dirt, rocky, rock scrambling

Canine compatibility: Dogs permitted
Fees and permits: None for hiking; campfire and wilderness permits required for overnight trips
Land status: Siskiyou Wilderness, Klamath National Forest
Trail contact: Happy Camp Ranger District, 63822 Highway 96, Happy Camp 96039; (530) 493-2243; www .fs.usda.gov/klamath

FINDING THE TRAILHEAD

From the intersection of US 101 and CA 199, drive northeast on CA 199 for 24.2 miles. Turn right onto well-signed Little Jones Creek Road. Drive on paved Little Jones Creek Road, also signed as FR 17N05, for 10 miles, following signs for the Doe Flat Trailhead. After 10 miles the pavement ends in a clearing, where the road forks. Make a hard left onto FR 16N02, following the sign indicating the Bear Basin Butte lookout. Continue on this well-maintained dirt road for 3.5 miles to the Doe Flat Trailhead.

From interior parts of Northern California, it is best to follow I-5 north into Oregon to Grants Pass. From there head south on OR/CA 199, crossing back into California. Turn left onto Little Jones Creek Road 11.5 miles south of the California-Oregon state line. **Trailhead GPS:** 41°48'50.67"N / 123°42'24.82"W

WHAT TO SEE

The Siskiyou Mountains are the northernmost subrange of the Klamath Range and, along with the Trinity Alps, are part of the largest mountain block within the Klamath region. This crescent-shaped mountain range extends in a large arc from the Siskiyou summit in southern Oregon west toward Grants Pass before turning south into California. These mountains form the divide between the Klamath River and Rogue River watersheds. Though the highest peak in the range lies in Oregon, the California half of the range is more rugged. Much of this area is protected within the 179,846-acre

The trail to the Devil's Punchbowl passes deep and mysterious forests.

Siskiyou Wilderness. This large wildland area has numerous tall, rocky peaks; the long, deeply cut canyon of Clear Creek; and a few beautiful lake basins. Preston Peak is by far the largest and highest mountain in the region and the dominant landmark of the area.

Lakes are not as numerous in the Siskiyous as they are in other wilderness areas in the Klamath Mountains. Though the few that are scattered around the wilderness area do have a charm and beauty all their own, the only one that attains a degree of grandeur that places it in the upper echelons of the Klamath's limnic jewels is the Devil's Punchbowl. The hike to the Punchbowl leads through a beautifully unusual forest filled with Brewer's spruce, a species that only grows in the Klamath Mountains. Along the way, the trail passes pretty Buck Lake, which makes a good option for hikers looking for an easy foray into the woods without having to tackle the steep climb necessary to reach the Devil's Punchbowl. Later in the hike the trail is graced with excellent views of the Clear Creek drainage and mighty Preston Peak, looming above its domain.

The hike begins at the Doe Flat Trailhead, where there is a good perspective on the canyon formed by the cumbersomely named South Siskiyou Fork of the Middle Fork of the Smith River. The path departing from the trailhead is the remnants of an old road leading to Siskiyou Pass. Though parts of the path retain the road's old width, other sections cut into cliffs have eroded away, leaving only a narrow path. The old road soon turns north and begins climbing up to Siskiyou Pass, a wide saddle in the divide separating the

A view down into the lonely canyon of Clear Creek.

Smith and Klamath River watersheds. Soon a series of boulders block off the old road and a singletrack trail veers off to the right and soon crosses over the pass into Doe Flat.

Turning west, the path traverses the hillside above the flat. Brewer's spruce becomes increasingly common along the path here. Their long, dangly branchlets, the reason these trees are sometimes called "weeping spruce," gives them a distinctive appearance. Finally, about 1.5 miles from the trailhead, the path arrives at the signed junction with the spur leading to Buck Lake. To get there, turn right and follow the path uphill over rocky outcroppings and a low ridge. The path then drops down to the small lake. Buck Lake is not a superlative specimen, but it is very pretty. Forest surrounds much of the lakeshore, but the south wall has some exposed rock that enhances the lake's appearance. If you are looking for a shorter hiking option, this is a good place to turn around and head back to the trailhead.

To continue on to the Devil's Punchbowl, return to the main trail and turn right. The trail then makes an undulating traverse of the increasingly steep hillside. The outlet of Buck Lake is crossed shortly after returning to the main path, and a short distance later the trail crosses a large creek that has a steady flow well into October. From the Buck Lake spur, the path makes a gradual descent for about 1.8 miles before you arrive at a fork in the trail. The path to the left is signed for Clear Creek, the Siskiyou Wilderness's main drainage. Your route, signed for the Devil's Punchbowl, makes a sharp turn to the

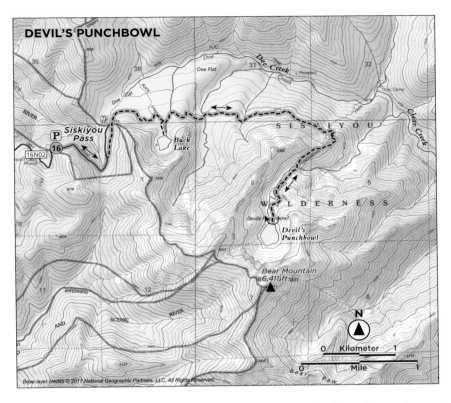

right and immediately begins to climb. For the next 0.3 mile, the trail ascends a series of brutally steep switchbacks that will get your lungs and legs burning. While climbing, look through breaks in the trees to catch glimpses of awesome Preston Peak for the first time. Fortunately the switchbacks do not last too long, though once the trail straightens out, it continues to climb a little farther before descending again. The switchbacks have finally brought you from the Doe Flat drainage around the shoulder of a ridge and into the drainage of the Punchbowl's outlet creek. As you approach, the rocky spires and cliffs begin to appear. The trail descends to and crosses the creek before arriving at a bare granite bench. To the east is a fantastic view of Preston Peak.

At this rocky bench the trail becomes much rougher as it negotiates the rocky terrain. In some places the way is obvious; in others the trail disappears and you need to follow cairns over slabs of rock. Ahead lie the great cliffs of the Punchbowl. They soar out of the lake and climb nearly 2,000 feet to rocky crags high overhead. These cliffs surround the water on almost all sides. Only a gap on the north side of the bowl allows the outlet creek to escape. The route passes through this gap. At times the way descends or climbs steep rock slopes, and you may need to use your hands. Halfway between the creek crossing and the Punchbowl, you will pass a smaller lake. Despite not being the main attraction, it

Fall color clings to the steep cliffs at the Devil's Punchbowl.

is a scenic body of water in its own right. Numerous paths skirt the lake here, some down by the water, some higher up on the slope. Both lead to the rocky bench to the south. Once at the bench, it is an easy scramble to the edge of the Devil's Punchbowl. This lake, with its dark cliffs and sapphire waters, is an incredible sight. Few lakes have such vertical cliffs, which almost completely encircle it. In addition to enjoying the staggering scene, be sure to test the bowl's incredible echo. Few places can equal the incredible reverberation of the lake's tight confines and tall cliffs. After enjoying this awe-inspiring place, retrace your steps to the trailhead.

MILES AND DIRECTIONS

0.0 Start from the Doe Flat Trailhead, and follow an old road into the Siskiyou Wilderness.

0.9 Cross over Siskiyou Pass, moving from the Smith River watershed to the Klamath River watershed.

1.5 Turn right at the spur leading to Buck Lake.

1.7 Reach the edge of pretty Buck Lake. Return to the main trail. (*Option:* If Buck Lake is your destination, turn around here.)

3.6 Begin climbing the steep switchbacks.

4.25 Cross the Punchbowl's outlet creek.

5.0 Reach the Devil's Punchbowl. Retrace your path to the trailhead.

10.0 Arrive back at the trailhead.

17. **NORTH YOLLA BOLLY MOUNTAINS**

WHY GO?

This hike travels through the remote North Yolla Bolly Mountains, which lie at the southern tip of the Klamath Mountains. Here a network of trails climb through a lush mountain basin to small alpine lakes and then continues higher to the summit of Black Rock Mountain, one of the range's two high peaks.

THE RUNDOWN

Start: Stuart Gap Trailhead

Distance: 7.2 miles out and back to Black Rock Lake or 8.6 miles out and back to Black Rock Mountain (*Option:* connect both destinations for a strenuous 9.8-mile lollipop via an off-trail scramble)

Hiking time: 4–6 hours for each option

Difficulty: Moderate/moderately strenuous

Elevation gain: 750 feet (to Black Rock Lake); 2,000 feet (to Black Rock Mountain)

Season: Summer, fall

Trail surface: Packed dirt, duff, rocky

Canine compatibility: Dogs permitted

Fees and permits: None

Land status: Yolla Bolly–Middle Eel Wilderness, Shasta-Trinity National Forest

Trail contact: Yolla Bolla Ranger District, 2555 Highway 36, Platina 96076; (530) 352-4211; www.fs.usda .gov/stnf

Other: Water is available in creeks and in Black Rock Lake.

FINDING THE TRAILHEAD

From Red Bluff on I-5, drive west for 55 miles. Turn left onto FR 30 / Wildwood–Mad River Road just after crossing the bridge over Hayfork Creek. Drive south on this paved road for 9 miles to Pine Root Saddle. Turn left onto FR 35 and continue for 10 winding, paved miles to Stuart Gap. At this five-way junction, turn right onto FR 28N62, which is signed for the Stuart Gap Trailhead. Drive this good dirt road for nearly 2 miles until it ends at the trailhead. **Trailhead GPS:** 40°13'15.77"N / 122°58'44.27"W

WHAT TO SEE

It is hard to imagine that a California wilderness area within sight of an interstate freeway would be considered remote, but that is certainly the case with the Yolla Bolly–Middle Eel Wilderness. Encompassing 182,589 acres of mountainous terrain, the Yolla Bollies are one of the least-visited major wildlands in Northern California. Most of the area occupies the highest reaches of the North Coast Range, including South Yolla Bolly

The rocky north face of Black Rock Mountain rises high above Black Rock Lake.

Mountain (sometimes known as Mount Linn), the range's highest point. However, at the northern edge of the wilderness lies the North Yolla Bolly Mountains. Though they fall within the official boundary, they are distinct from the rest of the Yolla Bollies. Geologically they are situated on the fault line that divides the North Coast Range from the Klamath Mountains. Their precise classification is a bit ambiguous, but because the headwaters of the South Fork of the Trinity River (a river that falls firmly within the Klamath Mountains sphere) lie on their northern and southern slopes, it is easy to associate the North Yolla Bollies with the Klamaths.

Regardless of which mountain region they fall into, these isolated peaks are very scenic. The North Yolla Bollies have a well-developed trail network, which makes exploring them a pleasure. The trails are focused on Pettijohn Basin, the bowl that lies between North Yolla Bolly (the highest peak in the northern part of the wilderness) and Black Rock Mountain. In addition to old-growth forests, the basin is home to small meadows and a pair of small lakes, each lying at the foot of one of the two peaks. The trail network also climbs up to the rim of the basin, where it is possible to climb to the summit of the high peaks. The best destinations are those on the Black Rock Mountain side of Pettijohn Basin. Black Rock Lake is easily the prettier of the two small lakes, and the summit of the namesake mountain boasts a panoramic vista and the ruins of an old lookout tower. Both peak and lake make great destinations for easy to moderate day hikes.

Unfortunately, visiting both lake and summit via the trail network is ambitious. For those set on observing both, a very scenic lollipop hike can be constructed with a short, steep 0.5-mile off-trail scramble. This combines both the beautiful lake and the vistas from high on the basin rim. This route should be attempted only by hikers with good route-finding experience.

The hike up to Pettijohn Basin begins at the Stuart Gap Trailhead. The trail enters the woods immediately and begins climbing at a moderate, steady grade. After a few switch-backs the trail reaches the top of a ridge and follows it south toward the basin. Breaks in the forest canopy offer glimpses across the large bowl toward the rocky face of Black Rock Mountain. About 1.0 mile from the trail you will cross the boundary into the Yolla Bolly–Middle Eel Wilderness. The name Yolla Bolly means "snowy mountain" in the language of the Wintu, one of the prominent Native American tribes in the northernmost parts of California. Incidentally, the word "balley," which means "mountain," has survived as a general moniker for peaks in the Klamath Mountains. Names such as Shasta Balley, Weaver Balley, and even Bully Choop are common throughout the range.

After crossing the wilderness boundary, the trail continues to climb for another 0.25 mile before reaching the junction with the trail to Black Rock Lake. If the lake is your destination, turn right here and follow the trail into the heart of Pettijohn Basin. The path passes through scattered patches of meadow and crosses the fledgling East Fork of the South Fork of the Trinity River. The true headwaters of the South Fork flow off the south side of the North Yolla Bollies. About 1.6 miles after leaving the main trail, you cross a small stream as the trail traverses a wide gully. If you intend to hike the lollipop, you will need to head up this gully toward the rim of the basin. There is a very faint trail to follow, but it fades out in numerous places, only to appear again higher up. Whether you can follow the path or not, simply hike up the basin in a southerly direction. The route steepens considerably as you near the top, but it is never too steep to hike. Once you cross over the rim, the trail to Black Rock Mountain lies just a few steps away. Either turn right for Black Rock Mountain or turn left to head back down into Pettijohn Basin.

Continuing on toward Black Rock Lake, stay on the main trail and climb back out of the gully, maintaining a western heading. The trail then rounds a shoulder and drops down to the lake, 0.7 mile past the gully. Though not large by Klamath Mountains standards, it is the largest alpine lake in the Yolla Bolly–Middle Eel Wilderness and certainly the prettiest. The dark cliffs of Black Rock Mountain loom 1,500 feet above the lake, adding a great deal of drama to the small body of water. If this is your destination, turn around and follow the trail back to the trailhead. If you are doing the lollipop, head back to the gully and turn right, beginning the climb up to the rim of the basin.

If your destination is Black Rock Mountain rather than Black Rock Lake, stay left on the main trail in Pettijohn Basin, about 1.25 miles from the Stuart Gap Trailhead. This is the route that will lead to the rim of the basin. However, just a short distance from the fork leading to Black Rock Lake, you will reach another junction. This time a spur branches off to the east and heads to North Yolla Bolly Lake. This small lake lies at the foot of North Yolla Bolly, the second-highest peak in the wilderness area. Though there is a fair amount of exposed rock, this lake lacks the dramatic backdrop of Black Rock Lake. Stay right at the junction and keep climbing through Pettijohn Basin. Finally, after 1.5 miles of ascending the increasingly steep wall of the basin, the trail makes a few switch-backs and then reaches the rim.

The long ridge above Pettijohn Basin connects North Yolla Bolly to Black Rock Mountain. Though there are some trees, much of the ridge is bare, and there are great views in all directions. To the east lies the rugged western face of North Yolla Bolly, which rises above the basin. To the west is the brooding mass of Black Rock Mountain. Looking south, the vast interior of the Yolla Bolly–Middle Eel Wilderness unfolds as a series of dark ridges and high peaks. As you scan the view to the north, the Trinity Alps, Mount Shasta, and Lassen Peak are all highlights. Shortly after you reach the rim and the views improve, you arrive at a four-way junction. To the left the path leads to the Rat Trap Gap Trailhead and the off-trail scramble to the summit of North Yolla Bolly. The path to the south takes you to Cedar Basin and the true headwaters of the South Fork of the Trinity River. Instead, turn right and follow the rim toward Black Rock Mountain.

As you hike, you pass through vast swaths of purple lupine, which cover much of the rim in season. When the crest gets higher and rockier, the route moves to the south side

North Yolla Bolly and fields of lupine line the rim of Pettijohn Basin.

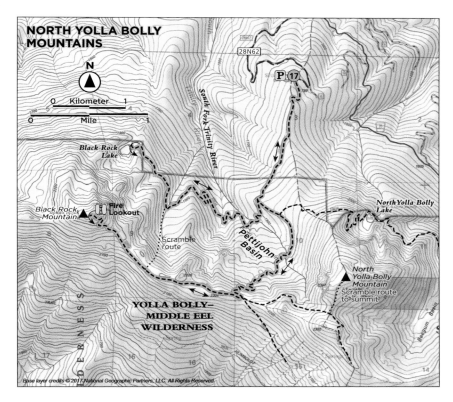

of the ridge. It eventually climbs back onto the true crest, right about where the off-trail scramble from Black Rock Lake reaches the top of the rim. From here the trail continues a short distance to the base of Black Rock Mountain. Note how the rock on the south side of the peak is black and sunbaked and surrounded by dense brush. On the shadier north side, there are more trees and the rock has a cleaner, grayer appearance. The path then makes a short, steep ascent up some switchbacks to the rocky summit of Black Rock Mountain. The ruins of an abandoned lookout tower are found on the top. Even without being able to climb a little higher into the tower, the vista from the top is magnificent. Whether doing the lollipop or just the peak, return to the trailhead by hiking back along the ridge and then down through Pettijohn Basin.

MILES AND DIRECTIONS

0.0 Start at the Stuart Gap Trailhead and begin climbing toward Pettijohn Basin.

1.25 Reach the junction with the trail leading to Black Rock Lake. Here you can head either to Black Rock Lake or the summit of Black Rock Mountain.

BLACK ROCK LAKE:

1.25 Turn right and traverse the interior of Pettijohn Basin.

2.85 Pass a small stream in a wide gully. (*Option*: Following the gully upstream is the strenuous off-trail route to the rim of Pettijohn Basin, which forms a loop connecting Black Rock Lake and Black Rock Mountain.)

3.6 Arrive at Black Rock Lake. Retrace your path to the trailhead.

7.2 Arrive back at the trailhead.

BLACK ROCK MOUNTAIN:

1.25 At the junction with the Black Rock Lake Trail, keep to the left and continue climbing.

1.45 Pass the spur leading to North Yolla Bolly Mountain.

2.75 Arrive at a 4-way junction on the rim above Pettijohn Basin. Turn right and begin the hike across the rim toward Black Rock Mountain.

4.3 Reach the top of Black Rock Mountain.

8.6 Return to the trailhead.

Approaching Black Rock Mountain from Pettijohn Basin

18. CANYON CREEK

WHY GO?

Canyon Creek is a journey into the heart of the Trinity Alps, boasting large waterfalls, meadows, glittering lakes, towering alpine peaks, and old mining relics. This is the most direct route into the splendid core of the Trinity Alps' granite wonderland.

THE RUNDOWN

Start: Canyon Creek Trailhead
Distance: 16.0 miles out and back
Hiking time: 8–10 hours or overnight
Difficulty: Difficult
Elevation gain: 2,700 feet
Season: Late spring through fall
Trail surface: Dirt, rocky, rock scrambling
Canine compatibility: Dogs permitted

Fees and permits: None for hiking; campfire and wilderness permits required for overnight trips
Land status: Trinity Alps Wilderness, Shasta-Trinity National Forest
Trail contact: Weaverville Ranger District, 360 Main St., Weaverville 96093; (530) 623-2121; www.fs.usda .gov/stnf

FINDING THE TRAILHEAD

 From Weaverville, head west 8 miles on CA 299. At Junction City veer right onto Canyon Creek Road. Drive north 12 miles on the winding, narrow road and park at the trailhead. Weaverville can be reached from Eureka or Redding on CA 299. **Trailhead GPS:** 40°53'15.34"N / 123°1'27.64"W

WHAT TO SEE

The Trinity Alps are one of Northern California's most spectacular mountain ranges. With the exception of the glacier-clad flanks of Mount Shasta, this is the most alpine region in the northernmost part of the state. Here there are towering granite peaks, powerful waterfalls, jewellike mountain lakes, expansive meadows, and deep, remote forests. Indeed, all the best features of a mountain paradise are found in the Trinity Alps. Encompassing 525,627 acres, the Trinity Alps Wilderness is the second-largest wild area administered by the USDA Forest Service in California. This is a vast land where mountains and wilderness seem to go on and on, and the sense of unending primeval adventure is unequalled anywhere else in California outside of the Sierra Nevada. It is to that grandest of mountain ranges that the Trinities are often compared. The juxtaposition of the ranges is appropriate, as their similarities encompass more than just their wild character. A look at the geologic map of California reveals that the composition of the Trinity Alps and the entire Klamath Mountains is the same as that of the Northern Sierra. One finds large expanses of metamorphic rock punctuated by enormous plutons of granite. It is as

Canyon Creek Falls

though the extreme north end of the Sierra Nevada was wrenched away from the rest of the range and shoved out toward the coast.

The center of the Trinity Alps is a cluster of tall peaks that range between 8,500 and 9,000 feet. This area contains the grandest collection of peaks and lakes in the entire Klamath Mountains system (though the tallest peak, Mount Eddy, lies in the nearby Trinity Divide). Most of the major waterways of the Trinities start here, including the South Fork of the Salmon River, the North Fork of the Trinity River, and the Stuart Fork of the Trinity River. Another large system is that of Canyon Creek, whose headwaters are at the foot of Thompson Peak, the highest mountain in the Trinity Alps and second highest in the Klamath Mountains. This large creek cuts through the granite heart of the range as it makes a remarkably straight southward dash to the Trinity River. For hikers looking to explore the core of the Trinities, Canyon Creek provides the most direct option to reach this sublime mountain paradise. Though the trip is long, it can be done as a day hike. For hikers not interested in pressing all the way to the lakes that lie at Canyon Creek's headwaters, there are plenty of spectacular shorter options, including some of the best waterfalls in Northern California, set in the large granite canyon surrounded by ragged peaks. The direct access to epic scenery, as well as the number of destinations possible in Canyon Creek, makes this one of the more popular trails in the Trinity Alps. Though solitude can still be found here, be prepared for some company.

The hike begins at the Canyon Creek Trailhead. The woods here are a mix of hardwoods and conifers. Oaks are the dominant species here. The path travels north, on the east side of Canyon Creek. The creek itself can be heard but not seen, since it lies far below. A short distance from the parking area, the trail veers right and crosses Bear Creek. Stay to the left, off the Bear Creek Trail, and climb out of the Bear Creek drainage. Soon the trail turns north again. The canopy is thick, but the west side of Canyon Creek is visible. The lower stretch of the canyon is composed of dark metamorphic rock. The transition to granite is swift, and soon the bright rock dominates the view. A short distance from Bear Creek, a careful observer will spy an impressive falls cascading down the west side of Canyon Creek.

The east side of the canyon gets steeper as you press deeper into the canyon. At 2.5 miles from the trailhead, a short spur splits off to the west. This route leads down to a small island (called McKay Camp) in Canyon Creek. The island can be reached via a large log bridge over the creek. This is the first good campsite and roughly marks the end of the lower portion of the canyon. The Sinks, a rockslide covering the creek, are a short distance upstream from the island. During low water the creek disappears under the rocks, only to reappear a short distance away. Until now, the path has been fairly level. From McKay Camp you begin to switchback up the canyon wall. Continuing this trend, the switchbacks are evenly graded, and the trail is not steep. At the top of the switchbacks, you cross open granite for the first time, providing the first real view of the upper canyon. The scene remains constant and impressive from this point on. This is also the only point on the main trail with a reasonably clear view of Canyon Creek Falls.

From the top of the switchbacks, the route continues to traverse the side of the canyon. Soon it crosses a seasonal stream and briefly veers to the west, about 4.0 miles from the trailhead. Shortly after crossing the stream, a rough, unmaintained route heads southwest to the base of Canyon Creek Falls. The route is hidden in the brush and may be hard to spot, but at times it is marked by cairns. The view from the base of the falls is one of the most memorable parts of the Canyon Creek hike and should not be missed. If you are looking for a shorter hike, this is a good place to turn around. Back on the main path, it turns north again and comes alongside Canyon Creek for the first time. Here you can stand on the cliff above the creek and observe an impressive cataract that is often mistaken for Lower Canyon Creek Falls. Later in summer, when the water is low, this is an excellent swimming hole.

After the cataract, the path generally continues north for several miles. About 0.5 mile from the falls, the route passes through Canyon Creek Meadows. The meadow is extensive, although most of it lies to the west of the trail and is often broken up by small pockets of trees. After traveling through the meadow for about 1.0 mile, the creek turns west while the route maintains its northerly direction. At the base of a steep slope, the route begins switchbacking through a thick grove of trees. At the base of the slope, look

The Boulder Creek Lakes basin can be seen beyond the top of Middle Canyon Creek Falls.

Thompson Peak and the
Wedding Cake preside over
icy Upper Canyon Creek Lake.

for a use trail leading to the base of awesome Middle Canyon Creek Falls. This is another excellent waterfall and not to be missed. Like the first cataract, this also makes a good destination for a shorter day hike. Past the switchbacks, maintain course for about 0.5 mile before reaching the junction with the trail that leads to the Boulder Creek Lakes. This large granite bowl contains both the Boulder Creek Lakes and the Forbidden Lakes, as well as several great waterfalls. There are also magnificent views of the granite high country at the heart of the Trinity Alps. Reaching the lakes requires a steep but fairly short climb from Canyon Creek. This area is better done as an overnight. Even if you are not heading up to the lakes, there are awesome views of the basin from the trail just prior to the junction.

From the intersection with the Boulder Creek Lakes Trail, the Canyon Creek Trail continues north another mile to another set of switchbacks. At the top of the switchbacks, another large waterfall becomes visible. This is often mistaken for Upper Canyon Creek Falls, which actually lies just a little downstream. An excellent campsite is located on an island at the base of the falls. Above the cataract, continue for almost 1.0 mile through another meadow. Things get a little confusing at this point. The trail originally stayed on the east side of the creek, climbing from the meadow up to the outlet of Lower Canyon Creek Lake. This route is still extant and apparent, and people often mistakenly continue up this old trail. However, if you take this path, you will need to ford the outlet

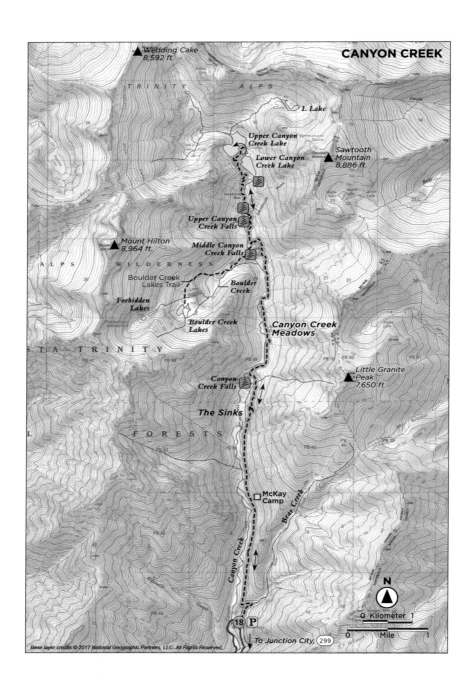

CANYON CREEK

Wedding Cake
8,592 ft.

TRINITY ALPS

L. Lake

Upper Canyon
Creek Lake

Lower Canyon
Creek Lake

Sawtooth
Mountain
8,886 ft.

Upper Canyon
Creek Falls

Mount Hilton
8,964 ft.

Middle Canyon
Creek Falls

ALPS

WILDERNESS

Boulder Creek
Lakes Trail

Boulder
Creek

Forbidden
Lakes

Boulder Creek
Lakes

Canyon Creek
Meadows

STA-TRINITY

Little Granite
Peak
7,650 ft.

Canyon
Creek Falls

The Sinks

FORESTS

McKay
Camp

Bear Creek

Canyon Creek

N

0 Kilometer 1

0 Mile 1

18 P

To Junction City, 299

of the lake in order to reach Upper Canyon Creek Lake. This is can be dangerous, especially early in summer, since the outlet flows directly into a series of impressive cataracts. To avoid this, the trail has been rerouted across the creek, below the falls, and then up to the lake. Although the new trail is signed, the marker is not clearly visible. Instead, look for faint trails leading to the west and a series of large iron pipes in the creek. These are remnants of a nineteenth-century mining operation. A small mining community known as Stonehouse once existed on this site.

Once across the creek, the trail all but disappears as it climbs a series of granite slabs up to the outlet of Lower Canyon Creek Lake. Cairns mark the way, although the route is generally obvious. The outlet of Lower Canyon Creek Lake is a massive cascade that tumbles over a series of granite slabs, forming a maze of waterfalls. From the outlet the lake becomes visible, and one of the great vistas of the Trinity Alps unfolds to the north. Thompson Peak, the highest point in the Trinities, towers 4,500 feet above the lake in true alpine splendor. Craggy Wedding Cake provides an appropriate companion. From here the trail continues to skirt the lake and then makes a short climb up to Upper Canyon Creek Lake. The view from here is slightly better than from the lower lake. It is made more impressive by the sheer wall that drops straight into the north end of the lake. The mighty peaks, glittering lakes, and massive granite cliffs combine to form an exceptional mountain paradise. All in all, this is one of the most sublime slices of Northern California.

MILES AND DIRECTIONS

0.0 Start at the Canyon Creek Trailhead, immediately crossing over into the Mount Shasta Wilderness.

2.5 Pass McKay Camp, an island campsite in Canyon Creek.

3.0 The Sinks are located below the trail, just upstream from McKay Camp.

3.9 Cross the first large creek (sometimes dry) after the switchbacks and look for a spur trail on the left leading to Canyon Creek Falls.

5.5 A use trail branches off to the left leading to the base of Middle Canyon Creek Falls.

6.0 Reach the junction with the trail leading to the Boulder Creek Lakes.

7.0 Pass Lower Canyon Creek Lake.

8.0 Arrive at the outlet of Upper Canyon Creek Lake. Retrace your path to the trailhead.

16.0 Arrive back at the trailhead.

19. **BEAR LAKES**

WHY GO?

The hike to the Bear Lakes is a journey into glaciated alpine splendor with granite crags, rushing creeks, large lakes, and lots of potential for off-trail exploration on the outskirts of the Trinity Alps.

THE RUNDOWN

Start: Bear Lake Trailhead
Distance: 8.5 miles out and back
Hiking time: 5–7 hours or overnight
Difficulty: Moderately difficult
Elevation gain: 2,800 feet
Season: Summer, fall
Trail surface: Dirt, rocky, rock scrambling
Canine compatibility: Dogs permitted

Fees and permits: None for hiking; campfire and wilderness permits required for overnight trips
Land status: Trinity Alps Wilderness, Shasta-Trinity National Forest
Trail contact: Weaverville Ranger District, 360 Main St., Weaverville 96093; (530) 623-2121; www.fs.usda .gov/stnf

FINDING THE TRAILHEAD

From Weaverville drive north on CA 3 for 47 miles. Turn left onto Bear Creek Loop. Note that the loop intersects CA 3 twice; you will want to take the second of the two. (The first one no longer connects to the trailhead, as a bridge has been washed out.) Once on Bear Creek Loop, proceed south for 1.6 miles to the trailhead.

In summer this hike can also be reached easily from the Mount Shasta area. To do so, begin on I-5, north of the town of Weed. Take exit 751 for Edgewood. Turn west and drive to the junction with Old Stage Road/Old 99. Turn right onto Old Stage/ Old 99. Continue north for a couple hundred yards and then turn left onto Stewart Springs Road. After 4 miles FR 17 splits off to the right. Follow this paved road, which is only open during summer and fall, for 23 miles to the intersection with CA 3. Turn left, drive 1.3 miles, and turn right onto Bear Creek Loop. The trailhead is 1.6 miles down the road. **Trailhead GPS:** 41°11'39.75"N / 122°39'5.57"W

WHAT TO SEE

The Bear Lakes are, without doubt, the most spectacular in the chain of lakes that line the northern and eastern perimeter of the Trinity Alps. Of all the numerous lakes found on these fringes of the range, it is the Bear Lakes that most closely approach the scale and awesome granite scenery found in the congregation of high peaks and large lakes that lie at the heart of the Trinities. The Bear Lakes do not need such a comparison to recommend them, for they are stunning in their own right. Surrounded by soaring white towers and almost completely enclosed in a giant granite bowl, Big Bear Lake is a marvelous

Mount Shasta and Mount Eddy rise far to the east beyond Bear Creek.

sight. Just prior to the lake is a stretch of polished granite where Bear Creek pours through rock chutes and over small ledges to form a great series of little cascades. For hikers willing to scramble off-trail, this hike also leads to Little Bear and Wee Bear Lakes. Though these are not as large as their nearby sibling, they are still set among extremely rugged rocky landscapes and are among the prettiest lakes in the Trinity Alps.

This hike used to begin on the west side of Bear Creek. The bridge that once provided access has been wiped out. From the new trailhead the trail now descends down to Bear Creek near its confluence with the Trinity River. This is the only hike in the Trinity Alps Wilderness where you can access the main fork of the Trinity. After fording Bear Creek, the trail climbs up to the old trailhead. From there the path begins to climb in earnest, ascending a few switchbacks before finally settling in and establishing a parallel course alongside Bear Creek. Though the trail and the creek follow each other, the path generally does not get close enough to comfortably access the water. After you climb for about 1.0 mile from the old trailhead, a bridge provides access to the north side of the creek. An attractive series of cascades falls into a small pool just upstream from the bridge. It is the prettiest spot thus far on the hike. After crossing the creek, the Bear Lakes Trail breaks hard to the east for a short distance and then begins a long series of switchbacks. The trail is ascending a ridge that separates the main branch of Bear Creek from one of its largest tributaries. As the trail climbs, listen for the sound of rushing water to the left and right of the trail.

At the top of the ridge, the switchbacks are left behind and a long, steady ascent of Bear Creek's drainage begins. The path passes through mixed forest of oak, pine, and cedar before climbing higher into forest where the oaks diminish and firs become more prevalent. Looking back to the east as you climb, notice the ridge that was denuded by fire long ago. Snags still persist amid the brush that has claimed the area. Soon the trail's

Towering granite cliffs surround Bear Lake.

grade becomes a bit more moderate and it nears the creek again. Look for a pair of enormous ponderosa pines on the south side of the trail. The area is filled with old-growth trees, but even so, these two trees are gargantuan. It is unusual to find two giants so close together. Just beyond the trees is a fantastic campsite right next to a raucous portion of Bear Creek that includes a nice bench constructed of granite stones.

Continuing on the Bear Lakes Trail, the path steepens again and soon passes through a series of clearings cleared by past avalanches. For the first time, the craggy cliffs of the Bear Lakes basin come into view. Though the full grandeur of the basin has not yet been revealed, it is still an inspiring sight after climbing for so long under the forest canopy. As the route progresses, it eventually crosses numerous seeps that create small streams or mucky areas along the trail. Though the roar of Bear Creek is audible, it has passed into a large thicket of willow that renders the creek invisible. As if to compensate for the loss of the creek, the basin's cliffs become more prominent with every step forward.

Finally the trail breaks out of the willow and brush and climbs onto a series of white granite slabs. Bear Creek tumbles down a series of cascades, pouring from one granite shelf to another and sliding over the smooth granite face. The cliffs of Big Bear Lake's cirque loom overhead. To the east, Mount Eddy and mighty Mount Shasta dominate the horizon, reminders that the Bear Lakes, as awesome as they are, are still on the very outskirts of the Trinity Alps. A well-constructed trail climbs these benches on the north side of the creek, on the fringe of the granite slabs. In some places rock steps have been constructed, easing the ascent. Though not the final destination of the trail, the cascading creek is mesmerizing and entices hikers to pause and relax awhile amid the playful water.

Just prior to reaching Big Bear Lake, the trail enters a brushy thicket and crosses Bear Creek one final time. A short distance later, you are deposited at the east end of the

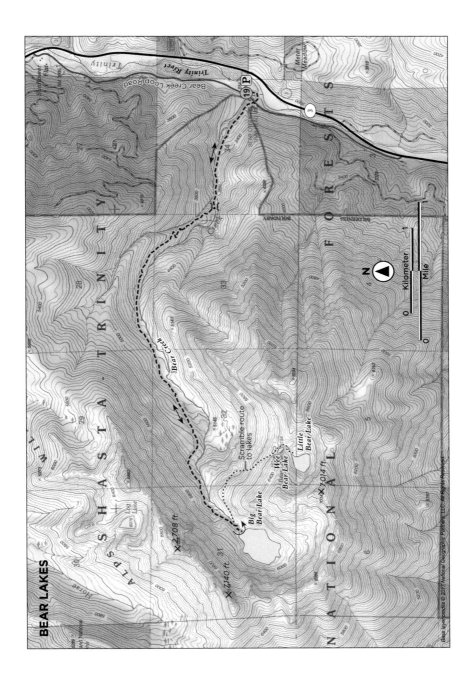

BEAR LAKES

Blaze layer credits © 2017 National Geographic Partners, LLC. All Rights Reserved.

beautiful lake. At 28 acres and 73 feet deep, Big Bear Lake is one of the largest and prettiest lakes in the Trinity Alps. The granite cliffs, nearly 1,300 feet high, almost completely encircle the lake. Only at the far eastern end of the cirque are the magnificent cliffs breached and the lake permitted to drain. Sharp spires line the top of the cliffs, mighty monuments to the creative forces that shaped the basin. The trail ends near the outlet of the lake, but it is possible to scramble over rock and through some brush to reach some great, rocky shoreline and a hidden valley on the lake's south side.

If you want to continue to Little Bear and Wee Bear Lakes, you must be prepared to make the 1.0-mile scramble over naked rock with no trail. The trip is worth the effort. To reach the lakes from Big Bear Lake, return to the cascades over the granite slabs. About two-thirds of the way up toward the lake from the base of the cascades (roughly parallel with where the trail first reaches the slab area), a pair of tall pine trees grow next to the creek. Cross the creek and begin climbing up the ridge on the far side and make a gradual climbing traverse to the east. Cairns have been placed to mark the route. Once the ridge has been climbed, a massive granite face is exposed to the south. This dramatic landmark is visible from Mount Shasta and throughout the Trinity Divide. Again, cairns mark the way along the traverse, but they are not necessary at this point. Spy the notch to the south and climb toward it. Upon reaching the notch, Wee Bear Lake is revealed. This lake may be small, but it is very pretty, especially from the south side, where some of the great towers above Bear Lake make a dramatic backdrop. Follow the use trail around the lake to the south side and then proceed through the woods, continuing to follow the faint path. You will soon arrive at Little Bear Lake. Like the big lake, this lake too is located in a granite bowl with a serrated ridgeline of rugged spires rising behind it. Though not as large as Big Bear Lake, it is just as pretty and receives only a fraction of the usage. When you are done enjoying the lake, you must scramble back down to the Bear Lakes Trail and then follow it back to the trailhead.

MILES AND DIRECTIONS

0.0 Start from the trailhead and drop down near the Trinity River; cross Bear Creek before climbing back up to the old trailhead. The trail then crosses the boundary of the Trinity Alps Wilderness and begins ascending Bear Creek's canyon.

1.0 Cross the bridge over Bear Creek.

3.9 Exit the forest cover and begin crossing the granite slabs that lie below Big Bear Lake.

4.25 Arrive at Big Bear Lake. Return the way you came.

8.5 Arrive back at the trailhead.

20. **GULCH LAKES LOOP**

WHY GO?

This beautiful loop in a remote corner of the Trinity Alps Wilderness ascends one meadow-clad canyon and descends into another, adjacent canyon with more meadows and a raucous creek. The highlight of the loop is a pair of superb lakes nestled in giant granite cirques at the head of each canyon.

THE RUNDOWN

Start: Long Gulch Lake Trailhead, 2 miles past Carter Meadows Campground
Distance: 9.2-mile loop (*Option:* easy 3.6 miles out and back to Long Gulch Lake)
Hiking time: 5–6 hours
Difficulty: Moderate
Elevation gain: 1,900 feet
Season: Summer, fall
Trail surface: Packed dirt, rocky, duff

Canine compatibility: Dogs permitted
Fees and permits: None
Land status: Trinity Alps Wilderness, Klamath National Forest
Trail contact: Scott River Ranger District, 11263 N. Highway 3, Fort Jones 96032; (530) 468-5351; www .fs.usda.gov/contactus/klamath
Other: Water is available in creeks and Long Gulch and Trail Gulch Lakes.

FINDING THE TRAILHEAD

Beginning in the small hamlet of Callahan on CA 3, drive north on CA 3 a short distance and turn left onto Callahan-Cecilville Road, which is also named FR 93. Continue for 12.3 miles to the signed turnoff for Carter Meadows Campground, which is on FR 39N08. Do not confuse this with the Carter Meadows Summit Trailhead, which will be at 11.8 miles. Continue 0.5 mile past the trailhead to the turnoff for the campground. Once on the very well-graded dirt road, proceed 2 miles to the Long Gulch Lake Trailhead. The trailhead is well signed and located just beyond the crossing of Long Gulch Creek. **Trailhead GPS:** 41°12'57.19"N / 122°55'14.82"W

WHAT TO SEE

Most of the Trinity Alps lie in the large Trinity River watershed, its creeks and rivers flowing south before joining the main stem of the Trinity. However, the northern fringe of this vast block of mountains drains two other rivers that are also tributaries of the Klamath River. The northeast corner is the headwaters of the Scott River; the remote mountains a little farther west are the source of the Salmon River. The mountains where these rivers begin are the Scott and Salmon Mountains, respectively. Near the nexus of the two ranges lies a pair of beautiful lakes, Long Gulch Lake and Trail Gulch Lake, tucked away at the end of rocky, beautiful canyons. These canyons are filled with large

meadows and ancient forests. A fantastic loop trail connects all these features and presents an excellent opportunity to explore these isolated mountains. The loop accesses both lakes and has expansive vistas into the heart of the Trinity Alps.

The trailhead for the hike up to Long Gulch Lake begins right next to Long Gulch Creek, but the trail quickly swings away from the water as it climbs into the canyon. The first part of the route is an old jeep road, but a good singletrack path has been worn into the old roadbed. After about 0.75 mile the old road emerges from the trees, enters a beautiful little meadow, and crosses the boundary into the Trinity Alps Wilderness. A rocky spire lines the crest of the ridge on the west side of the canyon, enhancing the view from the grassy field. Here the old roadbed ends, becoming true singletrack for the first time. The path crosses Long Gulch Creek, entering an even larger meadow that climbs up the east side of the canyon.

Beyond the large meadow, the trail begins to climb up the craggy ridge that forms the west side of the canyon. Views improve and make the somewhat steeper trail more enjoyable. Willows line the path to the west, marking the route of Long Gulch Creek. Though the water can be heard, it once again cannot be seen from the trail. Soon you encounter the first of many sets of switchbacks that make the loop easier. This set ascends a large rocky slope, passing large boulders as it ascends to the top of a bench. Views to the north, looking down the length of Long Gulch, are good. Once on the bench proceed a little farther before you finally arrive at a signed trail junction with the spur that leads to Long Gulch Lake. This beautiful 14-acre lake is 0.3 mile off the trail and makes a great destination for an easy day hike if you want to skip the longer loop. A nearly vertical granite cliff towers high above the south end of the lake, giving it a very a dramatic feel. To return to the trail for the full loop, simply retrace your steps to the junction.

Back on the main trail, the path continues to the south. It soon arrives in a large, rocky clearing, where you begin another set of switchbacks that lead to the rim of Long Gulch Lake's basin. Eventually the path straightens out as it reaches the rim of the canyon. From here there are fantastic views of Long Gulch Lake 600 feet below, as well as down the length of Trail Gulch toward the granite crags of the Russian Wilderness. By climbing to the top of the canyon rim, you have passed from the Salmon River watershed into that of the Trinity River.

Once on the ridge, descend a short distance to the south before arriving at a four-way junction. The first trail splitting off to the left follows the course of the North Fork of Coffee Creek. This is signed as the trail to the Schlomberg Site, where there are the remains of a cabin. The second trail to split off to the left drops down to Steveale Meadow and the South Fork of Coffee Creek. To continue the loop, stay all the way to the right at the junction. The narrow path maintains a level grade here, initially passing through a few grassy patches with views to the east of Peak 7,794, the triple-divide peak that towers high above the nearby South Fork Lakes. Soon the trail enters a densely wooded area. Other than one brief view of the rocky north face of Billys Peak, the trail will remain beneath the forest canopy until it arrives at the rim above Long Gulch Lake. One set of switchbacks help ease the grade before the path finally clears the forest and emerges on the rim above Trail Gulch Lake, where great views of the interior of the Trinity Alps await. Once again, Billys Peak is a highlight of the vista.

Looking west from the rim above Long Gulch, there is one of the finest vistas of the trail. The granite cliffs of Trail Gulch Lake's cirque soar high above the meadow-lined lake that lies nearly 1,000 feet below. In a separate basin on the far side of the cirque lies

Excellent views of Trail Gulch Lake highlight the descent into the lake's basin.

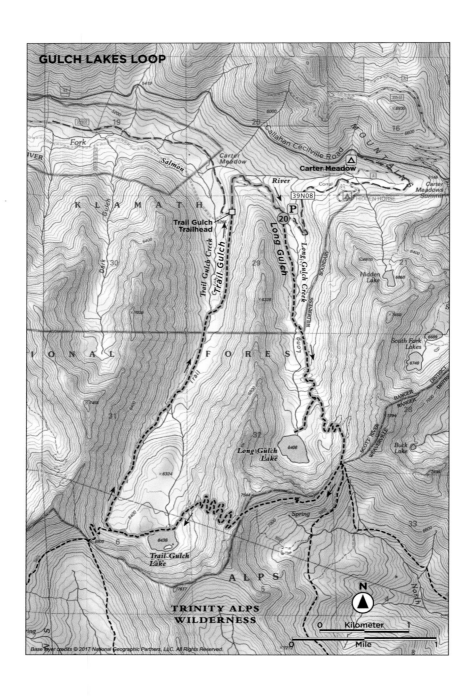

GULCH LAKES LOOP

the lone summit of Deadman Peak. From the rim, the trail begins to make a descent into Trail Gulch. It soon arrives at a switchback. Continue past the trail and veer off the trail a bit to the south to scramble to a point above a large boulder field. This point has the best views of Trail Gulch Lake and the head of Trail Gulch. Return to the trail and proceed down a series of switchbacks. Views are good at times, but there is also a fair amount of forest cover.

Finally, having dropped nearly 1,000 feet, hikers are deposited at beautiful, 10-acre Trail Gulch Lake. Willow thickets block access to the lake, where the trail finally levels off. Take an obvious side trail to the left to clear the thicket and enter a lovely meadow on the edge of the lake that is dotted with numerous granite boulders. Note the large rocky island in the lake. This makes a great swimming destination on hot summer days. Following the main trail, the path stays just north of the lakeshore. After crossing Trail Gulch Creek, the path pulls alongside the lake. There is easy access to the water along here and great views of the canyon wall on the east side of the lake.

Beyond the lake, the route descends a broad, boulder-filled gully as it heads west. Stay right at a signed junction. Beyond this point the trail turns to the north and begins its descent of Trail Gulch. The grade is very moderate and the path pleasant. Though there is some forest cover in parts, there is a fair amount of open country with good views of Trail Gulch's cliffs and Trail Gulch Creek. Small meadows pop up occasionally, adding some variety as well. Be sure to note the destruction wrought by large avalanches along the trail. About 1.0 mile from the junction the trail edges close to the main fork of Trail Gulch Creek. Another 0.75 mile farther the route crosses over the creek. At this point the trail strays away from the creek and continues another 0.8 mile to the Trail Gulch Trailhead. To complete the loop, stay to the right and walk along the road for another 0.8 mile back to the Long Gulch Trailhead.

MILES AND DIRECTIONS

0.0   Start from the Long Gulch Lake Trailhead and follow the trail clockwise.

1.5   Turn right to follow the spur to Long Gulch Lake.

1.8   The spur trail ends at the edge of Long Gulch Lake. Follow the trail back to the junction to continue the loop. (**Option:** If Long Gulch Lake is your destination, turn around here.)

2.5   Reach the rim above Long Gulch Lake.

3.8   Arrive at the overlook above Trail Gulch Lake.

5.3   The trail pulls alongside Trail Gulch Lake.

5.8   Stay right at a junction and turn north into Trail Gulch.

7.8   At the Trail Gulch Trailhead, keep to the right on the dirt road and follow it back toward the Long Gulch Trailhead.

9.2   Arrive back at the trailhead, completing the loop.

21. **TAYLOR AND HOGAN LAKES**

WHY GO?

This hike into the northern section of the small Russian Wilderness offers the opportunity to visit beautiful lakes in large granite bowls and spring-fed meadows in a rugged and remote mountain range boasting incredibly diverse forests.

THE RUNDOWN

Start: Taylor Lake Trailhead
Distance: 7.5 miles out and back to Hogan Lake (**Option:** easy 2.0 miles out and back to south end of Taylor Lake)
Hiking time: 4 hours or overnight
Difficulty: Moderately difficult
Elevation gain: 1,425 feet to Hogan Lake
Season: Summer, fall

Trail surface: Packed dirt, rocky
Canine compatibility: Dogs permitted
Fees and permits: None
Land status: Russian Wilderness
Trail contact: Salmon/Scott River Ranger District, 11263 N. Highway 3, Fort Jones 96032; www.fs.usda.gov/klamath

FINDING THE TRAILHEAD

 From junction of CA 3 and Sawyers Bar Road/Main Street in Etna, drive west on Sawyers Bar Road for 11 miles to Etna Summit. Just past the summit, turn left onto FR 41N18, signed for Taylor Lake. Follow the road for 2.3 miles to the trailhead. The road is mostly a good dirt road, but significant sections, especially on steep terrain, are paved. There is a large paved parking area. **Trailhead GPS:** 41°22'3.35"N / 122°58'28.88"W

WHAT TO SEE

Tucked between the major wildlands of the Trinity Alps and Marble Mountains, the diminutive Russian Wilderness can at times be overlooked. At only 12,521 acres, it is miniscule compared to its more famous neighbors. However, size is not necessarily indicative of the quality of the scenery and the Russian Wilderness packs an extremely scenic punch. Consisting of a crest of high mountain terrain that serves as a connecting bridge between the high-elevation regions of the Marbles and Trinities, the Russians are one of the most scenic areas in the Klamath Mountains. Composed primarily of granite, this alpine area boasts more than two dozen lakes within the wilderness border, with several more just outside the boundary. Dark gray cliffs and peaks rise beautifully above the sparkling waters and deep, remote forests. The biodiversity in this area is of particular note. Amazingly, seventeen conifer species have been documented in 1 square mile of these mountains—more than anywhere else in the world.

The mountains of the Russian Wilderness form the divide between the Scott and Salmon Rivers. These are narrow, steep mountains; consequently, the trails tend to climb steeply up drainages to rugged lake basins. The Pacific Crest Trail is one of the few exceptions to the tendency toward steepness, but it is marked by long approaches to the wilderness from both the north and south. Perhaps the best way to experience the beauty of the Russian Wilderness is to hike to Taylor and Hogan Lakes, located at the extreme northern end of the wilderness area. Both lakes exhibit the beauty that is a consistent feature of the lakes in this wildland. For hikers looking for a short trip, Taylor Lake is the most easily accessed body of water not only of the Russian Wilderness but of any wilderness in the Klamath Mountains. Easy access does not mean minimal scenic quality, however, and the lake's rugged basin is a beautiful sight. For those who want a longer and more demanding hike, the trail continues to Hogan Lake, where granite cliffs tower nearly 1,700 feet above the lake's cool waters. Spectacular Big Blue Lake is found 800 feet above Hogan Lake, accessed by a rocky scramble if strong hikers want a challenging addition to this hike. *Note:* Returning to the trailhead from Hogan Lake requires a 1,000-foot ascent.

The trailhead for the hike to Taylor Lake is at the south end of the large trailhead parking area. The lake is an easy 0.25-mile walk, and the trail is wide and level enough to accommodate a wheelchair. Easy access to this wild lake was the intent, and the trail engineers did an excellent job of making Taylor Lake an achievable destination for almost anyone. A few carved log benches are found along the way. In short order the trail pulls alongside Taylor Creek just before hikers are deposited at the north end of the lake, with good views of the craggy cliffs rising above the water. A trail continues to the left, along

Taylor Lake is a beautiful and easily accessed alpine lake.

Peak 7,684 looms above the trailhead, on the far side of Taylor Creek's canyon.

the east shore of Taylor Lake. If you are not planning on continuing to Hogan Lake or are looking for access to the water, take this trail, which wraps around to beautiful meadows at the lake's southern end. From here there is a good view of prominent Peak 7,684.

If you plan to continue the hike to Hogan Lake, you need to backtrack a few yards from where the trail first arrives at Taylor Lake. Look for a sign mounted onto a tree that indicates the directions to both Taylor and Hogan Lakes. The sign can be easy to miss, so keep an eye out for it. At the sign there is a set of logs that cross over the deep gully containing Taylor Creek. Cross the logs and pick up the trail on the other side. Even recent topographic maps incorrectly identify the trail to Hogan Lake following the path on the east side of the lake before bending around the south end and climbing up the divide that separates the lake basins. The trail now crosses over Taylor Creek and follows the west side of the lake before ascending the divide. Attempting to reach the divide from the south side of the lake necessitates cross-country hiking.

Once across the creek, the trail follows the lake for a short distance before beginning a series of switchbacks that moderate the 400-foot climb up to the divide. From the top there are filtered views of the Marble Mountains to the north. The trail levels off, passes through some stunted forest, and then begins a descent along the flanks of a basin that forms a secondary headwater to Taylor Creek. Some of the trees in this area have been blackened by fire. In about 0.4 mile from the top of the divide, the trail passes through an area composed of black rock and sparse trees. To the east the face of Peak 7,684 rises

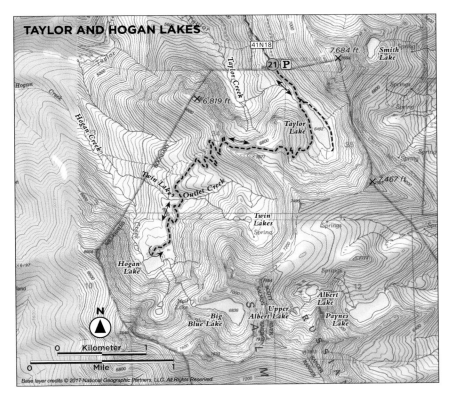

TAYLOR AND HOGAN LAKES

above the parking area, which can be made out despite being partially obscured by forest cover.

In the midst of the black rock, the trail makes the first of a long series of switchbacks that constitute the descent to Hogan Lake. At the second switchback, watch for a use trail leading off to the south. This path leads to the small Twin Lakes. As you continue the descent, the forest gives way to a large burned area. Burnt snags still stand, but the forest has already begun its regenerative process. The burned areas form a patchwork all the way to Hogan Lake. At the bottom of the switchbacks, the route crosses over the often dry creek that flows from the Twin Lakes. Shortly after that, the trail enters a small meadow. Hogan Lake lies only a little farther away. The trail arrives at the lake's north shore, where there are some excellent campsites. Awesome granite cliffs loom above the lake, and the sound of water cascading down them is audible. There are several good spots to relax on the forested shoreline and enjoy the view. If you want to attempt Big Blue Lake, the very steep route begins on the southeast side of the lake and initially ascends the large boulders of a talus slope. From there, though no trail exists, the way is fairly obvious, as you must angle toward the ridge directly overhead. Don't forget that to return to Taylor Lake, and ultimately the trailhead, you must make the 1,000-foot

Soaring cliffs rise out of Hogan Lake's west shore.

climb back up to the divide above Taylor Lake. Though the price is hefty, Hogan Lake is worth it.

MILES AND DIRECTIONS

0.0   Start from the trailhead and head south on an easy, wide path.

0.4   Arrive at the north shore of Taylor Lake. To continue to Hogan Lake, backtrack a little from the shore and cross the outlet creek on logs near the trail sign mounted in a tree. Follow the trail around to the west side of the lake. (*Option:* If you are heading to the meadows at the Taylor Lake's south shore, stay left here and continue another 0.4 mile until the trail fades out in the meadows. Turn around there.)

1.25   The trail reaches a high shoulder above Taylor Lake after ascending a series of switchbacks.

1.7   The trail begins a long series of switchbacks that descends 1,000 feet to Hogan Lake.

3.7   Arrive at Hogan Lake. To get to Big Blue Lake from here, continue around the east side of the lake and scramble up a large talus slope and along some ledges before arriving at the awesome lake. When heading back to Taylor Lake, remember that it is necessary to make the 1,000-foot ascent.

7.1   Return to the north shore of Taylor Lake.

7.5   Arrive back at the trailhead.

22. **SHACKLEFORD BASIN**

WHY GO?

Passing through one of the prettiest lake basins in the Marble Mountains, this lollipop hike visits three distinctly different and beautiful lakes set in scenic rocky basins.

THE RUNDOWN

Start: Shackleford Trailhead
Distance: 13.0-mile lollipop
Hiking time: 6–7 hours
Difficulty: Moderate
Elevation gain: 2,075 feet
Season: Summer, fall
Trail surface: Packed dirt, rocky
Canine compatibility: Dogs permitted

Fees and permits: None
Land status: Marble Mountains Wilderness, Klamath National Forest
Trail contact: Scott River Ranger District, 11263 N. Highway 3, Fort Jones 96032; (530) 468-5351; www .fs.usda.gov/contactus/klamath
Other: Water is available in creeks and in a handful of lakes.

FINDING THE TRAILHEAD

Beginning in Fort Jones, drive south on CA 3. Turn right onto Scott River Road and proceed 7 miles. Turn left onto Quartz Valley Road and continue for 4 miles. Turn right at the sign indicating Shackleford Trailhead and follow this road for 7 miles to the trailhead. **Trailhead GPS:** 41°33'45.49"N / 123°2'55.83"W

WHAT TO SEE

An expansive mountain stronghold, the Marble Mountains are one of the greatest sub-ranges of the Klamath Mountains. Preserved in the 225,114-acre Marble Mountains Wilderness, this mountain range is filled with unusual geography, rugged peaks, and numerous lakes. Though there are granite plutons scattered around the Marbles, as the name suggests, there is a significant amount of marble present as well. However, most of the range is composed of a mélange of different rock types that include sedimentary and ultramafic rock. The end result of this geologic mixture is a beautiful mountain range that beckons hikers to explore its unique charms. One of the best places to do this is in the Shackleford Creek Basin. Here you will find a collection of some of the best lakes in the Marble Mountains Wilderness, as well as oddly colored peaks indicative of the region's geology. The journey leads along pretty Shackleford Creek for a few miles before making a lovely loop through the lake basins, where you will find some of the best scenery in the Klamath Mountains.

The hike starts at the Shackleford Trailhead, heading west. A trail from the stables below quickly merges with the wide path. A short distance from the trailhead, a large sign mounted on a tree indicates passage into the Marble Mountains Wilderness. This is the

The hike to the lakes follows Shackleford Creek.

second-largest wilderness in the Klamath Mountains after the Trinity Alps to the south. Soon the sound of rushing Back Meadow Creek is audible. Cross the creek and continue on the main trail. Up until this point, the path has stayed north of large Shackleford Creek. Now, about 1.0 mile from the trailhead, it pulls in close to the water. The creek and the trail now maintain a parallel course for nearly 1.75 easy miles. Along the way you pass through a few small meadows and cross Long High Creek. This creek tumbles precipitously down the side of the canyon from Calf Lake, which lies 2,000 feet overhead.

At 2.75 miles from the trailhead, you arrive at the first fork in the trail. The path coming in from the left is the end of the loop section of the hike. Stay right and begin climbing up the trail. The trail makes a few lazy switchbacks as it works its way up a rocky ledge and then levels off again just as you arrive at a second junction. The trail branching off to the right leads to Calf Lake and other destinations, including an awesome rock scramble over a pass and down to the ABCD Lakes. Stay left at the trail and continue heading west, where you soon pass above small Log Lake. This diminutive body of water is ringed by trees and has numerous snags in it. Still, it is nice to have a landmark indicative of the increasingly attractive surroundings. Beyond Log Lake the trail passes through large open areas where the trees have been knocked down by avalanches. Meadows are spread out beneath the avalanche zones and offer the first really good views of the canyon. Once again the trail begins to climb as it presses deeper into the canyon. Soon the route pulls near the creek again as it tumbles down a narrow, rocky gorge.

Above the small gorge you can see the canyon headwall as you continue to climb. The forest begins to thin and passes through several small patches of meadow. You will know you are near the end of the climb when the trail runs along the base of some small cliffs. This end of the canyon is much rocker than any point up until now, and the scenery is much more interesting. After a couple of short switchbacks alongside the creek, the trail arrives at beautiful Summit Lake, 3.5 miles from the trailhead. As you arrive at the lake, stay left where the trail forks. The path to the right climbs out of the basin and connects to the Pacific Crest Trail. Stark cliffs rise above the west side of the lake and make a fine backdrop above the water, but it is the view from the south side that is the most memorable. From there tall russet-colored peaks rise above the west end of Shackleford Creek's canyon.

From Summit Lake continue hiking as the trail climbs just a little more. Just a few yards beyond Summit Lake lies small Summit Meadow Lake. As the name implies, the lake is indeed surrounded by meadow and is near the trail's summit. You arrive at the high point of the hike just a few hundred feet past the lake. At the top of the pass, the trail begins to descend toward Campbell Lake. Much of the terrain here is rocky, and views of the rugged peaks that ring the large basin that lies at the southwestern head of Shackleford Creek's canyon are good. After a few switchbacks you arrive at the bottom of the basin, where a network of meadows cover much of the floor. Make your way through the meadows for 0.3 mile to the junction with the spur trail leading to Cliff Lake.

Campbell Lake

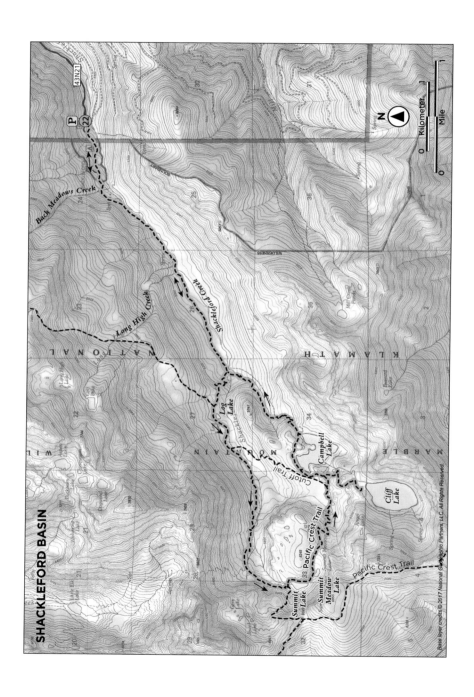

SHACKLEFORD BASIN

The side trip to Cliff Lake is well worth the effort. The deepest and among the largest bodies of water in the Marble Mountains, the lake is also one of the most spectacular. As the name implies, it is situated at the base of a long series of cliffs that stand 800 to 1,000 feet above the lake. Getting there requires a 0.65-mile climb on a trail that switchbacks up 350 feet through rocky ledges and alongside the lake's outlet creek. When you arrive, the outlet is below the trail on the right. There are good views from here, but the extensive shoreline has plenty of other good vantage points from which to observe the large, deep lake and the striking cliffs. After enjoying the beauty of this place, head back down to the junction with the main trail and turn right.

Campbell Lake is only a short walk from where the Cliff Lake spur intersects the main trail. The lake lies on the right, and from the shore you can see peaks of dark rock rising high to the south. Though not as dramatic as Cliff Lake, Campbell Lake is a worthy destination in its own right. Much of the shoreline is lined with trees, but there are long sections of rocky benches along the water, especially on the southwest side, that make good places to take a break. The trail wraps around the lake's west side and then the north. Be sure to stay right at an old trail that veers left to lead down to Shackleford Creek near Log Lake. On the north side of the lake, the path cuts inland a little to climb a low rise before arriving at a small dam that was built to raise the water level of the lake. Many lakes in the Klamath have old dams on them, but most have been broken to allow the water to return to its natural level. The small stone dam on Campbell Lake is still intact, making the lake a little larger than it would be naturally. The view west from the dam toward the Cliff Lake basin is particularly good. Beyond Campbell Lake the route descends a series of switchbacks as it runs parallel to the outlet creek. At 1.15 mile from the dam, the path crosses Shackleford Creek and reconnects to the main trail. From here it is an easy 2.75-mile walk back to the trailhead.

MILES AND DIRECTIONS

0.0   Start at the Shackleford Trailhead.

2.75   Turn right onto the trail to Summit Lake.

3.35   Pass Log Lake on the left.

5.45   Arrive at Summit Lake.

6.0   Top out on the divide between Summit and Campbell Lakes.

7.0   Turn right to take the spur trail to Cliff Lake.

7.6   Reach beautiful Cliff Lake.

8.3   Returning from Cliff Lake, turn right back onto the main trail and arrive at Campbell Lake.

9.0   Arrive at the Lake Campbell dam.

10.15   Turn right and rejoin the main trail back to the trailhead.

13.0   Arrive back at the trailhead.

23. MOUNT EDDY

WHY GO?

This incredible hike through red and yellow mountains journeys through lush meadows, past beautiful lakes in a glacial valley, and to the top of an ultra-prominent peak that boasts what might be the most dramatic vista in the northernmost part of California.

THE RUNDOWN

Start: Across the road from the Deadfall Meadow Trailhead.
Distance: 8.2 miles out and back to Mount Eddy (**Option:** Moderately easy 3.2 miles out and back to Middle Deadfall Lake)
Hiking time: 4–5 hours
Difficulty: Moderately strenuous
Elevation gain: 2,580 feet to Mount Eddy
Season: Summer, fall
Trail surface: Packed dirt, rocky

Canine compatibility: Dogs permitted
Fees and permits: None
Land status: Shasta-Trinity National Forest
Trail contact: Mount Shasta Ranger District, 204 West Alma St., 96067; (530) 926-4511; www.fs.usda.gov/main/stnf/
Other: Water is available in Deadfall Meadow and the Deadfall Lakes.

FINDING THE TRAILHEAD

From Mt. Shasta City, drive north on I-5 through the town of Weed. Take the Edgewood/Stewart Springs exit. Turn left and drive under the freeway, then turn right onto Old Stage Road / Old 99. Continue north for a couple hundred yards and then turn left onto Stewart Springs Road. After 4 miles, FR 17 splits off to the right. Follow this road for 10.2 miles to the Deadfall Meadow Trailhead, located on the right at a hairpin turn in the road. The trail is across the road. Note that you pass the Parks Creek Trailhead at 9.2 miles. This can be used as an alternative trailhead.
Trailhead GPS: 41°20'5.26"N / 122°31'15.26"W

WHAT TO SEE

Mount Eddy may not be a well-known mountain, but it deserves far more recognition than the scant little it gets. In terms of the region's geography, the peak holds many important positions. It is not only the highest point in the Trinity Divide, one of the easternmost of the Klamath Mountains' subranges, but at 9,025 feet is also the tallest peak in the entire Klamath Mountain range. Incidentally, it is also the highest summit in the coterminous forty-eight states west of I-5. Not only is it a tall peak, it is also very prominent, rising more than 5,000 feet above the three rivers that flow around its base. The headwaters of these three rivers—the Trinity, Sacramento, and Shasta—are all located on Mount Eddy, making the summit a triple-divide peak. Yet, for all these interesting

Mount Eddy rises dramatically above Upper Deadfall Lake.

statistics, the fact remains that Mount Eddy is simply a spectacular and very beautiful mountain.

Perhaps all these features are often overlooked because Mount Eddy was fated to fall in the incomparable shadow of Mount Shasta. In spite of its size, height, and beauty, it seems to shrink until almost unnoticed due to the overwhelming scale of the neighboring volcano. Despite this, Mount Eddy deserves to be recognized as the premier hiking destination it is. The trip to the summit passes through some of the most beautiful terrain in the Klamath Mountains. Beginning in Deadfall Meadow, the trail climbs up to picturesque Deadfall Basin. Here there are a trio of beautiful lakes and numerous scenic ponds. Climbing beyond the basin leads through an unusual forest en route to the summit of Mount Eddy, which lies just above tree line. The vista from the top is truly epic, encompassing much of Northern California and well into southern Oregon. Best of all, its proximity to Mount Shasta means it has one of the finest views of California's largest mountain.

The parking area for Mount Eddy lies across the road from the start of the trail. A small sign marks the beginning of the path. Descend a few feet into the meadow, where the trail soon weaves through some dense brush. To the west rise the red and gray towers of the nearby Scott Mountains, a forgotten subrange of the Klamaths that hides fine peaks and pretty lakes for those willing to explore their lonely trails. While making your way across Deadfall Meadow, there are a couple of crossings of small, spring-streams; some sections of the trail may get especially muddy through here. On the far side of the meadow, cross vigorous Deadfall Creek then follow as it turns to the east. It maintains a course through the woods, running parallel to the edge of the meadow. It soon crosses a creek that drains Lower Deadfall Lake before reaching another crossing of Deadfall Creek, about 0.6 mile

from the trailhead. Once on the east side of the creek, the trail climbs steadily up a slope through more trees before breaking out into the meadow again. The pattern of alternating patches of forest and meadow continues for 0.9 mile after the second crossing of Deadfall Creek before you arrive at a four-way junction with the Pacific Crest Trail and the historic Sisson-Callahan Trail, about 1.5 miles from the trailhead.

The intersection with the Pacific Crest Trail lies at the edge of Deadfall Basin. This large, glacier-carved canyon has sheer cliffs and a wide, U-shaped floor typical of valleys carved by great sheets of moving ice. It also has large, deep lakes, remnants of the glaciers that shaped this landscape. Many hikers coming to Deadfall Basin prefer to do so via the Pacific Crest Trail from Parks Creek Pass. This is a good route with nice views. It is twice as long as the Deadfall Meadow route but has half the elevation gain. To continue to Mount Eddy, pass the Pacific Crest Trail and begin hiking on the Sisson-Callahan Trail. In the nineteenth century this trail was the main route by which the Scott Valley residents and those around the base of Mount Shasta travelled. Immediately after the junction with the Pacific Crest Trail, several use trails veer to the right off the main path. These lead down to large Middle Deadfall Lake, the largest and deepest in the basin (825 feet elevation gain from the trailhead). The lake is backed by cliffs composed of red and russet-colored rock called peridotite. This ultramafic rock is ubiquitous in the Klamath Mountains, but it is rare to find it in large quantities outside the range. The rock produces poor soils, and many plants in the Klamath Mountains have specially adapted to survive in the harsh environment.

Past Middle Deadfall Lake, the Sisson-Callahan Trail climbs through the basin, passing a pond where the summit of Mount Eddy becomes visible for the first time. The peak lies just above a dramatic red and orange cliff that is streaked with large veins of white rock. A little past the pond, the trail arrives at Upper Deadfall Lake. Nestled at the base of the multicolored cliff, the meadow rings by far the prettiest lake in the basin. Spring-fed streams flow out of the base of the cliff and meander through verdant meadows before feeding into the lake. After traveling along the edge of the lake, the Sisson-Callahan Trail skirts the edge of the meadows while climbing up the south wall of the basin. After a short climb the trail arrives at a junction with the route that leads to the top of Mount Eddy. The Sisson-Callahan Trail continues south, descending into the canyon of the North Fork of the Sacramento River. From there it follows the river from its headwaters almost all the way to its confluence with the South Fork near Lake Siskiyou, on the outskirts of Mt. Shasta City.

Turning left onto the summit route, the path climbs moderately along the rim of the basin. Shortly after leaving the Sisson-Callahan Trail, keep an eye out for foxtail pine. These trees have red bark and short branches with needles arranged in small clumps that resemble a bottle brush or "foxtail." These trees grow throughout the Klamath Mountains but are cut off from the rest of the range, which lies 400 miles to the south in the southeastern Sierra Nevada. Proceed along the rim of the basin for 0.3 mile after leaving the Sisson-Callahan Trail. Views of the lakes down in the basin are great, and in the distance the Scott Mountains line the horizon. The path then cuts away from the rim and begins a long series of switchbacks up toward the summit of Mount Eddy. The forest grows sparse as you near the top, and the views get increasingly better.

After climbing the switchbacks for 0.8 mile, the trail emerges on the summit, and for the first time the mighty cone of Mount Shasta appears in all its tremendous glory. It is a worthy reward after the long climb, though the rest of the panorama on the summit is

Mount Shasta highlights the spectacular summit panorama.

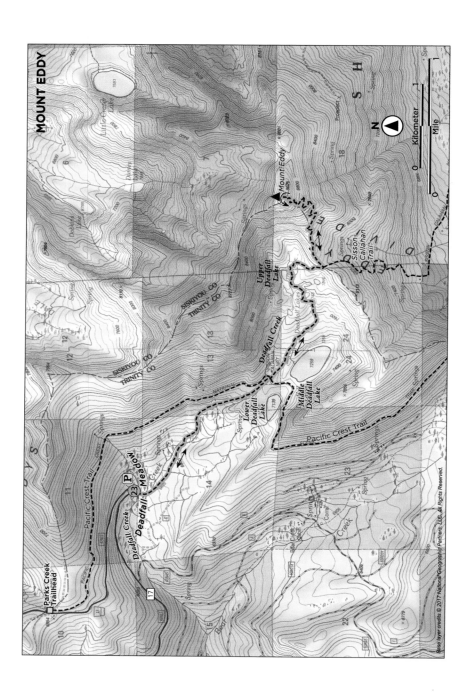

MOUNT EDDY

nearly as grand. It stretches from Lassen Peak, at the southern end of the Cascade Range, 150 miles north to Mount McLoughlin, the tallest peak in southern Oregon. To the south, many of the local landmarks around Mount Shasta, including the granite turrets of the Castle Crags, reveal how rugged the Trinity Divide is. To the west, most of the Klamath Mountains are visible, including the North Yolla Bollies, the Marble Mountains, the Scott Mountains, the Russian Wilderness, and the Red Buttes. However, it is the fang-like peaks and ridges of the mighty Trinity Alps that draw the eye. For those looking for an even better view of Mount Shasta, follow a faint trail east across a saddle to rocky Point 8,881. The north side of the saddle is home to a large snowfield that lasts all through summer most years. From the point you can see the seldom-visited Eddy Bowl falling away toward pyramidal Black Butte, which lies at the foot of Mount Shasta. The magnificent volcano is unbelievably large and is a jaw-dropping sight. After enjoying the summit vista, return the way you came back to the trailhead.

MILES AND DIRECTIONS

0.0 Start at the trailhead and make your way across Deadfall Meadow and Deadfall Creek.

0.6 Cross Deadfall Creek a second time.

1.5 The trail intersects the Pacific Crest and Sisson-Callahan Trails at the mouth of Deadfall Basin. Continue into the basin on the Sisson-Callahan Trail, passing large Middle Deadfall Lake at 1.6 miles. (*Option:* If Middle Deadfall Lake is your destination, turn around here.)

2.5 Pass alongside beautiful Upper Deadfall Lake.

2.9 Turn left onto the spur trail leading to the summit of Mount Eddy.

4.1 Arrive at the summit of Mount Eddy and enjoy the glorious view. Retrace your steps back to the trailhead at Deadfall Meadow.

8.2 Arrive back at the trailhead.

24. HEART LAKE

WHY GO?

Climbing from the shores of large Castle Lake to the rocky bowl of tiny Heart Lake leads hikers into a world of rugged cliffs, small ponds, and delicate meadows overshadowed by an incomparable view of mighty Mount Shasta.

THE RUNDOWN

Start: Castle Lake Trailhead
Distance: 2.0 miles out and back
Hiking time: 1–2 hours
Difficulty: Moderately easy
Elevation gain: 670 feet
Season: Summer, fall
Trail surface: Packed dirt, rocky
Canine compatibility: Dogs permitted
Fees and permits: None

Land status: Castle Crags Wilderness, Shasta-Trinity National Forest
Trail contact: Mount Shasta Ranger District, 204 W. Alma St., Mt. Shasta 96067; (530) 926-4511; www.fs.usda .gov/main/stnf/
Other: Water is available at Castle and Heart Lakes.

FINDING THE TRAILHEAD

From Mt. Shasta City, drive west on West Lake Street, crossing over I-5. At the stop sign, turn left onto Old Stage Road. After 0.25 mile veer right onto WA Barr Road. Continue south, crossing over the dam that impounds the Sacramento River and forms Lake Siskiyou. Just past the dam, make a left turn onto Castle Lake Road, which climbs for 7 miles to the road's end at Castle Lake. **Trailhead GPS:** 41°13'48.75"N / 122°22'53.55"W

WHAT TO SEE

The Trinity Divide's small Heart Lake is a lovely jewel of alpine goodness. The lake is nestled in a rocky bench at the foot of cliffs that rise nearly 500 feet to the summit of Castle Peak. Far below, beneath the great cliffs that fall away from Heart Lake's rocky bench, lie the clear waters of Castle Lake, the largest lake in the region and certainly among the most beautiful. Yet despite Heart Lake's enviable setting, it is set apart by one utterly unbeatable feature. Of all the alpine lakes in the vast Klamath Mountains, none have a finer view of Mount Shasta. The great volcano lies only a few miles to the east. Nothing in the intervening space imposes itself between Heart Lake and the mountain, rendering the view of Mount Shasta absolutely magnificent.

The hike to Heart Lake is surprisingly easy and scenic. To begin the hike, walk east from the trailhead toward Castle Lake's outlet. This area has some of the best views of Castle Lake and the cliffs above it. Though it is difficult to perceive their height from

Heart Lake is hidden on a rocky bench in the cliffs above Castle Lake.

here, they tower more than 1,100 feet above the water. Heart Lake is set in a bowl on a narrow bench about three-fourths of the way to the top of the cliffs. After admiring the view, cross over the outlet creek and then stay right as the trail forks. The path to the left is an unofficial route that leads to the nearby campground and the woods farther downstream.

Past the fork, the trail to Heart Lake turns south and begins to climb up the side of the ridge that hems in Castle Lake on the east. Though the trail passes through a dense thicket of willows, you can still look out over the lake and observe its large basin. The willows are soon replaced by conifers as the path climbs more steeply. The trees close in around the path, and for a short distance there are no views of note. This is the steepest part of the hike. Fortunately the sharp grade and the dense forest fade away as you climb up onto Heart Lake's rocky bench.

Here the trail splits. The path to the left goes over a low rise and then drops down to Little Castle Lake, another beautiful alpine lake. Stay right here and continue climbing, though the grade is not nearly as steep. Be sure to stay on the most obvious path as you go. Numerous use trails have been worn into this area and can make getting to Heart Lake a little confusing if you are not paying attention. Not long after the trail splits, the path skirts the base of some rock outcroppings. Beyond these outcroppings, the number of use trails deceases significantly and the route becomes obvious.

Stunning views of Castle Lake and Mount Shasta are found around Heart Lake.

As you continue to climb up the bench, you enter a beautiful alpine world. Scattered trees, large clumps of grass, and boulders all lie at the foot of steep slopes rising above the trail. The views to the north stretch all the way into southern Oregon. Soon the trail climbs steeply up to a saddle. From there, drop down to diminutive but beautiful Heart Lake. The trail crosses Heart Lake's small outlet stream and continues along its north shore. A pond lies just past the lake, and a small patch of meadow is adjacent to the pond. It is a lovely setting and begs to be savored.

However, as beautiful as it is at Heart Lake, it is the imposing presence of Mount Shasta that makes this such an exceptional spot. From the lake's outlet the mountain dominates the scene to the north. To the left of Mount Shasta, the dark turret of Black Butte, a prominent landmark around Mt. Shasta City and an impressive peak in its own right, can be seen. Beyond it rises the crest of the Cascade Range, topped by a peak known as the Goosenest. Fuji-like Mount McLoughlin in southern Oregon is visible on the horizon. Mount Eddy, the tallest peak in the Trinity Divide, also makes a notable appearance in the tremendous panorama.

Heart Lake's position in the Trinity Divide actually makes it ideally located for hikers to enjoy both sunrise and sunset on Mount Shasta. Perhaps the best way to observe these events is from the south side of Heart Lake, when the winds are still. The alpenglow on Mount Shasta reflects perfectly in the lake's still waters, casting a marvelous reflection. Teddy Roosevelt once said, "I consider the evening twilight on Mount Shasta one of the grandest sights I have ever witnessed." There are few places better than Heart Lake from which to witness the dazzling light display on Mount Shasta. When you must finally return, follow the trail back to the parking area.

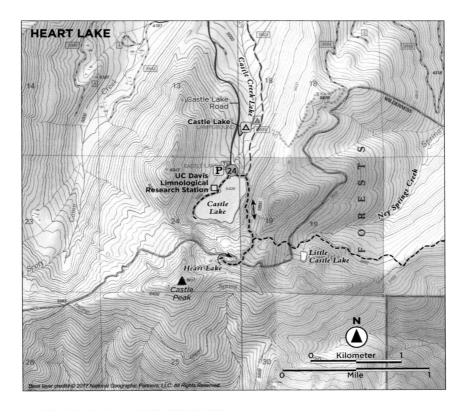

MILES AND DIRECTIONS

0.0 Start from the Castle Lake Trailhead and cross over the lake's outlet. Stay right and then begin climbing above the east side of Castle Lake.

0.5 At the unsigned junction with the route to Little Castle Lake, stay right and continue hiking to the southeast.

1.0 Arrive at Heart Lake. Turn around and retrace your steps.

2.0 Arrive back at the trailhead.

The Cinder Cone and the Fantastic Lava Beds are quintessential Cascades terrain.

CASCADES

THE CASCADE RANGE is one of the great mountain ranges of the American West—a land of mighty glacier-clad peaks, vast forests, and numerous volcanic features. This iconic range is typically associated with the states of Washington and Oregon rather than California. Yet the range pushes deep into Northern California, occupying the northeast corner of the state. Mount Shasta is the largest and second-highest mountain in the entire range, and Lassen Peak, the southernmost major volcano in the Cascades, is one of only two to have erupted in the twentieth century.

The Cascade Range in California can be divided into three main regions. The southern region is the Lassen Cascade. The focal point of this region is 10,457-foot Lassen Peak and the surrounding Lassen Volcanic National Park. The national park contains its namesake peak as well as several other volcanoes, cinder cones, and remnants of the long-decimated stratovolcano known as Mount Tehama. Active geothermal features are found throughout the park, as are lava flows and other signs of volcanic activity. Outside the national park, summits such as Thousand Lakes Volcano and Mount Burney, as well as the lava flows of the Hat Creek Valley, are testimony of past volcanic activity.

Separated from the Lassen Cascade by the Pit River, the Shasta Cascade region extends north to the Oregon border. The obvious highlight is solitary Mount Shasta. One of only two 14,000-foot peaks in California that is not located in the Sierra Nevada, the colossal mountain stands in isolation from the rest of the range, towering 10,000 feet above the surrounding landscape. Clad with the largest glaciers in California, Mount Shasta is both a visually stunning landmark and a fantastic hiking destination. Other parts of the Shasta Cascade include the Medicine Lake Highlands which are to the east and several volcanic peaks on the crest as it extends north into Oregon.

The third region of the Cascades in California is not technically part of the Cascade Range. East of the Lassen and Shasta regions lies the expanse of rolling hills, small, low mountain ranges, and wide valleys known as the Modoc Plateau. This high-desert area, like the Cascades, is a volcanic region. Cinder and spatter cones, vast lava flows, lava tubes, and other evidence of extensive volcanic activity are abundant. On the east side of the plateau are the lofty peaks of the Warner Mountains. This remote range is a classic example of fault-block mountains. Several layers of successive lava flows have been exposed in the uplifting process, resulting in awesome cliffs.

Unlike most of Northern California's other great mountain regions, there is not a significant amount of wildland remaining around the Cascades. The largest wilderness block is around Lassen Volcanic National Park. Mount Shasta itself is protected, as are the Lava Beds and the highest elevations of the Warner Mountains. The rest of the range is exposed to development.

25. SOUTH GATE MEADOW

WHY GO?
This spectacular hike traverses the flanks of majestic Mount Shasta, one of the most massive mountains in America. The trip to South Gate Meadow combines delicate meadows and barren volcanic terrain with spectacular vistas of glaciers and distant mountain ranges.

THE RUNDOWN
Start: Panther Meadow Campground and Trailhead
Distance: 4.8-mile reverse lollipop
Hiking time: About 3 hours
Difficulty: Moderate
Elevation gain: 1,275 feet
Season: Summer, fall
Trail surface: Packed dirt, rocky, loose scree, cross-country
Canine compatibility: Dogs not permitted in the Mount Shasta Wilderness.

Fees and permits: None
Land status: Mount Shasta Wilderness
Trail contact: Mount Shasta Ranger District; 204 W. Alma St., Mt. Shasta 96067; (530) 926-4511; www.fs.usda.gov/stnf
Other: Water is available at South Gate Meadow.

FINDING THE TRAILHEAD
From I-5, take the Central Mount Shasta exit. Merge onto Lake Street and head east for 1 mile, passing through the intersection with Mount Shasta Boulevard. As the road bends to the north, continue onto Washington Street for 0.1 mile before continuing onto Everitt Memorial Highway. Once on this road, continue for about 12.5 miles to the Panther Meadow Campground for the Panther Meadow Trailhead. **Trailhead GPS:** 41°21'17.25"N / 122°12'11.52"W

WHAT TO SEE
Dominating the region that surrounds it like no other mountain in California, Mount Shasta is an utterly awe-inspiring landmark. Visible from more than 100 miles distant, the mountain thrusts upward into the sky like an enormous, solitary, icy spike. Due to its immensity, it is often hard to discern the scale of this mighty mountain. At 14,179 feet it is the fifth-highest peak in California. It is also the second-highest peak in the Cascade Range, after Washington's Mount Rainier. While not quite as tall as Mount Rainier, Mount Shasta is much larger, totaling an incredible 120 cubic miles in volume. Mount Shasta is an outlier from the main crest of the Cascade Range and is unconnected to any other nearby mountains. This means it is almost completely surrounded by flatland and rises more than 10,000 feet above the surrounding landscape. Also noteworthy are the seven glaciers that cling to the mountain's upper slopes. Located on the northern and

Looking north toward the Gate, a gap between Sargents Ridge and Red Butte

eastern sides, the Hotlum, Whitney, Wintun, and Bolam Glaciers are California's four largest. The other three are scattered around Mount Shasta's southern slope.

While Mount Shasta is a popular destination for mountaineers looking to reach its summit, it is not as well known as a hiking destination. This means many of the trails are almost empty, and even the popular ones are not very heavily trod. Though all the trails on the mountain are very scenic, the best way to experience what Mount Shasta has to offer is to hike to South Gate Meadow. The terrain of this hike alternates between lush forests, delicate meadows, and barren volcanic landscapes. The journey ends at spring-fed South Gate Meadow, where there are awesome views of the mountain's rugged spires and the Konwakiton Glacier, all surrounded by explosive wildflower displays and the singing of small creeks. Adding to the hike's features is a loop on the return section that features more meadows and some of the best and most far-reaching vistas of the hike.

To begin the hike, depart from the Panther Meadow parking area and pass through the walk-in campground. In short order the trail reaches the meadows and splits. The trail coming in from the left is the final leg of this hike, joining the trail by way of the Panther Meadow spring and the Old Ski Bowl. Stay to the right and continue through the small meadow, crossing rivulets of water and occasionally using well-placed stones to avoid stepping on the fragile grass. Look for good views of Mount Shasta looming to the north. Several other landmarks, including Green Butte, Shastarama Point, and Thumb Rock, are all prominently visible with the main bulk of the mountain, while Gray Butte rises prominently above the meadow to the east.

Beyond the meadow, the trail enters a grove of old-growth Shasta red fir and begins to climb. After 0.7 mile the trail forks at a saddle. Going to the right leads to the summit of Gray Butte, a worthy trip in itself that reaches the peak's summit in another 0.9 mile and yields one of the finest vistas of Mount Shasta to be found anywhere. Those who want to add 1.8 miles to the hike are well rewarded for their effort. Staying left at the saddle, the trail ascends a shallow gully before climbing over a low ridge, entering the Mount Shasta Wilderness as you do. Here you arrive at the edge of a large, moonscape valley, only 0.2 mile from the junction with the Gray Butte Trail.

Descend into the valley, which is nearly devoid of trees, though a few small, hearty hemlocks manage to survive here. To the east, the sheer crimson cliffs of Red Butte rise above the valley, while views of Mount Shasta once again open up to the north. It is an astoundingly beautiful sight despite the barren landscape. Cross the sandy valley floor and swing close to the base of Red Butte before arriving at another junction 1.3 miles from the trailhead. The trail arriving from the west is the route to the Old Ski Bowl. This is the beginning of the return leg of the loop.

Proceeding from the junction, the trail climbs a low saddle and then makes a few switchbacks while descending into a narrow, rocky canyon. This is the South Gate, which forms a pass between the base of Sargents Ridge and Red Butte. (A corresponding North Gate, on the opposite side of Mount Shasta, makes another very scenic hike.) The path weaves through the boulders for some time before reentering the forest. While making a gradual descent through the trees, the path crosses a few small spring-fed streams, the largest of which usually has water flowing well into autumn. Soon the trail climbs briefly before emerging from the forest at the edge of beautiful South Gate Meadow 2.2 miles from the trailhead.

The spectacle from the edge of the meadow is tremendous. Lining the horizon is the long crest of Sargents Ridge, marching inexorably toward the summit of Mount Shasta.

The mighty towers of Mount Shasta are a stark contrast to the lush gardens of South Gate Meadow.

Mount Shasta is a stunning sight from upper Panther Meadow.

Several ragged towers dot the ridge, adding to its immensity. Near the top, the upper half of the Konwakiton Glacier is apparent. Below the ridge and closer, a series of low volcanic hills and cliffs mark the perimeter of the meadow area. Beneath these unfold the braided folds of the meadow itself, with small creeks flowing noisily through them. Around mid-July the meadow explodes with wildflowers, offering colorful contrast to the verdant oasis amid the barren volcanic terrain. The official trail ends at the edge of the meadow but established tracks lead through the meadow itself. Small flags placed by rangers mark the route. Do not deviate from the route and trample the fragile meadow. If you are looking to go farther into South Gate Meadow, stay to the right, following the larger path and climb through the meadow. Soon a large cascade pours down a steep slope. The trail makes a short, hard climb alongside the cascade before leveling off. From here the trail leads to the large complex of springs that are the source of life at South Gate Meadow.

When it is time to leave the meadow and continue the hike, retrace your steps back through the woods and the South Gate before reaching the junction with the trail coming from the Old Ski Bowl. Turn right here to complete the loop. The path initially traverses the side of a ridge before crossing a small basin. Though the basin is desolate, a small ribbon of meadow runs west, toward a saddle at the head of the basin. This is diminutive Hummingbird Meadow. A small spring feeds a tiny stream that runs the short length of the meadow before running underground. As the trail climbs toward the saddle, it threads a route that lies between the meadow on the right and a large boulder field to the left. After a few switchbacks, the trail reaches the top of the saddle, where it departs the Mount Shasta Wilderness.

From the top of the saddle you are treated to awesome views of the Trinity Divide and the sawtooth horizon formed by the vast Trinity Alps. The hulking, orange massif of Mount Eddy is the most eye-catching feature, though the rugged collection of spires that form the Grey Rocks and the awesome Castle Crags are highlights farther to the south. Views reach as far as distant Shasta Bally and Bully Choop Mountains, more than 60 miles to the south. The large canyon of the Sacramento River can be seen winding its way through the expanse of forested ridges. This view continues as you descend the west side of the saddle, toward the Old Ski Bowl trailhead. After dropping 350 feet, the path reaches the parking area. From here, drop down into the gully on the extreme east end of the pavement, following a vague use trail. The path fades out quickly, but simply maintain a course due south for 0.1 mile over the open, rocky terrain before intersecting a wide trail leading to Upper Panther Meadow.

Depending on where you hit the trail, there may be another trail junction. If you encounter this, stay to the left and follow the path straight to the cliffs immediately to the east. If you missed the junction, simply turn left onto the trail and follow it the short distance to the meadow. Once at the verdant oasis, follow the flat stones across the grass and wildflowers, enjoying the awesome views to both the north and south. Once back in the woods, you will reach a spur trail that leads a short distance to the springs that feed the meadow, a worthwhile trip with a magnificent view of the Castle Crags. Staying the course on the main trail, you soon cross the meadow's main stream, where there is one of the best views yet of Mount Shasta, rising majestically above Panther Meadow. Only a few feet from the stream crossing is another junction. Turn left here and descend the trail through a hemlock grove before emerging at Lower Panther Meadow, where the trail rejoins the original route. Stay right and follow it back through the campground to the parking area.

MILES AND DIRECTIONS

0.0 Start from the trailhead at Panther Meadow Campground; bear right and hike to the meadow.

0.2 Reach the far end of Panther Meadow and begin climbing through old-growth red fir forest.

0.65 At the junction turn left onto the trail signed for South Gate Meadow.

0.85 Come out of the forest to a great view of the Valley of the Moon. Begin to hike down into the valley.

1.3 On the far side of the valley, arrive at the junction with the trail coming from the Old Ski Bowl. Hike through the narrow gap of the South Gate.

1.65 Leave the South Gate and reenter the forest.

2.15 Arrive at the edge of gorgeous South Gate Meadows.

2.9 Return through the South Gate and go right onto the trail that leads to the Old Ski Bowl.

3.2 Climb alongside small, delicate Hummingbird Meadow.

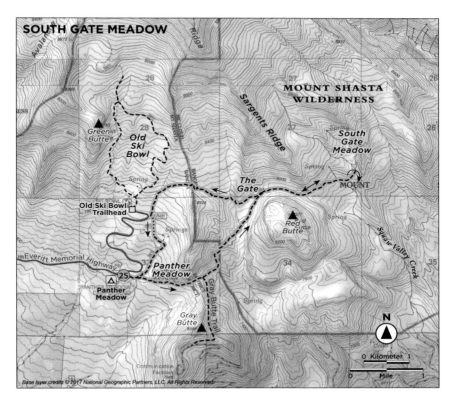

3.5 Reach the top of a ridge at the boundary of the Mount Shasta Wilderness. Begin the descent into the Old Ski Bowl.

4.0 Arrive at the Old Ski Bowl trailhead. Drop down the embankment at the east end of the parking area, and follow the faint track through the rocks and sand.

4.15 At a three-way junction, stay straight and continue to the south.

4.25 Stay to the left and hike down to lower Panther Meadow.

4.6 Turn right to return to the trailhead.

4.8 Arrive back at the trailhead.

26. MCCLOUD RIVER FALLS

WHY GO?

This beautiful hike travels along the McCloud River, one of Northern California's most beautiful, as it passes through a scenic volcanic canyon. The trip is highlighted by the river's three waterfalls, each different from the others.

THE RUNDOWN

Start: Lower Falls Picnic Area
Distance: 4.2 miles out and back
Hiking time: 2–3 hours
Difficulty: Easy
Elevation gain: 300 feet
Season: Spring, summer, fall
Trail surface: Rock, paved, packed dirt
Canine compatibility: Dogs permitted
Fees and permits: None

Land status: Shasta-Trinity National Forest
Trail contact: McCloud Ranger District, 2019 Forest Rd., McCloud 96057; (530) 964-2184; www.fs.usda .gov/stnf
Other: Water is available at Lower Falls. The section of the trail between Lower Falls and the Fowlers Campground is wheelchair-accessible.

FINDING THE TRAILHEAD

From the main intersection in McCloud, drive east on CA 89 for 5.5 miles. Turn right at the signed turnoff for Fowlers and Lower Falls. Drive 0.7 mile and veer right to go to Lower Falls. Pass the turnoff for the Fowlers Campground and continue 0.6 mile to the Lower Falls Picnic Area. **Trailhead GPS:** 41°14'25.98"N / 122°1'30.21"W

WHAT TO SEE

One of the loveliest rivers in Northern California, the McCloud River drains a large area on the southeast side of Mount Shasta. The river begins in the lowlands that lie between the Lassen and Shasta Cascades and flows west. For many miles it is a slow, meandering waterway, collecting water from springs, meadows, and tributary creeks. As it nears the town of McCloud, the river gathers steam and surges through a canyon cut into the volcanic terrain. Here tuff, basalt, and other rocks of volcanic origin line the river and contribute to the formation of the river's three waterfalls. The large cataracts occur when bands of erosion-resistant basalt cross the river and the water mostly pours over it rather than cuts through it.

The McCloud River Trail follows the river for 15 miles from the Algoma Campground to the Pine Tree Hollow Loop. The premier section of the trail lies between Lower McCloud and Upper McCloud Falls. It is possible to extend the hike in either direction, either heading upstream from Upper Falls or doing the 1.0-mile Pine Tree

Lower McCloud Falls

Hollow loop from Lower Falls. This description addresses only the falls portion of the hike, but either extension is a good option for more hiking.

Begin at the Lower Falls Picnic Area. There is a large vista point overlooking the falls at the north end of the picnic area. Lower McCloud Falls is the smallest and simplest of the three waterfalls. Just before the falls the river flows through slabs of bulbous lava rock to a point where the rock has given away and a gorge formed beneath it. The river pours off the slabs and into the gorge, a drop of about 12 feet. This area is popular with swimmers, who enjoy the sun-warmed rocks and jump into the pool beneath the falls. Do not attempt this when water levels are high.

From the observation deck, follow the path to the left and descend the stone stairs to the slabs next to the river. Follow the paved trail as it runs parallel to the river. The path then veers into a shallow gully and switchbacks up the side. This detour eases the grade and makes it feasible for wheelchairs to travel this section of the hike. Once out of the gully, the route moves back toward the river but is now well above it. Fences line some sections of the cliffs. As the river bends to the east, the path skirts the outer edge of the Fowlers Campground.

Leave the campground area 0.5 mile from Lower Falls and make an almost imperceptible descent back down to the river. Once past Fowlers, the trail becomes a normal dirt path. It runs alongside the McCloud River, passing large trees and boulders scattered

Middle McCloud Falls is one of the prettiest waterfalls in Northern California.

around the canyon bottom. Keep an eye out for Pacific yew trees, identifiable by their flat, short needles and stringy red bark. About 1.0 mile from Lower Falls, the river has exposed a large, washed-out section of the canyon wall. Here you can observe stratified rock aggregate mixed in with volcanic soils, as well as eroded hoodoo-like formations, all evidence of this area's fiery creation.

Just past this large cut bank, you arrive at the base of Middle McCloud Falls. This is the jewel of the McCloud waterfalls and a powerful, spectacular sight. Nearly 50 feet high and more than 100 feet wide, it is an impressive sheet of falling water. When the large cataract is swollen by spring snowmelt, it is an awe-inspiring display. A large pool lined with huge boulders is located at the base of the waterfall, another popular swimming hole. From the base of the falls, the trail switchbacks up the side of the canyon, culminating in a flight of wooden stairs built onto the side of the basalt cliffs. The trail levels off at the top of the stairs and leads to two more fenced observation points 150 feet above the waterfall. From this perspective you can see the river both upstream and downstream from the falls. Note the large boulder situated precariously on the precipice of the waterfall. You can also look west from here and see the high peaks of the Castle Crags Wilderness.

The trail continues beyond the observation points, built onto a narrow ledge with a fence providing safety from the exposure. Beyond the fence the trail narrows as it passes

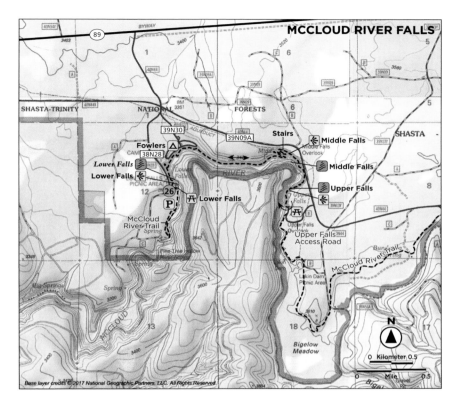

beneath dark basalt cliffs. Trees filter views of the river here, but you get a sense that it is much swifter moving than it is below Middle Falls. A second fence appears along the trail 0.35 mile from the top of Middle Falls, indicating your arrival at Upper Falls, though the crashing water is audible by this point, giving away the waterfall's presence. This waterfall is very different from the other two. Though the falls are only 25 feet high, the river has cut a slot through a 60-foot, roughly hewn columnar basalt cliff. The cataract surges through the slot and seems to burst directly out of the cliff. The path has several vantage points above the falls and passes alongside the narrow slot as well. You can gaze down into the frothy gorge where the river pours from one pool to the next before pouring out of the cliff.

Beyond Upper Falls, the trail follows the more sedate river to a small picnic area next to the water. This makes a good turnaround point. To add more distance to the trip, consider following the McCloud River Trail for another 0.5 mile to the decommissioned Lakin Dam and the large bayou-like meadow that lies behind it. Retrace the route to Lower Falls to finish the hike.

Upper McCloud Falls pours through a notch in a basalt cliff.

MILES AND DIRECTIONS

0.0 Start at the Lower Falls Picnic Area and follow the paved path north along the river.

0.25 Arrive at Fowlers Campground.

0.5 Leave the campground area and follow the McCloud River east.

1.25 Reach the base of Middle McCloud Falls.

1.6 The trail passes the observation points high above the falls.

1.9 Arrive at Upper Falls.

2.1 Turn around at the small picnic area just upstream from Upper Falls.

4.2 Arrive back at the picnic area.

27. LAVA BEDS

WHY GO?

Traveling across the high desert of Lava Beds National Monument, this hike offers views of distant volcanoes and up-close exposure to extensive lava flows. Near the trailhead is one of the park's many lava tubes, where permanent ice is slowly melting.

THE RUNDOWN

Start: Merrill Ice Cave Trailhead
Total distance: 6.7-mile lollipop
Hiking time: 3–4 hours
Difficulty: Easy
Elevation gain: 510 feet
Season: Year-round
Trail surface: Packed dirt, rocky, loose dirt and cinders, cross-country
Canine compatibility: Dogs not permitted

Fees and permits: Entrance fee
Land status: Lava Beds Wilderness, Lava Beds National Monument
Trail contact: PO Box 1240, Tulelake 96134; (530) 667-8113; www.nps.gov/labe
Other: There is no water available on this hike. If you are going to enter the Merrill Ice Cave, it is necessary to get a pass at the visitor center.

FINDING THE TRAILHEAD

From I-5 in Weed, drive northeast on CA 97 for 54 miles. Turn right onto CA 161 and continue 17.2 miles. Turn right onto Hill Road and drive south for 12.8 miles. Turn right onto the main park road and pass through the Lava Beds National Monument entrance station. Continue for 7.4 miles then turn right onto Merrill Cave Road. The trailhead lies 1 mile away. **Trailhead GPS:** 41°43'41.29"N / 121°32'58.21"W

WHAT TO SEE

Lava Beds National Monument preserves a large patch of high-desert terrain at the western edge of the Modoc Plateau. This high upland in the northeast corner of California boasts numerous volcanic features, including lava flows, cinder cones, and old craters. The Lava Beds contain one of the highest concentrations of these features as well as an amazing number of lava tubes. Human history has also left its imprint on the Lava Beds, as it was the home of the Modoc War in the late nineteenth century. Activity at the national monument takes two forms. Hikers travel trails on the surface that visit volcanic and historic sites; others venture beneath the surface and explore the lava tubes. This hike begins near the entrance to one of the lava tubes and then travels into the wild high desert of the Lava Beds hinterlands. There you can visit the dark, twisted walls of the Callahan Lava Flow and scramble to the top of Whitney Butte, an old cinder cone that affords excellent panoramic views across the Modoc Plateau and deep into southern Oregon.

Mount Dome and distant Mount McLoughlin, the highest peak in southern Oregon, are visible from the trail.

Before heading out to Whitney Butte, consider the short walk over to the Merrill Ice Cave. There is not much ice left in the cave, but early in the twentieth century a nearby resort offered ice skating events in the lower chamber. The ice may be receding rapidly, but the cave is still a good introduction to one of the premier features of the Lava Beds. In addition to the ice, the tube is noteworthy because it is actually two tubes stacked one on top of the other. Staircases, ladders, and walkways lead down into the caves. These were built to protect the ice. Other lava tubes have fewer precautions, and you are free to explore.

Once you have checked out the Merrill Ice Cave, head back to the parking area and begin hiking on the Whitney Butte Trail. The dusty path crosses the high-desert terrain in a northwesterly direction. The land here may be semiarid, but the hearty desert vegetation is ubiquitous. In addition to the desert brush, there are lots of junipers and even some scattered ponderosa pines. To the east of the trail rises the cinder cone of Schonchin Butte, topped by a lookout tower. The hike up this cone is another popular trek in the Lava Beds. After hiking 0.5 mile you will make an unheralded entrance into the Lava Beds Wilderness. The low hump due north is another cinder cone called Bat Butte. The trail now turns west and skirts the edge of an old lava flow. Unlike the flows that lie ahead, this lava has sections covered with soil, grasses, and junipers. Still, the dark rock that is exposed reveals its volcanic origin.

As you hike through the high desert, look to the north, out over the Klamath Basin. Large, conical Mount Dome lies just 7 miles to the north and is the most obvious feature visible from the trail. The border with Oregon is only 18 miles away, and numerous prominent landmarks in the Beaver State are visible. The most notable is pyramidal Mount McLoughlin, which rises 60 miles to the northwest. Just east of this mountain, southern Oregon's highest at 9,495 feet, is the forested rim of the Mount Lakes Wilderness. This ancient caldera is a collapsed volcano similar to Crater Lake, except glaciers breeched the rim and the interior is now able to drain. Numerous beautiful lakes still inhabit the crater, however. About 2.0 miles from the trailhead, Whitney Butte comes into view. This large cinder cone is covered with yellow grass and junipers, but the conical shape indicates its nature. Follow the path around the north side of the butte, as it slips through a gap between the cinder cone and the walls of another old lava flow.

As the path bends around to the west side of Whitney Butte, the dark, craggy walls of the Callahan Lava Flow come into view. Unlike the other lava flows along the trail, the vast Callahan flow looks fresh, as though it cooled yesterday. The trail leads right up to the base of the lava, where its destructive path finally came to a halt. The trail ends here, at the boundary of the national monument. However, rather than simply retrace your

From Whitney Butte, Mount Shasta can be seen beyond the stark Callahan Lava Flow.

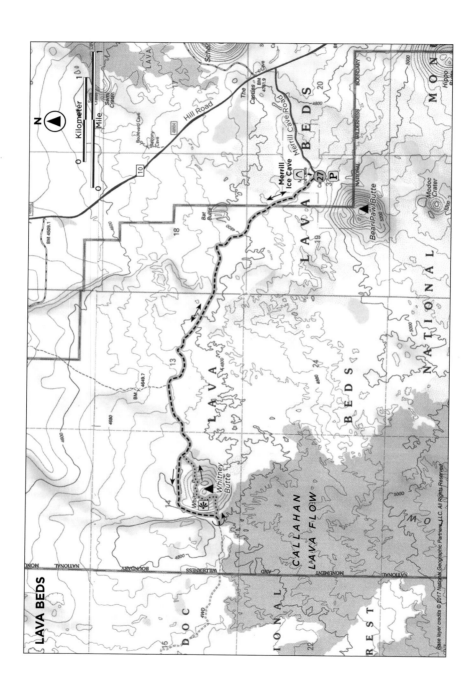

steps from the edge of the lava, turn east and scramble up the slope of Whitney Butte. At the top you will find that the cinder cone has two craters. The view from the top is excellent as well. To the north, Mount Dome in California and Mount McLoughlin in Oregon are obvious. To the south, more lava flows and cinder cones rise nearby. The view west, however, is the most memorable. Here lies the vast expanse of the dark Callahan Lava Flow. Beyond it is the white, glacier-clad tower of Mount Shasta, 40 miles to the west. This is a good place to eat a snack and enjoy the view. When you are ready to head back, either return the way you came or walk along the north rim of the cinder cone and then descend through the junipers on the northeast side. ***Note:*** It is necessary to cross the high desert to get to the trail from here. Be sure to maintain a northeasterly orientation. This will ensure that you intersect the trail. When you find the path, follow it back to the trailhead.

MILES AND DIRECTIONS

0.0 Start at the trailhead and make the quick trip to the Merrill Ice Cave. After exploring the ice cave, hike northwest on the Whitney Butte Trail.

0.5 Enter the Lava Beds Wilderness.

2.9 Round the north side of Whitney Butte.

3.3 Arrive at the Callahan Lava Flow. Return the way you came or scramble up the side of Whitney Butte.

3.5 Reach the rim of Whitney Butte. Follow along the rim on the north side of the butte before descending cross-country to the northeast.

4.1 (Approximate) rejoin the Whitney Butte Trail and turn right, following it back to the trailhead.

6.7 Arrive back at the trailhead.

28. PINE CREEK BASIN/ PATTERSON LAKE

WHY GO?

This hike explores the breathtaking but remote Warner Mountains in the far northeast corner of California. An easy hike to a pair of small lakes and the entrance to a large meadow-filled basin is a good introduction to the range. A longer hike continues to the crest of the range, where a striking lake and stunning vistas await.

THE RUNDOWN

Start: Pine Creek Trailhead
Distance: 11.2 miles out and back to Patterson Lake (*Option:* easy 4.5 miles out and back to Pine Creek Basin)
Hiking time: 7 hours or overnight
Difficulty: Strenuous
Elevation gain: 2,920 feet (Patterson Lake)
Season: Summer, fall
Trail surface: Packed dirt

Canine compatibility: Dogs permitted
Fees and permits: None
Land status: South Warner Wilderness, Modoc National Forest
Trail contact: Warner Mountain Ranger District, 710 Townsend St., Cedarville 96104; (530) 279-6116; www.fs.usda.gov/modoc
Other: Water is available in creeks and lakes.

FINDING THE TRAILHEAD

From the junction of CA 299 and US 395 in Alturas, head south on US 395. At the south end of downtown, turn left (east) on CR 56, which is also named E. McDowell and Parker Creek Road, depending on where on the road you are. The road winds for 13 miles, climbing up to a levee and passing a reservation casino before dropping into a shallow canyon. Eventually the road enters Modoc National Forest and becomes FR 31. Although the pavement ends, the road is in excellent condition and is passable by regular-clearance vehicles. After 13 miles the road reaches a junction with CR 5, a good gravel road. Turn right and head south on CR 5 for 9.8 miles to the signed turnoff for the Pine Creek Trailhead. Turn left and proceed to the end of the road. **Trailhead GPS:** 41°21'30.80"N / 120°17'2.39"W

WHAT TO SEE

Hidden away in the far northeast corner of California are the superb Warner Mountains. Not technically part of the Cascade Range, they lie at a geologic crossroads. To the west, the lonely expanse of the Modoc Plateau unfolds in a sea of lava flows, cinder cones, and high desert punctuated by occasional small mountains and high forest. To the east is the vast Great Basin, the bowl that lies roughly between the Sierra Nevada and the Rocky

Pine Creek Basin viewed from the creek crossing.

Mountains, where there is no outlet for rivers to reach the sea. Sitting on the divide between these two regions, the Warners are an extremely scenic mountain region. Volcanic in origin, the range is composed of layers of lava flows that have been thrust upward. The southern end, which is the most rugged, is protected as the South Warner Wilderness. With peaks rising to just under 10,000 feet, ten named lakes, verdant meadows, and lively creeks all complemented by a well-developed trail network, these mountains are a hiker's paradise. Yet due to their remoteness, they receive only light use.

This hike travels through extensive forest cover in a glacially carved canyon to Pine Creek Basin—a wide, meadow-filled valley just below the crest of the Warners. Strange volcanic rocks, ponds, and a pair of small lakes add interest to the journey. The leisurely first part of the hike ends at the base of Pine Creek Basin, where you can enjoy views of the basin and explore the lakes. If you're looking for a more challenging trip, the hike continues through Pine Creek Basin, climbing up to the crest of the Warners and then following the Warner Summit Trail to spectacular Patterson Lake, the largest and most beautiful lake in the range.

Begin the trip by hiking east on the Pine Creek Trail. A small creek flows to the north of the trail, but it is only occasionally visible. Promptly pass the boundary of the South Warner Wilderness and continue hiking through peaceful forests. Nearly 0.75 mile from the trailhead you will pass a few small ponds. Press on and in another 0.7 mile encounter

The Warner Summit Trail has great views of Squaw Peak and the Surprise Valley.

some larger, deeper ponds. In drought years these may shrink significantly. Past the small ponds you will see unusual white rocks with a strangely stratified appearance. These are old ash deposits, remnants of some of the volcanic activity that formed these mountains. At the rocks you begin to get a sense of the size of the canyon, as tall cliffs can be seen rising to the north. After the unusual rocks, the trail climbs a pair of switchbacks before arriving at a beautiful little lake located at the base of Pine Creek Basin, about 2.6 miles from the trailhead.

The small lake is ringed with meadow, and a gap in the trees on the east side permits views of the gentle crest of the Warners. Just north of the small lake is an even larger lake fed by Pine Creek. The tall cliffs of the north side of the canyon rise beautifully above the lake, which is surrounded by more of the unusual, stratified rock. No trails lead to this lake, so some route finding is necessary. Unlike the small lake at the base of Pine Creek Basin, this second lake is not spring fed and relies on water from Pine Creek to sustain it. In drought years it may dry up, leaving a large meadow.

Just past these lakes, the trail continues briefly until it arrives at the meadows of Pine Creek Basin. Here a great view of the broad bowl is revealed. The basin is filled with aspens, willows, conifers, lush grass, and sagebrush. Nearly 2.0 miles wide, this glacier-carved cirque is watered by innumerable springs, which sustain the abundant vegetation. The springs all combine to form Pine Creek, which exits at the basin and flows through the canyon toward the trailhead. For hikers only looking for a taste of the Warners, this area makes a good destination. You can relax in the meadows or explore the small lakes at its base. Follow the trail back when it is time to return.

If you want get more than just a taste of the Warners, the best destination is the crest of the range and awesome Patterson Lake. To get there, follow the trail into Pine Creek Basin. Cross over the creek and, after passing through a short stretch of forest, begin the long ascent up the north side of the large bowl. The trail makes a series of switchbacks up the grassy slopes, climbing steadily the entire way. Views of Pine Creek Basin to the south are especially good along the middle section of the climb. High overhead, the forested mass of Warren Peak looms darkly.

From the vantage point of the trail, Warren Peak and the rest of the Warners do not look particularly rugged, with the long, sweeping slope climbing up toward the crest. However, as the trail passes through clumps of whitebark pine, it reaches the top of the range 4.6 miles from the trailhead and the whole character of these mountains is revealed. Much like the great Sierra Nevada, these mountains are a classic anticline range. Situated on a fault that has been uplifted, they have a long gradual slope on the west side and suddenly drop off precipitously on the east side. On the east side of the Warners, this means

The cliffs of Warren Peak are an awesome backdrop to Patterson Lake.

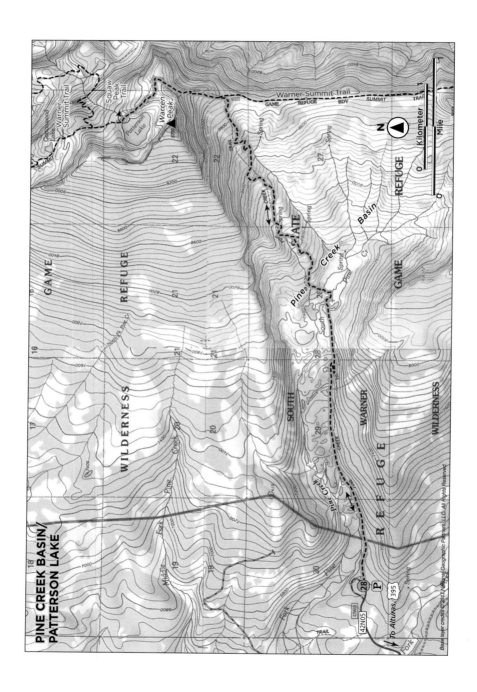

PINE CREEK BASIN/
PATTERSON LAKE

massive bands of exposed lava flows, steep cliffs, craggy peaks, and volcanic formations situated atop broad benches, all cloaked in a patchwork of forest, meadow, and barren volcanic soils. Needless to say, the view from the crest is incredible.

For some hikers, this may be a good destination in itself. With the stupendous view, it is worth the climb all on its own. Patterson Lake lies 1.0 mile to the north and requires 400 more feet of climbing. Once on the crest, the Pine Creek Trail ends at the intersection with the Warner Summit Trail, an epic backpacking route that makes a loop along the crest of the range and through the canyons and meadows on the flanks of its eastern escarpment. To get to Patterson Lake, turn left on the Summit Trail and head north. After a short switchback, the trail makes a traverse of stratified volcanic ash. On the far side of the traverse, you reach the highest point on the trail.

Here you are blessed with the most magnificent view of the trip. To the south, the great bowl of Owl Creek Basin lies immediately below, topped by bands of cliffs and the high, rounded tower of Dusenbery Peak, which lies well to the east of the main crest. Beyond, the gently sloped summit of Eagle Peak, the highest in the Warners, is visible. Looking north, part of Patterson Lake can be observed; beyond that, the turret of Squaw Peak is a prominent landmark. In the west, the distant tower of Mount Shasta thrusts prominently skyward, while in the east the long depression of the Surprise Valley and its alkali lakes lie 5,000 feet below. On the far side of the valley are the seemingly unending deserts of Nevada. It is a phenomenal spot.

From this high point, follow the trail down to Patterson Lake, passing through incredible fields of lupine in July and August. Cross over the lake's outlet stream and end the hike on the lakeshore, gazing up at this unique alpine gem. Patterson is a large, deep lake set in a rocky cirque beneath Warren Peak. Deep into summer, snow clings to cliffs that rise 700 feet above the water. Numerous layers of successive lava flows are exposed in the cliffs, broken apart as the mountains were thrust upwards. It is a breathtaking sight. Good campsites are abundant around Patterson Lake. If you aren't spending the night, enjoy your time here before returning the way you came.

MILES AND DIRECTIONS

0.0 Start from the trailhead and head east.

0.75 Pass the first set of ponds.

1.4 Pass the second set of ponds.

2.25 Arrive at small lake and the beginning of Pine Creek Basin. (*Option:* Turn around here if this is your destination.) To continue to Patterson Lake, head into the basin, cross Pine Creek, and begin climbing.

4.6 Arrive at the crest of the Warners. Turn left onto the Warner Summit Trail.

5.1 Top out on the pass above Patterson Lake.

5.6 Reach Patterson Lake. Retrace your steps from here when it is time to return.

11.2 Arrive back at the trailhead.

29. SUSAN RIVER

WHY GO?
This unique hike travels on a rails-to-trails conversion alongside the beautiful Susan River. It passes over several bridges and through two tunnels before looping back on a trail that climbs high to the rim of the Susan River Canyon and follows it back to the trailhead.

THE RUNDOWN
Start: Hobo Camp day use area
Distance: 9.4-mile loop
Hiking time: About 5 hours
Difficulty: Moderate
Elevation gain: 400 feet
Season: Year-round
Trail surface: Gravel road, packed dirt
Canine compatibility: Dogs permitted
Fees and permits: None
Land status: Bureau of Land Management

Trail contact: Eagle Lake Field Office, 2550 Riverside Dr., Susanville 96130; (530) 257-0456; www.blm .gov
Other: The trailhead at the Hobo Camp day use area opens at 8 a.m. but is gated at sunset. Gate closure times change according to the season and are posted near the entrance. Be aware of the time, and adjust plans accordingly. Water is available in the Susan River.

FINDING THE TRAILHEAD

Starting on CA 36 in downtown Susanville, head south on Richmond Road for 0.4 mile. Turn right onto South Street, drive to its end, and turn right onto Hobo Camp Road. Follow this gravel road to its end at the Hobo Camp day use area. **Trailhead GPS:** 40°25'2.67"N / 120°40'25.72"W

WHAT TO SEE
The Susan River begins just east of Lassen Volcanic National Park, flowing from Caribou Lake for 67 miles to Honey Lake. This large, typically dry lake occupies one of several endorheic basins that make up the Great Basin. After passing through upland forest, the river runs through a deeply cut canyon before reaching Susanville and emerging into the wide valley containing Honey Lake. The canyon lies at the nexus of the Sierra Nevada and the Cascade Range. The Diamond Mountains, one of the northernmost extensions of the northern Sierra Nevada, lie just a few miles south; the volcanic Cascades are the primary watershed of the Susan River. The canyon itself exhibits a variety of volcanic features, including basalt, breccia, and cooled lava rocks.

The railroad once traveled through the canyon to connect Susanville with the timber-rich mountain areas around Westwood, 20 miles to the west. When the railroad ceased operation, the Bureau of Land Management and USDA Forest Service acquired the right-of-way. The tracks were removed and the route became the famed Bizz Johnson Trail, an excellent rails-to-trails conversion. Named for the congressman who was instrumental in bringing the project to fruition, the trail is a centerpiece of revitalization. Today the trail stretches 25.5 miles from Susanville to Westwood and is a popular destination for hikers, bikers, and equestrians. In addition to the beautiful canyon, the trail passes through high-mountain forests, following the Susan River for 16 miles before heading through remote country to Westwood. This hike follows the river along 4.4 miles of the trail just west of Susanville. Along with the highlights of the river and canyon cliffs, this section has numerous crossings over reconstructed railroad bridges and passes through two long tunnels. Rather than simply retracing your steps, a singletrack trail following the southern rim of the canyon offers the chance to make a loop hike and get an elevated perspective on this small but scenic river.

Start the hike at the Hobo Camp day use area, an area surrounded by shady ponderosa pines. Pass through the picnic area and follow the trail along the side of a hill a short distance to where it joins the Bizz Johnson Trail. The main trailhead lies at the old railroad depot, 1.0 mile to the southeast in Susanville. The spur from Hobo Camp joins the main

The Susan River flows under one of many bridges as the Bizz Johnson Trail enters an old tunnel.

Elevated views of the Susan River are one of the great features of the Southside Trail.

trail just after it crosses the Susan River on an old girder bridge. Turn left onto the Bizz Johnson Trail. Immediately pass a dirt road on your left that leads to the equestrian staging area and then, just a few yards away, pass the junction with the South Side Trail. This is the return portion of the loop. Although the sounds of CA 36 are audible when you first enter the canyon, the sounds quickly fade as the noise of the Susan River and the wind rushing through the trees become dominant.

About 0.5 mile from Hobo Camp, the Bizz Johnson Trail crosses the first of several old railroad bridges leading to the north side of the river, where it will remain for most of the journey to the railroad tunnels, which lie 3.5 miles from the first crossing. Once on the north side of the river, the trail maintains a course between the water and the cliffs of the Susan River Canyon. After traveling 1.9 miles from the first crossing, the Bizz Johnson Trail crosses back to the south side of the river and 0.1 mile later crosses back to the north side. The rugged old bridges have heavy wooden planks on the roadbed. From this pair of bridges, continue along the river for 2.0 more miles before arriving at the first tunnel, 4.0 miles from Hobo Camp.

The tunnels are both about 0.1 mile long and cut through rocky volcanic outcroppings that press up against the river. Timbers line much of the long, straight passages. There are no lights inside the tunnels, but they are just short enough for the sunlight to provide meager illumination, making flashlights unnecessary. For those uncomfortable

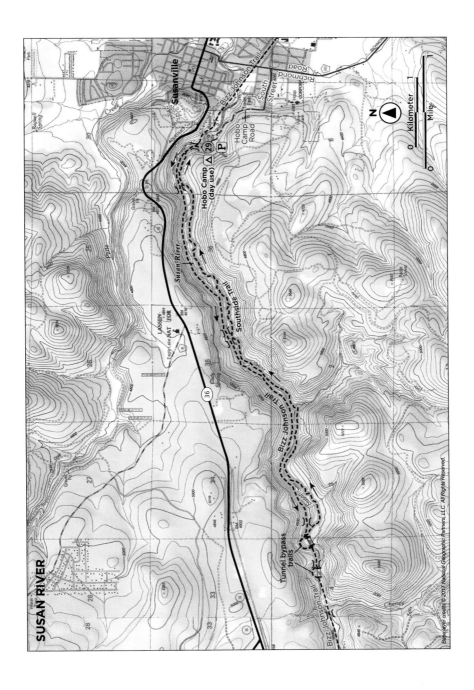

SUSAN RIVER

with confined spaces, bypass trails provide a means to avoid the tunnels. Pass through the first tunnel and then immediately cross over the Susan River. In 0.1 mile cross another bridge and enter the second tunnel. Once you have emerged on the other side, you have reached the turnaround point. Turn right and take the bypass trail back around the volcanic outcropping. Rejoin the Bizz Johnson briefly and cross over the Susan River twice before arriving back at the entrance to the first tunnel. Turn left here onto the bypass trail and follow along the river until you arrive at a trail junction with the South Side Trail. Veer right onto the trail to begin the loop back to Hobo Camp.

As its name implies, the South Side Trail follows along the southern bank of the Susan River. This route was constructed for mixed use, so be alert for bikers passing through. From the tunnel, the bypass trail initially climbs to a pleasant plateau populated by ponderosa pines. After 0.5 mile it passes an optional side trail that climbs steeply up an old dirt road. Skip the road and continue on the singletrack, which makes a rocky descent to the river's edge. The trail continues at the river's level for 1.5 miles before climbing back to the top of the cliffs high above the Susan River. Despite only being on the other side of the river from the Bizz Johnson Trail, it is amazing how separated the two trails feel. The South Side Trail then follows the contours of the canyon for 2.0 more miles, often with good views down toward the river, until it merges back with the Bizz Johnson Trail. From there take the short spur back to Hobo Camp.

MILES AND DIRECTIONS

0.0 Start from Hobo Camp on the spur that connects to the Bizz Johnson Trail.

0.1 Turn left onto the Bizz Johnson Trail.

0.5 Cross first bridge over the river.

1.9 The trail crosses two bridges in quick succession.

4.0 Reach the first tunnel. Hike through it, immediately cross the Susan River twice, and then enter the second tunnel.

4.4 Upon exiting the second tunnel, turn right onto the tunnel bypass trail.

4.75 Before reentering the second tunnel, turn left onto another tunnel bypass trail.

4.9 While on the tunnel bypass trail, veer right onto the South Side Trail. Follow it back toward Hobo Camp.

9.3 Merge onto the Bizz Johnson Trail and then turn right onto the spur leading to Hobo Camp.

9.4 Arrive back at Hobo Camp.

30. THOUSAND LAKES WILDERNESS

WHY GO?

This classic Cascade hike climbs through remote forest up to Everett and Magee Lakes, two of the prettiest lakes in the California Cascades. Hikers looking for a longer outing can continue farther as the trail leads into the crater of an ancient volcano and then climbs to a peak on the crater rim, where a marvelous view awaits.

THE RUNDOWN

Start: Cypress Trailhead
Total distance: 11.2 miles out and back (**Option:** moderate 7.0 miles out and back to Everett Lake)
Hiking time: 4–7 hours or overnight
Difficulty: Strenuous
Elevation gain: 3,000 feet (Magee Peak)
Season: Summer, fall
Trail surface: Packed dirt, rocky, cinders

Canine compatibility: Dogs permitted
Fees and permits: None
Land status: Thousand Lakes Wilderness, Lassen National Forest
Trail contact: Hat Creek Ranger District, 43225 E. Highway 299, Fall River Mills 96028; (530) 336-5521; www.fs.usda.gov/lassen
Other: Water is available at Everett and Magee Lakes.

FINDING THE TRAILHEAD

Starting at the intersection of CA 89 and CA 44 in the village of Old Station, drive north on CA 89 for 11.3 miles then turn left on FR 34N19, which is also signed as FR 26, just north of the forest service's Hat Creek Work Station. The road climbs to the south and then crosses a ridge and heads west. At approximately 8 miles, turn left onto FR 34N60. Proceed to the road's end at the Cypress Trailhead. The road is signed to the trailhead.

From the intersection of CA 89 and CA 299, 5 miles east of Burney, drive south on CA 89 for 10.4 miles. Turn right onto FR 34N19 and follow the directions above. **Trailhead GPS:** 40°44'17.73"N / 121°36'28.16"W

WHAT TO SEE

Just north of the Lassen area, a number of tall, extinct volcanoes line the crest of the Cascades as the range extends north toward Mount Shasta. The tallest and most impressive is preserved in the Thousand Lakes Wilderness, a compact 16,582-acre wildland. Often referred to as the Thousand Lakes Volcano, this tall peak boasts an impressive crater that was breached by glaciers. These large sheets of ice flowed east and excavated the Thousand Lakes Valley. While not having nearly as many lakes as the name implies, the valley

The volcanic Red Cliffs reflect in the still water of Everett Lake.

does have eleven named lakes and a seemingly limitless number of small, shallow ponds. The main part of the valley contains seven lakes and the preponderance of the ponds. Higher up near the crater are four more lakes, including excellent Everett and Magee Lakes. These jewels make great destinations on their own for a moderate 7.0-mile hike. For a more ambitious outing, hikers can continue through the gap in the crater, pass through its interior, and then ascend to a peak on its rim.

To begin the hike, follow the trail east from the Cypress Trailhead. You will immediately cross over rocky Eiler Gulch, which is usually dry. Once on the far side of the gulch, the trail begins a long climb toward the Thousand Lakes Valley. Watch for the cypress trees growing alongside the trail, from which the trailhead gets its name. After 0.9 mile a sign marks the entrance into the Thousand Lakes Wilderness. About 0.2 mile farther the trail splits. Going left here leads to nearby Eiler Lake, a worthwhile side trip if time permits. The lake, the largest in the Thousand Lakes Wilderness, lies 0.7 mile ahead. Instead, take the right fork; cross Eiler Gulch and then continuing hiking through the woods. In 0.5 mile from the first fork, the trail splits again. Going left here leads into the heart of the Thousand Lakes Valley, the large, lake-filled depression that lies between the Thousand Lakes Volcano and Freaner Peak. Stay right here again, and continue climbing gently through the forest.

Soon after the fork the trail makes numerous, short switchbacks up a steep slope. Once above these, another long, steady ascent begins, this time the base of the moraine left here by the glacier that breached the volcano's crater and scooped out the Thousand Lakes Valley. As the trail passes through brushy sections, you can catch glimpses of the wooded valley and some of the cinder cones that dot the area. Nearly 1.5 miles after the last trail junction, the route passes a large, shallow pond ringed with trees. Late in the year this pond has dried up and become a meadow. Upper and Lower Twin Lakes lie to the northwest and southeast of this pond, set back off the trail. From the north end you can see the high peaks of Thousand Lake Volcano crater's rim. Press ahead on the trail, and in short order arrive at beautiful Everett Lake, 3.5 miles from the trailhead.

Everett and Magee Lakes are quintessential Cascades lakes. Set in glacial valleys, ringed with trees, and backed by towering volcanic cliffs, they look like they would be at home in southern Oregon or some other classic part of the Cascade Range. Of the two, Everett is larger and prettier, but Magee Lake still holds its own. The cliffs behind them are dominated by a blocky turret and the tall Red Cliffs, which are actually grayer in appearance. These are all part of the Thousand Lakes Volcano's crater rim. As you move to the corner of Everett Lake, you can see reddish, pyramidal Crater Peak, the highest point on the rim. If this is as far as you are going, enjoy the view for a while a then retrace your steps to the trailhead.

To continue on to the rim of the Thousand Lakes Volcano, follow the trail that climbs north between Everett and Magee Lakes. This path makes a steady ascent through the crater's breech that lies between the Red Cliffs and Crater Peak. As you climb, you get more good views of the turret that dominates the view from the lakes. Once inside the crater, the forest thins a little and the walls rise 400 to 500 feet. The trail soon turns south and begins a series of switchbacks up a treeless volcanic slope. The climb is short and the grade moderate, and soon you reach the rim of the Thousand Lakes Volcano. Lassen Peak greets you as you reach the top. It is an awesome view after spending much of the hike in the deep wilderness woods.

Distant Mount Shasta seen from the crater rim of the Thousand Lakes Volcano.

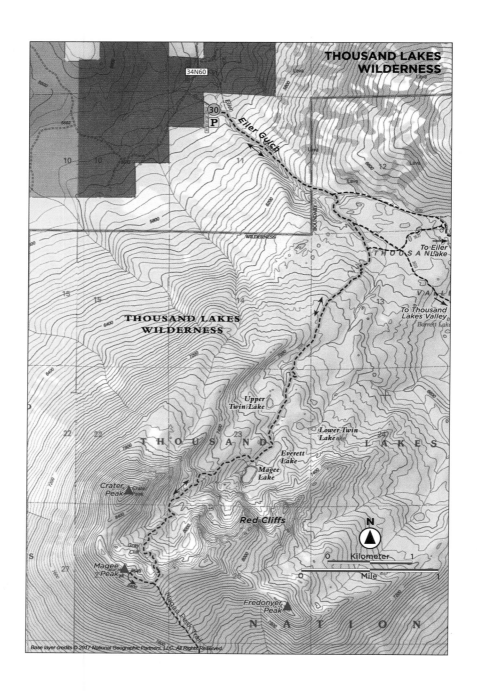

The trail follows the contours of the rim as it climbs to the south. Watch for a faint trail heading off down the south face of the mountain. This is the old Magee Trail, which accessed the lookout tower that was once perched on Magee Peak. The peak, really just a raised part of the rim on its west side, is the official end of the trail and yields a spectacular vista. Mount Shasta is the most prominent landmark, but the great mountain stronghold of the Trinity Alps strikes a jagged horizon to the northwest. The Sacramento Valley, North Coast Range, and Lassen Peak and its attendants all demand attention. Crater Peak is the tall rise on the rim just a little farther to the north. From here follow the trail back to the Cypress Trailhead.

MILES AND DIRECTIONS

0.0 Start at the trailhead. Just beyond, cross over Eiler Gulch and begin a long, steady climb up to the Thousand Lakes Wilderness.

1.1 Stay right at the first fork in the trail.

1.6 Stay right again at the second fork.

3.5 Arrive at Everett Lake. (*Option:* If this is your destination, retrace your steps to the trailhead.) To continue to Magee Peak, take the trail that climbs north from between Everett and Magee Lakes.

4.5 After passing through the gap in the crater rim, arrive at the interior of the crater.

5.25 Reach the top of the crater rim.

5.6 Arrive at the top of Magee Peak and enjoy the vantage point. Follow the trail back when done.

11.2 Arrive back at the trailhead.

31. **LASSEN PEAK**

WHY GO?
The ascent of Lassen Peak is a hard but thrilling hike to the summit of the southernmost volcano in the Cascade Range. The mountain towers above the surrounding landscape and offers incredible vistas almost every step of the way to the top of this active volcano.

THE RUNDOWN

Start: Lassen Peak Trailhead
Distance: 5.0 miles out and back
Hiking time: 3–4 hours
Difficulty: Moderately strenuous
Elevation gain: 2,000 feet
Season: Summer, fall
Trail surface: Packed dirt, sandy, rocky, rock scrambling

Canine compatibility: Dogs not permitted
Fees and permits: Entrance fee
Land status: Lassen Volcanic National Park
Trail contact: PO Box 100, Mineral 96063; (530) 595-4480; www.nps.gov/lavo

FINDING THE TRAILHEAD

From Red Bluff on I-5, drive east on CA 36 for 46 miles to the junction with CA 89. Turn left and drive north on CA 89 for 12.2 miles, pausing to pay the entrance fee at Lassen Volcanic National Park. The trailhead is 1 mile past Lake Helen.
  The trailhead can also be reached from Redding by driving east from I-5 on CA 44 for 47 miles. Near the entrance to Lassen Volcanic National Park, turn right onto CA 89 and follow this road through the park for 21.8 miles to the trailhead. **Trailhead GPS:** 40°28'29.52"N / 121°30'20.66"W

WHAT TO SEE

Lassen Peak, the centerpiece of Lassen Volcanic National Park, is the southernmost major volcano in the Cascade Range and one of only two volcanoes in the coterminous United States to erupt in the twentieth century. At 10,457 feet, it is the second-highest peak in the California section of the Cascades, second only to towering Mount Shasta. It is also one of the largest plug dome volcanoes in the world. This type of volcano is the result of extremely viscous lava being pushed up to the earth's surface. Since the lava is so sticky, it does not flow far or swiftly and tends to pile vertically rather than flowing quickly and covering a large surface. Plug domes often form in previously erupted volcanoes. In the case of Lassen Peak, the mountain has formed out of the ruins of prehistoric Mount Tehama, which once towered thousands of feet higher than Lassen Peak does today. Mount Tehama was obliterated in a fiery cataclysm, and in its place Lassen Peak emerged from the decimated landscape. Today the mountain towers over much of

Brokeoff Mountain, Mount Diller, and Eagle Peak greet hikers as they climb Lassen Peak.

Northern California, a dramatic landmark and powerful reminder of the colossal forces that remain at work inside our planet.

The hike to the top of Lassen Peak is a classic national park adventure. Though it is steep and strenuous, the short duration enables children to make the hike. Families and school groups can often be seen climbing the trail, huffing and puffing, hooting and hollering, and generally having fun as they go. The route ascends innumerable switchbacks as it climbs up a ridge on the mountain's south side. Once on top, you have the opportunity to enjoy the 360-degree panorama, looking down onto the twisted rock of Lassen Peak's crater and being proud to have made it to the top of an active volcano.

Lassen Peak towers majestically over the large trailhead, beckoning hikers to climb it. Large rocky crags halfway up are dominated by the enigmatic ocular-shaped formation called the Eye of Vulcan. The trail initially climbs steeply to the north and then makes a single switchback before leveling off in a grove of hemlock. This is the only level spot on the entire hike. At one of several interpretive displays found along the route, the trail turns to the east and begins climbing again. In 0.6 mile you begin the seemingly ceaseless switchbacks that lead to the top. These first switchbacks are well spaced between turns as they traverse the slopes of the mountain, but the higher you get, the shorter the distances between the turns.

Once you begin the long series of switchbacks, the trail passes through clumps of whitebark pine. These get sparse as you gain elevation. Eventually the trees are reduced to little more than shrubs, evidence of the harsh winter conditions that exist on Lassen Peak. The thinning forest means the views improve as you climb. The first thing to draw attention is the large cluster of peaks immediately to the south of Lassen Peak. The remnants of Mount Tehama, these peaks include Brokeoff Mountain, Mount Diller, Ski

Heil Peak, and Eagle Peak. Brokeoff Mountain is the remnant of Mount Tehama's southern slope and is the second-highest point in the national park. Just east of these peaks is where you'll find the geothermal features of Bumpass Hell. When the wind is right, you can detect the smell of hydrogen sulfide emanating from the fumaroles around the base of Lassen Peak.

After climbing for about 1.5 miles, the switchbacks round a corner and begin climbing up the edge of a steep ridge. This is the halfway point on the hike, and a few interpretive displays give hikers cause to pause. Where the previous switchbacks made wide traverses, these are very short and are stacked one upon the other in very rapid succession. The trail's position on the ridge is such now that the lands east of Lassen Peak are now visible. Ghostly snags, the remnants of the 2012 Reading Fire, lie below the mountain. Beyond them rise broad Prospect Peak, a shield volcano, and the stark Cinder Cone, one of the most fascinating features in the eastern part of the park. Snowfields are often found along this part of the hike, clinging to the slopes of a steep bowl on the mountain's southeast side.

The tightly stacked switchbacks finally come to an end at a small bench about 1.75 miles from the trailhead. The path does not level off, despite the small patch of level ground, and continues to climb. However, the switchbacks once again begin to stretch out as they ascend the final shoulder leading to the summit. A little more climbing finally delivers hikers to a point on the volcano's crater rim. Here a series of interpretive displays are installed, and hikers can relax on flat ground. From here a great view unfolds, highlighted by massive Mount Shasta, viewed above Lassen Peak's crater.

From the level spot, the trail descends along the crater rim and crosses a permanent snowfield before fading out in the jumble of rocks directly below the summit spire. Use trails lead to the top, though many hikers are satisfied with having reached the crater.

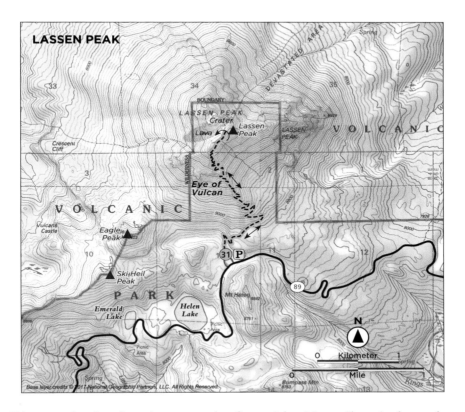

Either way, the view from the top stretches from mighty Mount Shasta in the north to the headwaters of the Yuba River, just north of Lake Tahoe in the Sierra Nevada. Spend some time taking in all the sights and enjoying being on the summit of a beautiful yet active volcano. When you are ready to return, follow the trail to the trailhead, enjoying the views all the way down.

MILES AND DIRECTIONS

0.0   Start at the trailhead and begin climbing steeply up a set of switchbacks.

1.25 Halfway to the summit, round a corner and begin a series of short, tightly stacked switchbacks.

1.75 Pass a small, level bench before climbing more switchbacks toward the top of Lassen Peak.

2.5   Arrive at the summit. Return the way you came.

5.0   Arrive back at the trailhead.

32. **WARNER VALLEY**

WHY GO?

A fascinating hike that visits a pair of active geothermal areas in the southwestern corner of Lassen Volcanic National Park, the hike through Warner Valley also boasts exceptional meadows, springs, and creeks.

THE RUNDOWN

Start: Warner Valley Trailhead
Distance: 6.8-mile lollipop with side trips
Hiking time: 3–4 hours
Difficulty: Moderately easy
Elevation gain: 740 feet
Season: Summer, fall
Trail surface: Packed dirt, wood boardwalk, rocky
Canine compatibility: Dogs not permitted

Fees and permits: Entrance fee
Land status: Lassen Volcanic Wilderness, Lassen Volcanic National Park
Trail contact: PO Box 100, Mineral 96063; (530) 595-4480; www.nps .gov/lavo
Other: Water is available at the trailhead.

FINDING THE TRAILHEAD

From CA 36 at the north end of downtown Chester, drive west on Feather River Drive. Turn left onto Chester Warner Valley Road. Drive 12.7 miles to where the pavement ends. Veer left to continue driving on Warner Valley Road, now a gravel road. Continue for 3 miles to the trailhead, stopping to pay the entrance fee in Lassen Volcanic National Park. The trailhead will be on the left. **Trailhead GPS:** 40°26'34.98"N / 121°23'50.49"W

WHAT TO SEE

Among the highlights of Lassen Volcanic National Park are the geothermal features that are scattered around the base of Lassen Peak. These features are all remnants of Mount Tehama, an ancient volcano that was annihilated in a final eruptive event. Though that mountain is now gone, Lassen Peak has taken its place, and the fiery forces that formed the mountain and then destroyed it are still at work beneath the surface of the earth. These are manifest in the fumaroles, mudpots, and hot springs found in several locations in the southwestern part of the park. One of the best ways to experience the geothermal features in the park is to hike the trails of the Warner Valley. Though Bumpass Hell may be the largest geothermal area in Lassen Volcanic National Park, the sites around the Warner Valley are less crowded and more varied and make for a more diverse hike. Here the trip combines a large, beautiful creek, broad meadows, and rocky cliffs with the geothermal areas of the Devils Kitchen and Boiling Springs Lake. In terms of peaceful, natural beauty and geologic interest, this hike is tough to beat.

This hike is made by connecting a few different trails to form a loop with spurs radiating out to the geothermal areas. Each of these areas can be done as shorter but still rewarding hikes. Whether doing the whole loop or just doing one of the parts, all options begin at the Warner Valley Trailhead. From there, follow the Pacific Crest Trail through well-watered meadows. The path follows alongside Hot Springs Creek. At 0.2 mile cross the creek on a sturdy bridge and climb gently up a slope. Drakesbad Guest Ranch comes into view just as the trail crosses some small streams. On cold mornings, note the steam rising from the naturally heated water of the streams. Just below this point the water is gathered into Drakesbad's swimming pool. Just past these springs the path arrives at a junction. If you wish to skip the trip to Devils Kitchen and just head to Boiling Springs Lake, turn left here.

To continue to Devils Kitchen, stay straight and follow the path downhill. The trail enters the woods and then crosses over Hot Springs Creek again on another stout bridge. Once across, your path is joined by a trail coming from Drakesbad. Veer left and head west as you parallel the creek. A long boardwalk leads to a small bridge across a pretty stream. You then enter a large, beautiful meadow, where cliffs rising at the far end of the Warner Valley make a fine sight beyond the grassy expanse. The trail cuts across the heart of the meadow, occasionally crossing more boardwalks when it encounters wetter areas. The path then reenters the woods on the north side of the valley. Continue hiking through the quiet forest until you arrive at the junction with the route to Drake Lake, 1.3 mile from the trailhead.

Hot Springs Creek
flows through the
Devil's Kitchen.

A vista above Boiling Springs Lake offers a glimpse of Lassen Peak.

Stay straight at the Drake Lake junction and continue hiking through the woods. The trail, which has been pleasantly level for almost the entire hike, now begins to climb. Around 0.9 mile from the junction with the trail to Drake Lake, you arrive at the hitching post for equestrians. Horses are not permitted beyond this point. The path then descends steeply to Hot Springs Creek. Cross the creek on a large bridge to begin the loop through Devils Kitchen. The second-largest geothermal area in Lassen Volcanic National Park, the area is a fascinating glimpse into the powerful forces that continue to shape the geography of the park. After crossing the bridge, turn right at the junction to make the loop. The ground around geothermal features can become brittle, and it is possible to fall through and be severally burned or killed. Be sure to stay on the trail to ensure safety. The sounds of hissing hot springs and burping mudpots is complemented by the quiet roar of the fumaroles as they vent steam. The smell of hydrogen sulfide, a classic companion of geothermal activity, is detectable. After making the short but intriguing loop through Devils Kitchen, cross back over the creek and climb up to the hitching post. From there head back to the junction with the trail to Drake Lake.

If you want to simply head back toward the trailhead or go directly to Boiling Springs Lake, stay left at the junction with the route to Drake Lake. To take the loop around Warner Valley, turn right and follow the trail heading to the south. After descending gradually, cross a small stream before arriving at Hot Springs Creek. There is no bridge here, and the creek is wide and swift. Just upstream of the trail is a log that hikers use to get to the other side when the water is high. Cross the log carefully, and then relocate the trail. A short climb leads to another junction. Turn left here and head east, through the forested south side of Warner Valley. Springs flowing just below the trail on the left feed streams that flow into the large meadow in the middle of the valley. Pass the most productive

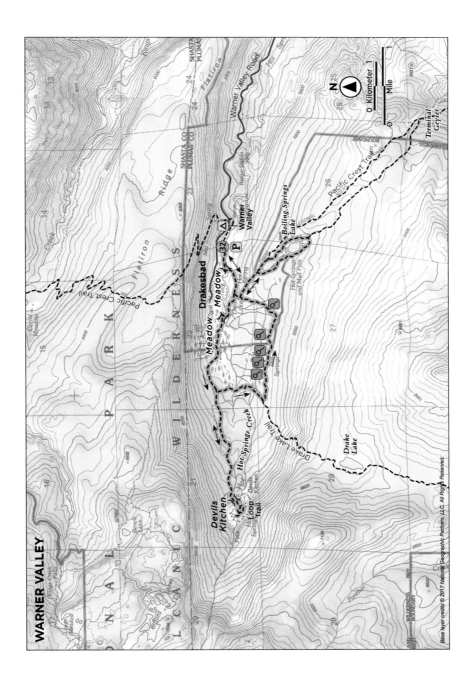

streams just before the trail turns north and arrives at a trail intersection near Drakesbad. To get to Boiling Springs Lake, turn right onto the Pacific Crest Trail.

Climb gradually toward the lake for 0.2 mile before the reaching the beginning of the Boiling Springs Lake loop trail. Veer right onto the loop and emerge out of the forest onto barren terrain rendered inhospitable to life by the geothermal forces that surround it. The path, defined by an outline of rocks, crosses this red and yellow wasteland, staying near the edge of the cliffs that drop down into the lake. The sounds of fumaroles and mudpots are audible, and the scent of hydrogen sulfide becomes strong as you approach the south end of the lake. The path dips back into the woods and winds around some gullies before arriving at a junction with the Pacific Crest Trail. Stay left and promptly arrive at one of the most memorable spots on the hike. Directly above the mudpots, the turquoise lake and its red and yellow shoreline lie between you and awesome Lassen Peak. Past the vista point, continue around the rim of the lake before the trail splits. The Pacific Crest Trail goes right; the lake loop stays left. Both return to the same point. The lake route is a little more interesting, so stay left and head back to the junction with the Pacific Crest Trail by the hot springs near Drakesbad. Turn right onto the Pacific Crest Trail and follow it back to the trailhead.

MILES AND DIRECTIONS

0.0 Start at the Warner Valley Trailhead.

0.4 At a junction near Drakesbad, stay straight to go to Devils Kitchen.

0.6 Turn left and follow the trail through a series of meadows.

1.5 Stay to the right at the junction with the Drake Lake Trail to continue toward Devils Kitchen.

2.2 Arrive at Devils Kitchen, where there is a short loop.

2.5 Complete the loop and return to the Drake Lake Trail.

3.4 Turn right onto the trail to Drake Lake.

3.8 Turn left onto the trail back to Drakesbad.

4.8 Turn right to hike the trail leading to Boiling Springs Lake.

5.0 Reach Boiling Springs Lake and begin the loop around the lake.

6.0 Complete the loop and follow the trail back toward Drakesbad.

6.2 Turn right when returning to the main trail; immediately turn right again onto the Pacific Crest Trail and head back toward the trailhead.

6.8 Arrive back at the trailhead.

33. BUTTE LAKE–SNAG LAKE LOOP

WHY GO?

This hike is a journey into the remote backcountry of eastern Lassen Volcanic National Park. In addition to the deep isolation, it visits two large, unusual lakes; passes by dark lava flows and the beautiful Painted Dunes; and offers a short, steep side trip to the top of the Cinder Cone.

THE RUNDOWN

Start: Butte Lake Trailhead in east corner of day use parking area
Distance: 13.0-mile loop (**Option:** Going in the opposite direction from the trailhead, it is an easy 3-mile out-and-back hike to the Cinder Cone.)
Hiking time: 6–7 hours or overnight
Difficulty: Moderate
Elevation gain: 1,000 feet
Season: Summer, fall
Trail surface: Packed dirt, rocky, cinders, sand

Canine compatibility: Dogs not permitted
Fees and permits: Entrance fee
Land status: Lassen Volcanic Wilderness, Lassen Volcanic National Park
Trail contact: PO Box 100, Mineral 96063; (530) 595-4480; www.nps .gov/lavo
Other: Water is available at the trailhead.

FINDING THE TRAILHEAD

From Redding, drive 71 miles east on CA 44 to the signed turn for the Butte Lake Campground. Drive south on the well-maintained gravel FR 36N18 for 6.5 miles to the Butte Lake Campground. After the self-pay entrance station, veer left and park at the day use parking area.

From Susanville, drive west on CA 36 for 5 miles then turn right onto CA 44. Continue for 35 miles to the signed turnoff for Butte Lake Campground, and follow the directions above. **Trailhead GPS:** 40°33'53.75"N / 121°18'2.67"W

WHAT TO SEE

The eastern side of Lassen Volcanic National Park is a more subdued landscape than the dramatic western side. Rather than the towering height of Lassen Peak, the action of the geothermal features, and the high, alpine terrain of the mountainous remnants of Mount Tehama, there are expansive forests, large isolated lakes, and lonely creeks. The area is not without its volcanic geology, however. Extensive lava flows, spectacular painted pumice dunes, and the stark Cinder Cone are highlights on this loop deep into the park's remote backcountry. The Fantastic Lava Beds, a large flow emanating from the Cinder Cone, are the focal point of the loop, making their presence felt in all three sections of the hike. The first portion follows along the edge of Butte Lake, where the lava pushed into the

The Fantastic Lava Beds, the Cinder Cone, and Lassen Peak are a fascinating sight beyond Butte Lake.

water along the west shore. The next section of the hike works its way around large Snag Lake, which was created when the Fantastic Lava Beds flow dammed up Grassy Creek and caused the water to fill a large depression. The last section of the hike passes beneath the walls of the lava itself, as well as past the Painted Dunes and the Cinder Cone. Exposure to other forms of volcanic activity—forms no less beautiful than their more famous counterparts on the west side of the park—makes this an engaging hike.

The hike begins in the east corner of the day use parking area. Head out on the trail, which follows above the shore of Butte Lake. After 0.5 mile the path climbs up and away from the lake and then tops out on a bluff above the lake. From there it descends steeply through some boulders back down toward Butte Lake. At the bottom the trail crosses Butte Creek, the lake's outlet. There is no bridge, but rocks, logs, and a collection of snags on the lakeshore are convenient means of keeping your feet dry. On the far side, a trail runs along the creek. Locate it and turn right, heading back along the water.

Butte Lake is a large, L-shaped body of water. Its most distinctive feature is the long western shoreline that marks the northern end of the Fantastic Lava Beds. The black, broken lava looks as though it flowed right into the water and then stopped. The narrow path follows the shoreline for 1.3 miles, the lava flows continuing the entire length of the lake. Along the way, the views of the Cinder Cone rising above the Fantastic Lava Beds improve. Soon the view is further improved when Lassen Peak peers through the gap between the Cinder Cone and large, wide Prospect Peak, a shield volcano that is one of the eastern park's most prominent peaks.

At the south end of Butte Lake, the trail passes through a beautiful stand of aspen before passing the trail to Widow Lake. Stay right and begin a long 2.5-mile section through forest on the east side of the Fantastic Lava Beds. This unremarkable section of trail slowly climbs up a low rise and then makes a gradual descent to Snag Lake, which lies 4.85 miles from the trailhead. At Snag Lake, a deep sense of isolation seems to permeate in a way that few destinations in Lassen Volcanic National Park can rival. The lake is just too far out of the way to get very much traffic. However, it is a beautiful destination, and the hike around the lake is one of the best sections of the trail.

The path initially follows along the wooded east shore of the lake. Though trees filter the view of the water, the presence of the lake is reassuring after the long, uneventful wooded passage between Butte and Snag Lakes. The path crosses a few spring-fed streams before veering away from the lake and passing the trail to Juniper Lake and arriving at the edge of Grassy Creek, the primary creek flowing into Snag Lake. Grassy Creek flows out of Horseshoe Lake, another large, remote lake in the eastern Lassen backcountry. Cross the creek and continue west, crossing patches of meadow intermingled with the forest. The trail briefly turns south before reaching the trail heading north from Juniper Lake, the largest of the eastern Lassen Lakes. Turn right on this trail and head north.

Now begin the best section of the hike, which stretches from here to the Cinder Cone. The western shore of Snag Lake was severely burned long ago, and the hills above the water are bare except for some brush and some living trees. A few snags, not the source of the lake's name, are also found here. The land has long been recovering from the fire, and the loss of the forest has opened up good views to the east. Mount Hoffman, one of the highest peaks in the eastern part of the park, dominates the view from the lake. Not all is desolate here, though, as large patches of meadow line the southern part of the lake, making good places to take a break. As the trail proceeds north, the ravages of the fire are

Mount Hoffman looks down on Snag Lake.

more profound and the land more barren, though a small spring-fed stream does provide a contrast to the burnt hills.

As you have worked your way around the lake, one constant has been the presence of the Fantastic Lava Beds to the north. Snag Lake was formed when the lava impounded Grassy Creek and caused it to flood the small valley. The lake has no outlet, and it is interesting to note that Butte Lake has no inlet. Water manages to travel through the porous lava flow, allowing water from Grassy Creek to sustain Butte Lake. When the trail arrives at the far north end of the lake, you encounter the Fantastic Lava Beds up close for the first time. Right where lakeshore and lava meet, there is a perfect, sandy beach with some shady trees nearby. Mount Hoffman looms above the far side of the lake. It is a great place to pause, enjoy the unique geology, and bid farewell to Snag Lake.

When you leave Snag Lake, the trail follows along the base of the Fantastic Lava Beds. What has been a distant point of interest in the hike will be a constant, immediate presence for the rest of it. As you head north, note that different colors begin to appear in the lava, embellishing the jagged, irregular shapes the molten rock cooled into. After following along the edge of the lava beds for about 1.0 mile, the forest begins to thin and eventually disappears altogether as the trail emerges on a wide plain of gray pumice. With level terrain and no trees, the view becomes immense as Lassen Peak, Prospect Peak, and the Cinder Cone all make their appearance again.

As you approach the base of the Cinder Cone, you pass the western edge of the Painted Dunes, one of the most interesting features in the park. These are best appreciated from the top of the Cinder Cone, where you can look down on the red and yellow pumice dunes. However, the climb to the top of the Cinder Cone is challenging because it is

The Cinder Cone boasts spectacular views of the Painted Dunes, Fantastic Lava Beds, and Snag Lake.

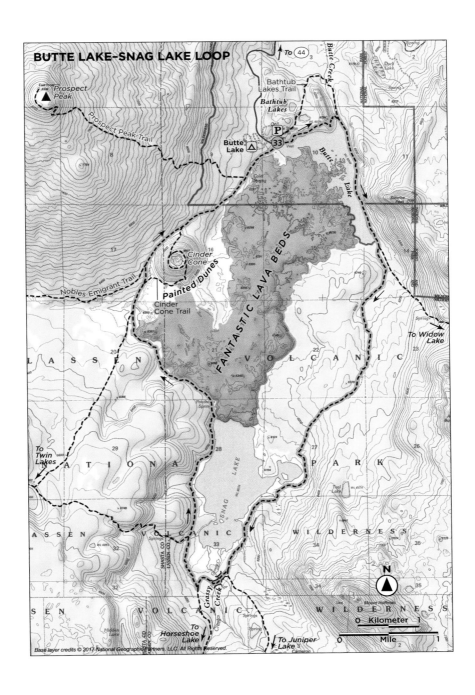

BUTTE LAKE–SNAG LAKE LOOP

both steep and on loose cinders, which tend to inhibit progress. If you have the energy after hiking 11 miles at this point, then veer right onto the first trail you encounter near the Cinder Cone. This path quickly reaches a second fork, where you stay right. You then hike through the Painted Dunes, where there are good views of Lassen Peak. Both in the dunes and on the cone, be sure to stay on the trail. Walking on the pumice and cinders damages their natural appearance for others.

After climbing to a low shoulder on the south side of the cone, the real effort begins. Here you must ascend a steep, cindery trail. Fortunately it does not last long, and when you reach the top, you are treated to one of the best vistas in the park. Lassen Peak looms to the west, while the full panorama of the Fantastic Lava Beds, Painted Dunes, and Snag and Butte Lakes is revealed. It is magnificent. After exploring the network of trails that ring the Cinder Cone's crater, descend the trail on the cone's north side to reconnect to the main trail and head back to the trailhead.

If you choose not to climb the Cinder Cone, continue north, rounding its base and climbing toward the gap between the cone and the forested base of Prospect Peak. Here you turn right onto the Nobles Emigrant Trail, a route used by nineteenth-century pioneers to enter California. Follow this trail east, passing the trail coming down from the Cinder Cone and then running parallel to the Fantastic Lava Beds. Follow this landmark 1.4 miles back to the trailhead.

MILES AND DIRECTIONS

0.0 Start from the Butte Lake Trailhead and head east (left).

0.8 After crossing Butte Creek, turn right and follow the trail along the east shore of Butte Lake.

2.2 After leaving Butte Lake, stay right where the trail forks.

4.9 Arrive at Snag Lake.

6.7 Stay right at the junction with the trail to Juniper Lake and then cross Grassy Creek.

7.0 Turn right and join the trail coming from Horseshoe Lake.

9.0 Leave Snag Lake and begin following along the edge of the Fantastic Lava Beds.

10.8 Reach the junction with the trail to the top of the Cinder Cone. Turn right to make the ascent; stay left to bypass.

11.0 If you skipped the Cinder Cone, turn right onto the Nobles Emigrant Trail.

11.6 Pass the trail climbing down from the Cinder Cone.

13.0 Arrive back at the trailhead.

34. CARIBOU WILDERNESS

WHY GO?

With numerous lakes and beautiful forest, this hike through the Caribou Wilderness explores lightly traveled volcanic country just east of Lassen Volcanic National Park.

THE RUNDOWN

Start: Caribou Lake Trailhead, immediately south of Caribou Lake.
Distance: 8.5-mile lollipop
Hiking time: About 4 hours
Difficulty: Moderately easy
Elevation gain: 650 feet
Season: Summer, fall
Trail surface: Packed dirt, rocky, duff
Canine compatibility: Dogs permitted

Fees and permits: Entrance fee
Land status: Caribou Wilderness, Lassen National Forest
Trail contact: Almanor Ranger District, 900 E. Highway 36, Chester 96020; (530) 258-2141; www.fs.usda .gov/lassen
Other: Water is available at numerous lakes.

FINDING THE TRAILHEAD

From Susanville, drive west on CA 36 for 5 miles. Turn right onto CA 44 and continue for 17.9 miles. Turn left onto Mooney Road and drive 4.3 miles. Turn right onto gravel Silver Lake Road and proceed 5 miles. As you enter the Silver Lake area, turn right onto FR 32N10. Stay on this road for 0.8 mile then turn left for the Caribou Lake Trailhead. **Trailhead GPS:** 40°30'8.50"N / 121°9'52.62"W

WHAT TO SEE

In many ways the 20,833-acre Caribou Wilderness is an extension of the eastern half of Lassen Volcanic National Park. Both regions are shaped by volcanism and feature tranquil forests and numerous lakes. They even share a border, creating one large wildlands block. One significant difference separates these two regions. Lassen, blessed with national park status, receives significantly more visitors than the Caribou Wilderness. For hikers looking to lose themselves in beautiful forests with several deep lakes and gentle, rolling topography, the Caribou Wilderness is the place to go. This hike utilizes the wilderness's most accessible trailhead and makes a lollipop through a dense collection of lakes and ponds. Most of the trip crosses an old lava flow that has long been covered by vast forestlands. The highlight of the hike is Turnaround Lake, a deep lake backed by a 400-foot-high butte.

To begin the hike, climb up a short hill to Caribou Lake, near the small dam that increases the lake's volume. Caribou Lake is the source of the Susan River, which flows east from here. From the trailhead, follow the path east as it stays close to the shore of

A peaceful morning at Caribou Lake.

Caribou Lake. Like nearly all bodies of water in this area, the lake is ringed with trees. Soon you enter the Caribou Wilderness and then arrive at a fork about 0.75 mile from the trailhead. This is the beginning of the loop portion of the hike. Go left here and pass alongside a large unnamed pond. The trail turns back to the west and begins the only notable climb of the hike. Most of the wilderness occupies an old lava flow, and to reach the interior you need to climb up the cliffs that form the edge of the flow.

Once you have reached the top, the trail continues climbing gently a little more until you reach the spur that leads to Emerald Lake. Like many of the lakes in the Caribou Wilderness, this fine lake sits in a rocky bowl with a tree-lined shoreline. The trail to Emerald Lakes continues south to Cypress Lake. Instead, return to the main trail, turn left, and continue to the west. Pass a long, shallow pond and then arrive at the spur that accesses Gem Lake. Though similar to Emerald Lake, Gem Lake is twice the size and in a rockier bowl. Return again to the main trail; turn right and begin a long passage through forest where scattered boulders help break the forest monotony. After 0.8 mile arrive at North Divide Lake.

Unlike the lakes encountered so far, North Divide Lake does not sit in a rocky bowl. This oddly shaped lake spreads out over a wider area and even has some small patches of meadow on its northwestern fringes. At the west end of the lake, the trail splits. Going left here leads to Long Lake and the large collection of smaller lakes accessed from Hay

Meadow. Instead, turn right and head north. This section of the trail is the only place where you may encounter running water on the hike. In late spring and early summer, a pretty creek runs from North Divide Lake to Black Lake and then Turnaround Lake. The former is reached 0.8 mile after North Divide Lake.

The trail continues past Black Lake a short distance before it splits. The path to the right is the way back to the trailhead. However, before taking this route, stay to the left at the fork and hike a little farther to beautiful Turnaround Lake. With the exception of Caribou Lake at the trailhead, Turnaround Lake is much larger than the other lakes on this trail. A rocky butte rises 400 feet above the west side of the lake, an unusual occurrence in this fairly flat wilderness. The east shore is a good place to pause, take a break, and enjoy the view of the lake. When you are ready to continue hiking, head back to the fork and turn left to complete the loop through the wilderness.

As you head back toward the trailhead, the path crosses somewhat more rugged terrain than it has elsewhere on this hike. The trees are a little sparser and the terrain a little rockier. You will pass numerous small ponds and, 1.2 miles from the junction by Turnaround Lake, arrive at the edge of Jewel Lake, another pretty lake set in a rocky bowl. From here the trail descends a lazy switchback as you head off the old lava flow. Once you reach the

Turnaround Lake is among the larger
lakes in the Caribou Wilderness.

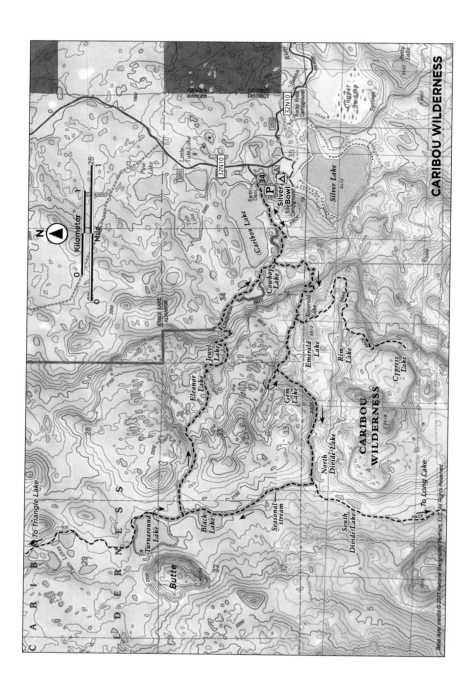

CARIBOU WILDERNESS

bottom, follow the trail through the forest for 0.6 mile before you reach Cowboy Lake. This lake sits at the foot of the old lava flow, which makes a craggy backdrop. If it weren't so shallow, it would challenge Turnaround Lake as the prettiest on this hike. Cowboy Lake is only moments away from the end of the loop. When you arrive at the intersection with the trail from Caribou Lake, turn left and follow it back to the trailhead.

MILES AND DIRECTIONS

0.0 Start at the Caribou Lake Trailhead.

0.75 Stay left when the trail splits to begin the loop.

1.7 Turn left to take the spur trail to Emerald Lake.

2.3 Turn right to take the spur trail to Gem Lake.

3.7 At the west end of North Divide Lake, turn right and head toward Turn-around Lake.

4.7 Pass the trail that leads to Jewel Lake and back to the trailhead.

4.9 Enjoy the view at Turnaround Lake.

5.1 Turn left to go to Jewel Lake and the trailhead.

6.4 Pass Jewel Lake.

7.8 Just beyond Cowboy Lake, turn left to return to the trailhead.

8.5 Arrive back at the trailhead.

The beauty of the surrounding mountains is evident from the Orland Buttes.

SACRAMENTO VALLEY

THE CENTRAL VALLEY is California's vast interior heartland. Essentially a giant basin in the center of the state, it is surrounded by a diverse assemblage of mountains that climb high above the expansive plain. Reckoning clockwise from San Francisco Bay, the valley is bound by the North Coast Range, the Klamath Mountains, the Cascade Range, the Sierra Nevada, the Transverse Range, and the South Coast Range. Out of these mountains flow a stunning collection of rivers. Most of these are part of the extensive watersheds of the Sacramento and San Joaquin Rivers. The Sacramento River watershed includes the McCloud, Pit, Feather, Yuba, and American Rivers. The San Joaquin River watershed includes the Mokelumne, Stanislaus, Tuolumne, Merced, and, at high water, the Kings Rivers. The water from all these major rivers converges in the vast Sacramento–San Joaquin Delta and then empties into San Francisco Bay. It is an amazing river system. The three southernmost rivers of the Sierra Nevada—the Kings, Kaweah, and Kern Rivers—flow out of the mountains into the southernmost part of the Central Valley, which is an endorheic basin and has no access to the sea.

Once a giant marshland, this is now the most agriculturally productive zone on the planet. Almost any kind of fruit, vegetable, or other type of agrarian yield can be produced here. The water demands of agriculture are supported by a complex hydrologic system that harnesses the water of the rivers and distributes it throughout the Central Valley. A series of reservoirs built on the rivers has helped to maintain this system during drought conditions.

The Central Valley is divided into three sections. The northern section, drained by the Sacramento River, is referred to as the Sacramento Valley. South of the delta is the San Joaquin Valley. At the southernmost end of the entire basin is the endorheic Tulare Basin. All three sections are agricultural engines, though the Sacramento Valley has seen the least such development.

Throughout its entire length, more than 400 miles from north to south, the valley floor is unrelentingly flat. By and large there is little to attract hikers. Even more important, there are few trails upon which to hike. The one minor exception is the northern part of the Sacramento Valley. A few volcanic intrusions have produced a small amount of topography amid the great flatness. Occurrences such as the Orland Buttes are not the kind of rugged terrain for which the state is known, but they do offer a surprising amount of beauty, especially in spring. They also give hikers a good perspective on the great scale of the valley as they traverse these rare elevated areas and can see the level expanse bounded by great mountains to the east and west and the great icy cone of Mount Shasta looming majestically in the north. When the grass here is green, the mountains white with snow, and sun shining on blooming wildflowers, many may be moved to ask why there are not more trails in this area of unexpected beauty.

35. **IRON CANYON**

WHY GO?

This hike makes a pleasant loop through volcanic tablelands at the extreme northern end of the Sacramento Valley. Views of many peaks around the valley are abundant, highlighted by a historic overlook high above the Sacramento River as it leaves the mountainous terrain and begins the long meander to the sea.

THE RUNDOWN

Start: Iron Canyon Trailhead
Distance: 3.6-mile lollipop
Hiking time: 1–2 hours
Difficulty: Easy
Elevation gain: 250 feet
Season: Year-round
Trail surface: Packed dirt, rocky

Canine compatibility: Dogs permitted
Fees and permits: None
Land status: Bureau of Land Management
Trail contact: Redding Field Office, 355 Hemsted Dr., Redding 96002; (530) 224-2100; www.blm.gov

FINDING THE TRAILHEAD

 From I-5 in Red Bluff, take exit 649 for Antelope Boulevard/CA 36. Turn onto CA 36, which is also CA 99. Proceed east for 2 miles. Turn left on CA 36 when it splits off from CA 99. Continue for 5.2 miles and turn left into the large gravel parking area for the Iron Canyon Trailhead. **Trailhead GPS:** 40°15'9.63"N / 122°8'47.21"W

WHAT TO SEE

The Sacramento River, California's longest and largest river, begins in the high peaks just west of Mount Shasta. From there it is a wild waterway, flowing south through the mountains until it reaches massive Lake Shasta. Beyond the large reservoir the river flows through a more subdued land of hills and tall, cut banks. It still manages to retain some of its mountain character and has numerous rapids and riffles. Finally the river enters Iron Canyon, a nearly 400-foot-deep gash through a volcanic ridge. On the far side of the canyon, there are no ridges or rolling hills and the river enters the vast flatlands of the Sacramento Valley. To the south the expanse unfolds all the way to the river's great delta at the inlet to San Francisco Bay. The vantage at the rim of the canyon is this hike's main objective. From the canyon rim, you are treated to an excellent view of the last wild stretch of the great river, as well as great views of the mountain peaks that form the perimeter of the valley.

Starting from the gravel parking area, the trail heads west and quickly drops down into a rocky gully. After climbing up the far side, the trail splits. This is where the

The Sacramento River flows through Iron Canyon.

return portion of the loop rejoins the trail. Stay left, maintaining a course that runs parallel to the gully. The terrain here is largely flat grassland with scattered boulders and oak trees. The sparse forestation means there are far-reaching views, especially to the west, where the Yolla Bolly Mountains form the western wall hemming in the Sacramento Valley.

After crossing a shallow draw, the trail continues west for 0.6 mile before passing beneath a power line and then immediately crossing the rocky channel of a dry stream-bed. Once across, the path briefly merges with an old dirt road before veering west back onto singletrack. You only have a little farther to travel along the road before finally being deposited at the precipice of impressive Iron Canyon, about 1.5 miles from the trailhead. Turning north, follow the trail along the rim of the canyon, enjoying the views down to the Sacramento River. A little over 0.25 mile along the rim leads to a large interpretive display, immediately south of a rocky prominence that is the highest point on the cliffs of Iron Canyon. The sign reveals that this was likely the location where famed mountain man Jedediah Smith surveyed the surrounding mountains and determined to head west to the coast rather than continue along the Sacramento River to the north.

Continuing past the sign, it is possible to climb out on the rocky point for excellent views. Be sure to watch out for poison oak growing among the rocks. Just to the north, the trail accesses a second set of rocks that are a little easier to climb onto but offer equally pleasing views. The rocky vista points offer a great perspective of the mountains around the Sacramento Valley, including the Trinity Alps and Mount Shasta. However, the highlight is the Sacramento River and its canyon. Here you can observe the river's passage through the rugged gate before it enters the great expanse of the valley to the south.

Beyond the vistas at the edge of Iron Canyon, the trail turns away from the river and heads northeast, passing through treeless grasslands. Though the canyon is no longer visible, the views remain expansive. Crossing back under the power lines, the trail turns east. Turtle Creek lies just to the north, though the creek is not visible. Scattered boulders and oak trees are found throughout this area. Several old dirt roads and use trails deviate off the main path along this section of the route, but the proper course is easy to discern. To the east, the Tuscan Buttes, a pair of rounded hills topped by radio towers, are the most interesting feature lying a short distance away. Lassen Peak and Brokeoff Mountain are among the prominent summits on the horizon.

After maintaining this course for some time, you turn south. The number of oak trees increases as the trail nears the rocky gully encountered at the beginning of the hike. Here the paths intersect. Turn left, cross the gully, and complete the short walk back to the trailhead.

Lassen Peak and Brokeoff Mountain are among the many tall peaks that ring the valley.

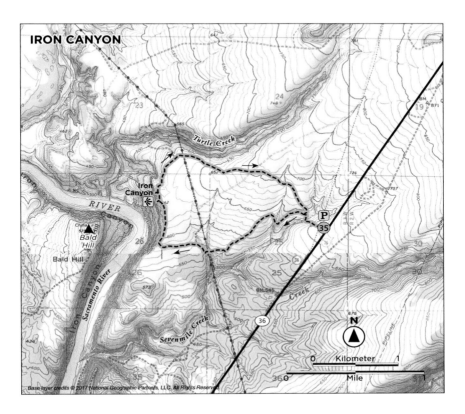

MILES AND DIRECTIONS

0.0 Start at the Iron Canyon Trailhead.

0.2 After crossing the gully, stay left at the trail junction.

1.5 Arrive at the rim of Iron Canyon.

1.75 An interpretive display provides the history of the vista point.

3.4 Complete the loop and turn left to return to the trailhead.

3.6 Arrive back at the trailhead.

36. ORLAND BUTTES

WHY GO?

The trip through the Orland Buttes explores an area of relief amid the flat sea of the Sacramento Valley. Passing alongside Black Butte Lake, the trail offers awesome spring scenery and views of the mountains that ring the valley.

THE RUNDOWN

Start: Overlook parking lot near Black Butte Dam
Distance: 5.1-mile lollipop
Hiking time: 2–3 hours
Difficulty: Easy
Elevation gain: 525 feet
Season: Year-round; best in spring
Trail surface: Packed dirt, rocky, road
Canine compatibility: Dogs permitted

Fees and permits: None
Land status: US Army Corps of Engineers
Trail contact: Sacramento District, 19225 Newville Rd., Orland 95963; (530) 865-4781; www.spk.usace.army .mil/Locations/Sacramento-District -Parks/Black-Butte-Lake

FINDING THE TRAILHEAD

From I-5 in Orland, take exit 619 for Orland/Chico. Turn right onto Newville Road and drive west for 7.7 miles. At the US Army Corp of Engineers headquarters, turn left onto the park road and stay straight to where the road ends at the parking area for the observation point. **Trailhead GPS:** 39°48′44.60″N / 122°20′11.33″W

WHAT TO SEE

Despite being prominently visible from I-5, the Orland Buttes are generally overlooked by hikers and travelers, even though they are a rare example of rugged relief rising from the great flat expanse of the Sacramento Valley. The buttes are a rugged remnant of an ancient volcanic mudflow, a rare occurrence on the west side of the valley. To the northeast, in the foothills of the Cascade Range, there is evidence of extensive volcanic activity, but the Orland Buttes are the only significant volcanic outlier in this area. The surrounding land and the hills that lie to the west are all composed of sedimentary rock. Fortunately for hikers, the relief offered by the buttes makes for a great and unique trail opportunity. The Sacramento Valley is unrelentingly flat, and the rugged volcanic upland yields dramatic views of the valley and the mountains that hem it in. As an added bonus, much of the valley around the buttes is undeveloped. This means that, aside from impounded Black Butte Lake, you have a chance to see what the valley looked like in its primeval state, before it became one of the most productive agricultural regions in the

The trailhead vista has a good view of Black Butte and Black Butte Lake.

world. There are many trails around the Orland Buttes, but the best is a loop that climbs to the top of Black Butte, the northernmost butte, where there is a great vista point. From there it loops down and travels through open grasslands back to the trailhead.

The hike starts at the overlook near the Black Butte Dam. From the vista, plateau-like Black Butte rises on the far side of the lake, its band of black basalt standing out against the grasslands. Head to the dam and cross over it. From the top of the dam, great views of the Sacramento Valley unfold, crowned by Mount Shasta rising dramatically above the mountains far to the north. Though not well signed, this route is considered the Osprey Trail. On the far side, the trail makes a wide turn by the lake's overflow channel. It then heads downhill, running parallel to the wide gully. About 0.75 mile from the trailhead, look for a narrow trail branching off to the left as the trail passes between some rocky patches. Turn left here, descend into the gully, and then climb out the other side.

Once out of the gully, the trail turns to the west and begins a gradual ascent up the long spine of Black Butte. In spring the green grass is intensely lush. The views begin to improve as the trail climbs. Note also that as you get higher, the dark basalt rock begins to be more pronounced. This is especially the case along the south side, where the band of dark basalt that is the highlight of Black Butte becomes more evident. Aside from a few trees found growing below the rim on the north side, there is not much more than grass here. About 1.45 miles from the trailhead, the spine narrows to a thin neck. The dark rock is more abundant here, forcing the trail to weave through large but scenic outcroppings, taking on the appearance of a wild rock garden.

The neck eventually narrows until it is just a few dozen yards in width and the rocks have become large and abundant. The true bulk of Black Butte now looms directly ahead. At the end of the neck, about 1.65 miles from the trailhead, watch for a wide trail heading downhill to the right. This will be the beginning of the return route to the trailhead. For now, climb up the slope of Black Butte on one of the numerous paths that wind

Volcanic outcroppings on Black Butte frame the distant South Yolla Bolly Mountains.

through the rocks. Follow these along the crest of the butte to the south end, where you'll find a network of railings. From here there are great views of the surrounding region. Black Butte Lake is directly below, and to the south the high peaks of St. Johns and Snow Mountains line the southern end of the Coast Range. The unusual Sutter Buttes rise abruptly from the floor of the Sacramento Valley to the southeast. The Coast Range extends north, where the often-snowy summit of South Yolla Bolly Mountain, also known as Mount Linn, is identifiable. The mountains that hem in the northern end of the valley, including pyramidal Bully Choop and Shasta Bally, are obvious. Cascade luminaries Lassen Peak and Brokeoff Mountain are highlights of the view as well. Much of the northern Sierra Nevada, including the awesome Sierra Buttes, completes the panorama to the southeast.

After enjoying the view, retrace your steps back to the base of Black Butte's slope, where the wide trail branches off from the narrow neck. Follow it down a switchback to an alternative trailhead. From the trailhead parking area, the Osprey Trail continues to the west, weaving through ravines and low hills to the Buckhorn Recreation Area, which has a large campground. Instead of following that path, continue up the road 0.1 mile and turn right onto an old dirt road. This path, now the Coyote Trail, heads east and runs parallel to the base of Black Butte's long spine. The dark rocks continue to be visible from the trail, as do many of the landmarks around the Sacramento Valley. After 0.5 mile from the alternative trailhead, the path passes a large stock tank on the left. In another 0.3 mile look for a narrow path branching off to the right. This connects back to the Osprey Trail as it emerges from the overflow channel. Taking this shortcut will shave 0.5 mile off the hike; otherwise, continue on the road to a junction at the edge of a large overflow pond. This pond is likely to have water in it in spring, but it dries up in summer as Stony

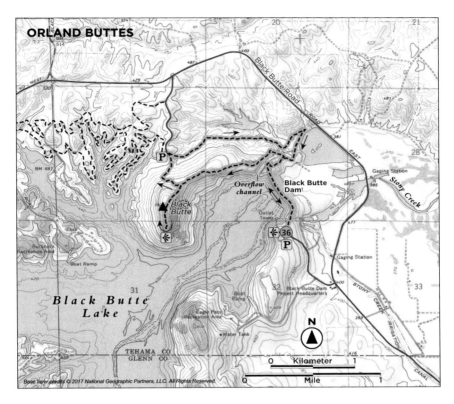

Creek's flow is reduced. Turn right here and turn right again in 0.2 mile. The trail then reconnects with the Osprey Trail and crosses the dam back to the trailhead.

MILES AND DIRECTIONS

0.0 Start at the overlook parking area and cross Black Butte Dam to begin the hike on the Osprey Trail.

0.75 Turn left onto the trail that passes through the lake's overflow channel.

1.65 Veer left off the main path and follow tracks through large rocks to the summit of Black Butte.

2.0 Arrive at the overlook atop Black Butte. Return to main trail.

2.8 Turn right off the park road onto an old dirt road, named Coyote Trail.

3.75 Pass the cutoff option to return to Osprey Trail near the overflow channel.

4.0 Turn right onto the road by a large overflow pond.

4.2 Turn right to return to the Osprey Trail and cross back over the dam.

5.1 Arrive back at the trailhead.

An unnamed lake near Twin Lakes is surrounded by wildflowers.

NORTHERN SIERRA

THE NORTHERN SIERRA is the most diverse region of California's greatest mountain range. Stretching from its meeting with the Cascade Range around Lake Almanor to the mountains along the rim of the Lake Tahoe Basin to the south, it is a range of contrasts, in both its geography and its uses. Great swaths of these mountains are blanketed in boundless forests, punctuated only by higher terrain that climbed enough in elevation to receive the scouring ministry of glaciers. These areas are the focal point of most hiking activity, while the great forests have been given over to other, non-recreational endeavors. Consequently, this is the least-wild section of the Sierra Nevada. Despite this, the Northern Sierra is an incredibly beautiful region, boasting some of the most superb and iconic landscapes in the entire Sierra Nevada. Lake Tahoe of course is one of the greatest alpine destinations in all of the American West. Though it is often overshadowed by the wondrous lake, the rest of the region lays its claim to great scenery as well.

Geologically the region is quite similar to the Klamath Mountains in northwestern California. There is a significant amount of sedimentary rock, with major intrusions of granite and ultramafic rocks. Pyroclastic mudflows, remnants of volcanic activity that once occurred in this area, are also present in the Northern Sierra. Indeed, it was volcanic activity that was responsible for the formation of Lake Tahoe.

While volcanism was partially responsible for the creation of Lake Tahoe, the high country was shaped by glaciers. The terrain at the northern end of the range is relatively low in elevation and gentle in its topography. As you move south, the range gets higher. This resulted in more glacial activity; consequently, there is now more rugged terrain with rocky peaks and lake basins. Most of these areas, notably the Bucks Lake and Lakes Basin areas, lie along the Sierra Crest. Farther south, the area along the crest was home to glaciers, but the high peaks of the Yuba River headwaters were also heavily scoured by the large sheets of ice. The headwaters area is one of the few areas not on the main divide that has a high concentration of lakes and craggy peaks.

Most of the northern Sierra Nevada is drained by the Feather, Yuba, and American Rivers. The Feather River is particularly notable for having the Sierra's largest watershed basin. It was along these rivers, especially the American River, that gold was discovered and California's destiny established. The area was mined extensively, and many of the communities throughout the Northern Sierra were first established as mining camps.

Numerous highways cross the Northern Sierra, providing good access to this region. I-80 roughly divides the range between the more lightly used but larger northern area and the smaller southern area, which is the heavily used Lake Tahoe region. In the south, US 50 accesses the Lake Tahoe area directly; in the north, CA 70, CA 49, and CA 20 all cross the range and provide easy opportunities to reach some of the area's beautiful high country.

37. INDEPENDENCE TRAIL–JONES HOLE LOOP

WHY GO?

This classic Gold Country hike combines an exciting crossing of a boardwalk, suspended on cliffs and elevated on tall trestles, with a deep gorge, plunging waterfalls, and one of the largest rivers in the northern Sierra Nevada.

THE RUNDOWN

Start: Signed pullout on CA 49 for both the East and West Independence Trails
Distance: 4.0-mile loop
Hiking time: About 2 hours
Difficulty: Easy
Elevation gain: 450 feet
Season: Year-round; waterfalls and river at their fullest in spring, swimming best in late summer
Trail surface: Packed dirt, wooden boardwalk, dirt road
Canine compatibility: Dogs not permitted

Fees and permits: None
Land status: South Yuba State Park
Trail contact: 17660 Pleasant Valley Rd., Penn Valley 95946; (530) 432-2546; www.parks.ca.gov/?page_id=496
Special considerations: There is a significant amount of poison oak on this route.
Other: The Independence Trail is wheelchair-accessible from the trailhead to Rush Creek.

FINDING THE TRAILHEAD

From Nevada City, drive east on CA 20 then turn left onto CA 49, signed for Downieville. Drive on CA 49 for 6.3 miles to a pullout signed for the Independence Trail. Only 4 or 5 cars can park in this pullout, but there are several more pullouts nearby to accommodate more vehicles. **Trailhead GPS:** 39°17'29.50"N / 121°5'50.38"W

WHAT TO SEE

South Yuba River State Park's Independence Trail is billed as the nation's first wheelchair-accessible wilderness trail. Both the state park and the trail were made possible by years of tireless effort by noted naturalist John Olmsted, who was responsible for numerous state parks around California. The Independence Trail has eastern and western sections, divided by CA 49. Both offer wheelchair-accessible sections, fascinating history, impressive trail engineering, and beautiful scenery. However, the western half can also be combined with other trails to form a great loop. This option includes an intriguing section of precariously perched boardwalk that crosses a deep, waterfall-filled gorge with access to the South Fork of the Yuba River.

The reconstructed flume
clings to the cliffs above
Rush Creek.

A small waterfall lies
upstream on Rush Creek.

The hike begins where the Eastern and Western Independence Trails meet. Turn right to take the western route and immediately pass through a low tunnel beneath CA 49. The Independence Trail is essentially a repurposed flume that once carried water to a nearby hydraulic mining operation. The width and smooth floor of the channel were seen to be ideal for wheelchairs, and the idea for the trail was born. Other accessible features like well-constructed boardwalks and observation platforms augmented the trail, providing mobility-impaired hikers an opportunity to experience and enjoy the wilderness.

On the far side of the tunnel beneath CA 49, the trail heads west, and in 0.2 mile it splits. The path on the right heads down to the Yuba River at Jones Hole. This is the route of the loop's return. Stay left and follow the old flume. Paths have been worn on the rim of the flume for those who want to hike on a typical singletrack trail. For the next 1.0 mile, the Independence Trail follows the contours of the hillside. At times the slope is too steep, and bridges are constructed in order to maintain the gentle grade of the trail. An observation platform offers a glimpse of the Yuba as it roars through the canyon almost 500 feet below.

About 0.8 mile beyond the point where the trail forks, you arrive at the highlight of the hike, an elaborately constructed bridge over the deep gorge of Rush Creek. The bridge begins as a boardwalk section situated on the steep, rocky slope of the gorge. As it traverses the canyon and nears the creek, large trestles support the bridge as it crosses the water. North of the bridge, a set of tiered waterfalls pour over rocky lips and fall into inaccessible pools. The sheer cliffs of the gorge are very narrow, giving the canyon an almost slot-like appearance. On the south side of the bridge, the creek flows 30 feet below. Adjacent is a complicated structure that features wooden switchbacks and an observation deck to provide wheelchair access to the creek itself. Just upstream from the

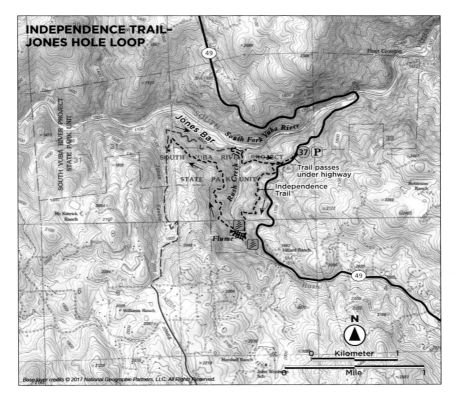

creek is another small waterfall. Unfortunately, the wooden ramp is closed off due to structural issues.

After crossing over Rush Creek, the boardwalk continues along the western side of the gorge, slung perilously over the steep canyon walls. It is an unusual and beautiful section of trail, where the path itself is integrated into the landscape and hiking experience. Beyond the bridge, however, it quickly becomes clear that hikers generally turn around at the flume complex. An old wheelchair-accessible restroom has fallen into a sorry state of disrepair, and the dense vegetation, while not overtaking the trail, makes wheelchair travel past this point unrealistic. Nonetheless, the path is pretty and has a lonely, forgotten feeling. Persevere for another 1.4 miles before being deposited on the edge of a dirt road.

Turn right on the road and follow it downhill. The roar of the Yuba River gets louder as you go. The road bends around the shoulder of a ridge and descends to a cluster of clearings, where some unofficial campsites have been established. Several spurs lead down to vantage points above the water and over to Jones Bar, a level spot along the river. In summer Jones Bar is a popular swimming hole, but in spring the Yuba River is a raging torrent and must be avoided. Stay on the main road, which soon ends at a footbridge across Rush Creek. Cross the bridge and turn left, where a short spur leads to the best

The South Fork of the Yuba River flows furiously in spring but by summer this area is a pleasant swimming hole.

place to view the river safely. When done, head back toward the bridge and briefly follow the trail upstream along Rush Creek. The path turns east and makes the steep but short climb back up to the Independence Trail. Once there, it is only 0.2 mile back to the trailhead.

MILES AND DIRECTIONS

0.0 Start at the trailhead, take the Independence Trail west, and pass under CA 49.

0.2 Stay left at the junction with the trail to Jones Bar.

1.0 Arrive at the fascinatingly built bridge over Rush Creek.

2.4 Turn right onto a dirt road and descend toward the Yuba River.

3.4 The dirt road ends at Rush Creek. Cross the footbridge, observe the Yuba River, then begin the climb back up to the Independence Trail.

3.8 Rejoin the Independence Trail.

4.0 Arrive back at the trailhead.

38. FEATHER FALLS

WHY GO?
Feather Falls is one of the great waterfalls of California. The loop hike to the falls features lush foothill forests, large creeks, and views of the Middle Fork of the Feather River's deep canyon crowned by Bald Rock Dome. The highlight is awesome Feather Falls, thundering hundreds of feet down a sheer cliff.

THE RUNDOWN
Start: Feather Falls Trailhead
Total distance: 8.0-mile loop
Hiking time: 4–5 hours
Difficulty: Moderate
Elevation gain: 1,000 feet
Season: Year-round; waterfall fullest in spring
Trail surface: Packed dirt, rocky
Canine compatibility: Dogs permitted

Fees and permits: None
Land status: Feather Falls Scenic Area, Plumas National Forest
Trail contact: Feather River Ranger District, 875 Mitchell Ave., Oroville 95965; (530) 534-6500; www.fs .usda.gov/main/plumas
Special considerations: There is a significant amount of poison oak on this route.

FINDING THE TRAILHEAD
From CA 70 in Oroville, drive east on CA 162/Oroville Dam Boulevard for 1.4 miles. Turn right onto Olive Highway and follow this road for 6.6 miles. Turn right on Forbestown Road and continue for 6.2 miles. Turn left onto Lumpkin Road. Drive this windy road for 11 miles and turn left onto Bryant Ravine Road. The Feather Falls Trailhead lies 1.7 miles ahead. Signs indicate the direction to Feather Falls at most of the later turns. **Trailhead GPS:** 39°36'52.00"N / 121°16'0.64"W

WHAT TO SEE
The foothills of the Sierra Nevada are generally not known for spectacle and grandeur, descriptives usually saved for the range's magnificent high country. Feather Falls may be the most spectacular destination in all of the foothills. Indeed, it is one of the few waterfalls in California, or anywhere else in the United States, that can stand shoulder to shoulder with the waterfalls of Yosemite. Plunging 410 feet down a vertical cliff, it is an incredible and humbling sight. Yet for all their beauty, the falls are only part of the charm of this excellent hike in the foothills of the Sierra Nevada. Peaceful forests surround crashing creeks and part sporadically to produce great views of the Feather River, its deep canyon, and prominent Bald Rock Dome. The hike is a loop. The first half travels to the falls in 4.5 gentle miles; the return trip is only 3.5 miles but features a steep climb back up to the trailhead. It can be hiked in either direction, but doing the long section

first lets the anticipation build on the way to the falls and then delivers you back to the trailhead faster.

Begin at the trailhead and make an easy descent into foothill forest. Just under 0.5 mile from the trailhead, you arrive at a fork. A sign indicates that the route to the left reaches the falls in 3.5 miles, while the upper route, to the right, is 4.5 miles. It seems the mileages here are the entire distance per route, including the sections from the trailhead to the fork and once the trails converge to the falls. Stay to the right and hike down the trail as it gently follows the contours toward Frey Creek.

When you arrive at Frey Creek, you are greeted by a surprisingly large flow of water as it cascades down a steep rocky slope. In spring this can have a ferocious amount of water in it. Cross the creek on a large wooden bridge, getting an up-close view as you go, and then continue hiking along the contours of the canyon, eventually beginning to descend again.

Watch for views of Bald Rock Dome in the distance. This dome, reminiscent of the domes around Tuolumne Meadows, is a notable landmark above the Middle Fork of the Feather River as it passes through awesome Bald Rock Canyon. Not much of the canyon is visible from the trail, but its tall sheer cliffs end in a jumble of giant granite boulders over which the Feather River pours in one large cascade after another. The granite in this area is part of the Bald Rock Pluton, one of several large granite intrusions in the Northern Sierra. Much of the exposed granite of this pluton, including the canyon, Bald Rock Dome, and Feather Falls, is preserved in the Feather Falls Scenic Area.

After traversing the high, steep slopes for 2.3 miles, the trail is rejoined by the shorter path coming out of Frey Creek's canyon. From here the path climbs up and around a shoulder high above the Feather River. In wetter years part of the river is stilled here,

Feather Falls

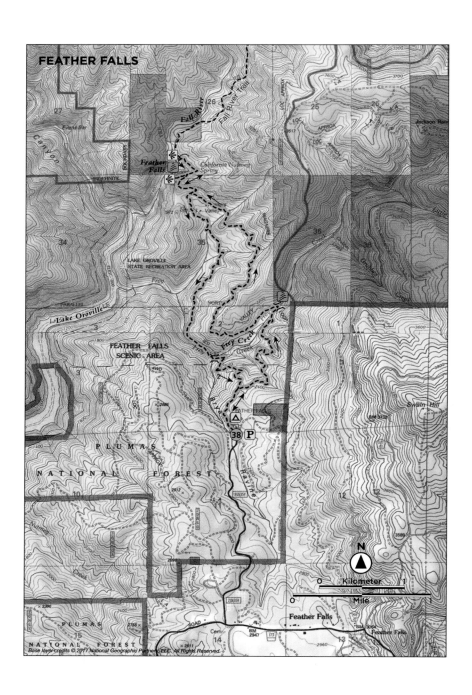

where Lake Oroville reaches its maximum extent up the canyon. A vista point with some displays tempts you to stay and enjoy the view, but the thundering sound of Feather Falls, now becoming audible for the first time, should encourage you to press on.

As you round the shoulder and descend toward the falls, you encounter railings that have been installed to ensure safety on the steep slopes. The rocky path soon reaches a fork. To get to the falls, turn left, walk a little farther, and descend a stairway to a wooden causeway built over a rocky saddle. Across the causeway is the Feather Falls observation deck, perched precariously over the abyss on a giant rock column. Across the chasm is powerful Feather Falls. A significant tributary of the Feather River, Fall River pours through a narrow gap in the cliff and runs down a giant oblique granite slab, widening as it falls. It then hits a large bulge in the cliff and explodes into several parallel streams as it plummets down the face of the cliff. It is a marvelous sight.

It is possible to get other perspectives of the falls. Return to where the spur to the observation platform left the main trail. Turn left and follow the narrow, rocky path as it arcs around the head of the chasm. It then climbs up near the top of the falls. You can very carefully scramble over the rocks down to the lip, where the falls pour off the cliff. A fence has been installed for safety. When you have had your fill of the falls, follow the path back past the spur to the vista and then continue back to where the two trails joined. To complete the loop, stay to the right here.

The latter part of the loop makes a long descent toward Frey Creek. Tucked away in the bottom of the canyon, the area is lusher than the forest the higher trail passes through. As you near the bottom of the canyon, the trail pulls alongside Frey Creek then crosses it and begins the climb back up to the trailhead. This is the only really steep grade on the hike. Fortunately it is not long, and the forest service has even installed benches along the trail. After climbing for 0.75 mile, you reach the junction with the higher trail. From there it is a quick walk back to the trailhead.

MILES AND DIRECTIONS

0.0   Start at the Feather Falls Trailhead.

0.4   Stay right at the fork to take the higher trail to Feather Falls.

1.6   Cross Frey Creek.

3.9   The trails of the loop rejoin.

4.3   At a short spur, turn left and descend to the Feather Falls observation platform. To return, retrace your steps to where the trails met.

4.8   Stay right to take the shorter, steeper trail back to the trailhead.

6.8   Cross Frey Creek and begin climbing up toward the trailhead.

7.6   Rejoin the higher trail.

8.0   Arrive back at the trailhead.

39. BUCKS LAKE WILDERNESS

WHY GO?

A short hike that ventures into the Sierra Nevada's northernmost wilderness area, this trip leads to Gold Lake, a beautiful mountain lake set at the base of stark cliffs.

THE RUNDOWN

Start: Trailhead near the Silver Lake boat launch
Distance: 3.4 miles out and back
Hiking time: 2–3 hours
Difficulty: Easy
Elevation gain: 600 feet
Season: Late spring through fall
Trail surface: Packed dirt, rocky
Canine compatibility: Dogs permitted

Fees and permits: None
Land status: Bucks Lake Wilderness
Trail contact: Mt. Hough Ranger District, 39696 State Highway 70, Quincy 95971; (530) 283-0555; www.fs.usda.gov/plumas/
Other: Swimming is not permitted in Silver Lake. Permits are required for overnight camping in the Bucks Lake Wilderness.

FINDING THE TRAILHEAD

Starting on westbound Lawrence Street in downtown Quincy, turn left onto Crescent Street/CA 70. In 1 block turn right onto Bucks Lake Road/Quincy Oroville Highway. Continue on this road for about 9 miles. After passing through the rural community of Meadow Valley, turn right onto Silver Lake Road, which is also FR 24N29. Proceed 6 miles, staying on the main road the entire way, until arriving at the Silver Lake Campground. The trailhead is at the end of the road, just past the campground, next to the lake's dam and boat launch. **Trailhead GPS:** 39°57'30.31"N / 121°8'4.21"W

WHAT TO SEE

Though granite, the rock that is so closely identified with the Sierra Nevada, is exposed in the deep canyon formed by the North Fork of the Feather River, there isn't much visible at higher elevations as you move south from the Sierra Nevada's northern terminus at Lake Almanor. The first encounter with what would be recognized as a classic Sierra landscape is in the Bucks Lake Wilderness. This highland area reaches elevations above 7,000 feet, the northernmost part of the Sierra Crest to do so. The area is part of the divide that separates the Feather River's north and middle forks. Interestingly, this is the only portion of the Sierra Nevada north of I-80 to be designated as a wilderness area. The hike to Gold Lake explores the most scenic part of the Bucks Lake Wilderness and makes a great introduction to what hiking in this range's high country offers.

Beginning at the trailhead near the boat launch into Silver Lake, the trail crosses over the lake's dam. Tall rocky cliffs provide a scenic backdrop to this fine mountain

Silver Lake's impressive headwall highlights the beginning of the hike.

reservoir. Though it was originally a natural body of water, the lake's volume has been significantly increased by the dam impounding its outlet. The lake functions as the water source for the nearby Meadow Valley community, and though boating and fishing are permitted, swimming is not. Once across the dam, the trail begins climbing and promptly passes a sign marking entry into the Bucks Lake Wilderness. In short order the wide path climbs up to the top of a low ridge. An old jeep trail continues along the shoreline of Silver Lake to the right. At the top of the ridge, a broad vista unfolds, stretching from Lassen Peak in the Cascade Range to the north down to the spire-like Sierra Buttes to the south.

The trail soon crosses the side of the ridge and makes a gradual ascent as it traverses the ridge's flank. Note that this ridge is, in fact, a glacial moraine. At one time large ice flows descended the rugged cliffs to the west and inched their way east, carving out the basins that now contain Gold and Silver Lakes. The moraine is the mountain debris left over as the glacier pushed it aside. Little of the debris is visible now, and the moraine is covered in a thick blanket of brush. There is little shade as the trail climbs, but this means there are good views that help motivate hikers to push onward. The most notable sight is the large granite basin immediately to the south that contains Gold Lake. The large, rocky bowl is capped by the dark mass of 7,020-foot Spanish Peak, the second-highest point in the Bucks Lake Wilderness. The sound of Jacks Meadow Creek flowing out of

Gold Lake and crashing down into its namesake meadow below the trail fills the air as you hike up the moraine.

About 1.0 mile from the trailhead, the path finally turns south, moving off the moraine and onto the granite cliffs that make up the crest of the Bucks Lake Wilderness. The trail, once crossing dirt and duff, now becomes very rocky and is routed along the ledges and cracks of beautiful granite boulders. The route immediately arrives at a junction with the Granite Gap Trail, which climbs up to nearby Rock Lake and the Pacific Crest Trail. Stay to the left and continue to undulate across the cliffs toward Spanish Peak. Be sure to look down into the basin, watching for Jacks Meadow Creek flowing over naked rock into the meadow below.

Soon you will cross the small outlet stream from Rock Lake cascading over the trail. From here the path makes a short ascent up to a rocky saddle. At the top, the large cirque holding Gold Lake finally unfolds. The lake is larger than you might expect. The sound of several snowmelt streams flowing into the lake is audible, though it can be hard to spot them, since much of their flow is hidden beneath riparian vegetation. Nearly 1,000 feet overhead, the dark volcanic protrusion of Spanish Peak dominates the vista. The maintained section of the trail essentially ends at this point, but well-established use trails

The dark face of Spanish Peak is a looming presence above Gold Lake.

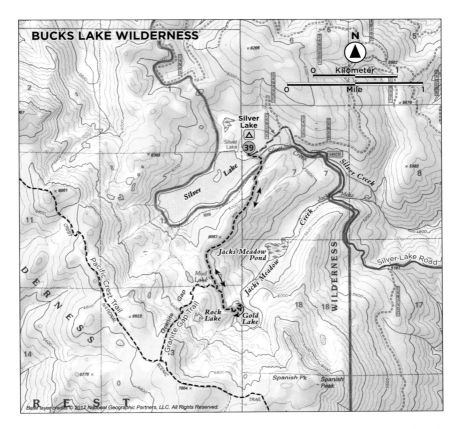

BUCKS LAKE WILDERNESS

descend to the lake. There is not much in the way of overnight camping sites here, but there are nice granite slabs at the water's edge to relax on or swim from. A narrow path also leads to the lake's outlet, where the outlet creek cascades over the granite. When it is time to return, follow the trail back to the trailhead.

MILES AND DIRECTIONS

0.0 Start at the trailhead and head south, crossing over Silver Lake's dam.

0.1 Enter the Bucks Lake Wilderness and start the climb up the side of a long glacial moraine.

1.0 Stay left at the junction with the Granite Gap Trail. This is where the route to Gold Lake climbs off the moraine onto the granite cliffs.

1.5 Cross over Rock Lake's small outlet stream.

1.7 Arrive at Gold Lake. Return the way you came.

3.4 Arrive back at the trailhead.

40. **FRAZIER FALLS**

WHY GO?

The hike to Frazier Falls is an easy walk through pleasant forest and rugged rocks that leads to an overlook above one of the tallest waterfalls in the northern Sierra Nevada.

THE RUNDOWN

Start: Paved path from Frazier Falls Trailhead
Distance: 1.0 mile out and back
Hiking time: About 1 hour
Difficulty: Easy
Elevation gain: None
Season: Late spring, summer, fall
Trail surface: Paved
Canine compatibility: Dogs permitted

Fees and permits: None
Land status: Lakes Basin Recreation Area, Plumas National Forest
Trail contact: Beckwourth Ranger District, 23 Mohawk Rd., Blairsden 96103; (530) 836-2575; www.fs.usda .gov/plumas
Other: This trail is wheelchair-accessible.

FINDING THE TRAILHEAD

Starting in Graeagle, drive southwest on CA 89 for about 1.5 miles. Turn right onto Gold Lake Highway, which is also FR 24, and continue 1.7 miles. Turn left onto a road signed for Frazier Falls. Continue on this narrow, paved road for 4.2 miles before arriving at the Frazier Falls Trailhead. **Trailhead GPS:** 39°42'29.66"N / 120°38'45.74"W

WHAT TO SEE

Frazier Falls is one of the highlights of the Lakes Basin Recreation Area. Interestingly, it is one of the few trails in the basin that does not lead to a lake. Instead, the short hike gives waterfall lovers a chance to enjoy the cataract crashing 175 feet off a sheer cliff composed of metamorphic rock. It is one of the taller waterfalls in the northern Sierra Nevada. Even better, it is one of the most easily accessible waterfalls in the area. A paved ADA-compatible trail leads from the trailhead to the falls in just over 0.5 mile, meaning people of all physical ability levels are able to enjoy this marvelous spectacle. The trail passes through rocky terrain before crossing over Frazier Creek and arriving at the observation deck. Even though it is a short, easy hike, it is highly scenic and a great way to get easy exposure to the type of terrain found in the Northern Sierra.

The paved path departs the trailhead to the east. It maintains a level course through forest before entering a rocky area, where low walls rise a dozen feet or so above the trail. Though brush still covers some parts of the rock, the forest has largely receded from the trail, giving the area a more open feel despite there not being many views. After 0.25 mile

Frazier Falls

Rocky cliffs line Frazier Creek's canyon.

of winding through the rock, the trail reaches a wooden bridge across Frazier Creek. This large creek flows out of nearby Gold Lake, the largest lake in the Lakes Basin Recreation Area. As you cross the bridge, the sound of the falls becomes audible.

After the bridge, the trail climbs gently up onto a narrow ridge. Here the views of the surrounding terrain open up. Most likely to catch your eye is the set of glacier carved cliffs to the east. The path curves to the north before arriving at the observation deck. Perched on the opposite side of a narrow canyon, it is easy to gaze across the narrow gorge at Frazier Falls. The creek races over the lip of a sheer cliff and crashes into a protrusion of erosion-resistant rock. It then leaps out and cascades the rest of the way down to the bottom of the canyon. It is an inspiring sight, especially when Frazier Creek is engorged with spring snowmelt. This is also a good opportunity to look northward, down the creek's watershed, to get a sense of what much of the Northern Sierra is like. A vast sea of pine forest and rounded mountain summits is revealed downstream. After enjoying the view, follow the path back to the trailhead.

MILES AND DIRECTIONS

0.0 Start from the Frazier Falls Trailhead on the paved path.

0.25 Cross over Frazier Creek on a large wooden bridge.

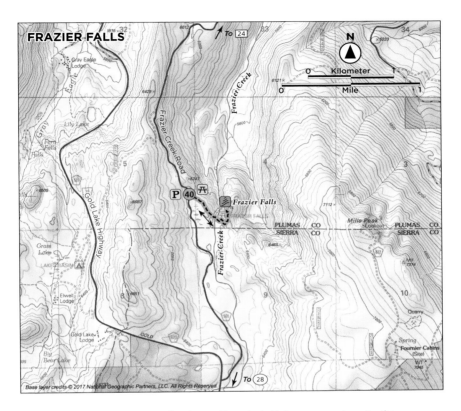

0.5 Arrive at the Frazier Falls observation deck. Retrace your steps to the trailhead.

1.0 Arrive back at the trailhead.

41. LAKES BASIN

WHY GO?

Enjoy a journey through the Lakes Basin Recreation Area, a mountain region defined by numerous lakes, rugged cliffs, and beautiful alpine scenery.

THE RUNDOWN

Start: Trailhead near center of Lakes Basin Campground
Distance: 6.0-mile loop
Hiking time: 3–4 hours
Difficulty: Moderate
Elevation gain: 1,100 feet
Season: Summer, fall
Trail surface: Packed dirt, rocky, duff

Canine compatibility: Dogs permitted
Fees and permits: None
Land status: Plumas National Forest
Trail contact: Beckwourth Ranger District, 23 Mohawk Rd., Blairsden 96103; (530) 836-2575; www.fs.usda.gov/plumas

FINDING THE TRAILHEAD

Beginning in central Graeagle, drive east on CA 89 for a little over 1 mile. Turn right onto Gold Lake Highway and continue for 6.7 miles. Turn right onto Elwell Lodge Road and proceed 0.4 mile to the entrance of the Lakes Basin Campground. Drive to the center of the campground, where there is a small parking area at the trailhead.

Coming from Sierra City, drive east from the small downtown on CA 49 for 5 miles. Turn left onto Gold Lake Highway and continue for 8.8 miles. Turn left onto Elwell Lodge Road and proceed 0.4 mile to the entrance of the Lakes Basin Campground. Drive to the center of the campground, where there is a small parking area at the trailhead. **Trailhead GPS:** 39°42'8.78"N / 120°39'42.51"W

WHAT TO SEE

The section of the Sierra Nevada's crest that lies between the Middle Fork of the Feather River and the North Fork of the Yuba River is one of the Northern Sierra's most scenic parts. This is an area with numerous deep mountain lakes set among rugged cliffs and a few high, notable peaks. The mountains here are generally composed of metavolcanic rock, which is common in this part of the Sierra Nevada. This is the first part of the Sierra to exhibit really extensive glaciation over a large amount of terrain. Notably, there are more than a half dozen lake basins here, most with several lakes scattered within them. Though it is known collectively as the Lakes Basin region, the name in particular belongs to a large basin at the northern end of the area. This basin is, after the awesome Sierra Buttes, probably the most scenic part of the greater Lakes Basin complex. Boasting an impressive ten named lakes and several small unnamed ponds, this is an area bursting with beautiful mountain scenery. Complemented by meadows, rushing creeks, and even a small waterfall, the Lakes Basin beckons to be explored. Fortunately, this is easily accomplished, since the forest service has constructed a great network of trails that allow for numerous hike variations, including a few loops. This hike is not difficult, but those looking for an easier option should consider doing this hike in reverse and heading toward Big Bear and Silver Lakes.

Most hikers intent on enjoying the Lakes Basin's trails start at the large main parking area between the campground and the Elwell Lakes Lodge. However, a good alternative that sees less use and offers more diversity on the hike is to start at the smaller trailhead in the middle of the Lakes Basin Campground. Starting from here, the trail immediately crosses a bridge that spans a large creek that feeds into Gray Eagle Creek, the primary outlet of the Lakes Basin. This creek originates from Big Bear Lake and will be encountered again at the end of the hike. Once across the creek, the trail passes through a lodgepole forest and almost immediately skirts meadow-bound Grass Lake. The trail continues through the forest, occasionally weaving around large rock outcroppings. In 0.75 mile the trail arrives at another bridge, this time over the primary branch of Gray Eagle Creek. On the far side of the bridge, it is possible to descend some bare rock slabs to observe a nice little waterfall. The creek plunges over several small cascades as it drops 30 or so feet.

Back on the trail, it now begins to climb over rocky benches. Stay to the left when a trail heads off to the northwest. This leads to the nearby Gray Eagle Lodge. The trail passes a scenic, unnamed, rockbound lake. The imposing flanks of Mount Elwell now loom overhead. This is one of the few prominent peaks in the Lakes Basin area. Past the lake, the trail continues its easy climb through the rocky landscape. The sound of crashing water soon becomes audible as the trail arrives at the small dam that impounds impressive

The trail boasts great views of the cliffs lining Long Lake.

The craggy face of Mount Elwell, seen from the south side of Mud Lake.

Long Lake, about 1.75 miles from the trailhead. Here a trail crossing the dam joins the route, having originated at the main Lakes Basin Trailhead.

The path stays just above the shore of Long Lake as it heads west. Soon it begins to climb steeply as it traverses the flank of Mount Elwell. This section of trail is fairly steep, but you are compensated with increasingly good views of Long Lake and the cliffs that form the east side of the Sierra Crest. Though the rocky cliffs offer a more subdued alpine vision than other mountains elsewhere in California, they are nonetheless extremely attractive. During the ascent, the path crosses a large talus slope. Here the trail nearly gives out completely, becoming a line of boulders arranged into an easily followed straight line set amid the chaotic jumble. After climbing 400 feet, the route once again becomes a normal dirt trail as it crosses onto a low shoulder of Mount Elwell, where views of the Lakes Basin below are great. This is the highest point on the hike.

At a junction with a trail leading to the top of Mount Elwell, stay to the left, turning south and beginning a descent into a basin nestled into the cliffs on the west side of Long Lake. The basin contains small Mud Lake, though the whole area is much prettier than the name indicates. Once the path reaches the bottom of the basin, it skirts the edge of the cliffs, crossing several snowmelt streams that flow early in summer. Though the trail does not pass alongside Mud Lake, this section of the trail is still quite pretty. The white rock of the cliffs contrasts nicely against the meadow basin floor and is punctuated by lodgepoles. On the south side of the basin the trail climbs again, this time nearing the creek that cascades out of the Hellgramite Lakes' small basin. Having climbed out of the bowl containing Mud Lake, the trail passes alongside the easternmost of the Hellgramite Lakes, named for a species of fly larva that lives in freshwater. Beyond these small lakes, the trail begins its long descent back toward the trailhead.

Silver Lake is the first of four lakes that line the final leg of the hike. After skirting its northern shore, the trail swings back toward Long Lake for one last look at this large body of water. This view is highlighted by the craggy face of Mount Elwell above Long Lake. Turning back to the east, you will soon arrive at Cub Lake, followed in short order by Little Bear Lake. The latter is larger than it looks from the trail, since half the lake curves obliquely beyond a spit of land. Lastly, the journey leads to Big Bear Lake. This is the largest lake on the hike other than Long Lake. With the rocky cliffs of the Sierra Crest making an impressive backdrop, it is a good place to stop and enjoy the scenery before completing the hike.

Just past Big Bear Lake, there is a junction with the route to Round Lake, a worthy side trip if you have the stamina. Stay left and parallel the creek that flows out of the Bear Lakes. The creek soon veers away from the trail, which maintains a northward heading. About 0.25 mile from Big Bear Lake, the trail splits. If you stay left, you will arrive at the Lakes Basin's main trailhead. Instead, turn right and cross the creek, entering into Elwell Lakes Lodge. Pass through the lodge and walk along the dirt road. When the road merges with the main road leading the trailhead, look for a sign indicating the point where the trail leading to the Lakes Basin Campground resumes. From here it is a pleasant 0.25-mile walk through a large aspen grove back to the campground trailhead.

MILES AND DIRECTIONS

0.0 Start at the trailhead in Lakes Basin Campground. Immediately cross a bridge over a large creek.

0.75 Cross a second bridge over Gray Eagle Creek. A small waterfall is located just off the trail.

1.75 Arrive at the Long Lake dam; after a short distance along the lakeshore, begin a climb up a large talus slope.

2.4 Stay left at a junction with the trail leading to the summit of Mount Elwell.

3.75 Pass one of the Hellgramite Lakes.

4.2 Arrive at Silver Lake then proceed on the trail, passing an overlook above Long Lake.

5.0 After encountering Cub and Little Bear Lakes, the trail reaches the edge of Big Bear Lake.

5.2 Stay left at the intersection with the Round Lake Trail.

5.45 Turn right onto the trail to Elwell Lakes Lodge.

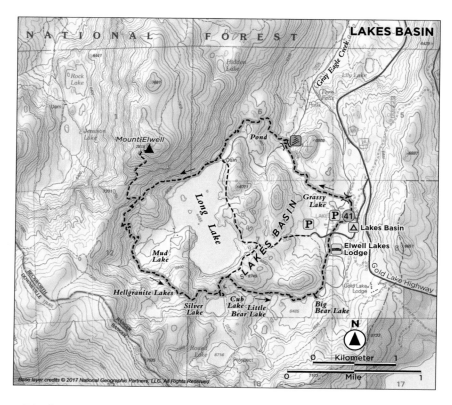

5.6 Stay straight through the lodge compound, and then proceed down the dirt road that accesses the lodge.

5.75 Cross the paved road to the signed trail leading to the Lakes Basin Campground.

6.0 Arrive back at the trailhead.

42. **SIERRA BUTTES**

WHY GO?

The trip to the summit of the stunning Sierra Buttes is one of the classic hikes of the Sierra Nevada. The trail features lakes large and small and incredible views, culminating in an exciting ascent to a marvelously exposed lookout tower. Three different trailheads offer differing lengths and difficulties, but the full hike described here features the most magnificent vistas and incredible scenery.

THE RUNDOWN

Start: Sardine Lakes trailhead
Distance: 12.0 miles out and back, with shorter options (see below)
Hiking time: 7–8 hours
Difficulty: Strenuous
Elevation gain: 3,100 feet
Season: Summer, fall
Trail surface: Packed dirt, rocky road, metal stairs

Canine compatibility: Dogs permitted
Fees and permits: None
Land status: Tahoe National Forest
Trail contact: Yuba River Ranger District, 15924 Highway 49, Camptonville 95922; (530) 288-3231; www.fs.usda.gov/main/tahoe
Other: Water is available at the Tamarack Lakes.

FINDING THE TRAILHEAD

From Sierra City, drive east on CA 49 for 5 miles. Turn left onto Gold Lake Highway and drive for 1.3 miles. Turn left onto Packer Lake Road. In 0.3 mile stay straight to continue onto Sardine Lake Road. Trailhead parking is in large pullouts on both sides of the road. **Trailhead GPS:** 39°37'17.51"N / 120°36'58.55"W

WHAT TO SEE

As you move south from the Lake Almanor area, the Sierra Nevada's northern boundary, the first truly significant peaks you will come upon are the awesome Sierra Buttes. It is here that you will encounter a splendid jumble of towering, seemingly inaccessible spires that loom majestically above large lakes. Indeed, it is the Sierra Buttes that provide the first hint of the staggering mountain landscapes that have made the Sierra famous. It stands to reason, then, that it is at the Sierra Buttes that you will find the first really epic Sierra Nevada hike. It is a challenging journey, climbing more than 3,000 feet to the very top of the Buttes, where a notoriously precarious fire lookout stands in splendid isolation above the abyss. The stairs making the final climb to the tower are bolted into the rock, allowing for a safe but spectacularly exposed ascent. It is an unforgettable experience.

The journey to the top of the Sierra Buttes begins on the side of the road that leads to the Sardine Lakes. The wide path was once a four-wheel-drive road but is now officially recognized as the Tamarack Connector Trail. Follow the old road as it makes a series of switchbacks up the side of the glacial moraine that hems in the Sardine Lakes on their north side. The trail passes through the woods for the duration of the switchbacks, with views kept to a minimum. After 1.0 mile you come around a bend and a staggering scene is revealed. The massive collection of crags rises dramatically above the large Sardine Lakes. It is easy to imagine a glacier pouring off the rocks and forming the moraines as it trails debris to its side. If you look carefully, you can see the lookout tower that is your destination. It seems impossibly far away from here.

Take heart and continue the steady climb up the flank of the moraine. Though they are similar in size, Upper Sardine Lake is actually the larger of the two. After a long, climbing traverse of the moraine, you pass the Sardine Overlook spur trail. Though the vista from the overlook is good, skip it and keep climbing. After 2.2 miles the trail begins to switchback steeply up the side of the moraine to a saddle.

From the top of the saddle, descend through the forest into a small basin. As the trail levels out, it passes numerous rock outcroppings and a substantial amount of scree. Just as at the beginning of the hike, the trail here was once an old jeep road. As the path winds and weaves through the rocky terrain, you get good views to the north toward the valley drained by Packer Creek. Watch for the occasional rock thrust upward, giving the area a bit of an unusual appearance. The path eventually crosses a rocky saddle and then makes a gentle descent until it crosses a creek, the first running water on the hike, and deposits you at the Tamarack Lakes.

Though they are not large, in terms of scenic qualities the Tamarack Lakes are in the upper echelon of mountain lakes in the Northern Sierra. Ringed by patches of meadow,

Staggering views of the Sardine Lakes and the Sierra Buttes are constant on the Tamarack Connector Trail.

willow, and pine, the lakes are backed by the ragged towers of the Sierra Buttes' northern shoulder. Few lakes north of I-5, perhaps only the Sardine Lakes, can boast such a dramatic backdrop. The name Tamarack is found throughout much of California's mountains. It was a moniker often applied by nineteenth-century naturalists to lodgepole pines. Today when you see the name, you are almost guaranteed to find lodgepoles present in that location, and these lakes are no different.

When you arrive at the Tamarack Lakes, you find a rocky road climbing up from the north and continuing around the west side of the lakes. Though four-wheel-drive vehicles are still permitted on this route, this is also the path that leads up from the Tamarack Lakes Trailhead, an option described below. Follow the road around the lower lake. The path splits, with the left visiting the upper lake, the prettier of the two. Return to the path on the right, an old road that begins to climb up the side of the lake's basin. In 0.5 mile you will reach a four-way junction. The wide road turns west here and climbs up to the top of the ridge. A narrow footpath, a shorter option, continues straight ahead. However, the road is more scenic as it takes better advantage of the Pacific Crest Trail, which has great summer wildflowers and better views. Turn right and follow it steeply up to the crest of the ridge. Once on top, you immediately encounter the Pacific Crest Trail. (**Option:** The shortest option to the summit of the Sierra Buttes joins the route here. See the Pacific Crest Trail Route below.) Turn left here to continue the hike.

Once on the Pacific Crest Trail, you pass rocky knolls that are covered with wildflowers through much of summer. Views of the north shoulder of the Sierra Buttes improve as you climb, as does the perspective to the east. When the Pacific Crest Trail eventually splits off to the right, stay left and follow the crest of the ridge. Soon the singletrack trail option on the route from the Tamarack Lakes joins the trail on the left. From here the path curves along the rim of the uppermost part of the lakes' basin, with good views down to the crystalline pools of water set amid the forest. The trail eventually veers away from the edge and begins to climb through dense forest up the Buttes' shoulder. The trees get larger as you climb, and eventually large boulders begin to line the trail.

As you near the top of the shoulder, watch for well-established use trails heading off to the left. Follow one of these to the rim, where you are blessed with an astounding vista. Below lies Young America Lake, a large alpine gem tucked into a wide, rocky cirque high in the jumble of the Sierra Buttes' spires. Beyond Young America Lake, the Sardine Lakes are visible between the two moraines that flow from the Sierra Buttes. In the distance, the headwaters of the North Fork of the Yuba River can be seen. It is an inspiring sight and a hopeful indicator that you are near the top. Return to the main trail and turn left (toward the southwest). You will shortly arrive at a clearing that looks like it was once the end of an old four-wheel-drive road. Pick up the trail on the other side and commence climbing the final set of switchbacks on the trail. In 0.25 mile you reach the top of the switchbacks on the side of the fire lookout's dirt access road.

Once you reach the road, you know you are just below the summit. Turn left and follow the road as it switchbacks up the last couple hundred feet to the base of the fire lookout. As you bend around a large crag, the lookout and its flying staircase are

The north side of the Sierra Buttes reflect in Upper Tamarack Lake.

finally revealed. Before you climb the stairs, pause and read the monument to the young men who installed the staircase. It must have been an exciting and harrowing effort. Start climbing the stairs, which are broken into three flights. Though they are securely mounted to the rock and have stout railings, the exposure here at the top of the Sierra Buttes can be unnerving. Press on to the top, and then make your way over to the base of the lookout.

Climb the final set of stairs up to the catwalk. When you reach the top, you are treated to a staggering 360-degree panorama of Northern California. Mountains, remote ridges, the Sardine Lakes, and even the great Central Valley lie at your feet. Walk out to the infamous northeast corner of the lookout and note that the catwalk extends out into space, the crags of the Sierra Buttes lying far below. It is exhilarating. From here, make the journey back to your starting trailhead.

MILES AND DIRECTIONS

0.0 Start at the Sardine Lakes Trailhead, up the Tamarack Connector Trail.

1.0 The trail swings onto the flank of a long moraine, revealing an amazing view of the Sierra Buttes.

1.8 Stay right at the junction with the Sardine Overlook Trail.

2.5 Reach the top of a saddle and begin descending toward the Tamarack Lakes.

3.4 Arrive at the Tamarack Lakes. From there continue on the Tamarack Connector Trail, which begins climbing to the Pacific Crest Trail between Upper and Lower Tamarack Lakes.

4.2 Turn left onto the Pacific Crest Trail.

4.5 Stay left when the Pacific Crest Trail veers off to the right.

5.25 Follow a short spur trail to the Young America Lake overlook.

5.6 Turn left onto the dirt road just below the summit.

6.0 Arrive at the Sierra Butte lookout tower. Turn around to retrace your steps.

12.0 Arrive back at the trailhead where you started.

OPTIONS

The entire trip to the top is more than some hikers have the time or desire to take on. Thankfully, the summit is still within reach. Of two alternative trailheads, the first offers a more modest but still awesome hike that begins near the Tamarack Lakes, while the second begins on the Pacific Crest Trail and leads directly to the summit. Both are shorter

Inaccessible Young America Lake is hidden in a cirque high above the Sardine Lakes.

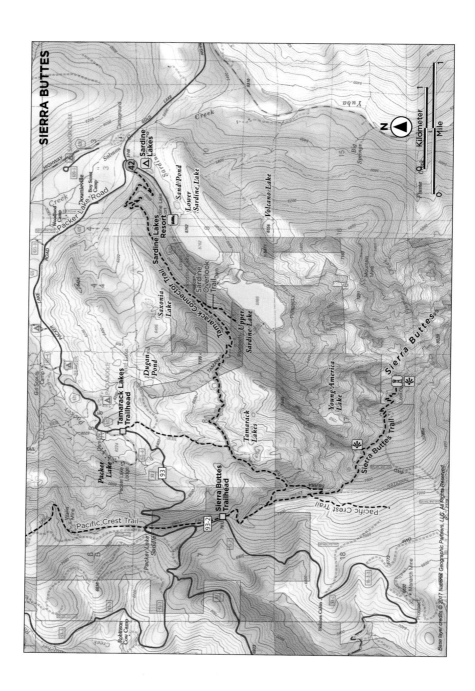

SIERRA BUTTES

than the full hike and require less climbing, though they still demand some serious exertion to get to the top. Of course there are also variations.

TAMARACK LAKES ROUTE

This 6.8-mile out and back is moderately strenuous.

Finding the trailhead: From Sierra City, drive east on CA 49 for 5 miles. Turn left onto Gold Lake Highway and drive for 1.3 miles. Turn left onto Packer Lake Road. In 0.3 mile turn right to stay on Packer Lake Road. Stay on this road for 2.8 miles and then turn right into the Tamarack Lakes Trailhead. **Trailhead GPS:** 39°37'18.51"N / 120°39'11.69"W

If you are looking for a shorter route to the top of the Sierra Buttes, want to still enjoy the beautiful Tamarack Lakes basin, but are not keen on making the entire hike, this is an excellent option. The Tamarack Lakes Route climbs from near Packer Lake to the Tamarack Lakes where it joins the main route described in this chapter. This option requires 2,300 feet of elevation gain. From the parking area on Packer Lake Road, cross the pavement and arrive at the trailhead. (*Caution:* Four-wheel-drive vehicles are permitted to drive on this road so stay alert for their presence.) Begin hiking up the wide, rocky road. Stay right at the fork and continue up the hill. You will soon be hiking alongside the creek flowing out of Lower Tamarack Lake. From here it is only a short distance up to the lakes, 0.9 mile from the trailhead. Continue from milepost 3.4 of the featured hike where the Packer Lake Trail joins the Sierra Buttes Trail, heading southwest.

PACIFIC CREST TRAIL ROUTE

This is a 5.0-mile out and back that is moderately easy.

Finding the trailhead: From Sierra City, drive east on CA 49 for 5 miles. Turn left onto Gold Lake Highway and drive for 1.3 miles. Turn left onto Packer Lake Road. In 0.3 mile turn right to stay on Packer Lake Road. Stay on this road for 4.3 miles. After 2.6 miles you pass Packer Lake and the road becomes CR 621/FR 93. This paved road then winds steeply up into the mountains and arrives at a junction with multiple roads. Veer left and stay on the pavement. Drive 0.3 mile and stay straight to continue onto dirt FR 93-2. Continue 0.2 mile down to the Sierra Buttes Trailhead on the Pacific Crest Trail. **Trailhead GPS:** 39°36'41.45"N / 120°39'55.07"W

While this route lacks many of the epic views of the Sierra Buttes offered by the full hike, it is still very scenic. Further, it is the most direct and popular route and is significantly shorter. The trailhead is higher than the other two options but still demands an elevation gain of 1,600 feet. To hike this route, head south from the Sierra Buttes Trailhead on the Pacific Crest Trail. You immediately begin to climb a steep path that switchbacks a few times before leveling off at the top of the ridge. Once the grade eases, you are quickly joined by the old jeep road coming up from the Tamarack Lakes, 0.5 mile from the Sierra Buttes Trailhead. Continue as for the featured hike, starting at milepost 4.2 by going straight on the PCT.

43. GLACIER LAKE

WHY GO?

This hike through one of the most extensively glaciated high-country regions in the Northern Sierra is packed with far-reaching vistas, beautiful peaks, and alpine lakes. The trail leads from a tremendous trailhead vista to tiny Glacier Lake, set beneath the rocky crags of the Black Buttes.

THE RUNDOWN

Start: Trailhead on east side of parking area
Distance: 7.4 miles out and back
Hiking time: 3–4 hours
Difficulty: Moderately easy
Elevation gain: 1,150 feet
Season: Summer, fall
Trail surface: Packed dirt, rocky
Canine compatibility: Dogs permitted

Fees and permits: None
Land status: Tahoe National Forest
Trail contact: Yuba River Ranger District, 15924 Highway 49, Camptonville 95922; (530) 288-3231; www.fs.usda.gov/main/tahoe
Other: Water is available at Glacier Lake.

FINDING THE TRAILHEAD

From I-80, 74 miles east of Sacramento or 24 miles west of Truckee, take the CA 20 exit for Nevada City/Grass Valley. Continue on CA 20 for 3.8 miles then turn right onto Bowman Lake Road/FR 18. Drive 6.3 miles on this paved road. Turn right onto Grouse Ridge Road and drive 5.1 miles on this bumpy but easily drivable dirt road. Just after passing the Grouse Ridge Campground, turn right into the large trailhead parking area. **Trailhead GPS:** 39°23'28.00"N / 120°36'32.34"W

WHAT TO SEE

The headwaters of the South and Middle Forks of the Yuba River consist of a large knot of heavily glaciated mountains. Dozens of lakes and countless tarns occupy broad plateaus, shallow valleys, and rolling terrain situated beneath tall peaks. The area is primarily composed of granite, but, as is common in the Northern Sierra, there are notable intrusions of gabbro and sedimentary rocks. Though it lacks any form of legal protection, the heart of this mountainous area is essentially a wilderness area. Indeed, the Yuba River headwaters are one of the largest wildlands in the Northern Sierra that lack formal protections. Part of the reason for this is the presence of numerous large reservoirs that were initially constructed for hydraulic mining and hydroelectric purposes. Despite the presence of these lakes around the periphery of the mountains, hikers can still travel to the interior and enjoy classic Sierra Nevada scenery.

The distant peaks of the Sierra crest line the horizon beyond Sanford Lake and Red Mountain.

The hike begins at the trailhead between the Grouse Ridge Campground and the fire lookout tower. The trailhead alone is worth the drive, as it is blessed with an incredible panorama that stretches from the Black Buttes to the east to the Sierra Buttes in the northeast and all the way up to Lassen Peak, 90 miles to the north. The trail departs from the trailhead on the east side of the parking area. It goes downhill and joins the trail coming from the campground to the south. Turn left at the trail and begin a steady descent down toward the rolling woodlands to the northeast. When you first reach the trail, another incredible view greets you. Directly below the trail, Sanford Lake peaks out from behind a band of trees. The mountains drop off into a deep canyon just past the lake, and in the distance rises the gray bulk of Red Mountain, capped by its namesake red crags. In the distance beyond the crimson peak, you can see the high country of the Granite Chief Wilderness to the left of the summit, and the majestic Crystal Range in the Desolation Wilderness rises far in the distance on the right.

Continue your descent and enter a heavily wooded area. After 0.5 mile pass the trail on your left that leads to Milk, Island, and Feeley Lakes. The trail continues to lose elevation for another 0.5 mile before leveling off in the midst of dense forest. A short distance after you reach the level forest bottom, another trail branches off to the left. This time the path leads to the Crooked Lakes and Sawmill Lakes. Stay right and continue hiking through the easy terrain. Though it is not readily visible from the trail, long Sand Ridge now rises to the north. The forest prevents much opportunity to observe the ridge, but the presence of small granite domes around the trail are good compensation. Watch for small tarns through the trees just south of the trail.

Nearly 2.0 miles from the trailhead, the trail skirts the edge of a lovely meadow that has excellent wildflowers in summer. At the meadow you get your only good opportunity to spot the rounded top of Sand Ridge. As you near the far end of the meadow, look just south of the trail for a pond that is in the advanced state of becoming a meadow. As you leave the pond behind, the trail begins to climb earnestly. It follows a small stream that lasts until about midsummer. This is the only running water until you reach Glacier Lake. After climbing along the water for a little while, the trail levels off and enters another area with large trees, providing a little more shade before you hit the open terrain near the Black Buttes.

Just beyond the small wooded area, the trail climbs again, this time over bare rock that is dotted with bright wildflowers. The path levels off again and passes a few beautiful tarns on the left. A faint track leads past the clear waters and up to the edge of a bluff. Here there is a fantastic vista of English Mountain and the awesome crags of the Sierra Buttes. Though most of the lakes themselves are not visible because of forest cover, the area directly below this lookout is the Five Lakes Basin. Only the westernmost of the lakes can be seen from this spot.

Head back to the trail and continue climbing one last time until you are finally deposited on a rocky knoll above Glacier Lake. You can see the lake, but this area is still too wooded to get a great view. From here you can either head south along the lake toward the base of the Black Buttes or north toward the outlet of the lake. The latter offers better

The spur trail leads to a great view of the Sierra Buttes and the Five Lakes Basin area.

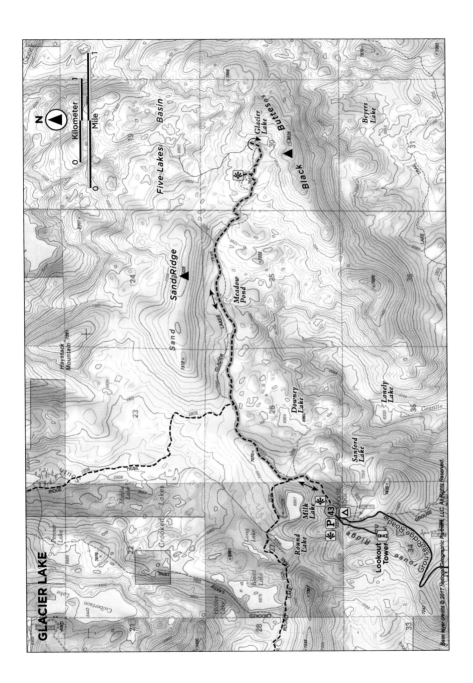

The brooding towers of the Black Buttes form a dramatic wall above Glacier Lake.

views. Follow use trails down to the water and along the shoreline. Cross over the lake's outlet to a rocky shoreline. Here you can see the towering, dark towers of the Black Buttes, possibly the most rugged crags in the Yuba headwaters area. Snow clings to the cliffs well into summer, sometimes all the way into August. The outlet of the creek flows north in the Five Lakes Basin. A rough path follows the stream. If you want to explore these lakes set in lovely granite bowls, a better option is to head back to the knoll above the lake and follow a more established trail from there. Otherwise, when you are ready to return to the trailhead, follow the trail back the way you came.

MILES AND DIRECTIONS

0.0 Start at the Grouse Ridge Trailhead, where there is a spectacular panorama. Follow the trail down the hill and turn left when you join the trail coming from the campground.

0.5 Stay right at the junction with the trail to Milk Lake.

1.0 Stay right again when the trail to Sawmill Lake branches off to the left.

2.0 Pass a small meadow below Sand Ridge.

3.7 Arrive at Glacier Lake. Return the way you came.

7.4 Arrive back at the trailhead.

44. FIVE LAKES BASIN

WHY GO?

This hike offers quick access to the Granite Chief Wilderness, climbing through rugged terrain to the peaceful Five Lakes Basin.

THE RUNDOWN

Start: Trailhead on right (north) side of Alpine Meadows Road
Distance: 4.2 miles out and back
Hiking time: 2–3 hours
Difficulty: Moderately easy
Elevation gain: 1,000 feet
Season: Summer, fall
Trail surface: Packed dirt, rocky
Canine compatibility: Dogs permitted
Fees and permits: None
Land status: Granite Chief Wilderness, Tahoe National Forest

Trail contact: Truckee Ranger District, 10811 Stockrest Springs Rd., Truckee 96161; (530) 587.3558; www.fs.usda.gov/main/tahoe
Other: Much of this trail is on a forest service right-of-way through private land. Please respect the property owners and do not leave the trail until it enters the Granite Chief Wilderness. Water is available at the Five Lakes.

FINDING THE TRAILHEAD

Drive on CA 89, either 3.5 miles north from Tahoe City or 10 miles south from Truckee. Turn west onto Alpine Meadows Road and drive for 2.1 miles. The trailhead is on the right side of the road, and parking is in several wide spots along the pavement. **Trailhead GPS:** 39°10'45.93"N / 120°13'47.31"W

WHAT TO SEE

Occupying a high spot on the Sierra Nevada crest to the northwest of Lake Tahoe, the Granite Chief Wilderness is a pocket of wildlands that is heavily influenced by several notable geologic regions. The heart of the wilderness is a granite core that is encroached by both volcanic and sedimentary rocks. Consequently, the wilderness has a very diverse appearance. The Granite Chief Wilderness lies on the divide between the American and Truckee Rivers. The latter is the outlet of Lake Tahoe and flows east to Pyramid Lake in Nevada; the former is one of the principal tributaries of the Sacramento River. While the western boundary of the wilderness is located in fairly remote country, the eastern side is beset by civilization. Both the famous Squaw Valley and Alpine Meadows ski areas are located directly adjacent to the Granite Chief Wilderness.

The hike to the Five Lakes Basin threads the needle between these developed areas and climbs a series of rugged slopes and cliffs to reach the small cluster of lakes. The trip up to the Granite Chief Wilderness takes you from civilization into a primeval world where rivers are born and the land is untouched by the civilizing forces just a few miles away. The proximity to Lake Tahoe makes this a good option for hikers visiting the lake area who want a quick shot into the high mountains that surround the lake.

The hike begins on the north side of Alpine Meadows Road. The trail begins climbing immediately as it passes through dense brush. A few groves of trees offer a little shade as you climb, but in the open areas you begin to get good views of the Bear Creek Drainage. Large dark rock outcroppings line the drainage, protruding from the dense forest that cloaks the area. The creek begins in the large basin occupied by the Alpine Meadows ski area, which also comes into view as you climb. The large bowl where the ski resort is located is composed of volcanic rock, as is the rock the trail passes at the beginning of the hike.

The trail climbs a few small switchbacks before continuing its traverse to the west. After 0.6 mile the trail begins a series of short switchbacks that are stacked upon one another. As you gain elevation, look above you and note the light-colored granite outcropping capped by dark volcanic rock. The trail is nearing the transition zone where the main granite pluton of the Granite Chief Wilderness abuts the volcanic pyroclastic flow that overlaid this area. This arrangement, where the ancient volcanic flows covered the granite bedrock only to be subsequently cleared away, is typical of the Central Sierra.

Once you reach the top of the switchbacks, the trail continues on the side of the canyon a little farther before it reaches a hairpin turn that rounds the shoulder of the ridge you have been climbing. Here the scenery shifts dramatically. As you round the bend, a line of granite cliffs is revealed to the west, rising above a small, wooded valley. The brushy volcanic slopes of the first part of the trail are replaced by crags of light-colored,

The climb to the Five Lakes Basin offers good views on the complex geology of the Alpine Meadows area.

The largest of the Five Lakes
has a good perspective on
Squaw Peak.

wind-eroded granite. This rock has a somewhat different composition than the cliffs on the other side of the valley. At the hairpin turn, note the towers of a ski chairlift. These were installed for a proposed lift that would connect Squaw Valley and Alpine Meadows. The upper terminus of the towers is near the summit of KT-22, the peak directly above the trail. The plan met with significant opposition, and only the towers have been put into place.

From the hairpin turn, the trail climbs up the flanks of the little valley. As you climb you pass alongside more eroded granite. In late spring and early summer, the valley echoes with the sound of snowmelt streams racing over the rocks. By midsummer these are usually long gone. As the trail nears the end of the valley, it begins to swing north. You can look above and note the upper flanks of Squaw Peak, the highest point in Squaw Valley.

As you round the headwall of the canyon, the trail levels off and a sign greets you at the boundary of the Granite Chief Wilderness. For the first time the trail is on public land and it is permissible to leave the path. However, stay on the trail as it enters a shady forest and press on for about 0.2 mile. As the trail maintains its westerly course, you can see the first of the Five Lakes below the trail. It is not a large lake, but it does entice hikers to head down to it. Staying on the trail, proceed through the forest until you reach the shores of the largest and prettiest of the Five Lakes. From the south shore, Squaw Peak makes a fine backdrop, though you can make out a chairlift terminal from this point, a reminder

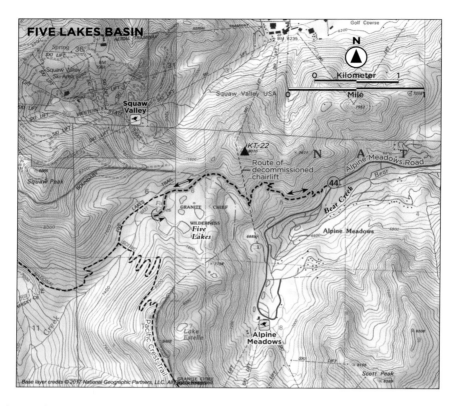

that civilization is encroaching on this wilderness. The Five Lakes do not occupy a typical glacial cirque like most alpine lakes in the Sierra Nevada. Instead they are nestled into a depression right on the crest of the Sierra Nevada. The Five Lakes Trail continues a little past the lake and connects to the Pacific Crest Trail. Enjoy the pristine setting and explore the lakes in the basin. When you are done, return the way you came.

MILES AND DIRECTIONS

0.0 Start at the Five Lakes Trailhead.

1.0 Round a hairpin turn and enter a granite valley.

2.1 Arrive at the largest of the Five Lakes. Retrace your path to the trailhead.

4.2 Arrive back at the trailhead.

45. **RUBICON TRAIL**

WHY GO?

Following the contours of Lake Tahoe, the Rubicon Trail explores one of the few stretches of wild shoreline on the spectacular lake. Fiercely blue waters, wide ranging vistas, and a great waterfall all combine to make this a memorable hike.

THE RUNDOWN

Start: Trailhead near Lester Beach
Distance: 9.8 miles out and back (shuttle possible)
Hiking time: 4–5 hours
Difficulty: Moderate
Elevation gain: 900 feet
Season: Spring, summer, fall
Trail surface: Packed dirt, rocky, pavement
Canine compatibility: Dogs not permitted

Fees and permits: Entrance fee
Land status: D. L. Bliss State Park
Trail contact: PO Box 266, Tahoma 96142; (530) 525-7277; www.parks .ca.gov/?page_id=505
Other: This hike can be done as a partial shuttle when the bus operated by the Tahoe Transportation District is running. Operation times vary per season.

FINDING THE TRAILHEAD

Starting at the junction of CA 89 and US 50, drive north on CA 89 for 10.7 miles. Turn right onto Lester Beach Road at the entrance to D. L. Bliss State Park. Drive on this road through the park, passing the campgrounds and following signs to the Rubicon Trail until the road ends at the trailhead. The parking area is not large and can fill up quickly. It is best to get an early start. **Trailhead GPS:** 38°59'54.81"N / 120°5'51.15"W

WHAT TO SEE

Lake Tahoe is the superlative landmark of the northern Sierra Nevada. The massive lake is the largest alpine lake in North America, the sixth-largest lake by volume in the United States, and the second-deepest lake in North America. Yet despite its statistical greatness, it is the mesmerizing beauty of the fiercely blue water and the ring of mountains surrounding it that make Lake Tahoe such an incredible hiking destination. For hikers, the only problem is the paucity of great trails in a natural or even wild setting. Much of the mountain terrain around the lake may be wilderness, but the lake's shoreline has experienced its share of development. Thankfully, the Rubicon Trail satisfies the need for hikers looking to experience Lake Tahoe at a primeval level.

The hike on the Rubicon Trail begins near Lester Beach in D. L. Bliss State Park. The path then winds south, first above then along the shore. It crosses over Emerald Point

The distant Carson Range and the deep blue water of Lake Tahoe are visible from a precarious section of the Rubicon Trail.

and then heads west along the north shore of beautiful Emerald Bay before arriving at Vikingsholm and Eagle Falls. The trail has little elevation gain and can be completed as a long out-and-back hike. During summer months, a bus connects Emerald Bay and D. L. Bliss State Parks along CA 89. It is possible to shorten the trip by utilizing this option, but the bus does not go all the way down to the trailhead, and a couple miles of road must also be hiked. If time is not pressing, the hike along the lake is much more enjoyable.

The Rubicon Trail begins at the small trailhead near Lester Beach. This trail can get busy and the parking lot full, so start early if you want to get a parking spot. The bonus to an early start is the morning light coming in from the east and illuminating the shoreline, coves, and mountains to the south as you hike. You are also blessed with a quiet, serene lake before the powerboats start heading out for the day. The first part of the hike is one of the best. Head east from the trailhead and immediately enjoy a great view of the north half of Lake Tahoe. As you round the granite crags above Rubicon Point, the trail is routed along a narrow ledge about 150 feet above the water. In some places the rocks above overhang the path and you have to duck and weave along this section. Iron bars with chain fencing have been installed for safety, and wooden bridges cross gaps in the ledge. It is a wonderful section of trail and one of the most memorable.

All too soon the ledge comes to an end above a cove, where you get your first good view to the south. The blue lake and white rocks of the shore contrast against the green trees. You also get a glimpse of Stevens and Red Lake Peaks, the headwaters of the Upper Truckee River to the south, and some of the mountains that line the eastern edge of the Desolation Wilderness high above the lake. Pass a trail that connects to the Lighthouse Trail. This path begins at the same trailhead and visits a small, old wooden lighthouse before joining the Rubicon Trail. From this junction the trail climbs gently to the south before turning west and entering a dense forest. This is the only part of the hike where there are no views of the lake. Eventually you emerge from the heavy canopy and can enjoy the lake again. The trail then makes a gradual descent toward the lake, reaching the edge about 2.0 miles from the trailhead.

Follow the rocky shoreline for 0.7 mile before turning inland to cut across Rubicon Point. Along the way there are opportunities to scramble down to the water or relax on large boulders next to the lake. The best place to access the water is right where the trail cuts inland, where a little beach lies just off the trail. To continue to Eagle Falls, follow the trail inland and in 0.4 mile arrive at the edge of Emerald Bay, perhaps the most iconic destination at Lake Tahoe.

Emerald Bay is the remnant of significant glacial activity. A large sheet of ice flowed out of the mountains, leaving moraines, debris from the glacier's path, piled up on either side. The hole scoured out by the glacier filled with water, walled in by the moraines, to create its current appearance. Similar in formation to nearby Cascade and Fallen Leaf Lakes, Emerald Bay was just close enough to Lake Tahoe to allow the water from the lake to creep in and claim it as part of Tahoe itself. Today it is one of the most popular corners of the lake. As you follow its shoreline west, tall mountains rise precipitously above the water. These mountains are part of the outstanding Desolation Wilderness. Note rocky Fannette Island in the middle of the bay. This is the only island in Lake Tahoe.

As you follow the Rubicon Trail west along Emerald Bay, you pass through Boat Camp, a campground for boaters, before crossing over a few small streams, the first significant running water along the trail. Shortly after that you pass beneath huge old ponderosa pines and arrive at Vikingsholm, a Scandinavian-style mansion built in 1929 and

Eagle Falls

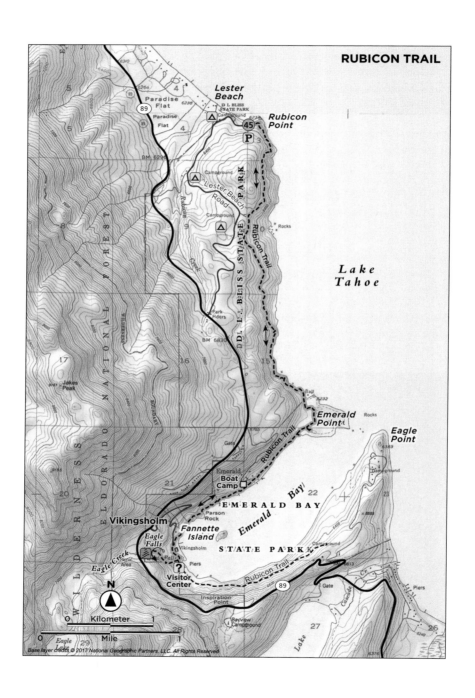

RUBICON TRAIL

now part of Emerald Bay State Park. Note that most of the foot traffic here approaches from a paved road to the right. The road functions as a footpath for visitors coming from the parking area up on CA 89. If you plan to use the shuttle, use this road to get to the bus stop.

Stay left and follow the path past the remarkable Vikingsholm. As you near the visitor center, veer right off the Rubicon Trail. The trail actually continues around the south shore of the bay, but Eagle Falls is a much better destination. Follow the path west from the visitor center and begin climbing alongside Eagle Creek. Pass a wooden bridge over Eagle Creek on your left and keep climbing a little farther before arriving at a vista point at the base of the falls. Eagle Falls cascades powerfully down the cliff and crashes into the rocks below. Higher up, Upper Eagle Falls can be seen through the trees, though CA 89 offers better views of this waterfall and access to it. Enjoy the cool spray and the view before returning to Vikingsholm. From there either shuttle over to D. L. Bliss State Park or retrace your steps back on the Rubicon Trail.

MILES AND DIRECTIONS

0.0 Start the hike by heading east on the Rubicon Trail. The path quickly turns south and passes over the fenced ledge section.

0.6 Pass the spur that connects to the Lighthouse Trail.

2.6 Cut inland across Rubicon Point.

3.0 Arrive at the north shore of Emerald Bay.

4.5 Turn left and walk past Vikingsholm toward the visitor center.

4.6 At the visitor center, turn right onto the trail to Eagle Falls.

4.9 Arrive at the base of Eagle Falls. To get back to the trailhead, retrace your steps on the Rubicon Trail.

9.8 Arrive back at the trailhead.

46. **TWIN LAKES (DESOLATION WILDERNESS)**

WHY GO?

The hike to Twin Lakes is an easy and exciting trip over granite slabs and along rushing creeks and waterfalls into the stunning backcountry of the Desolation Wilderness, the Northern Sierra's most extensive and breathtaking wildlands.

THE RUNDOWN

Start: Paved path from the Twin Lakes Trailhead

Distance: 6.6 miles out and back or overnight

Hiking time: 3–4 hours

Difficulty: Moderate

Elevation gain: 1,160 feet

Season: Summer, fall

Trail surface: Packed dirt, rocky, rock slabs

Canine compatibility: Dogs permitted

Fees and permits: None

Land status: Desolation Wilderness, Eldorado National Forest

Trail contact: Pacific Ranger District, 7887 Highway 50, Pollock Pines 95726; (530) 644-2349; www.fs.usda .gov/eldorado

Other: The trailhead parking area is small and the trail serves a few destinations. If the lot is full, an overflow parking area is available 0.9 mile west by the visitor center. Water is available in creeks and lakes.

FINDING THE TRAILHEAD

From Sacramento, drive east on US 50 for 76 miles. Turn left onto Wrights Lake Road and continue north for 8.1 windy, paved miles to Wrights Lake. Near the small visitor center, turn right to continue on narrow, paved Wrights Lake Road for 0.9 mile to the end of the road at the Twin Lakes Trailhead. **Trailhead GPS:** 38°50'58.72"N / 120°13'32.72"W

WHAT TO SEE

The Desolation Wilderness is Lake Tahoe's great alpine backyard, full of high peaks, glittering lakes, and extensively glaciated valleys. It is here that the Sierra Nevada first completely reveals its iconic nature: a vast and wild expanse of granite and water, beckoning hikers to lose themselves in its sublime natural cathedral. It is here that John Muir's eloquent naming of the Sierra as "the Range of Light" is first proved unquestionably true. You may think that enjoying this alpine wonderland requires significant effort. Though long backpacking trips are common in the Desolation Wilderness, there are also plenty of shorter hikes that make perfect day trips. The finest of these is the hike into the Twin Lakes, located on the west side of the Crystal Range, the Desolation Wilderness's tallest and grandest range. The hike makes a steady ascent through a patchwork of forest and brush before breaking out onto open granite slabs. After running parallel to the cascade-laden South Fork of Silver Creek, the trail reaches the first of the Twin Lakes, set in a sensational granite bowl. From there you can push deeper into the basin, where wildflowers are abundant and beautiful Island Lake offers more unforgettable scenery.

From the trailhead parking area, follow the paved path north, past some private summer homes. A trail branches off to the right just before you reach a bridge that spans Silver Creek. Take this path and follow it through a series of meadows for 0.5 mile before that trail begins its ascent to Twin Lakes. The grade at the beginning of the trail is the hike's steepest. Press on, crossing a granite slab before reentering a brushy area. Soon the path pulls close to a small creek, which is audible as you climb.

After climbing for 1.4 miles you reach the boundary of the Desolation Wilderness, where the trail splits. The path to the right leads to Grouse and Smith Lakes. Stay left and promptly cross over the creek that flows from the aforementioned lakes. From here the route climbs to the northeast, crossing one bare granite bench after another. The large basin that contains the Twin Lakes slowly reveals itself as you near the wide entrance. Without trees to obscure the views, vistas to the west out over the middle elevations of the Sierra Nevada foothills are good, and whet the appetite for what lies just ahead.

The trail, often marked by cairns or lines of rocks along the path, finally pulls alongside Silver Creek 2.0 miles from the trailhead. The water pours over a lovely cascade just as you arrive alongside the creek. Just 0.2 mile farther, listen for a place where the sound of the water has gotten louder. Leave the trail here and carefully scramble over the granite down to the edge of a narrow gully. Here there is a very linear, rectangular gap in the

The trail to the Twin Lakes passes beautiful cascades on the South Fork of Silver Creek.

Alpine splendor at the Desolation Wilderness' Twin Lakes.

rocks where the creek shoots through and tumbles down a vein of rough rock, forming an unusual and beautiful waterfall.

Lower Twin Lake lies only 0.5 mile past the waterfall. The way there first crosses more granite slabs as the gates of the basin now tower majestically overhead. The path then passes through an area where a network of small ponds and meadows dot the granite landscape. Small rivulets of water flow between the ponds, compounding the beauty with their gurgling. Just beyond the tiny meadow is Lower Twin Lake. It is an inspiring sight. The landmarks are arrayed in just the right way, as though someone had designed them as an ideal mountain wonderland. The lake, bound by more granite slabs, is large and lovely. Behind it is a high, sheer granite cliff over which pours a stringy but sizable waterfall. Upper Lake, at nearly the same elevation as the lower lake, lies at the base of the falls. Surrounding all of this are towering peaks, which are among the tallest in the Northern Sierra.

From Lower Twin Lake, cross over the outlet and follow the trail deeper into the large basin. After passing through a pretty little meadow on the lake's north side, climb up a long granite slope before gently dropping down to small Boomerang Lake. The narrow path skirts the lake's south shore, crosses a narrow isthmus between it and a smaller pond, and then arrives at a small, unnamed lake surrounded by wildflowers. The view south from here toward towering Mount Price is one of the prettiest you will find anywhere. The trail continues, climbing a rock bluff, and deposits you at the edge of Island Lake. The wide expanse of the basin surrounds you here, soaring up the long slope toward Mount Price, which at 9,975 feet is just 8 feet shorter than Pyramid Peak, the highest point in the Desolation Wilderness. Ahead of you is Island Lake, backed by a dark gray cirque and flanked by Peak 9,441, which is partially composed of an unusual reddish rock. At your feet are delicate alpine gardens, laden with wildflowers watered by a matrix of small streams. There are many small tarns and meadows scattered around the basin. The

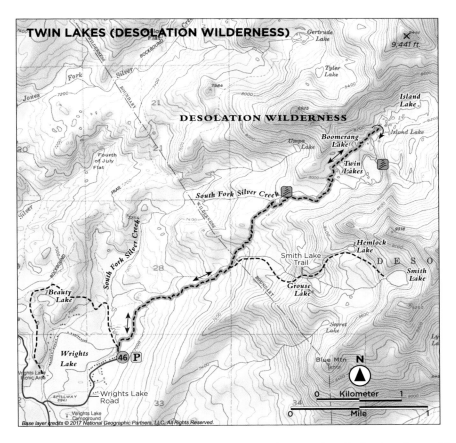

open, nearly treeless terrain makes cross–country travel easy, and exploring is a pleasurable and fruitful endeavor. When you have had your fill, return the way you came.

MILES AND DIRECTIONS

0.0   Start at the trailhead and follow the paved path north. Quickly turn right onto the trail just before the wooden bridge over Silver Creek.

1.4   Just after crossing the boundary into the Desolation Wilderness, stay left at the fork and cross a large tributary of Silver Creek.

2.0   Reach Silver Creek.

2.7   Arrive at Lower Twin Lake. Cross the outlet and hike east to continue to Island Lake.

3.3   Enjoy the serenity at Island Lake. Retrace your steps from here.

6.6   Arrive back at the trailhead.

47. DESOLATION VALLEY

WHY GO?

This memorable and beautiful hike pierces directly into the awe-inspiring Desolation Valley, in the heart of the Desolation Wilderness. The first half of the hike ascends above Tamarack Lake to a saddle dotted with scattered meadows. The latter half then makes a loop connecting massive Lake Aloha with beautiful Lake of the Woods, offering sublime vistas.

THE RUNDOWN

Start: Water taxi dock near Echo Chalet
Total distance: 7.9-mile lollipop (from water taxi landing)
Hiking time: 4–5 hours
Difficulty: Moderate
Elevation gain: 1,325 feet
Season: Summer, fall
Trail surface: Packed dirt, rocky
Canine compatibility: Dogs permitted; extra fee required for dogs on the water taxi
Fees and permits: Fee for water taxi; check with the Echo Chalet for prices.

Land status: Desolation Wilderness, Lake Tahoe Basin Management Unit
Trail contact: 35 College Dr., South Lake Tahoe 96150; (530) 543-2600; www.fs.usda.gov/ltbmu
Other: This hike requires a water taxi to reach the trailhead. For hikers who want to skip the water taxi, a 2.5-mile one-way walk on the Pacific Crest Trail from Echo Chalet leads to the pier at the end of Upper Echo Lake. Water is available at numerous lakes.

FINDING THE TRAILHEAD

From the junction of US 50 and CA 89 in South Lake Tahoe, drive west on US 50 for 8.6 miles. Just after Echo Summit, turn right onto Echo Summit Road/Johnson Pass Road. Proceed 0.6 mile then turn left onto Echo Lake Road/FR 11N05. Follow this road 0.9 mile to the Echo Lakes, where the water taxi departs for the trailhead. **Trailhead GPS:** 38°50'47.80"N / 120°4'42.86"W

WHAT TO SEE

If the Desolation Wilderness is the first occurrence of the Sierra Nevada's great glacier-polished granite landscapes, then the Desolation Valley is the first epic landscape where all the hallmarks of the Sierra come together in perfect harmony and grand scale. The valley is bounded on the west by the towering summits of the Crystal Range, the magnificent white rampart of the Sierra Nevada's main crest. Beneath the Crystal Range is a rolling plain of granite knobs and buttes and scattered lakes tucked into rocky bowls. It is a lovely place to explore. However, the most incredible feature in the valley is massive Lake Aloha.

Tamarack Lake and Ralston Peak are a gorgeous spectacle while hiking to Lake Aloha.

The enormous lake is entirely bounded by an extensive rocky shoreline with countless peninsulas, islands, and coves. It is a unique and tremendous sight. The east side of the valley is formed by the dark rocks of tall Jacks Peak, one of the highest summits in the Desolation Wilderness. It is a monumental and sweeping scene, one of the most fantastic sights in the Northern Sierra.

The most direct option to reach Desolation Valley by trail is to approach from the Echo Lakes. To accomplish this, you can either follow the Pacific Crest Trail for 2.5 miles along the northern shores of the lakes or take the water taxi across the lakes from the Echo Chalet. From the pier where the taxi delivers hikers, it is only 3.3 miles on the Pacific Crest Trail to the shores of Lake Aloha. This option shaves a significant distance off the hike and makes the trip to this most spectacular corner of the Desolation Wilderness an easier option. **Note:** A fee is charged for the taxi each way, and a minimum number of people are needed on each ride. Thankfully, during the summer months when the wilderness is accessible, there is usually not much difficulty getting the requisite number of people needed to make the water taxi cost-effective.

If you are taking the PCT all the way from the Echo Chalet, the trail picks up east of the chalet area and bends around the north side of the lower lake. Some of the trail was blasted into the bare granite above the water. If you are taking the water taxi, it is a quick and scenic ride through the lakes that involves an impressive maneuver through the narrow strait that separates the upper and lower lake. You disembark from the taxi at Upper Echo Lake's northwest corner. From the dock, walk east just a few yards to find the short trail that leads up to the Pacific Crest Trail. Turn left when you reach it.

From the junction of the Pacific Crest Trail and the short path from the Upper Echo Lake dock, head west, passing first through forested terrain before breaking out onto bare rock. As you climb up the rugged trail, look back to the east for a great view of the Echo Lakes. After climbing steadily for 0.7 mile, you enter the Desolation Wilderness and pass by the trail leading up the steep slopes to Triangle Lake. Stay left on the Pacific Crest Trail and enter a second wooded stretch before once again crossing more rocky terrain, where you soon arrive at the spur leading down to Tamarack Lake, about 1.1 miles from Upper Echo Lake.

Tamarack Lake is the largest of a trio of mountain lakes at the foot of tall Mount Ralston, which looms over the large basin. Though they seem separated by distance and geography, this is part of the same large glacial valley that contains the Echo Lakes. The spur down to Tamarack Lake is short, and if you have the time, it is worth dropping down and visiting this scenic spot. If you are looking for a shorter trip, exploring the other bodies of water in the basin, especially Ralston Lake, is a great option. Continuing the climb up from the spur trail, you soon get great views of Tamarack Lake from above. Ralston Peak continues to dominate the area, providing a stunning alpine backdrop to the glittering water. The view finally fades as the trail makes a few switchbacks through a steep meadow clinging to the upper end of the long valley. At the top of the switchbacks, pass another trail leading to Triangle Lake, then climb just a little farther before the trail finally levels off, the first time it has done so in the 2.0 miles since Upper Echo Lake.

The gentler grade complements the gentle terrain that lies above the lake basin you just climbed out of. Though you only catch glimpses of it from the trail, large Haypress Meadow covers an extensive area just off the path to the left. For the most part, the trail passes through a pleasant lodgepole forest. Several trails branch off this easy part of the hike. The first two you pass lead down to Lake of the Woods. The initial trail passed is the return route at the end of this hike's loop. After the two trails on the left, you pass two more on the right, both of which lead down to small Lake Margery, which lies just below the Pacific Crest Trail on the right.

After hiking 3.0 miles from Upper Echo Lake, you arrive at a junction. The path to the left is signed for Aloha Lake. However, this route leads to the very southeast corner of the lake and does not give you an opportunity to enjoy the beautiful shoreline. Instead, bear right and continue on the Pacific Crest Trail as it descends into the Desolation Valley for another 0.75 mile. Though the terrain is increasingly rocky, the dense forest on the left yields only very filtered views, hinting at the grandeur that lies ahead. Finally the trail levels off and you arrive at the shore of Lake Aloha.

The scene that unfolds when you arrive at the edge of the huge lake is nothing short of monumental. Lake Aloha occupies the entire northern half of the Desolation Valley. It fills in innumerable cracks, crevasses, and bowls that lie between an untold number of granite domes and crags. Hundreds of small rocky islands pop above the water. To the west is the awesome crest of the Crystal Range, the highest set of peaks in the Desolation Wilderness. Pyramid Peak, the tallest point, is on the far left; the highest point on the far right of the crest is Mount Price. The entire block of mountains is stark white granite, and it is obvious, even from this distance, that the glaciers have carved and polished the whole valley, including the high peaks.

When you reach the lake, the Pacific Crest Trail continues north, along the shore of Lake Aloha. Instead, turn left onto a trail coming from the south. This path also follows the lake's extensive shoreline but offers the opportunity to hike an excellent loop through parts of the southern half of the Desolation Valley. Head south on this path and enjoy the scenery as you go. Be sure to pause and explore some of the rocky terrain between the trail and the lake. After maintaining this course for 0.6 mile you reach the very southern end of the lake, where the trail splits. Stay left and then immediately stay right when the trail leading back up to the Pacific Crest Trail branches off.

After passing the Pacific Crest Trail connector, the trail climbs moderately up to a meadow-filled pass between a granite dome and the high slope of the eastern side of the Desolation Valley. If you are comfortable with cross-country rock scrambling, this is a good time to go west and scamper up to the top of Point 8,383. From this vantage one of the great panoramas of the Sierra Nevada is revealed. Here you can see the entire Desolation Valley, from the Crystal Range to the dark rocks of Jacks Peak, which forms the east side of the valley. Between these high towers is the great water-and-granite maze that is Lake Aloha. Looking south, you can see Lake of the Woods immediately below the dome and the jumble of rocks and lakes that is the southern Desolation Valley. The west side of Ralston Peak hems in the valley on the southwestern side, while far to the south

Aloha Lake is crowned by the granite splendor of the Crystal Range.

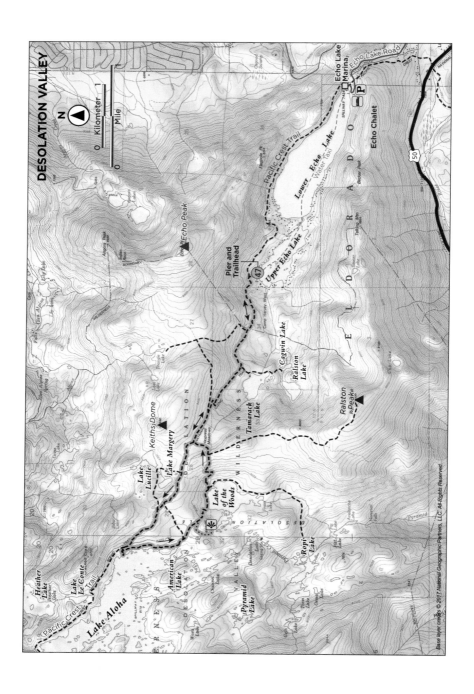

DESOLATION VALLEY

N

Kilometer 1

Mile

Echo Lake
Marina
Echo Lake Road

Echo Chalet

P

Lower Echo Lake

Water Taxi

Pacific Crest Trail

Pier and
Trailhead

47

Upper Echo Lake

Echo Peak

Caguin Lake

Ralston
Lake

Ralston
Peak

Tamarack
Lake

Keiths Dome

Lake
Margery

Lake
Lucille

Lake of the
Woods

Ropi
Lake

Pyramid
Lake

American
Lake

Lake Aloha

Lake
Le Conte

Pacific Crest Trail

Heather
Lake

E L   D O R A D O

D E S O L A T I O N   W I L D E R N E S S

D E S O L A T I O N   V A L L E Y

Base layer credits © 2017 National Geographic Partners, LLC. All Rights Reserved.

you can make out Thunder Mountain, near the Mokelumne Wilderness. It is a stunning vista and the highlight of the hike.

From Point 8,383 bid farewell to Lake Aloha. Return to the trail and continue to the south as it begins the descent to Lake of the Woods. A few switchbacks moderate the grade before you arrive at the lakeshore. Follow along the north end of the lake before arriving at a junction. The trail to the right continues south along Lake of the Woods and ends at nearby Ropi Lake. You want to stay left and begin to climb out of Lake of the Woods' basin. The path climbs steeply, though some switchbacks help make it more palatable. The trail passes through some of the thickest wildflowers of the hike, and you are treated to good views of the Crystal Range lining the horizon above Lake of the Woods. After climbing for 0.5 mile you reach the top of a ridge, where there is a junction with the trail leading to the top of Ralston Peak. Stay left here and descend through forest and meadow before arriving at the Pacific Crest Trail. Turn right and follow it back to the dock at Upper Echo Lake.

MILES AND DIRECTIONS

0.0 Start at the Upper Echo Lake dock and climb swiftly up to the Pacific Crest Trail. Turn left.

0.7 Enter the Desolation Wilderness and stay left to continue on the Pacific Crest Trail.

1.4 Pass the spur leading to Tamarack Lake on the left.

2.0 Reach the top of the pass and stay right to continue on the Pacific Crest Trail. Stay on this trail at all subsequent forks until you reach Lake Aloha.

3.8 Arrive at Lake Aloha. Turn left and follow the shoreline south.

4.4 At the very southern end of the lake, bear left then immediately stay right to go to Lake of the Woods.

4.7 At the top of the low pass, scramble up to the right for an awesome panorama from Point 8,383.

5.0 Arrive at Lake of the Woods.

5.2 Stay left and climb out of the Lake of the Woods basin.

5.7 At the top of the ridge, bear left at the junction with the Ralston Peak Trail.

5.9 Turn right back onto the Pacific Crest Trail, and follow it back to Upper Echo Lake.

7.9 Turn right onto the connector trail that accesses the pier at Upper Echo Lake and descend to arrive back at the dock.

Round Top looms high over the Pacific Crest Trail as it crosses an unnamed pass.

CENTRAL SIERRA

THE CENTRAL SIERRA is a large stretch of the Sierra Nevada between Lake Tahoe in the north and Yosemite in the south. In many ways, this is the forgotten Sierra, overshadowed by Lake Tahoe and the High Sierra. The terrain here is in several places gentler than the famous neighboring landscapes. Yet that does not mean it lacks beauty or great mountains of its own. Indeed, some of the most distinctive scenery in the Sierra is found here. Most notable of these is the high country of Carson Pass, which includes the serene meadows on the Upper Truckee River and the alpine lakes and meadows around majestic Round Top, one of the tallest peaks in the region. Another area of unusual beauty is the tree-line mountains that line Sonora Pass, where unique glacier-carved volcanic peaks hide lovely alpine lakes.

Volcanism is the unifying feature in the Central Sierra. Like most of California's greatest mountain range, the large granite pluton that constitutes most of the mountains is present here. However, unlike the rest of the Sierra Nevada, significant intrusions of volcanic pyroclastic flows have overlaid the granite. Much of the volcanic material was subsequently cleared out by glaciers and other erosive forces, leaving isolated blocks of the dark volcanic rock atop the granite bedrock. Every hike in this section of the guide travels through volcanic terrain. Most pass alongside the granite bedrock as well, affording hikers the opportunity to observe both layers and consider the forces that created and shaped this region.

Unlike most parts of the Sierra Nevada, the crest of these mountains sits a little closer to the range's true center. This means that large rivers flow off both sides of the range, rather than the typical arrangement of large west-flowing rivers and smaller creeks tumbling down the steep eastern side. In the Central Sierra, the Mokelumne and the Stanislaus Rivers flow west. Both join the San Joaquin not far from the Sacramento–San Joaquin Delta. A pair of rivers also flow east. The Walker and Carson Rivers rise in the Central Sierra and flow off the range into the Great Basin, where there is no outlet to the sea. Most of the high-country watersheds are protected in four large wilderness areas: the Mokelumne, Carson-Iceberg, Emigrant, and the northern half of the Hoover Wilderness.

The Central Sierra has some of the best road access of the range. Three trans-Sierra highways—CA 88, CA 4, and CA 108—cross the entire range over beautiful, high passes. This gives hikers good opportunities to get close to the backcountry in short order.

48. **MEISS MEADOW/ SHOWERS LAKE**

WHY GO?

This gorgeous hike on the Pacific Crest Trail follows the Upper Truckee River through verdant Meiss Meadow on the way to Showers Lake and affords a great view of Lake Tahoe to the north.

THE RUNDOWN

Start: Meiss Trailhead on CA 88
Distance: 10.3 miles out and back
Hiking time: 5–6 hours or overnight
Difficulty: Moderate
Elevation gain: 750 feet
Season: Summer, fall
Trail surface: Packed dirt, duff, rocky
Canine compatibility: Dogs permitted
Fees and permits: Parking fee

Land status: Dardanelles Roadless Area, Lake Tahoe Basin Management Unit
Trail contact: 35 College Dr., South Lake Tahoe 96150; (530) 543-2600; www.fs.usda.gov/ltbmu
Other: This hike begins in the Carson Pass Management Area. Water is available in the Upper Truckee River and Showers Lake.

FINDING THE TRAILHEAD

On Highway 88, drive east from Jackson for 60 miles or west for 28.5 miles from US 395 in Minden, Nevada. Turn into the Meiss Trailhead, on the north side of CA 88.

The trailhead can also be reached from South Lake Tahoe by driving south on CA 89 for 11.2 miles. Turn right onto CA 88 and continue west for 9 miles. Just beyond Carson Pass, turn right into the Meiss Trailhead parking area. **Trailhead GPS:** 38°41'48.15"N / 119°59'30.82"W

WHAT TO SEE

The Dardanelles Roadless Area is a pocket of wild mountains that lie at the far southern end of the basin that contains Lake Tahoe. This area occupies the transition zone where the large granite pluton around southern Lake Tahoe is first overlain with volcanic pyroclastic breccia. This heralds the beginning of the Central Sierra, where large expanses of granite are periodically capped by the remains of ancient volcanic activity. For hikers this means a strikingly different landscape than the granite beauty of Lake Tahoe and the Desolation Wilderness to the north. Instead, the areas where the volcanic rock remains tend to be more subdued, with rounded summits and ridges rather than towering crags. The gentler terrain does not mean that it lacks beauty. On the contrary, the Dardanelles area is one of the most scenic parts of both the Lake Tahoe region and the Central Sierra. Tall cliffs faced with dark strata and deeply eroded volcanic badlands rise above

Round Top and the Mokelumne Wilderness high country are a highlight of the climb from Carson Pass.

flourishing meadows. The Upper Truckee River flows lazily through the valley, collecting the water emerging from four large lakes and several unnamed tarns. Indeed, it is an exquisitely beautiful place.

This hike through the Dardanelles Roadless Area follows the Pacific Crest Trail from Carson Pass to Showers Lake. The lake is situated on a high bench, where the volcanic flows first cover the granite pluton of southern Lake Tahoe. To get there, you must climb over a scenic pass and then follow the Upper Truckee River through sublime Meiss Meadow. Just past Showers Lake, you can climb out onto granite slabs and gaze out at Lake Tahoe.

Begin at the Meiss Trailhead at Carson Pass. The trail sets out to the west and wraps around the lower flanks of Red Lake Peak. In about 0.8 mile the path leaves the woods and begins climbing up a treeless slope. As you climb up a series of switchbacks, the views south toward Round Top, a formidable peak in the Mokelumne Wilderness, get continually better. Above the switchbacks the trail makes one final traverse of the steep slopes and arrives at a saddle below a shoulder of Red Lake Peak. Looking north from here you can see the deep blue waters of Lake Tahoe in the distance. However, it is the southward vista of Round Top and its long, craggy ridges radiating out from the blocky summit that is most impressive. Despite the gently sloping terrain of the mountains on the north side of Carson Pass, the presence of Round Top and the adjacent peaks gives this area a much more rugged feel.

The wildflowers of Meiss Meadow contrast against the stark slopes of Red Lake Peak.

A surprising little lake greets you on the nearly treeless saddle. The trail passes it and continues north, through open fields filled with wildflowers in season. Cross a small stream flowing off Red Lake Peak. This stream is the southernmost headwaters of the Upper Truckee River. Below the trail it forms a deep gully in the volcanic soil and flows north, off the saddle. The trail runs parallel to it as you descend to Meiss Meadow. The large meadow occupies the broad floor of a beautiful valley surrounded by stratified volcanic mountains. Their texture alternates among desiccated badlands-like formations, craggy rock outcroppings, and smooth, grassy slopes. Though it differs from the usual grandeur of the Sierra Nevada, the setting of Meiss Meadow has its own beauty, the kind that emphasizes alpine serenity over rugged spectacle.

When you reach the meadow, cross over the newly formed Upper Truckee River and pass through a stand of scattered pines before reentering the meadow. As you do, the old Meiss cabin comes into view. Cross over the river again as the trail cuts across the meadow and then follows its eastern boundary. Wildflower displays in this area are astounding. Continue north, following the edge of the meadow until you reach the junction with the trail to scenic Round Lake, 2.8 miles from Carson Pass. This lovely lake is set at the base of a particularly imposing volcanic cliff topped by a large rock turret. It is a great alternative destination for this hike.

From the junction with the Round Lake Trail, which is also the Tahoe Rim Trail, press on to the north. The path stays along the edge of Meiss Meadow for a while before dipping into a stand of scattered pines. Beyond the pines you enter the widest part of the meadow, where it spreads out and fills much of the sweeping valley. The Upper Truckee meanders back into your path. When you cross it, note a path coming in from the east. This leads to nearby Meiss Lake, another attractive destination. Once you have crossed the small river, granite starts to appear for the first time on the hike. Climb over a low rise where a small lake is tucked into the forest before passing along the edge of a small meadow.

As you leave the meadow behind, the trail begins to climb. At first it passes beneath more forest, but it soon leads through more small patches of meadow. Look back toward the south to get a good, elevated perspective on Meiss Meadow and the wide valley it occupies. Finally the trail levels off and leads down toward the grassy shore of lovely Showers Lake. The lake sits at the point of transition between the volcanic mountains and the granite bedrock that underlies the region. On the south side of Showers Lake, the pyroclastic formations rise above the water; but on the north side, large granite outcroppings push up against the shore. Follow the trail toward the north end of the lake.

Granite crags around Showers Lake contrast the volcanic cliffs that ring the lake.

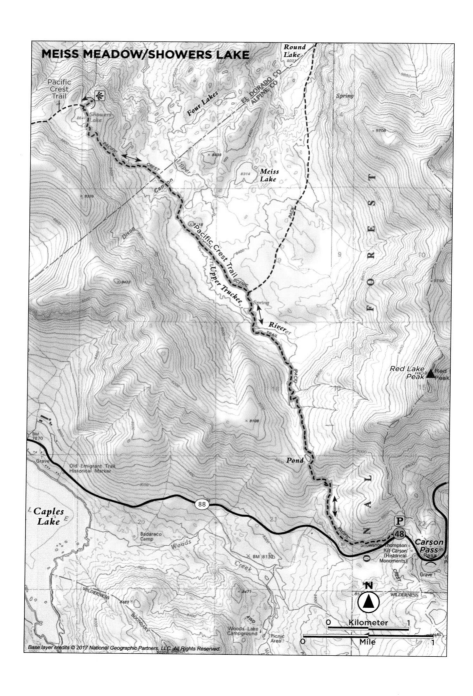

MEISS MEADOW/SHOWERS LAKE

Pacific Crest Trail

Showers Lake

Four Lakes

Round Lake
8032

Spring

EL DORADO CO.
ALPINE CO.

Meiss Lake
8314

FOREST

9708

9600

9704

Pacific Crest Trail

Upper Canon

Dixon

8402

PCT/TRCT

Canon

Upper Truckee

River

Spring

9750

Red Lake Peak

Red Peak

15

9108

Pond

BM 7870

Grave

Old Emigrant Trail Historical Marker

8000

Caples Lake

88

21

Badaraco Camp

Woods

Creek

BM 8132

Thompson Kit Carson (Historical Monuments)

Carson Pass

P 48

Grave

WILDERNESS BOUNDARY

8483

8471

WILDERNESS

Woods Lake Campground

Picnic Area

AWD

N

| 0 | Kilometer | 1 |
| 0 | Mile | 1 |

Base layer credits © 2017 National Geographic Partners, LLC. All Rights Reserved.

Distant Lake Tahoe and the Upper Truckee River watershed can be seen from a vista near Showers Lake.

As the Pacific Crest Trail descends briefly away from the lake, veer right by a campsite and follow a use trail out to a large granite crag. Scramble out on it and enjoy a fantastic panorama of the Upper Truckee River drainage, leading all the way down to the blue waters of Lake Tahoe. Relax and enjoy the view before heading back to the trailhead.

MILES AND DIRECTIONS

0.0   Start at the Meiss Trailhead.

1.2   Reach the saddle below Red Lake Peak.

2.1   Cross the Upper Truckee River at the beginning of the meadow.

2.8   Pass the trail leading to Round Lake.

3.4   Cross the Upper Truckee River for the third and final time.

5.15 Arrive at Showers Lake. Just beyond the north shore of the lake is a granite outcropping with a great view of Lake Tahoe. Retrace your steps back to the trailhead.

10.3 Arrive back at the trailhead.

49. **ROUND TOP LOOP**

WHY GO?

This magnificent loop through the high country of the Mokelumne Wilderness leads through epic wildflowers displays to a pair of gorgeous lakes situated at the foot of one of the most picturesque mountains in the Central Sierra.

THE RUNDOWN

Start: Woods Lake Trailhead
Distance: 5.3-mile loop
Hiking time: 3–4 hours
Difficulty: Moderate
Elevation gain: 1,220 feet
Season: Summer, fall
Trail surface: Packed dirt, rocky
Canine compatibility: Dogs permitted
Fees and permits: Parking fee
Land status: Mokelumne Wilderness, Eldorado National Forest

Trail contact: Amador Ranger District, 26820 Silver Dr., Pioneer 95666; (209)-295-4251; www.fs.usda .gov/eldorado
Other: This hike travels through the Carson Pass Management Area. Special rules, including camping restrictions, are in place. Water is available in creeks and Winnemucca and Round Top Lakes.

FINDING THE TRAILHEAD

Drive east from Jackson on CA 88 for 59.5 miles, or drive west for 30 miles from US 395 in Minden, Nevada. Turn south onto Woods Lake Road and drive 1 mile; turn right into the parking area.

The trailhead can also be reached from South Lake Tahoe by driving south on CA 89 for 11.2 miles. Turn right onto CA 88 and continue west for 10.6 miles. Turn left onto Woods Lake Road; proceed 1 mile and turn right into the trailhead parking area. **Trailhead GPS:** 38°41'28.68"N / 120°0'33.23"W

WHAT TO SEE

The awesome high country of the Mokelumne Wilderness dominates the scenery of the beautiful Carson Pass area. Round Top, the basalt neck of an ancient volcano, crowns the mountains to the south of the pass, setting a rugged, foreboding skyline against the horizon. Though the mountain may look intimidating, the lands at its feet are delightful and beckon hikers to come and explore their sparkling lakes, verdant meadows, and explosive wildflower displays. The lakes, large Winnemucca Lake and lovely Round Top Lake, are among the most beautiful in the Central Sierra. Add to these wonderful features awesome views of Carson Pass from the trail and you have all the pieces in place for a splendid hike in a stunning alpine setting.

Explosive wildflowers line the trail while climbing toward Round Top and Winnemucca Lake.

There are a few ways to get to Winnemucca and Round Top Lakes, but the best route is to hike the loop from the Woods Lake Trailhead. While this involves a bit more climbing than the route coming from Carson Pass, it offers more diverse scenery, the opportunity to hike along beautiful creeks, one of the best wildflower displays in the Sierra Nevada, and the chance to examine historic mining relics. Furthermore, it enables doing the hike as a loop, which increases the enjoyment of the hike by extending the new territory that can be explored.

Begin the hike at the Woods Lake Trailhead and follow the path south along the road. The trail promptly splits to begin the loop. The path to the right is the return leg of the hike. Turn left at the fork and cross Woods Lake Road. The path soon reaches a stout bridge and crosses over Woods Creek. Once on the east side of the creek, you veer south and follow along the bank. Woods Creek is large and sustained by snow high up on Round Top and the nearby Sisters that lingers deep into summer. After following the creek briefly, the route bends away from the creek and a low granite hill rises to your right. Unseen on its other side is Woods Lake, hidden in a deep granite bowl.

Once you leave the creek, the trail begins to climb. You maintain a steady grade, first through forest for about 0.7 mile, before eventually breaking out into a wide, grassy vale. In July and August the wildflowers erupt in a profusion of color. Round Top, in all its stately glory, rises majestically from the head of the valley. As you climb, the sound of crashing water can be heard, though it takes a little while for the creek to appear on the right. This is the outlet creek from Winnemucca Lake, which, along with the outlet creek from Round Top Lake, feeds into Woods Lake. Woods Creek proper does not begin until it flows from the lake. Keep climbing through the valley, crossing into the Mokelumne Wilderness 1.4 miles from the trailhead. Note the profusion of granite boulders in the valley. This is in keeping with the typical geology of the Central Sierra, where volcanic rock, typically ancient lava flows, overlays granite. The same conditions first occur just to the north in the Dardanelles area.

As you near the top of the valley, the path pulls alongside the creek and follows it as you close in on the end of the valley. Look to the north for an excellent view of volcanic Red Lake Peak. Climb a little farther until you finally reach the top as you arrive at the edge of Winnemucca Lake, 2.0 miles from the trailhead. The setting of the lake is as breathtaking as it is beautiful. At just under 9,000 feet above sea level, the lake is just below the tree line. The stunted trees are indicative of the harsh winter environment and limited growing season, though in summer wildflowers happily line the northern lakeshore in thick blankets. Ragged cliffs jut abruptly above the water, marching inexorably up toward the summit of Round Top, which commands the entire scene.

As you arrive at Winnemucca Lake, you pass a trail that parallels the north shore. This is the trail coming up from Carson Pass. Though it is not the route to Round Top Lake, it is worth following this path a little along the edge of the lake, since it offers good views of the wildflowers, lake, and cliffs. After enjoying the view, return to the main trail and follow it to the lake's outlet, where you turn to the west and begin climbing along the base of Round Top toward a high saddle. Snow lingers here and in early summer may block progress. As you climb, look back to the east for a good view of Winnemucca Lake from above.

Nearly 1.0 mile after leaving Winnemucca Lake, the trail arrives at Round Top Lake. Though much smaller than Winnemucca Lake, its location is just as grand. Round Top still towers 1,000 feet above the lake to the southeast, while the pair of peaks similar to

Round Top and one of the Sisters reflect in Round Top Lake.

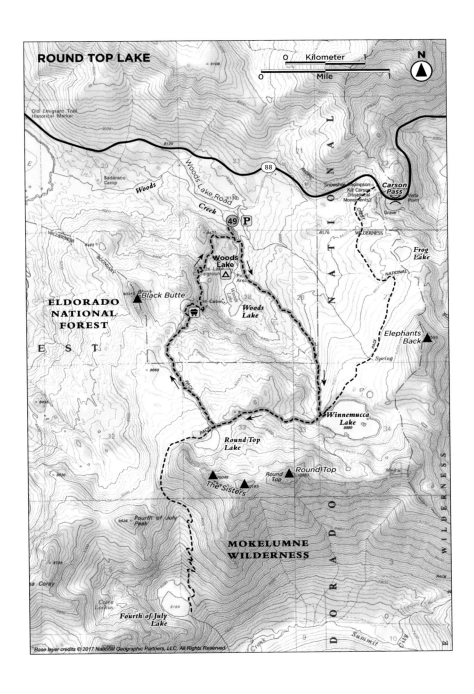

ROUND TOP LAKE

Round Top known as the Sisters cap a stately cliff that rises south of the lake. Higher than Winnemucca, Round Top Lake is even closer to tree line, and the trees are gnarled.

Near the lake's outlet is another junction. Staying straight here leads to remote Fourth of July Lake; the trail to the right leads to Woods Lake. Turn right here and begin the return portion of the hike. Be sure to look back and bid farewell to Round Top and the Sisters as you descend. This part of the hike follows Round Top Lake's outlet creek almost all the way down to Woods Lake. At first you wind through lush meadows, where you can still look south at the peaks behind you. However, a new landmark draws your eye. Immediately to the south is the dark knob of Black Butte. In the distance beyond it, the great towers of the Crystal Range in the Desolation Wilderness meet the horizon.

The trail eventually enters the cool forest and continues alongside the creek. About 1.0 mile after leaving Round Top Lake, you pass a pair of early twentieth-century trucks. These come as a bit of a surprise after having been in these high mountains. The trucks are remnants of a mining operation that once existed here. Other old industrial detritus is scattered about the area, and a large diversion chamber in the creek also testifies to the hard work that once was spent up here. Past the mine the trail begins the final descent toward Woods Lake. A sweeping switchback brings you to the edge of the creek, which is now a precipitous series of cascades crashing down the steep slope. Cross the creek and merge onto the old dirt road that once accessed the mines. Follow the old road through rocky terrain for about 0.4 mile before splitting off onto a singletrack trail. Below the trail is the Woods Lake Campground. From here it is only 0.3 mile farther to the beginning of the loop and then a short walk back to the trailhead.

MILES AND DIRECTIONS

0.0 Start at the Woods Lake Trailhead and follow the path south along the road.

0.1 When the trail splits, turn left; cross the road and then Woods Creek.

1.4 Enter the Mokelumne Wilderness

2.0 Arrive at Winnemucca Lake. From the outlet, follow the trail west.

3.0 Reach Round Top Lake. Turn south here to follow the loop.

4.0 Pass the old mining ruins.

5.2 Reach the end of the loop. Turn left to return to the trailhead.

5.3 Arrive back at the trailhead.

50. **WHEELER LAKE**

WHY GO?

This pleasant hike to pretty Wheeler Lake is a peaceful journey through a lovely forest dotted with occasional meadows and creeks.

THE RUNDOWN

Start: Across the highway from Sandy Meadow Trailhead
Distance: 8.5 miles out and back
Hiking time: 4–5 hours
Difficulty: Moderately easy
Elevation gain: 980 feet
Season: Summer, fall
Trail surface: Packed dirt, rocky, sandy
Canine compatibility: Dogs permitted

Fees and permits: None
Land status: Mokelumne Wilderness, Stanislaus National Forest
Trail contact: Calaveras Ranger District, 5519 Highway 4, Hathaway Pines 95233; (209) 795-1381; www.fs .usda.gov/stanislaus
Other: Water is available at Wheeler Lake.

FINDING THE TRAILHEAD

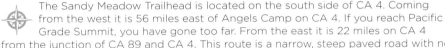

The Sandy Meadow Trailhead is located on the south side of CA 4. Coming from the west it is 56 miles east of Angels Camp on CA 4. If you reach Pacific Grade Summit, you have gone too far. From the east it is 22 miles on CA 4 from the junction of CA 89 and CA 4. This route is a narrow, steep paved road with no center divider. Use caution if coming from this direction. The parking area is located near a large stock corral. From the trailhead, cross the highway to where the marked trail resumes on the north side. **Trailhead GPS:** 38°30'54.85"N / 119°55'45.73"W

WHAT TO SEE

The southern Mokelumne Wilderness is a more subdued environment than other corners of the large Central Sierra wilderness. There are no high peaks like those that hold commanding positions above the northern and eastern sides of the wilderness. Instead, the south side is a region dominated by the usual Central Sierra combination of granite bedrock overlaid by prehistoric volcanic mudflows. The creeks here originate high in the volcanic terrain and drain northward through the granite bedrock to the North Fork of the Mokelumne River. It is a peaceful setting, blanketed in dense forests that open up for occasional meadows, one of the chief features of this hike. The journey through the southern Mokelumne Wilderness feels as though it has seen little human traffic as you pass through it and the dense forest. It has a sense of mystery and being lost. The highlight of the trip is pretty Wheeler Lake. The lake sits snugly at the bottom of a granite bowl, with gray cliffs rising above the lake on the west side. Above the lake to the south is the

Sheer cliffs line the Wheeler Lake basin.

high volcanic ridge that marks the southern boundary of the Mokelumne Wilderness. Although the bustling activity of the Lake Alpine area lies on the other side of the ridge, Wheeler Lake feels as though it has been lost to time.

The hike begins at the Sandy Meadow Trailhead on the south side of CA 4. A very short path leads to the highway, where you cross and pick the trail back up by a sign marked "Trail." The path initially climbs for 0.25 mile before it reaches a crest and begins a long descent that pierces deep into the woods. As you first begin to lose elevation, you pass through a pleasant meadow with fleeting glimpses to the east of rugged peaks. Press on a little farther, and about 1.0 mile from the trailhead you pass a large granite slab just off the north side of the trail. Scramble out onto this slab for a good vista of the interior of the Mokelumne Wilderness. The highlight is the brooding pinnacles of Reynolds Peak. Lying just north of Ebbetts Pass, it is part of a collection of volcanic peaks that line the crest of the Sierra Nevada.

Back on the trail, press on a little farther through the woods before you arrive at the edge of Sandy Meadow. When you reach the edge of grass, the trail splits. The path to the left is the old trail to Wheeler Lake. It has since fallen into disuse and is not in nearly as good condition as the newer trail, which this hike follows. Stay right and continue the steady descent as the trail turns north. While the path winds through granite boulders, you are joined by the sound of a seasonal creek that flows out of the meadow.

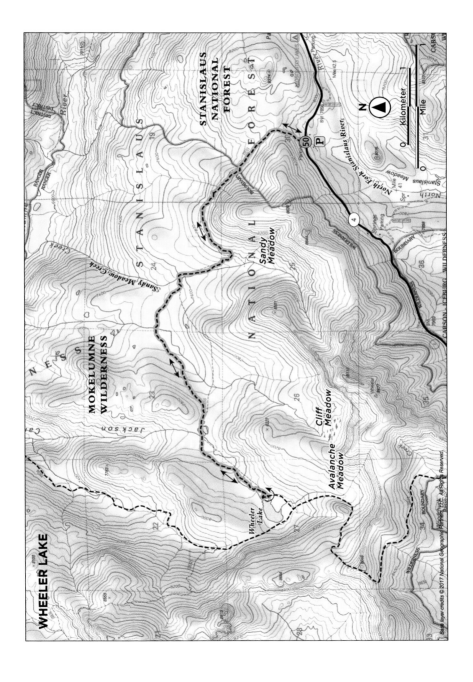

WHEELER LAKE

STANISLAUS NATIONAL FOREST

MOKELUMNE WILDERNESS

NATIONAL FOREST

STANISLAUS

Sandy Meadow

Cliff Meadow

Avalanche Meadow

Wheeler Lake

Sandy Meadow Creek

Jackson

CARSON-ICEBERG WILDERNESS

North Fork Stanislaus River

N

kilometer

Mile

Base layer credits © 2017 National Geographic Partners, LLC. All Rights Reserved.

You maintain this northward trajectory for 0.4 mile beyond Sandy Meadow before the trail turns west again. The sounds of a gurgling stream are heard before the trail arrives at the edge of the creek. Follow the channel for a little bit before arriving at a crossing. On the other side of the creek, the trail is level as it passes through a forest that is growing noticeably thinner. You promptly travel through patches of meadow, the first openings in the forest since leaving Sandy Meadow. This is followed by another long stretch in the woods, now feeling more lost and remote than ever, before you arrive at a beautiful, meadow-lined pond. Though it lacks the rugged cliffs that make Wheeler Lake so attractive, this pond features some of that lake's other great attributes. It has beautiful meadow along the shore, and lots of white boulders dot the area.

Just after the pond, the trail crosses another creek, this one originating from Wheeler Lake. Once you are on the other side, you begin the final climb up to the lake basin. As you climb, the trail passes over increasingly more frequent granite slabs. Cross over the creek a second time, and then quickly arrive at the edge of Wheeler Lake. After having traveled through the forest for so long, the large opening in the tree cover comes as a bit of shock to the senses. The lake occupies a two-tiered basin, with granite forming the lower layer and a volcanic layer sitting on top of it. A tall cliff rises to the west, while the dark brown ridge marks the southern end of the basin. On the north side of the lake, several granite rocks protrude from the water. The southern edge of the lake is lined by a large meadow. The lake once occupied much of the meadow's expanse, but it has silted up over time. Now the grassy area fills nearly half the lake's former extent. The trail continues toward this area, where it splits and heads off to a few destinations. Explore the lake and the meadow; then head back along the path to return to the trailhead.

MILES AND DIRECTIONS

0.0 Start at the trailhead and cross CA 4; resume hiking where a sign indicates the trail.

1.0 Pause on a granite slab and enjoy the view.

1.6 At the edge of Sandy Meadow, stay right at a junction and follow the trail to the north.

3.4 Pass a small pond.

4.25 Arrive at Wheeler Lake. Return the way you came.

8.5 Arrive back at the trailhead.

51. **NOBLE LAKE**

WHY GO?

This trip explores an unusual part of the Sierra Nevada, where tall, eroded volcanic peaks tower above a deep canyon, cliffs of dark, twisted rock loom above the trail, and a small, lovely lake is set in an open, grassy basin.

THE RUNDOWN

Start: Ebbetts Pass Trailhead
Distance: 8.6 miles out and back
Hiking time: 4–5 hours
Difficulty: Moderate
Elevation gain: 1,000 feet
Season: Summer, fall
Trail surface: Packed dirt, rocky
Canine compatibility: Dogs permitted

Fees and permits: None
Land status: Humboldt-Toiyabe National Forest
Trail contact: Bridgeport Ranger District, HC62, Box 1000, Bridgeport 93517; (760) 932-7070; www.fs.usda .gov/main/htnf
Other: Water is available at Noble Lake.

FINDING THE TRAILHEAD

The trailhead is located at Ebbetts Pass on CA 4, 114 miles east of Stockton and 12.7 miles west of the junction of CA 89 and CA 4. A signed gravel road heads east briefly from the highway to the trailhead. **Trailhead GPS:** 38°32'54.39"N / 119°48'21.72"W

WHAT TO SEE

Located alongside the Pacific Crest Trail, just south of Ebbetts Pass, Noble Lake is one of the more scenic lakes in the Central Sierra. It is snuggled into a small bowl in the midst of a broad, grassy basin. High volcanic peaks and ridges ring the basin, providing a dramatic backdrop to the lake. All the mountains in this setting, many just under 11,000 feet high, are volcanic in origin. They are part of a chain of volcanic peaks along the eastern edge of the Central Sierra that runs from Raymond and Reynolds Peaks in the eastern Mokelumne Wilderness down to the Leavitt Peak area in the Emigrant and Hoover Wilderness Areas along Sonora Pass. Occupying the middle space between these two areas are the eastern highlands of the Carson-Iceberg Wilderness. Although it is just outside the northeastern boundary of the Carson-Iceberg Wilderness, Noble Lake is a part of an essentially wild region. The hike to the lake explores the incredible terrain of these tall, volcanic mountains, yielding great views, unusual scenery, and beautiful wildflowers.

From the Ebbetts Pass Trailhead, follow the trail uphill until you intersect the Pacific Crest Trail. Turn left and continue uphill through forest cover a little more before crossing an open bluff. With fewer trees and on a prominent point, the trail has good views

Towering Highland Peak highlights the view across Noble Canyon.

out across Silver Creek's canyon. This large creek flows east from Ebbetts Pass and feeds into the Carson River. Lining the horizon above the watershed are the ragged towers of Raymond and Reynolds Peaks, primary features in the eastern Mokelumne Wilderness. You also catch your first glimpses of Silver and Highland Peaks, towering mountains that will be constant companions on this hike.

Leaving the bluff, the Pacific Crest Trail descends into a broad amphitheater. Here you begin to get a sense of the unusual terrain that is characteristic of this area. Dark cliffs, eroded into ceaseless cracks, crevices, and pinnacles, hold sway above the trail. Typical of the Central Sierra, the cliffs are the remnants of ancient volcanic mudflows. Flowing off the cliffs are several snowmelt streams that often run into August. The trail crosses these streams as it cuts across the large bowl. Many of them are choked with wildflowers in midsummer. On the east side of the amphitheater, the trail climbs to a high point in the woods and then rounds a hairpin turn. As you round the turn, there is a large rock you can scramble out onto; though the views are not much better than from the trail.

Once around the hairpin turn, you begin a long, descending traverse of the west side of Noble Canyon. The trail first cuts through a wooded area, but it will soon emerge onto the steep slope of the canyon. Awesome Highland Peak, a towering mountain with several layers of exposed strata, looms beautifully on the east side of Noble Canyon. Granite boulders, indicative of the bedrock these volcanic mountains rest upon, line the trail as you head downward, toward the end of the canyon. After heading downhill gently for a little over 1.0 mile, you reach the base of Noble Canyon's headwall.

At the head of the canyon, cross over a pair of small streams lined with masses of wild-flowers and contour to the east. You soon round a ridge and enter a delightful grotto. The creek originates from springs high above Noble Lake at the very upper end of the basin.

When you encounter it here, the creek is a beautiful ribbon of water leaping from rock to rock as it crashes down the boulder-choked slot in the cliffs. You approach the creek on a narrow path cut into the near vertical walls of the gully. Cross the creek and follow the trail as it cuts across the equally steep wall on the opposite side. The trail climbs past some wonderfully gnarled junipers and then arrives at a junction with the Noble Canyon Trail. This path heads north from here, following Noble Creek all the way to its confluence with Silver Creek. Stay right and continue around another ridge as you enter another gully.

Similar to the first creek, though not as large, the water flowing here is from Noble Lake. Cross over the small creek and begin a series of switchbacks that climb up a rugged volcanic wall. Brown rocks protrude from the barren soil, giving the area a moonscape appearance. As you near the top of the climb, you are treated to a spectacular view to the north. Seemingly only a stone's throw away, the crenellations of Raymond and Reynolds Peaks in the Mokelumne Wilderness are on the far left of the vista. Farther away, the solitary cone of Hawkins Peak rises out of gentler terrain, though it falls away steeply on its east side. Famed Grover Hot Springs lies at the foot of this steep slope, though you cannot see it from here. In the distance you can observe the tall summits of Freel Peak, Jobs Peak, and Jobs Sister, the highest peaks on the rim of the Lake Tahoe basin.

When you reach the top of the switchbacks, you follow the creek over open terrain only a short distance before arriving at beautiful Noble Lake. Among the more scenic lakes in the Central Sierra, its location also ranks among the more unusual. Most of the lakes in this part of the Sierra Nevada are set in granite bowls that have been overlaid by volcanic mudflows. The porous volcanic rock does not hold water as readily as dense granite does. Noble Lake, however, sits in a high basin composed entirely of pyroclastic

Rugged volcanic terrain surrounds Noble Lake.

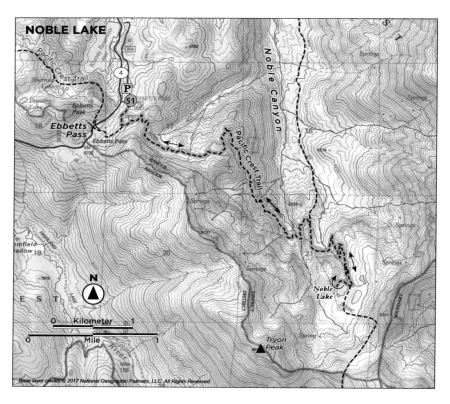

mudflow remnants. The Pacific Crest Trail skirts the east side of the lake before climbing over a pass at the top of the canyon and entering the North Fork of the Mokelumne River watershed. Hikers looking for a longer hike can climb up to the pass for a great view south. More likely you will want to relax at Noble Lake. Tryon Peak gazes down on the lake from the west, while the deeply eroded tower of Highland Peak is the focal point of the view to the north. It is a beautiful, unique place. Enjoy it before returning to the trailhead on the Pacific Crest Trail.

MILES AND DIRECTIONS

0.0 Start at the Ebbetts Pass Trailhead and climb toward the Pacific Crest Trail.

0.2 Turn left onto the Pacific Crest Trail.

1.5 Enter Noble Canyon and begin descending toward the base of the headwall.

2.8 Stay right at the junction with the Noble Canyon Trail.

4.3 Arrive at Noble Lake. Return the way you came.

8.6 Arrive back at the trailhead.

52. **SWORD LAKE**

WHY GO?

This hike leads through cool forests with periodic vistas of gentle granite terrain and along the base of an imposing volcanic tower to beautiful Sword Lake, one of the finest swimming holes in the Sierra Nevada.

THE RUNDOWN

Start: County Line Trailhead
Distance: 6.8 miles out and back
Hiking time: 3–4 hours or overnight
Difficulty: Moderately easy
Elevation gain: 846 feet
Season: Summer, fall
Trail surface: Packed dirt, rocky, rock slabs
Canine compatibility: Dogs permitted

Fees and permits: None
Land status: Carson-Iceberg Wilderness, Stanislaus National Forest
Trail contact: Summit Ranger District, 1 Pinecrest Lake Rd., Pinecrest 95364; (209) 965-3434; www.fs.usda.gov/stanislaus
Other: Water is available at Sword and Lost Lakes.

FINDING THE TRAILHEAD

From Sonora, drive east on CA 108 for 47 miles. Turn left on Clarks Fork Road and drive north for 0.9 mile, crossing over both the Middle and Clark Forks of the Stanislaus River. Turn left onto FR 6N06, signed for Fence Creek campground. Follow this dirt road for 6 miles to the County Line Trailhead. The road is at times bumpy but in good condition.

Coming from Sonora Pass, drive west on CA 108 for 17 miles. Turn right onto Clarks Fork Road and follow the directions above. **Trailhead GPS:** 38°22′41.41″N / 119°55′31.44″W

WHAT TO SEE

The classic manifestation of the Central Sierra is the rolling granite terrain capped by brown volcanic formations. This arrangement is common from just south of Lake Tahoe to just north of Yosemite. The volcanic layers were created by pyroclastic flows that covered the granite rocks only to be scraped away by passing glaciers. The dark rocks we see today are the remnants of the volcanic activity that once convulsed the entire central region of the Sierra Nevada. There is, perhaps, no better example of these geologic events than the Dardanelles. Rising like dark ramparts of an ominous fortress, the cliffs of the Dardanelles gaze down much of the western half of the Carson-Iceberg Wilderness.

The Dardanelles may be somber in appearance, but they remain a beautiful centerpiece to this overlooked part of the Sierra. One of the best ways to experience them is to make the hike out to beautiful Sword Lake. Nestled into a lovely trough amid the rolling granite terrain typical of the Central Sierra, the lake is an elongated jewel, perfect for swimming and catching reflections of the Dardanelles brooding high overhead.

Begin the hike by heading north on the County Line Trail from the trailhead. After passing through a large grassy area, the path begins to climb into the woods. At the end of the short climb, you pass the boundary of the Carson-Iceberg Wilderness just as you arrive at a large rock where there is a good vista to the south of the tall peaks of the western Emigrant Wilderness. The view disappears as you head north into the forest, but the trail soon enters a few small meadows where wildflowers complement the green grass. From the clearings you can just make out the tips of the Dardanelles above the trees. Past the meadows, the path begins to make a long, gradual descent toward Sword Lake. Remember that this long grade must be climbed up on the way back to the trailhead.

On the descent, the trail passes some large rocks, where you can look out over the far western end of the Carson-Iceberg Wilderness. Watch for the blue sliver of the Spicer Meadow Reservoir amid the trees. To the south you can see the brown volcanic hills that are the southernmost feature of the Mokelumne Wilderness. The trail continues north, passing an area that was devastated by a large landslide that flowed off the west end of the

The trail features several views of the Dardanelles.

Open vistas of rolling Central Sierra terrain are frequent along the trail to Sword Lake.

Dardanelles. The dense brush and young trees of this area are indicators that the land is deep into the recovery process.

After crossing the slide area, the trail reenters the woods and then makes a single switchback. As you exit the forest again, the path crosses a small stream that is usually reliable for most of the summer. Despite its short length, the stream, one of the sources of Dardanelles Creek, manages consistent flow thanks to springs in the permeable volcanic rock. Continue through some open, brushy terrain and then cross another small stream before arriving at a junction with the trail along Dardanelles Creek. Stay right here and enter a wide, forested gully. Granite boulders and outcroppings increase in frequency, complementing a few small ponds that line this section of the trail. The trail then turns west and in short order deposits you at the edge of beautiful Sword Lake.

The lake occupies a long gap flanked by a series of granite benches. Small beaches periodically break up the benches, allowing easy access to and from the water. When you first arrive at the lake, you are looking north along its axis. The granite highlands of the central Carson-Iceberg Wilderness, crowned by the volcanic cap of Bull Run Peak, a smaller formation akin to the Dardanelles, lie ahead. These provide a pretty backdrop to the lake. Continue on the trail, avoiding spurs that branch off to the right to access the water. After rounding a granite peninsula, the path leads to the west shore of Sword Lake. Here you get the best view of the awesome Dardanelles. The dark rock palisade

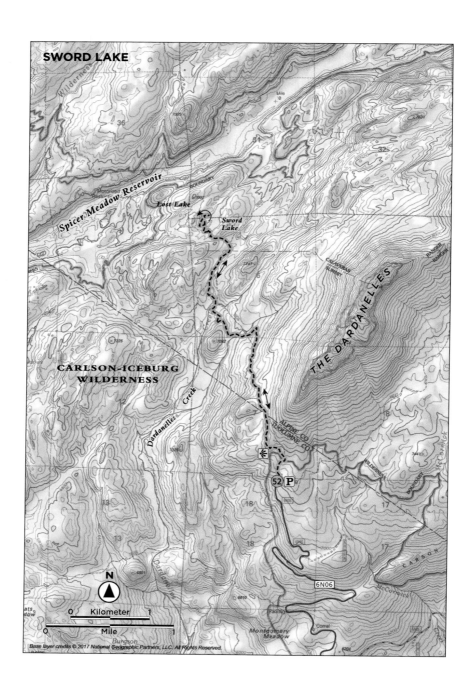

SWORD LAKE

Spicer Meadow Reservoir

Lost Lake

Sword Lake

THE DARDANELLES

CARLSON-ICEBURG
WILDERNESS

Dardanelles Creek

ALPINE CO
TUOLUMNE CO

52 P

N

Kilometer   1

Mile   1

6N06

Montgomery
Meadow

The imposing Dardanelles are a unique sight above granite-bound Sword Lake.

rises imposingly above the lake, yielding a unique and stunning backdrop to the serene body of water. From here you can enjoy excellent swimming, sunning on the exposed granite slabs, or exploring the surrounding area. Lost Lake lies just to the west, with large Spicer Meadow Reservoir beyond that. Follow the trail back to the trailhead when it is time to return.

MILES AND DIRECTIONS

0.0   Start from the County Line Trailhead and head north.

0.4   Arrive at a good vista point as you enter the Carson-Iceberg Wilderness.

2.1   Turn right at the junction with the Dardanelles Creek Trail.

3.4   Arrive at the edge of Sword Lake. Retrace your steps to the trailhead when it is time to return.

6.8   Arrive back at the trailhead.

53. BURST ROCK AND LAKE VALLEY

WHY GO?

This beautiful hike to Powell and Chewing Gum Lakes ventures into the gorgeous Emigrant Wilderness, which lies in the transition zone between the volcanic Central Sierra and the vast granite expanse of the High Sierra. The trail passes panoramic vistas, a meadow- and lake-studded valley, and plenty of beautiful granite high country.

THE RUNDOWN

Start: Gianelli Trailhead on FR 4N47
Distance: 9.0 miles out and back to Chewing Gum Lake. (**Option:** moderately easy 5.0 miles out and back to Powell Lake)
Hiking time: 3–5 hours
Difficulty: Moderate
Elevation gain: 1,460 feet Chewing Gum Lake
Season: Summer, fall
Trail surface: Packed dirt, rocky, rock slabs

Canine compatibility: Dogs permitted
Fees and permits: None
Land status: Emigrant Wilderness, Stanislaus National Forest
Trail contact: Summit Ranger District, 1 Pinecrest Lake Rd., Pinecrest 95364; (209) 965-3434; www.fs.usda.gov/stanislaus
Other: Water is available at Powell and Chewing Gum Lakes.

FINDING THE TRAILHEAD

From the junction of CA 108 and CA 49 in Sonora, drive east on CA 108 for 29 miles. Turn right onto Pinecrest Lake Road and follow this road for 0.4 mile. Turn right onto Dodge Ridge Road and continue for 3 miles, following signs to Dodge Ridge Ski Area. At the sign marking the entrance to Dodge Ridge, turn right onto Dodge Ridge Loop Road. Drive 0.5 mile until the road ends at an intersection with FR 4N26, which is also Crabtree Road. Turn left and proceed 1.6 miles to a junction with the road signed for Bell Meadow on the right. Stay left here and pass through the Aspen Meadows pack station on a dirt road. Once through the pack station, the dirt road, still FR 4N26, becomes pavement again for another 2.7 miles. When the pavement ends, stay straight onto FR 4N47, following this good dirt road for 4 miles to the large Gianelli Trailhead. **Trailhead GPS:** 38°11'54.24"N / 119°53'3.48"W

WHAT TO SEE

The 112,721–acre Emigrant Wilderness lies just northwest of Yosemite and in many ways is an extension of the renowned national park. Much of its area protects the same granite terrain that lies across its border to the south, with numerous lakes, tall peaks, and rugged

The view from Burst Rock contrasts volcanic crags against the stark granite landscape.

canyons that have all been sculpted by glacial activity. Yet the Emigrant Wilderness is also a land of transition. This is the land where the stark crystalline beauty of granite, the iconic rock that defines most of the High Sierra to the south, gives way to the dusky volcanism that is the hallmark of the central Sierra Nevada. The northern marches of the Emigrant Wilderness, including its highest peaks, are all volcanic in origin.

Since the southern end of the Emigrant Wilderness is part of a contiguous wildlands block with Yosemite, the best access is from the north. For this reason, the region is often associated with the Central Sierra. The volcanic terrain is typically the easiest part to access. One exception is the Burst Rock vicinity, which provides easy entry into the wilderness and dives quickly into the classic granite terrain of the Sierra Nevada, with wide vistas and beautiful lakes. The trip to Powell and Chewing Gum Lakes is a classic hike through this landscape, yet it lies right at the edge of where the terrain changes. The panoramas are of both granite mountains to the south and volcanic peaks to the north, offering an intriguing and beautiful contrast.

Begin the hike at the large Gianelli Trailhead. The path immediately begins to climb as it heads northeast toward a ridge. After a 0.5-mile linear climb, you near the ridge and begin to switchback up toward its apex. Near the top, an interpretive display recounts the history of this trail as a nineteenth-century emigrant route, the source of the wilderness area's name, and the harrowing experiences of the pioneers who passed through here. It

Looking down on Lake Valley, Chewing Gum Lake, and the interior of the Emigrant Wilderness

is humbling to think of the hardships people suffered to reach California and open the land up to those of us who enjoy it now.

Past the display, the sandy path levels out and reaches a sign marking the boundary of the Emigrant Wilderness. Just past this point you reach Burst Rock, about 1.3 miles from the trailhead. Here there are awesome views to the north. The rocky canyon below is the headwaters of the South Fork of the Stanislaus River. Beyond this rises a ridge topped by the volcanic turret of Castle Rock and the spires of the Three Chimneys. Here you can observe one of the final occurrences of the dark pyroclastic flows overlaying the granite bedrock that is typical of the Central Sierra. This phenomenon is common from this point all the way to the Dardanelles region that lies just south of Lake Tahoe. To the right of the Three Chimneys, two distant peaks stand out. On the left is Sonora Peak, the highest point in the Carson–Iceberg Wilderness. On the left is Leavitt Peak, the highest peak in the Emigrant Wilderness.

Continuing from Burst Rock, the trail makes an easy descent along a wooded slope. It soon levels off briefly as it passes a small pond bound by large boulders on one side. You then descend a little more before leveling off once again and arriving at an unsigned spur trail branching off to the left. Follow this path to pretty Powell Lake. The small lake is ringed with trees and meadow and has a nice rocky finger jutting out of its north shore. Beyond the lake the skyline is dominated by Castle Rock and the Three Chimneys,

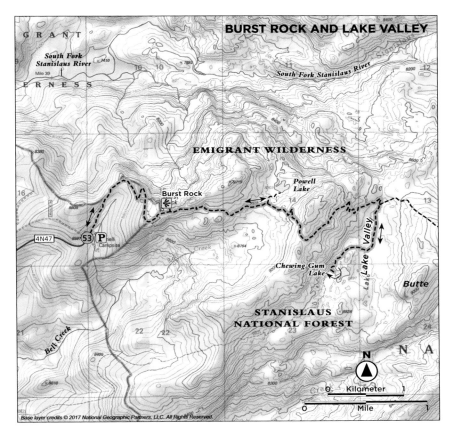

reminders that the volcanism of the Central Sierra is not far off. If you are looking for a shorter outing, this makes a good place to turn around.

If you are continuing on to Chewing Gum Lake, return to the main trail and proceed to the east. The path immediately begins climbing at a moderate grade as it traverses the flanks of a ridge. Soon you reach a saddle on the crest of the ridge and then begin to drop down its east side. Just beyond the saddle, the trail passes through a cluster of trees and then skirts a granite slab on the right. From here there is a great overlook high above Lake Valley. The large meadow and Chewing Gum Lake lie directly below this vista, and off to the southeast are the seemingly unending mountains of the Emigrant Wilderness and northern Yosemite.

Press on from here, descending the east flank of the ridge until the path enters a series of tight switchbacks. These finally end at level ground, where a short walk brings you to a junction. To the left the trail continues to Whitesides Meadow and Upper Relief Valley, both worthy destinations for another trip. Turn right here and follow the trail to the south. You quickly enter Lake Valley, where you cross a lovely meadow backed by a sheer

Classic Sierra Nevada beauty is found at Chewing Gum Lake.

granite cliff. The path soon veers west and passes through a rocky notch before crossing another, smaller meadow in a granite bowl. Just a little farther you arrive at Chewing Gum Lake, a splendid little lake set in the midst of small granite domes and fingers. A white butte rises beautifully behind it to the east. Scramble on the rocks and enjoy the cool water. Exploring the open, rocky terrain is easy and leads to the discovery of a few smaller ponds and more pockets of meadow nearby. From here, follow your footsteps back to the trailhead.

MILES AND DIRECTIONS

0.0 Start at the Gianelli Trailhead and immediately begin to climb.

1.3 Arrive at Burst Rock.

2.25 Reach Powell Lake. (**Option:** If this is your destination, turn around here.)

3.7 Turn right to take the trail into Lake Valley.

4.5 The trail ends at Chewing Gum Lake. Return the way you came.

9.0 Arrive back at the trailhead.

54. **BLUE CANYON**

WHY GO?

The short, steep hike up Blue Canyon is one of the best hikes in the volcanic high country around Sonora Pass. Excellent wildflowers, small waterfalls, and a sapphire lake all contrast sharply against the dark, barren canyon, where tall peaks loom ominously overhead.

THE RUNDOWN

Start: Small unsigned pullout on CA 108 next to Deadman Creek

Distance: 3.6 miles out and back

Hiking time: About 3 hours

Difficulty: Moderate

Elevation gain: 1,200 feet

Season: Summer, fall

Trail surface: Packed dirt, rocky, gravel

Canine compatibility: Dogs permitted

Fees and permits: None

Land status: Emigrant Wilderness, Stanislaus National Forest

Trail contact: Summit Ranger District, 1 Pinecrest Lake Rd., Pinecrest 95364; (209) 965-3434; www.fs.usda.gov/stanislaus

Other: Water is available in creeks and Blue Canyon Lake.

FINDING THE TRAILHEAD

The trailhead—a small unsigned pullout on CA 108 about 2.5 miles west of Sonora Pass—is 62 miles east of Sonora and 17.5 miles east of the junction of CA 108 and US 395. There is room in the pullout for 4 or 5 cars. If it is full, there is another pullout 0.2 mile west. You can also park here, though there are no trails connecting the pullouts, and conditions can be dangerous for foot traffic. Use caution if you must park in the second pullout. **Trailhead GPS:** 38°19'8.49"N / 119°39'49.29"W

WHAT TO SEE

The mountains around Sonora Pass are in many ways the high point of the Central Sierra. In practical terms, this is where you find the highest peaks in the region. Numerous summits rise above 11,000 feet, the highest being Sonora and Leavitt Peaks. Sonora Pass is also the area where the pyroclastic mudflows that overlaid much of the granite bedrock of the Central Sierra reach their greatest manifestation. Rather than simply appearing as dark caps set upon a granite pedestal, the entire mountain block is composed of the ancient volcanic flows. These mountains were then scoured by glaciers, giving them a distinctive appearance unlike any other part of the Sierra Nevada.

Surprisingly, there are not many trails exploring this unique and spectacular landscape. The Pacific Crest Trail offers the most extensive journey and is the only maintained

After climbing up from Deadman Creek, hikers get their first good view of Blue Canyon.

trail through the Sonora Pass high country. However, the best way to experience this amazing landscape is to hike through Blue Canyon, which is hidden away in the far northeast corner of the Emigrant Wilderness. The canyon is a short, narrow alpine glen that climbs steeply up to a fantastic cirque basin. Here, tiny Blue Canyon Lake sits at the base of massive cliffs that soar 1,000 feet above the water. The hike through the canyon is complemented by excellent wildflower displays as well as lively Blue Canyon Creek, which pours over a few small waterfalls and is a constant companion throughout the hike.

The journey starts on the side of CA 108 next to Deadman Creek. The trail up to Blue Canyon Lake is well established but not an officially maintained trail. That is evident immediately in the way the trail descends steeply through rocky terrain to the creek. Cross the water and then climb up the equally steep south side of the creek's narrow gully. Snow covering the trail at the higher elevations can linger deep into summer in some years. If the creek seems too deep and strong to ford, this is a good indicator that the higher sections of the trail may be snowed in. It is best not to attempt the hike if the creek crossing is too dangerous.

Once you have climbed out of the gully, the trail moderates its grade but continues to climb. It passes alongside a narrow gorge, where you can look down on Blue Canyon Creek as it tumbles over small waterfalls. Beyond the gorge the canyon widens and passes

through a lush plateau where grass and willow cover much of the canyon bottom. Blue Canyon Creek rushes by the trail. Be sure to look back toward the large granite bulge on the north side of CA 108. This is part of the granite bedrock common throughout the central Sierra Nevada. Continue climbing, crossing over a small creek flowing out of a basin high on the east side of the canyon.

After crossing the creek, you climb out of the lush part of the canyon. Ahead you can see there is a wall dividing the canyon into upper and lower sections. Above the wall, a horn-shaped tower looms above the lower canyon. As you climb, the few trees that populated the lowest part of the hike fade away and you enter an essentially treeless environment. As you approach the wall dividing the canyon, Blue Canyon narrows and you are forced by a rocky knoll to swing close to the creek. Here the trail gets very gravelly, which will be a constant state for much of the rest of the hike. Be extra careful on these sections, since the gravel can make the trail seem like it is covered in ball bearings. As you pass between the rocky knoll and the creek, you enter a lovely little bowl filled with wildflowers. The creek tumbles down a series of little waterfalls as it enters the bowl. Drop down and cross a small, often dry stream and head to the other side of the bowl, which is about 0.75 mile from the trailhead.

Climbing out of the bowl is the hardest part of the hike. The trail enters a steep, narrow gully and begins to climb. The gully is filled with gravel and can be difficult to climb. Stay close to the north side, where there is more bedrock exposed, which you can use to balance yourself. When you emerge from the gully, you will find you have ascended the wall that partitioned the canyon into upper and lower sections. You immediately cross a dry gully and then encounter the large creek flowing out of Deadman Lake, which is in a high basin to the southeast. A faint trail branches off along the south side of the creek to access the beautiful lake.

Past the creek flowing from Deadman Lake, continue your unyielding climb up through Blue Canyon. After hiking up the steep trail through open terrain for 0.3 mile, you descend a loose gravel slope down to Blue Canyon Creek. Cross the creek and follow the path into a narrow gully, where you have only a narrow margin between a wall of bluish-gray rock and the creek. Ahead of you, the head of the canyon is now evident as dark, dramatic spires thrust upward. Cross back over the creek as you emerge from the gully and make the final climb up to Blue Lake through explosive fields of wildflowers.

The lovely emerald waters of Blue Lake are fringed with a thick band of grass, especially on its north side. Wildflowers blanket the area, giving the outlet of the lake an idyllic feeling. A small grassy island lies just off the east shore of the lake. The lush border around the water is a striking contrast to the brooding, rocky cirque Blue Lake is set in. Dusky towers are set high atop a ridge, off which pour vast fields of scree. The vertical world of the cirque's headwall is broken up by a large rock glacier directly south of the lake. Here the rocky scree and talus descend from the ridgetop in a series of large mounds. These are the remnants of a glacier that once flowed here. When the glacier melted, it left the debris it was carrying behind in a shape that roughly matched parts of

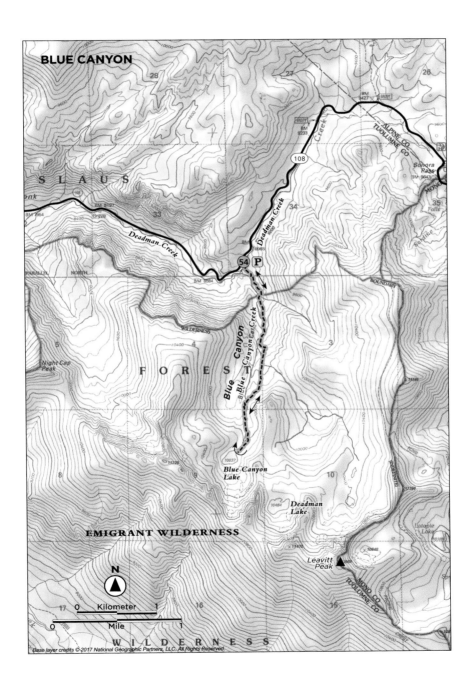

Ragged peaks gaze down on Blue Lake.

the glacier itself. It is a starkly beautiful landscape. Enjoy it for a while and then retrace your steps to the trailhead.

MILES AND DIRECTIONS

0.0 Start from the trailhead pullout and climb down to Deadman Creek. Cross the creek and climb up the other side.

0.75 Use caution while ascending a steep gully filled with loose gravel.

1.0 Cross the creek flowing from Deadman Lake.

1.8 Arrive at Blue Canyon Lake. Follow the trail to return to the trailhead.

3.6 Arrive back at the trailhead.

55. **SARDINE FALLS**

WHY GO?

An easy hike through the Sonora Pass area's meadows and forest leads to a beautiful mountain waterfall.

THE RUNDOWN

Start: Pullout on CA 108
Distance: 2.2 miles out and back
Hiking time: 1–2 hours
Difficulty: Easy
Elevation gain: 375 feet
Season: Summer, fall
Trail surface: Packed dirt, gravel
Canine compatibility: Dogs permitted

Fees and permits: None
Land status: Humboldt-Toiyabe National Forest
Trail contact: Bridgeport Ranger District, HC62, Box 1000, Bridgeport 93517; (760) 932-7070; www.fs.usda .gov/htnf/

FINDING THE TRAILHEAD

Begin at the junction of CA 108 and US 395, 17 miles northwest of Bridgeport. Drive west on CA 108 for 12.1 miles. Park in a pullout on the side of the highway where a gate is marked "No Motorized Vehicles." If the pullout is full, there are other pullouts along the highway nearby. **Trailhead GPS:** 38°18'52.26"N / 119°36'21.04"W

WHAT TO SEE

Although the dark volcanic peaks around Sonora Pass are strikingly different from much of the rest of the Sierra Nevada, the region presents an alpine beauty distinctly its own. One of the best ways to explore this area is to take a leisurely stroll along the trail to Sardine Falls. Though there are scenic meadows, creeks, and even Sardine Falls itself, the real attraction of this trail is the terrain that surrounds these features. The earthy, brown peaks are a stark contrast to the bright granite that lies just to the south in Yosemite, and the simple walk to the falls offers views aplenty of this unique part of the Sierra. The falls are just icing on the cake.

Though there is no formal trailhead, there are well-established pullouts along the highway where the trail begins. Locate the gate marked "No Motorized Vehicles" and follow the doubletrack, an old, closed jeep road, down into the meadow. The trail soon crosses a marshy spot and then pulls up alongside Sardine Creek. The path often disappears into the meadow at this point. Just maintain a course parallel to the creek. The path reemerges at a ford across the creek. Once on the other side, follow the trail across more meadow. The dark cliffs that lie ahead all climb to the 10,000- and 11,000-foot range. Sharp eyes may spot the Pacific Crest Trail passing beneath the tallest, most rugged of

The unusual alpine terrain around Sonora Pass highlights the walk to Sardine Falls.

the peaks. Beyond the meadow, the trail climbs gently, soon entering a forest of scattered lodgepole pine.

At 0.6 mile from the trailhead, the old jeep road comes to an end near McKay Creek and a singletrack trail climbs up a low hill. This is the only significant climb of the hike, gaining 100 feet quickly while passing through a dense thicket of young aspens. When the trail levels out, it crosses over a small stream before beginning a gentle ascent alongside McKay Creek. Wildflowers are a welcome presence along the trail as the dark cliffs begin to loom more dramatically overhead. The track eventually crosses one final stream before arriving at the waterfall, 1.1 miles from the trailhead. Sardine Falls is formed when McKay Creek plunges 50 feet over an erosion-resistant cliff composed of ancient pyroclastic mudflows. The white water is a refreshing contrast against the brown rocks. Note how much of the water from the falls has found an unusual route that passes through a fissure in a huge boulder. On the east side of the creek, there are some campsites should an easy overnighter be an option. If you want to extend the trip, faint use trails head west before climbing up the ridge to access the McKay Creek basin. When you are done enjoying the falls, retrace your steps to the trailhead.

Sardine Falls

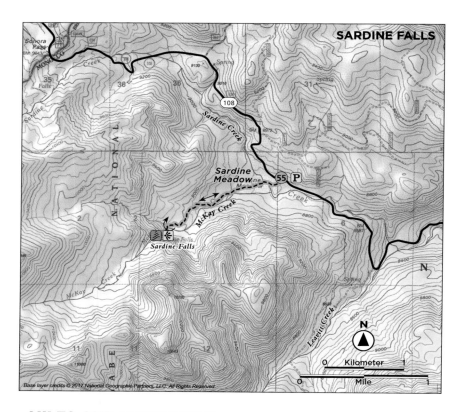

MILES AND DIRECTIONS

0.0 Start at the trailhead, passing the gate marked "No Motorized Vehicles."

0.15 Ford Sardine Creek and follow an old doubletrack dirt road through open meadow.

0.6 The old road climbs up a hill and narrows to a singletrack trail.

0.8 Cross a small creek and continue through patchy forest and wildflowers.

1.1 Reach the base of Sardine Falls. Return the way you came.

2.2 Arrive back at the trailhead.

56. LEAVITT MEADOW LOOP

WHY GO?

The scenic hike through Leavitt Meadow forms a tour through different regional influences, including desert terrain, high mountains, and the volcanism of the Central Sierra. Highlights include three pretty lakes and the beautiful Walker River meandering through the large meadow.

THE RUNDOWN

Start: Leavitt Meadow Campground day use parking area
Distance: 7.1-mile reverse lollipop (*Option:* easy 5.6-mile loop to Secret Lake and Leavitt Meadow, omitting other lakes)
Hiking time: 4–5 hours
Difficulty: Moderately easy
Elevation gain: 800 feet
Season: Late spring, summer, fall
Trail surface: Packed dirt, rocky, sandy
Canine compatibility: Dogs permitted

Fees and permits: Parking fee at the day use parking; no fee at the backpacker trailhead
Land status: Hoover Wilderness, Humboldt-Toiyabe National Forest
Trail contact: Bridgeport Ranger District, HC62, Box 1000, Bridgeport 93517; (760) 932-7070; www.fs.usda .gov/main/htnf
Other: Water is available at the trailhead, in numerous lakes, and from the Walker River.

FINDING THE TRAILHEAD

 From the junction of CA 108 and US 395, 17 miles west of Bridgeport or 48 miles south of Gardnerville, Nevada, drive 7 miles west on CA 108 to the entrance to the Leavitt Meadow Campground. The day use parking area is at the far end of the campground loop from the entrance. The backpacker trailhead is about 100 yards past the campground entrance. **Trailhead GPS:** 38°20'3.07"N / 119°33'6.65"W

WHAT TO SEE

Leavitt Meadow is a natural masterpiece that quietly invites hikers to explore the many treasures that can be found in the land of contrasts it occupies. The large, lush meadow lies at the meeting place of the volcanic Central Sierra, the icy heights of the High Sierra, and the arid expanse of the Great Basin. It beautifully exhibits features of all three regions. The sagebrush hills contrast against the lush meadow, while the pyroclastic peaks contrast against stark granite towers. The tranquility of the hidden lakes makes the swift Walker River all the more vibrant. The three influences all make their presence felt on this hike, making it one of the most scenic trails in the Central Sierra.

The hike includes stunning vistas of Leavitt Meadow, the Walker River, and the distant peaks of the High Sierra.

Begin the hike at the day use parking area in the Leavitt Meadow Campground. If the small parking area is full, use the backpacker parking area about 0.1 mile up CA 108 from the campground entrance. A signed path from there leads down to the day use trailhead. From here you immediately cross over the Walker River on a large steel bridge. An older bridge lies below, no longer used for the hike. The river rushes through an attractive, rocky gorge. The trail then enters a rocky area and turns south, where it promptly splits. Take the Secret Lake Trail to the left to hike the loop. This option gets all the climbing done at the beginning of the hike and also gives you a chance to familiarize yourself with the landscape from an elevated perspective.

The trail continues to the east, crossing a small meadow and then climbing into the rocky terrain above. The desert influence makes itself felt here, with sagebrush, mountain mahogany, and other vegetation typical of arid environments. The track turns south as you climb. Be sure to turn around and look to the north. There you will find the US Marine Corps' Mountain Warfare Training Center backed up against the mountains, sitting at the edge of large Pickel Meadow. The path continues to climb moderately as you reach the top of the ridge that rises out of the east side of Leavitt Meadow. The trail levels off a bit, and you can begin to make out the brown peaks that rise above the meadow's west side. Soon the path veers out onto the western shoulder of the ridge, and 1.4 miles from the trailhead, a magnificent vista unfolds.

From the vantage point on the ridge, you gaze out over large Leavitt Meadow. The great meadow is a flat, lush oasis amid the semiarid mountains. Patches of sagebrush, willow, and grass, all dotted with occasional juniper and pine, intermingle to form a lovely natural quilt. In the midst of the meadow, the Walker River emerges from granite gates and meanders through the broad valley. Above the west side of Leavitt Meadow rises a layered mountain block. At its base, rising a few hundred feet above the meadow, a weathered granite band is exposed. This is overlaid by the dark remnants of the pyroclastic flows that covered much of the Central Sierra. Though this geologic arrangement is encountered on several hikes in this part of the Sierra Nevada, at no other point is the phenomenon observed in such an arrangement. It is as though you are looking at a cross section of the mountains after one-half has been removed. More volcanic mountains, notably Poore Peak, rise east of Leavitt Meadow. Crowning the view, the grand escarpment of white High Sierra peaks that form the northern border of Yosemite, capped by 11,755-foot Tower Peak, lines the southern horizon.

Continuing south from this vantage point, the trail winds back away from the edge of the ridge, obscuring the view of Leavitt Meadow. After climbing a little more, the trail starts to descend the north end of the ridge. When you pass a large patch of barren, gray soil, watch for use trails heading off to the left. These eventually fade out, but pushing past their end a little ways leads to a great view of Poore Lake and Poore Peak. In early summer a tall ribbon of water tumbles down the side of the mountain toward the lake. Return to the main trail and proceed just a little farther until you arrive at the edge of Secret Lake. The cool waters seem out of place in this semiarid environment, but it is a welcome and beautiful sight. The lake is prettiest from the south shore, where Poore Peak rises above the clear water.

Press on from Secret Lake, following the trail as it winds through the dry forest and then descends the ridge to a junction with the Leavitt Meadow Trail. From here you can either turn right and head back to the trailhead through the meadow or turn left and make the easy hike over to Roosevelt and Lane Lakes, which are only 0.5 mile ahead. To reach the lakes, turn left and head south, following the path past a sign marking the entrance to the Hoover Wilderness.

The Walker River is a refreshing place to pause while hiking through Leavitt Meadow.

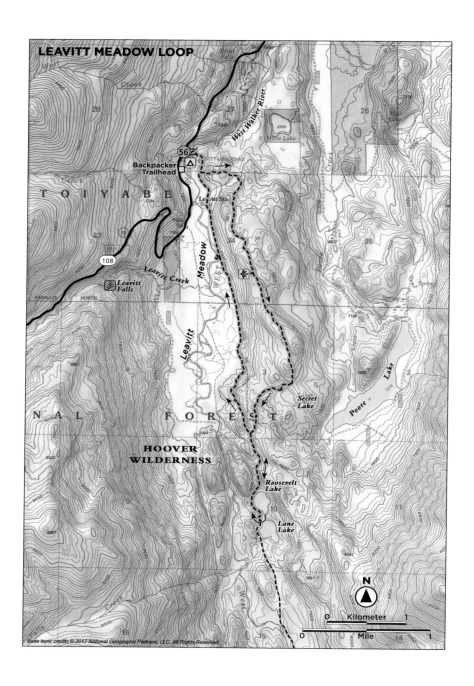

LEAVITT MEADOW LOOP

The trail to the lakes, sandy in places, climbs over a gentle rise and then makes a quick descent to the edge of Roosevelt Lake. The lake is set in a small bowl between the Walker River and the west side of Poore Peak, which rises impressively above the water. The trail skirts the lake's west side, providing easy access to the water in numerous places. From the south end of Roosevelt Lake, it is only a moment's walk to the shore of Lane Lake. It is surprising how similar the lakes are in terms of size and scenery. Both are pretty and make a good place to pause and relax.

To resume the hike, head back north, depart the Hoover Wilderness, and return to the junction with the Secret Lake Trail. From here continue north, losing elevation as you go. In 0.7 mile from the Secret Lake Trail, you finally leave the heavy forest cover behind and enter the Leavitt Meadow area. It is a memorable place—it is easy to imagine a tribe of Native Americans encamped by the river. The trail does not at first drop all the way down to the meadow itself. Instead it loses elevation very gradually as it follows along the sagebrush-covered base of the Secret Lake ridge. Despite not being down in the lush grass, the elevated perspective gives you great views along this entire section of the hike.

Near the middle of Leavitt Meadow, the Walker River finally swings close to the trail. You can follow one of several use trails down to the water, where there are swimming holes, rocky beaches, and swift, clear water. It is a great spot and worth the time to stop here as you approach the end of the hike. Back on the trail, you keep heading north as the river bends back to the west, though it stays close enough to hear. Low hills close in around the meadow as you reach the end of the loop. Climb up just a short distance and arrive at the junction that marked the beginning of the loop. From here it is only 0.3 mile back to the bridge over the Walker River and the trailhead.

MILES AND DIRECTIONS

0.0 Start at the trailhead and cross the bridge over the Walker River.

0.25 Turn left at the junction to begin the loop to Secret Lake.

1.4 A fantastic vista of Leavitt Meadow is just off the trail to the right.

2.4 Arrive at Secret Lake.

3.0 Turn left at the junction with the trail to Roosevelt and Lane Lakes. (*Option:* Turn right to return to the trailhead for a 5.6-mile loop.)

3.5 Reach Roosevelt Lake.

3.8 Arrive at Lane Lake. Retrace your steps to the junction with the Secret Lake Trail.

4.6 Return to the Secret Lake Trail junction. Stay left, continuing onto the trail to Leavitt Meadow.

5.3 Arrive at the edge of Leavitt Meadow.

6.8 Return to the junction at the end of the loop.

7.1 Arrive back at the trailhead.

Awesome Vernal Falls is one of the iconic highlights of the entire Sierra Nevada.

WESTERN SIERRA

FOR THE PURPOSES OF THIS BOOK, the Western Sierra consists of those parts of the Sierra Nevada that cover Yosemite National Park down to Kings Canyon and Sequoia National Parks. With the exception of CA 120's passage across Yosemite, this section of the Sierra can only be accessed from the western side of the mountain range. In many ways, this is the heart of the entire Sierra Nevada, both geographically and in the hearts of people. It is here that most of the range's great icons are found. When people think of California's greatest mountain range, they think of Yosemite and its great domes and waterfalls, of deep canyons cut by massive rivers, or of Sequoia National Park and its ancient trees of staggering proportions. This is the part of the Sierra where people grow up camping amid unending granite playgrounds of polished, exfoliating domes and beneath cliffs that strain your neck muscles trying to see them. In short, when people speak of the Sierra Nevada, this is the part of the range to which they most often refer.

This mountain region can be easily broken up into three distinct subregions: Yosemite, the San Joaquin watershed, and the Sequoia–Kings Canyon complex. All three subregions are accessed via good state highways that lead from major population centers in the Central Valley. The national parks are naturally the most popular and attract people from all over the world. The central area that lies between the two national park complexes does not draw nearly as many people.

Though all three areas cover a significant amount of the High Sierra, only the high country of Yosemite is covered in this book due to the good access available from Tioga Road. The rest of the backcountry must be accessed on foot and requires lengthy backpacking trips, most of which are beyond the purview of this book. What is covered in this guide are hikes that are found at higher elevations of the long western slope of the Sierra Nevada. Many of these explore the deep canyons carved by the Sierra's great rivers. These include the Hetch Hetchy Valley, Yosemite Valley, and Kings Canyon. One trail on the San Joaquin River, as it passes through the foothills, is also included. The remainder of the hikes explore the redwood groves and alpine terrain that lie west of the Sierra Crest.

Despite being one of the most heavily trafficked mountain regions in California, this is also the wildest. Most of Yosemite and Sequoia–Kings Canyon National Parks are protected as wilderness areas that stretch from the Sierra Crest all the way down to the lower elevations in the foothills. Smaller wilderness areas cluster around the parks, slightly increasing the total area that is protected. The region that lies between the parks also has substantial wilderness preservation, especially in the High Sierra sections, where the John Muir and Ansel Adams Wilderness Areas form a large bridge of pristine land that connects the parks. In the mid-elevation regions of the land between the national parks, there are only two small wilderness areas. These are, naturally, the focal points of much of the hiking and backpacking in this area.

57. **HETCH HETCHY**

WHY GO?

The hike through Hetch Hetchy contrasts the solemn beauty of the inundated Hetch Hetchy Valley with the overwhelming fury of some of the best waterfalls in Yosemite.

THE RUNDOWN

Start: Day use parking area adjacent to O'Shaughnessy Dam
Distance: 12.2 miles out and back to Rancheria Falls (*Option:* easy 4.7 miles out and back to Wapama Falls)
Hiking time: 2–6 hours or overnight
Difficulty: Moderate
Elevation gain: 750 feet
Season: Spring, summer, fall
Trail surface: Concrete, gravel, rocky

Canine compatibility: Dogs not permitted
Fees and permits: Entrance fee
Land status: Yosemite Wilderness, Yosemite National Park
Trail contact: PO Box 577, Yosemite National Park 95389; (209) 372-0200; www.nps.gov/yose
Other: Water is available at the trailhead.

FINDING THE TRAILHEAD

From Groveland, drive east on CA 120 for 23 miles. Turn left onto Evergreen Road, which is signed for Hetch Hetchy and Camp Mather, just before you arrive at the Yosemite entrance station. Follow this paved road for 7.4 miles, passing through Evergreen Lodge before arriving at Camp Mather. At Camp Mather, turn right onto Hetch Hetchy Road and proceed 9 miles to road's end at the trailhead.

Coming from Yosemite Valley, head west on Northside Drive to the junction with Big Oak Flat Road, signed for CA 120. Drive 9.5 miles to Crane Flat. Continue straight onto CA 120 and proceed 8.8 miles, passing through the entrance station then turning right onto Evergreen Road. Follow this paved road for 7.4 miles, passing through Evergreen Lodge before arriving at Camp Mather. At Camp Mather, turn right onto Hetch Hetchy Road and proceed 9 miles to road's end at the trailhead. **Trailhead GPS:** 37°56'47.25"N / 119°47'15.40"W

WHAT TO SEE

Hetch Hetchy Valley is in many ways a twin to Yosemite. Soaring granite monuments and sheer cliffs 2,000 feet high graced by magnificent waterfalls are the essence of this incredible valley. Yet not all is well—the Tuolumne River, one of the Sierra Nevada's most beautiful, is dammed, the valley flooded, and the beauty marred. It is said that the great naturalist John Muir, who fought to preserve this paradise, died of a broken heart when construction of the dam was approved. Having accepted that this is Hetch Hetchy's fate, hopefully just for the time being, the valley is still blessed with a tremendous amount of beauty that deserves to be appreciated and enjoyed. Yet this corner of Yosemite National Park remains one of the least visited.

The hike through Hetch Hetchy follows a narrow bench that contours along the valley's north wall. The prime destination is the mind-boggling power of awesome Wapama Falls. More than 1,000 feet high, this powerful waterfall hurtles down the cliff and explodes with a thunderous din into a storm of spray. This is easily one of the most spectacular waterfalls in California, but relatively few get to appreciate it. Tall, slender Tueeulala Falls, though not nearly as voluminous, is a graceful complement to its surging sibling. The highlight of this hike is the passage along a series of bridges below Wapama Falls. In spring and early summer these bridges offer a thrilling, mist-soaked passage through the maelstrom of Wapama Falls. For hikers looking to go farther, the trail continues deeper into Hetch Hetchy Valley to Rancheria Falls, a series of cascades and waterfalls along a large creek.

The trip starts at the day use parking area adjacent to O'Shaughnessy Dam. Walk down to the dam and cross over it. The dam was completed in 1923, built to supply water and electricity to the city of San Francisco. This was, and remains, a controversial decision. As you cross, be sure to survey the reservoir and the landscape of the valley. This is a good

Though the valley has been inundated, Hetch Hetchy remains beautiful.

place to familiarize yourself with the landmarks. The large spire thrusting up from the south side of the reservoir is Kolana Rock. Directly across the water is Hetch Hetchy Dome. Look for Tueeulala Falls and Wapama Falls below and to the left of the dome. Between them is a tall cliff that is reminiscent of mighty El Capitan in Yosemite Valley. Had the valley not been inundated, it is likely that these would all be landmarks as famous and beloved as others in Yosemite. Instead, they wait quietly for the few hikers who come to Hetch Hetchy to gaze at them in appreciation.

On the far side of the dam, you enter a wide tunnel bored into the granite cliff. Lights illuminate the dank passage, and after 0.1 mile of traveling through the rock, you emerge on a narrow bench just above the water. The views down the valley are still good here, but as you begin to head round the end of the valley to the cliffs on its north end, the view constricts a little. The path, an old road dating to the days of the dam's construction, soon makes a gentle climb and at 1.0 mile from the trailhead arrives at a junction with trails leading to Yosemite's northwestern backcountry.

The old road narrows and passes onto a broader granite bench. There are few trees along this section, and the views here are fantastic. In spring small seeps, snowmelt rivulets, and small wildflower gardens line the trail. About 0.5 mile beyond the trail junction, the path passes a particularly lovely area where a small stream flows over smooth granite slabs into small pools. The bench eventually narrows again and the trail enters a stretch of forest cover before crossing over Tueeulala Falls' creek. In spring there is a substantial amount of water here. This waterfall does not flow heavily for long, however; it has a very small watershed and is reduced to a trickle in summer.

After passing Tueeulala Falls' creek, the real excitement begins. You emerge from the trees and cross a talus slope where the trail drops down a short stretch of switchbacks. Pass some trees and arrive at the beginning of the bridges that cross the rocks below Wapama Falls. A couple things are important to note here. First, at the beginning of the first bridge, be sure to look up at the falls. This is the best spot to get a glimpse of its entire drop. In spring, when it is at its full intensity, the great height of the waterfall makes it appear to be moving in slow motion. Second, and more important, if the water is too high, the bridges are impassable and should not be attempted. Hikers have died trying to cross the bridges at highest water. The very first part of the first bridge is often the most heavily flooded, so you should have a good idea of the conditions right away.

If the conditions are good, cross the bridges. A total of five spans traverse the massive talus slope beneath Wapama Falls. As the water detonates when it hits the rocks at the base of the falls, it recollects itself into five channels and proceeds to pour through the large boulders that make up the talus. The mist from the falls blasts hikers as they walk along the bridges. When the wind shifts and the mist is blown elsewhere, there are moments when you can see the falls clearly. Cross the bridges to the far side and pause to enjoy the sight of massive Wapama Falls complemented by tall Tueeulala Falls beyond it. If you only intend to hike to Wapama Falls, this is the turnaround point.

To go on to Rancheria Falls, continue past Wapama Falls. The trail makes a long, shaded journey on the wooded bench of the valley's north side. The forest mostly consists

Slendor Tueeulala Falls and powerful Wapama Falls crash down the northern cliffs of Hetch Hetchy.

of oaks; poison oak also is found here, so stay vigilant. The trees often clear, revealing great views of the east end of the Hetch Hetchy Valley. At 4.5 miles from the trailhead, the path begins to veer away from the reservoir for the first time as it approaches Tiltill Creek. The trail drops down to the creek and crosses it on a steel bridge just above where the creek pours over a little waterfall. Once across the creek, the trail climbs up a treeless slope, reaching Rancheria Creek in 0.4 mile.

When you first arrive at Rancheria Creek, you are treated to a great view of a cataract that is often mistaken for Rancheria Falls. Here the large creek tumbles through a gap between huge granite rocks and then fans out over a wide, polished slab. The contrast between the narrow passage and the wide fan is striking and in some ways more memorable than Rancheria Falls itself. Keep climbing on the trail, passing a wooded area that is a popular backpacker camp. If you plan on making this trip an overnighter, this is the place to spend the night. Above the camp, the trail makes one final climb over a treeless slope. Here you can see Rancheria Falls proper. The creek races through a long, narrow chute and then widens out as it pours over a 15-foot drop. Pass the trail to Vernon Lake just before the route tops out at a bridge that spans the creek right as it enters the chute. It is an impressive sight, especially in spring when the creek is swollen. Follow the trail back to the trailhead when you are ready to return.

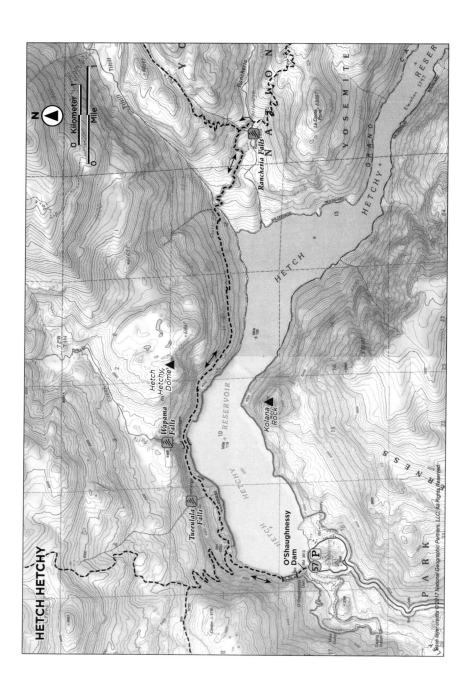

Distinctive cataracts are found along Rancheria Creek.

MILES AND DIRECTIONS

0.0 Start at the trailhead, cross O'Shaughnessy Dam, and enter a tunnel.

0.2 Emerge from the tunnel and follow the trail around to the north side of the valley.

1.0 Stay right at a trail junction.

1.9 Cross the creek below Tueeulala Falls.

2.25 Arrive at the bridges below Wapama Falls. (**Option:** Cross the bridges, adding 0.2 mile, then turn around and retrace your steps for a 4.7-mile hike.)

5.0 Cross Tiltill Creek.

5.4 Reach Rancheria Creek near a large, unusual cascade.

6.1 Just after passing the trail to Vernon Lake, arrive at the bridge that crosses the top of Rancheria Falls. This marks the end of the hike and the turnaround point.

12.2 Arrive back at the trailhead.

58. **PANORAMA TRAIL**

WHY GO?

The Panorama Trail is one of the greatest adventures in Northern California. With epic views nearly every step of the way, it highlights many of the grandest features in Yosemite, passing three staggering waterfalls and boasting constantly changing views of Half Dome and Yosemite Valley.

THE RUNDOWN

Start: Trailhead at Glacier Point
Distance: 8.5-mile shuttle
Hiking time: 4–5 hours
Difficulty: Moderate
Elevation gain: 800 feet
Season: Late spring, summer, fall
Trail surface: Packed dirt, duff, rocky, rock slabs
Canine compatibility: Dogs not permitted

Fees and permits: Entrance fee; bus fare to Glacier Point if taking the tour bus to the trailhead
Land status: Yosemite Wilderness, Yosemite National Park
Trail contact: PO Box 577, Yosemite National Park 95389; (209) 372-0200; www.nps.gov/yose
Other: Water is available at the trailhead and at the Vernal Falls bridge.

FINDING THE TRAILHEAD

From Yosemite Village, drive west on North Side Drive for 5.6 miles. At the junction with South Side Drive, turn left. This is signed for CA 41 and Wawona. Follow this one-way road for 0.9 mile and turn right onto CA 41/Wawona Road. Drive 9.2 miles and turn left onto Glacier Point Road. Follow the road for 15.7 miles to its end at Glacier Point. **Trailhead GPS:** 37°43'40.25"N / 119°34'23.82"W

WHAT TO SEE

There is perhaps no other trail that can claim as many awe-inspiring views as Yosemite's Panorama Trail. The hike begins with top-of-the world vistas at Glacier Point, quite possibly the Sierra's finest single overlook, and makes a long, circuitous descent to Happy Isles in Yosemite Valley. Though the perspective on iconic Half Dome changes over the course of the journey, the great dome is a constant companion throughout the hike. The Panorama Trail also leads past three monumental waterfalls, boasts sweeping views of the High Sierra, and offers several vantage points looking into Yosemite Valley. Considering that there is only one modest climb on the hike and that most of trip is downhill, you get an enormous amount of "bang for your buck."

The one catch with the Panorama Trail is that you must first get to Glacier Point. There are three options for doing this. The first option is to drive up there. This necessitates

The Panorama Trail is full of sublime views that include Half Dome, Vernal and Nevada Falls, and the High Sierra.

either leaving a vehicle at the top and getting a ride later to retrieve it or simply arranging a ride and completing the trip as a shuttle hike. The second option is to ride the Yosemite tour bus that travels from the valley up to Glacier Point. One-way tickets are available. The bus departs the Yosemite Lodge twice per day.

The last option is to hike a challenging grand loop from Yosemite Valley up the Four Mile Trail to Glacier Point and then come down the Panorama Trail. For capable hikers, this is by far the best option. It combines the awesome views of Yosemite Valley from the climb up, especially the ever-changing perspective of Yosemite Falls, with the incredible perspectives on the Grand Staircase as you descend back to the valley. This hike can even be done using the park's shuttle bus system. To do this, take the shuttle to the main lobby entrance of the Yosemite Lodge. Walk south from the shuttle stop, past some of the lodge buildings, and then turn right onto a paved bike path. Follow the path through Leidig Meadow and across the Merced River to the Swinging Bridge parking area. From there cross South Side Drive and turn right onto the park's loop trail. From there it is a quick walk to the Four Mile Trailhead and onward up to Glacier Point. The total loop is about 14 miles. It has the advantage of requiring no personal vehicles, and you can leave your car in camp or at the day use parking area.

However you get to Glacier Point, don't begin the journey back down to the valley without stopping at the point itself. It is quite simply one of the best, if not the best, vistas in the Sierra Nevada, or the rest of California, for that matter. From the edge of the overlook, you can gaze out over Yosemite Valley. Eagle Peak, Yosemite Falls, North Dome, Mount Hoffman, the Cathedral Range, Tenaya Canyon, Mount Watkins, Clouds Rest, Half Dome, and the Merced River can all be spotted from this impossibly magnificent spot. Back at the small store at the entrance to Glacier Point, you can look east. Half Dome once again looms just across the canyon, joined now by many of the peaks of the High Sierra, especially Mount Lyell, the tallest point in Yosemite, as well as the nearby Clark Range.

After admiring the views, it is time to depart, confident in the knowledge that there is plenty more spectacle yet to come. From Glacier Point the trail climbs briefly and then splits. The path to the right is the long Pohono Trail, which follows the south rim of Yosemite Valley all the way to the famous Tunnel View. Stay left and follow the trail as it descends a series of dusty switchbacks. The forest here burned decades ago, so the canopy is gone and views of the back side of Half Dome, the Panorama Cliffs, and the Merced River are astonishing. After 0.4 mile the trail straightens out and begins a long, shadeless traverse toward Illilouette Creek.

As the trail passes along the steep slopes below Glacier Point, the grand scenery persists unabated. One of the highlights comes 0.7 mile from the trailhead, where there are some large boulders alongside the trail that you can climb up for a particularly excellent view of Half Dome, Mount Broderick, Liberty Camp, and Vernal and Nevada Falls storming their way down the Grand Staircase toward Yosemite Valley. This is all topped by the snowy peaks of the High Sierra. Press on a little farther before reaching a junction with the Illilouette Creek Trail. This path continues straight and is one of the main travel arteries into southern Yosemite's backcountry. Turn left at the junction and begin another series of switchbacks.

At the bottom of the switchbacks, an obvious spur leads down to an exposed rock ledge, where you are treated to an astounding view of Illilouette Falls pounding down into narrow Illilouette Gorge. The large creek then cascades over a seemingly endless series of enormous boulders, all beneath the gaze of Half Dome. It is an unforgettable sight, but it is important to use extreme caution at this exposed overlook. Return to the trail and then continue down the last few switchbacks before arriving at a bridge that spans Illilouette Creek. As you cross the bridge, note how the creek fans out over large slabs of smooth granite. Climbing down to some of the rocky benches along the water, you reach a popular place to pause and eat a snack before continuing the hike. Use caution around the water, as this is just upstream from the falls.

When you are ready to press on, head back to the trail. The path follows the same course as the creek, and keen eyes can spot the lip of Illilouette Falls. You then begin a series of switchbacks. This is the only sustained climb on the Panorama Trail. Once you reach the top, it will be all downhill back to Yosemite Valley. After the first set of switchbacks, watch for an obvious spur trail branching off to the left, about 0.6 mile past the bridge over Illilouette Creek. This leads out to Panorama Point. The view is to the north, straight through the gap between Half Dome and Glacier Point. Oddly shaped North

Illilouette Falls thunders into a narrow gorge while Half Dome rises in the distance.

Mighty Nevada Falls hurtles off the cliff.

Dome and the majestic Royal Arches are highlights from this overlook. Head back to the trail and continue climbing.

After Panorama Point the trail finally moves out toward the rim of the Panorama Cliffs. These tall, sheer cliffs plunge more than 2,000 feet straight down to the Merced River. The trail is set back from the edge, but be aware that the drop-off is nearby. A couple sets of short switchbacks over bare granite help gain a little more elevation before the trail finally levels off. As it does, look back to the north and note that graceful and fantastically tall Yosemite Falls has come into view. This view, with its great depth as you look toward the tall waterfall, gives you a good sense of just how big Yosemite Valley really is.

Once the trail levels off, you make a long traverse along the rim. The views here are mostly filtered by trees clinging to the edge of the precipice, but you can still make out several details, most notably Half Dome, which looms less than 1.5 miles away. As you head east, the sound of Nevada Falls becomes audible, and soon you will be able to spot the towering white waterfall through the trees. However, before you get there you must lose a significant amount of elevation. The descent begins when you arrive at the junction with the trail to the Ottoway Lakes. Stay left here and travel a series of switchbacks that descend through a cool forest. At the bottom of the switchbacks, you arrive at a junction with the John Muir Trail, marking the official end of the Panorama Trail.

For hikers hungry for extra vistas of staggering proportion, it is worth hiking a little ways on the John Muir Trail to reach the iconic spot where you can observe Nevada Falls pouring off the cliff, with Half Dome, Mount Broderick, and Liberty Cap all perfectly arranged above it. Returning to the main trail, continue the final short distance before reaching the top of Nevada Falls. A stout bridge crosses the Merced River just as it makes its furious leap off the cliff. It is a scary and wondrous sight. Once across the bridge the trail turns to the right. It is possible to follow a path over the granite and descend to a ledge where a fence provides safety while you watch the mighty waterfall crash into the rocks, 580 feet below. From this angle, with the flying plumes of white spray, it is easy to see why it is named Nevada, which is "snowy" in Spanish.

From the top of the falls, the trail parallels the Merced River upstream a short distance before arriving at a junction. The John Muir Trail continues upstream into Little Yosemite Valley. The route back to Yosemite Valley bears left. Take the left turn and pass a composting toilet. Here the path begins the notoriously jarring trip down granite steps as it descends a seemingly endless series of short switchbacks built into a narrow gully. About halfway down, Nevada Falls comes back into view, offering even more dazzling opportunities to watch the dynamic waterfall.

When you finally reach the bottom of the switchbacks, the route leads into the woods. As you approach the river again, be sure to follow the granite slab out to an overlook where you get a truly spectacular view of the entirety of Nevada Falls. The shimmering white water plunges down the face of the cliff and then hits a steep slope, exploding into a whirlwind of mist and then charging down the slope to the rocks below. Like so many other sights on this hike, it is unforgettable. Proceeding, the path heads downhill, crosses some ledges above a gully, and then crosses a bridge over the Merced River. Below the span, the river churns through a narrow slot before pouring over a small waterfall and then spreading out in a cascade named the Silver Apron. You will soon reach a fork in the trail. The path to the left climbs up to the John Muir Trail. Stay right and hike over to the edge of the Emerald Pool, a wide, deep spot in the Merced River just upstream from Vernal Falls. Walk along the pool and then cross out onto granite slabs, where fences afford a safe view at the top of Vernal Falls.

The Mist Trail, which begins at the top of Vernal Falls, is the final leg of the hike down to Yosemite Valley, and it may just be the most exhilarating. From the granite slabs at the top of the falls, climb down rocky steps that have been wedged into a large crevice in the cliffs immediately south of the falls. A fence offers protection and balance as you descend. When you reach the bottom, more granite steps lead the way through the forest. The roar of Vernal Falls gets louder as you get lower. Soon the trail emerges from the forest cover and you are blasted by the mist jetting out from the bottom of Vernal Falls. The trail, still a series of granite steps, cuts through a stunningly green slope at the base of tall cliffs. The grasses here live in a perpetual rainstorm, constantly watered by the mist from the waterfall. Much of the water collects on the steps and flows in small streams down the trail.

After a steep descent, the trail passes through a tunnel formed by a large leaning slab of granite. The trail right before the tunnel is typically the most heavily saturated by the

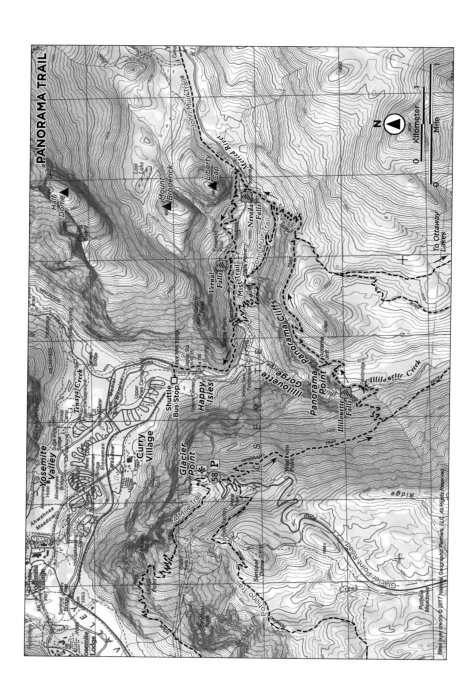

spray coming from the falls. Past the tunnel, the Mist Trail continues down a series of switchbacks and then finally straightens out as it nears the river. There are several opportunities to stop and look back toward the mighty waterfall. Vernal Falls is formed when the river surges over the edge of the cliffs and dives 318 feet to the rocks below. Where Yosemite Falls is grace with great scale and Nevada Falls is kinetic as it plunges, crashes, and spreads out, Vernal Falls is raw power. There is no unusual shape to the falls, just a large river hurtling itself off a cliff. It is breathtaking.

Once the trail has passed all the switchbacks, it makes a 0.4-mile journey down to the bridge over the Merced River. There is running water and restrooms here. As you cross the bridge, you are blessed with one final look at Vernal Falls. The river itself is impressive as it flows from one big rapid to the next, never pausing or resting for a moment. After the bridge the trail makes its final push to Happy Isles. It crosses a few large rockslide areas before traversing another ledge high above the river. Be sure to look down over the rock fence and see the river leap off a few short but compelling waterfalls. Descending rapidly, you soon arrive at Happy Isles. Follow the wide path to the loop road and then cross the bridge to the shuttle stop.

MILES AND DIRECTIONS

0.0   Start from the trailhead at Glacier Point and head south. Immediately stay left when the Pohono Trail branches off to the right.

0.75 Pass an excellent vista of Half Dome and Vernal and Nevada Falls.

1.6   At the junction with the Illilouette Creek Trail, stay left and descend a series of switchbacks.

2.1   Reach the overlook above Illilouette Falls.

2.4   Cross the bridge over Illilouette Creek.

3.2   Pass the spur to Panorama Point.

4.5   Stay straight when the trail to the Ottoway Lakes branches off to the right.

5.3   Stay straight when you reach the John Muir Trail.

5.7   Cross the bridge over the top of Nevada Falls.

5.8   Turn left off the John Muir Trail to begin the descent to Vernal Falls.

6.9   Stay right at the junction and follow the river to the top of Vernal Falls.

7.1   Reach the top of Vernal Falls

7.8   Cross the bridge over the Merced River and catch one last view of Vernal Falls.

8.5   Arrive at Happy Isles and pick up the shuttle.

59. **TUOLUMNE RIVER TO GLEN AULIN**

WHY GO?

This superb hike follows the gorgeous Tuolumne River from the peaceful setting of Tuolumne Meadows to the Glen Aulin High Sierra Camp, the beginning of the Grand Canyon of the Tuolumne. The river goes from serene and meandering to a whitewater torrent where the river races over countless cascades and a pair of great waterfalls.

THE RUNDOWN

Start: Parking area along gravel access road near Lembert Dome
Distance: 10.5 miles out and back
Hiking time: 5–6 hours
Difficulty: Moderate
Elevation gain: 800 feet
Season: Late spring, summer, fall
Trail surface: Packed dirt, duff, rocky, rock slabs

Canine compatibility: Dogs not permitted
Fees and permits: Entrance fee
Land status: Yosemite Wilderness, Yosemite National Park
Trail contact: PO Box 577, Yosemite National Park 95389; (209) 372-0200; www.nps.gov/yose
Other: Water is available from the Gaylor Lakes.

FINDING THE TRAILHEAD

Drive to Tioga Pass on CA 120 for 39 miles from Crane Flat in the west or 19 miles from the junction of CA 120 and US 395 in the east. Turn north onto the gravel road at the base of Lembert Dome. Park either in the parking area near the base of the dome or along the gravel road that leads to the Tuolumne Meadows pack station. This latter option gets closer to the beginning of the trail, but be aware that some areas are marked with No Parking signs. Parking is permitted on the road wherever signs are not posted. **Trailhead GPS:** 37°52'43.88"N / 119°21'30.50"W

WHAT TO SEE

The Tuolumne River is one of the great rivers of the Sierra Nevada. It begins on the flanks of the two highest peaks in Yosemite, Mount Dana and Mount Lyell. The Dana and Lyell Forks flow through spectacular alpine country before converging in Tuolumne Meadows. After making a tranquil passage through the vast meadow, the river makes a frenzied descent through the Grand Canyon of the Tuolumne before finally being tamed by the discordant dam at Hetch Hetchy. During the intense descent through the canyon, the river rushes over four unique and astounding waterfalls. This classic hike follows the Tuolumne River on its journey from Tuolumne Meadows to the beginning of the Grand Canyon of the Tuolumne. The vibrant meadows offer great views of the granite spires

A tranquil section of the Tuolumne River flows through a meadow while storm clouds brew over the Cathederal Range.

of the Cathedral Range. The trail then descends into the canyon, where the river bursts over one granite bench after another, culminating in the plunges of Tuolumne Falls and the White Cascade. The hike ends at the Glen Aulin High Sierra Camp, where activity buzzes but a relaxing mood still prevails.

Begin the hike at the road that leads to the Tuolumne Meadows pack station. Follow the road past a gate and continue through the meadow on a wide dirt path. The Tuolumne River, your constant companion for the duration of the hike, flows just to the left, quietly winding its way through the lush alpine meadow. In the distance you can see several of the sharp summits of the Cathedral Range, most notably Unicorn and Cathedral Peaks. In 0.4 mile the road forks. Take the path to the right, which bends around large Soda Spring and arrives at the old Parsons Lodge. Next to the lodge, the Pacific Crest Trail branches off to the north, becoming a singletrack trail as it enters the woods.

Follow the Pacific Crest Trail through an alternating succession of forest, meadows, and granite slabs for the next 2.5 miles. About halfway through this first part of the hike, the path pulls near the northern part of Tuolumne Meadows, though a small band of trees separates the trail from the grassy expanse. At 1.3 miles, cross fast-flowing Delaney Creek, which emerges from the Skelton Lakes, hidden high above the trail. Shortly after you cross the creek, a trail to the Young Lakes branches off to the right. Stay left and continue the easy, level hiking on the Pacific Crest Trail. After the junction the trail crosses some

Tuolumne Falls

rolling granite terrain with pockets of thick forest. Unseen from the trail, the Tuolumne River makes a raucous crossing of the same section of bedrock, flowing swiftly over the smooth rock in a series of lovely rapids.

After crossing the rolling, wooded terrain, the trail pulls alongside the river again as it makes a long bend around a lovely meadow. Unconnected to Tuolumne Meadows, this large verdant oasis amid the woods opens up the views and you can see the needlelike spires of the Cathedral Range. You can spot, from left to right, Unicorn Peak, the Cockscomb, dome-shaped Peak 11,268, Cathedral Peak, and Fairview Dome. While enjoying the inspiring view, follow the trail as it matches the contour of the river's bend around the north end of the large meadow.

After entering some trees the path emerges on a large, smooth granite slab that slides right down to the river. There is no trail across the slab, but the route is obvious. Down by the water, catch one final vista of the awesome Cathedral Range before you begin the journey into the Grand Canyon of the Tuolumne River. After leaving the viewpoint, the trail cuts through another short band of forest before crossing a second wide granite slab. Note that the river, which has been placid up to this point, now begins to run over a succession of benches, leaping from one short cascade to the next. It presages the watery tumult that lies just downstream. Follow the trail out onto a granite ledge above the increasingly dynamic river. The trail then veers away from the water and descends steeply off the ledge into a small wooded valley. The trail heads back to the river, where you arrive at a bridge that spans the Tuolumne River, 4.0 miles from the trailhead.

As you cross the bridge, look downstream and admire the rebirth of the river. For 4.0 miles the water has been glassy, gentle, and meandering. Now it is reborn as a frothing, whitewater torrent, surging down one granite ledge after another. It is an incredibly kinetic section of water. Cross the bridge and follow the trail to the right as it crosses more granite bedrock alongside the river. From here on, the trail follows one of the most exciting stretches of river in the Sierra Nevada. The trail mostly crosses bare granite and only occasionally veers away from the water in order to climb down off a large bench.

After following along the raging river for 0.75 mile after the bridge, the trail arrives at the base of magnificent Tuolumne Falls. Here the river pours over the precipice and plunges 70 feet to the rocks below. Near the top, the falls crash into a ledge and then fan out over the cliff below. It may not be as tall as some of the waterfalls around Yosemite Valley, but the power and fury of the falls are breathtaking. From Tuolumne Falls the trail continues along the whitewater for just a little farther before veering away from the water and descending to a junction. The path to the left is part of the High Sierra Loop and leads to McGee Lake and then onwards to May Lake, at the base of Mount Hoffman.

Stay right at the junction and follow the trail back toward the river. When you arrive at the water's edge, the trail crosses a bridge over the river. From the bridge you are presented with another fantastic scene. As you cross the bridge, you can watch the Tuolumne River cascade down another beautiful waterfall, the White Cascade. Here the river tumbles down a wide, rocky chute, slams into a large boulder, and explodes into numerous freefalls that spill into a lovely pool at the falls' base. Once across the river, the trail comes to a three-way fork. To the right the trail crosses a bridge over Conness Creek and arrives at the Glen Aulin High Sierra Camp. Staying straight continues on the Pacific Crest Trail, following Conness Creek as it heads north toward the northern boundary of Yosemite. Going left continues along the Tuolumne River, passing the epic trio of California, Le Conte, and Waterwheel Falls on the journey through the Grand Canyon of the Tuolumne.

Pause here and enjoy the scenery at Glen Aulin. The High Sierra camp here has canvas tents, a commissary, water, and places to sit and enjoy the awesome surroundings. The pool at the base of the White Cascade is a great swimming hole in summer, when the water level is not swollen with spring snowmelt. Another great option is to take the left turn after crossing the Tuolumne River. The trail climbs briefly over a granite knoll and then descends alongside the river as it fans out over a huge red slab of rock. It may not be as precipitous as some of the other waterfalls, but it is an impressive sight nonetheless. When you are ready to begin the hike back to Tuolumne Meadows, return the way you came.

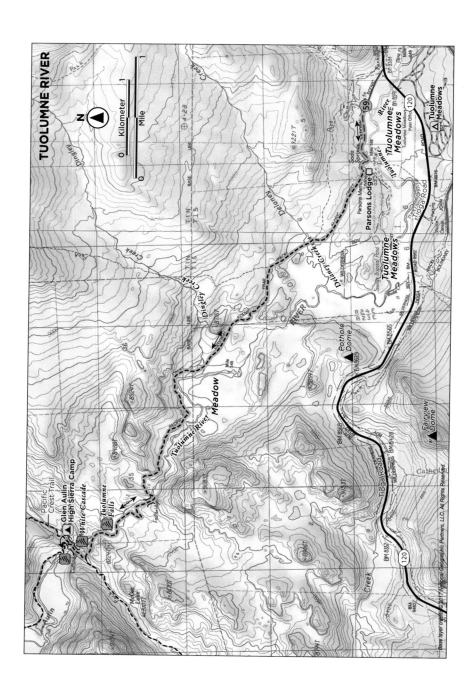

TUOLUMNE RIVER

Just past Glen Aulin, the Tuolumne River flows down another awesome cascade.

MILES AND DIRECTIONS

0.0 Start from the parking area along the gravel access road near Lembert Dome.

0.4 Arrive at Parsons Memorial Lodge and veer right onto the Pacific Crest Trail.

1.7 Stay left at the junction with the Young Lakes Trail.

2.7 The large meadow on the far side of the river offers great views of the Cathedral Range.

4.0 Cross over the Tuolumne River.

4.8 Pass the base of Tuolumne Falls.

5.1 Turn right at the junction with the trail to McGee Lake.

5.25 Arrive at Glen Aulin. Return the way you came.

10.5 Arrive back at the trailhead.

60. GAYLOR LAKES

WHY GO?

This spectacular hike through the high country of eastern Yosemite is a thrilling journey through gorgeous alpine lakes, wide meadows, and historic mining communities. There are incredible views of the High Sierra nearly every step of the way.

THE RUNDOWN

Start: Parking area west of park entrance station on CA 120
Distance: 4.4-mile lollipop
Hiking time: 2–3 hours
Difficulty: Moderate
Elevation gain: 1,300 feet
Season: Late spring, summer, fall
Trail surface: Packed dirt, rocky, duff
Canine compatibility: Dogs not permitted

Fees and permits: Entrance fee
Land status: Yosemite Wilderness, Yosemite National Park
Trail contact: PO Box 577, Yosemite National Park 95389; (209) 372-0200; www.nps.gov/yose
Other: Water is available from the Gaylor Lakes.

FINDING THE TRAILHEAD

Drive to Tioga Pass on CA 120 for 46.5 miles from Crane Flat in the west or 11 miles from the junction of CA 120 and US 395 in the east. The parking area is located on CA 120 immediately west of the park entrance station. **Trailhead GPS:** 37°54'36.82"N / 119°15'29.92"W

WHAT TO SEE

The high country of Yosemite is overflowing with gorgeous alpine lakes that are among the prettiest in the High Sierra. Most of these are found deep in the park's hinterland, where only backpackers go, and see few visitors. A smaller number of lakes are located within easy striking distance of Tioga Road, offering some good options for hikes that explore these alpine gems but do not require long trips to reach them. Of the lakes that can be accessed with relative ease, the Gaylor Lakes may be the most exquisite. The hike to the lakes is among the most dazzling, view-packed sections of trail in the Sierra Nevada. Yet despite the superb beauty of this hike, it is not among Yosemite's best-known trails, leaving it relatively uncrowded (by Yosemite standards of course). Those who do take this trip are richly rewarded with far-reaching vistas, lush meadows, awesome lakes, and rugged cliffs all bundled together, seasoned with some fascinating history, and enjoyed on a concise and scenic loop.

The hike begins by climbing immediately as you leave the trailhead. This trail means business as you climb steeply up the hillside. This is the only part of the hike with significant tree cover. Beyond this point travel is mostly through open meadow and rocky terrain. Though there are a few short switchbacks, the climb is generally steep and persistent. Fortunately it only lasts 0.5 mile before you near the top of the saddle, leaving the trees behind and revealing the first of several spectacular vistas.

Directly above the saddle rises 11,004-foot Gaylor Peak. From this point on the trail, it looks somewhat low and squat. Later in the hike you will get a different perspective on this beautiful peak. Looking north you see a large open meadow extending toward a block of granite cliffs. However, to the south is the real highlight of the view from the pass. Far below the trail, the open country around Tioga Pass—namely the fields of Dana Meadows—contrasts against the steeply rising slopes of Mount Dana, the second-highest peak in Yosemite. The view extends farther south, down the length of the valley drained by Parker Pass Creek. The tall Kuna Crest rises on the west side of the valley, while the east side is formed by the main crest of the Sierra Nevada. Both of these chains of peaks exceed 13,000 feet. On many hikes this view would be the climax, but on the trip to the Gaylor Lakes, this is just the opening round of staggering scenery.

From the pass, follow the trail as it drops down to Middle Gaylor Lake. As you near the bottom, the western horizon is broken up by the awesome needles of the Cathedral Range, one of Yosemite's iconic landscapes. From right to left, these peaks include Cathedral Peak, Tressider Peak, Unicorn Peak, the Echo Peaks, the Cockscomb, and the Matthes Crest. It is an amazing array of granite spires. The view of these giant stone daggers piercing the sky from out of the waters of Middle Gaylor Lake is unforgettable. Eventually you must continue the hike, crossing over the inlet into Middle Gaylor Lake and following the trail as it bears left. It climbs gently along the small creek until you arrive at the south shore of Upper Gaylor Lake, where the trail forks.

Gaylor Peak and the Gaylor Lakes join with the distant Kuna Crest and Cathederal Range to form a grand vista.

Though no trail leads to it, Lower Granite Lake is an easy-to-reach Sierra Nevada gem.

Both paths around Upper Gaylor Lake lead to the same place. The option to the left is more direct; the option to the right is much more scenic. Since the left-hand option tends to hold more snow, turn right. The narrow track hugs the edge of the lake as it passes between the water and the foot of Gaylor Peak. As you round the north side of the lake, you cross a patch of gray rocks where you can look south and catch another view of the Cathedral Range. Continue around the lake until you rejoin the path that traveled the west shoreline. Once the paths have rejoined, the trail climbs moderately up a gully. When you reach the top, turn around and look back to the south. This is possibly the most spectacular view of the hike. From here you can see both Upper and Middle Gaylor Lake lying at the foot of red Gaylor Peak. Beyond them rises the Kuna Crest, which includes the notable summits of Mammoth Mountain and Kuna Peak. A little farther west, the dark summit of Mount Maclure sits just above the Maclure Glacier, one of the largest in Yosemite.

After pausing to enjoy the view, continue along the trail for just a few moments before arriving at the ruins of the Great Sierra Mine. This extensive silver mine, the largest mining operation within the borders of Yosemite, was opened in 1881. The site of numerous buildings and heavy investment, the mine never produced much silver and was closed in 1884. Reopened briefly in the 1930s, it has since been left to be reclaimed by nature. A few small stone buildings remain, and you can investigate them and marvel at the hard labor necessary to construct buildings in such harsh conditions.

The Great Sierra Mine marks the official end of the Gaylor Lakes Trail. Hikers looking to return directly to the trailhead should retrace their steps from here. For those experienced with cross-country travel and route finding, a great loop can be made by heading west from the mine and descending a ridge to the crystalline Granite Lakes. These lakes

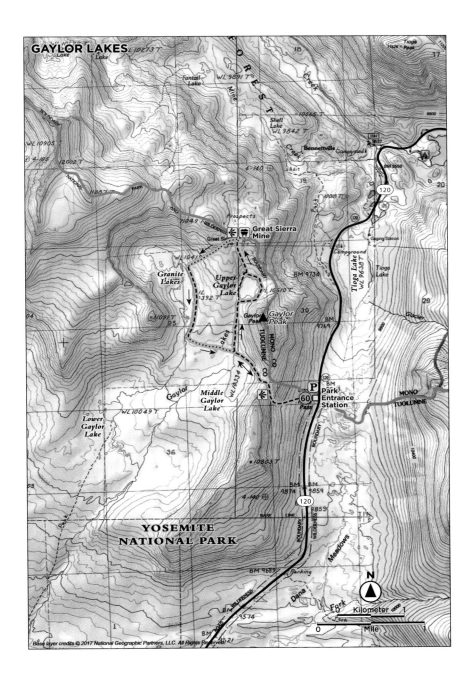

GAYLOR LAKES

YOSEMITE
NATIONAL PARK

Great Sierra
Mine

Granite
Lakes

Upper
Gaylor
Lake

Gaylor
Peak

Middle
Gaylor
Lake

Lower
Gaylor
Lake

Park
Entrance
Station

N

Kilometer
Mile

are nestled in a large, round basin with an amphitheater of sheer granite cliffs rising more than 700 feet above them. The two lakes are distinctly different. The upper body of water is a typical, round alpine lake. The other lake is situated at the mouth of the cirque basin, which is narrower than the inner area. This has pinched off the lake and given it a more elongated shape. Both are very scenic.

As you descend the trail-less ridge, aim for the rocky dike that separates the two lakes. Be sure to look south as you hike down. There you can see Mount Maclure again, but this time it is joined by Mount Lyell, Yosemite's highest peak, just to the left. Just beneath the summit you can clearly see the large icy sheet of the Lyell Glacier. Not only is this the largest glacier in Yosemite, it is the second-largest in the entire Sierra Nevada after the Palisades Glacier. When you reach the rocky dike, you can enjoy some small cascades as the water flows from the upper lake to the lower. Along the shore of Lower Granite Lake, there is a well-established use trail. Follow this to the south end of the lake at the mouth of the cirque. At that point the trail fades away, and you have to travel cross-country across a large meadow strewn with granite boulders. Head toward the ridge just to the right of Gaylor Peak. In about 0.4 mile you arrive at Middle Gaylor Lake. Lower Gaylor Lake lies lower in the meadow, but it is not nearly as pretty as its two siblings. At the middle lake you will pick up another use trail that follows along the water. Head around toward the north end of the lake, cross the inlet, and climb back up to the ridge above the trailhead. From there, follow the trail down to the trailhead.

MILES AND DIRECTIONS

0.0 Start from the trailhead at Tioga Pass and immediately begin climbing a steep slope.

0.5 Reach the top of the saddle, where there are great views to the south.

0.75 Arrive at Middle Gaylor Lake. Cross the outlet stream and follow the trail to the north.

1.3 Reach Upper Gaylor Lake. Stay right to follow the prettier path around the lake's south shore.

2.0 The official trail ends at the Great Sierra Mine. To continue, go cross-country down the slope to the west toward the Granite Lakes. (**Option:** Return the way you came for a 4.0-mile out-and-back hike.)

2.6 At the north end of Lower Granite Lake, locate the use trail that follows its shoreline and take it south.

3.1 At the end of Lower Granite Lake, the use trail disappears. Turn east and walk cross-country over the meadow toward Middle Gaylor Lake.

3.5 Arrive back at Middle Gaylor Lake. Retrace your steps from there.

4.4 Arrive back at the trailhead.

61. **SAN JOAQUIN RIVER GORGE**

WHY GO?

The hike to the San Joaquin Gorge explores a springtime land teeming with wildflowers and a beautiful oak savanna and visits the San Joaquin River as it races through a narrow granite gorge.

THE RUNDOWN

Start: Signed trailhead parking area on Smalley Road
Distance: 7.6-mile lollipop (**Option:** 1.8 miles out and back to San Joaquin River Gorge)
Hiking time: 3–4 hours
Difficulty: Moderate
Elevation gain: 1,580 feet
Season: Year-round, though spring is best; summer can be extremely hot.
Trail surface: Packed dirt

Canine compatibility: Dogs permitted
Fees and permits: None
Land status: San Joaquin River Gorge Management Area, Bureau of Land Management
Trail contact: 40060 Smalley Rd., Auberry 93602; (559) 855-3492; www.blm.gov
Other: Water is available at the trailhead.

FINDING THE TRAILHEAD

 From Fresno, drive east on CA 168 for 37 miles. Turn left onto Auberry Road and drive 2.9 miles. Veer left onto Powerhouse Road, drive 1.8 miles, then turn left onto Smalley Road. Continue for 4.4 miles, entering the San Joaquin River Gorge Management Area. Turn right into the parking area signed for the trailhead and campground. **Trailhead GPS:** 37°4'58.52"N / 119°33'15.30"W

WHAT TO SEE

The San Joaquin is the longest and largest river to flow out of the Sierra Nevada. After the Sacramento River, it is the second-longest river in California. Its immense watershed covers the entire area between Yosemite and Kings Canyon National Parks. As its various forks come together and collect water from its innumerable tributaries, the river passes through deep canyons on its way to the great Central Valley. During this long passage, the water has been harnessed for hydroelectric power generation. Despite the occasional impoundments necessary to make electricity, the San Joaquin still has several stretches where it is a wild, free-flowing mountain river. The last section where the river flows free through the mountains is preserved as the San Joaquin River Gorge Management Area. It lies between the Kerckhoff Dam and the high-water mark of Millerton Lake. Here the river makes one final dash through rugged terrain, one final surge through granite boulders, one final journey as the wild river it was born to be.

The San Joaquin River flows
through the rugged gorge.

Hikers are fortunate to have the opportunity to see the river as it charges swiftly through a rugged granite gorge. The deep trough, lined with white, rocky slabs and giant boulders, is an impressive sight and a reminder that the San Joaquin can still be a mean piece of water, despite having been harnessed to power the industry that lies downstream. However, the hike to the river offers more than just the gorge. Once across the excellent footbridge, the trail makes a loop through the wildland on the north side of the river. It climbs high up onto the craggy rim of the river's canyon, where awesome views of this beautiful foothill canyon wait. The hike is best done in spring, when temperatures are cool, the river is full, the grass is green, and wildflowers proliferate along the trail. Then, when the high country is still smothered in snow, the San Joaquin River Gorge may seem like paradise.

To begin the hike, follow the trail north from the parking area. The wide dirt path makes an easy descent toward the river, which lies 1.0 mile ahead. The path follows the contours of the hillside, winding around small knolls as it passes through oak woodlands and alongside some large hedges. In spring this section of trail features amazing wild-flowers that densely pack the hillsides and turn them pink. The trail crosses a few small springtime streams, but by summer these have all dried. As you descend you begin to catch glimpses of the gorge and hear the river as it shoots through. Finally, after making a steady descent, you arrive at the large footbridge across the river.

Though the gorge is the primary attraction on this part of the hike, pause and note the bridge before walking out onto it. It is certainly among the most impressive footbridges you will encounter anywhere. Anchored at both ends into the granite wall of the gorge, the bridge consists of two parallel arches that meet at the apex. From this is suspended the walkway, providing easy access to the wild, north side of the river. As you walk out over the water, you are treated to a long view down the linear gorge. Though the terrain here is almost semiarid, the granite slabs and boulders leave no doubt that this is indeed a river of the Sierra Nevada. It is reminiscent of sections of Northern Sierra rivers such as the Feather and the Yuba, which also flow through gorges that are similar in composition. While on the bridge, be sure to note the presence of the nearby Kerckhoff Powerhouse. Built in the 1920s, it was the first hydroelectric installation on the San Joaquin River.

After you have crossed the bridge, the trail turns upstream and climbs a short distance to a fork. This marks the beginning of the loop. It can be hiked in either direction, but going counterclockwise saves the good views of the canyon for later, leaving less hiking to be done after hitting the highlight. Turn left at the fork and commence hiking over the gently rolling hills that lie north of the river. The route initially heads west, toward the tall, flat-topped wall of Kennedy Table. This mountain is part of the remnants of an old lava flow that once covered this whole area. Squaw's Leap, a prominent high point on the south side of the San Joaquin, is part of this same formation, though the river long ago broke the two mountains apart from each other. After going west for 0.75 mile from the footbridge, the trail arrives at a junction. The path to the left follows along the river until it reaches Millerton Lake. Stay to the right and proceed on the trail as it finally bends around to the north. This begins the more strenuous climbing of the hike as you ascend the flanks of the canyon wall.

The trail makes a steady ascent to the north, but as it nears the steep slope that leads to the canyon rim, the path turns east. After a long switchback that rounds a rocky knoll, you keep climbing north. Soon, about 1.5 miles from the beginning of the loop, you cross an old dirt road. Stay alert and be sure to follow the trail rather than the dirt road. From

Expansive views of the San Joaquin River Gorge are found along the higher sections of the trail.

SAN JOAQUIN RIVER GORGE

here it is only a little more climbing before the path enters a lush notch in the cliffs and arrives at the rim of the canyon.

Once you have climbed to the top of the canyon, the trail turns east and follows along the rim. However, the views aren't really panoramic for a little while, since the trail stays back away from the edge. Nonetheless, the hiking is very scenic, and even though the view is filtered, you can still enjoy the sight of the large canyon below. Eventually the trail passes some rock outcroppings on the right, where you can scramble up and get a really detailed vantage point on the San Joaquin River Gorge. You can see the deep channel of the San Joaquin, as well as the Kerckhoff Powerhouse. Just to the right of the powerhouse, keen eyes can spot the footbridge through the trees. The various structures of the San Joaquin River Gorge Management Area dot the hillsides. In the distance rise the dark volcanic plateaus of Squaw's Leap and Kennedy Plateau. Beyond the breech between these mountains, the river is impounded to form Millerton Lake, after which is begins its lazy meandering through the vast Central Valley.

Moving on from the rocky vista, the trail begins to descend back toward the San Joaquin River. It makes a series of long switchbacks down a wide gully, dropping swiftly as it goes. Views of the upstream part of the gorge are good. Here the canyon is much narrower, and the steep walls are much closer to the river. Near the bottom of the gully, the trail bends back to the west and begins to run parallel to the river again, though it is much higher than the rocky gorge. You gradually lose elevation until you can see the Kerckhoff Powerhouse through the trees and hear the river flowing below. It is just a few more moments before you reach the junction where you began the loop. From here turn left, cross the footbridge, and follow the trail back up to the trailhead.

MILES AND DIRECTIONS

0.0 Start from the trailhead and begin the easy descent to the river.

0.9 Cross the footbridge over the San Joaquin River. (**Option:** Turn around here for a 1.8-mile out and back to the river.)

1.1 Stay left at the junction to begin the loop.

1.8 Stay right at another junction.

2.6 Keep right when the trail branches off a dirt road.

3.5 Arrive at the top of the ridge.

4.0 Come to a good view point overlooking the valley.

6.5 Reach the end of the loop. Retrace your steps from here.

7.6 Arrive back at the trailhead.

62. **TWIN LAKES**
(KAISER WILDERNESS)

WHY GO?

This hike enters the Kaiser Wilderness, an isolated block of high granite peaks on the west side of the Sierra Nevada. Hikers find sculpted granite peaks, beautiful lakes, meadows, and swift creeks.

THE RUNDOWN

Start: Rattlesnake Trailhead
Total distance: 6.3-mile lollipop
Hiking time: 3–4 hours or overnight
Difficulty: Moderately easy
Elevation gain: 930 feet
Season: Summer, fall
Trail surface: Packed dirt, rocky, sandy
Canine compatibility: Dogs permitted

Fees and permits: None
Land status: Kaiser Wilderness, Sierra National Forest
Trail contact: High Sierra Ranger District, 29688 Auberry Rd., Prather 93651; (559) 855-5355; www.fs.usda .gov/sierra
Other: Water is available in the Twin Lakes and from creeks.

FINDING THE TRAILHEAD

From Fresno, drive east on CA 168 for 67 miles. When the highway ends at the east end of Huntington Lake, turn right onto Kaiser Pass Road. Stay on this wide, paved road for 5.6 miles. It then narrows into a windy, twisting, narrow road and continues for 1.7 miles to Kaiser Pass. From the pass proceed 2.1 miles farther as Kaiser Pass Road descends to the north. At the intersection with FR 5, turn left and drive 2 miles on the bumpy but easily passable dirt road to the Rattlesnake Trailhead. **Trailhead GPS:** 37°19'25.92"N / 119°8'25.16"W

WHAT TO SEE

The Kaiser Wilderness protects a high, east-west-trending ridge that lies well to the west of the main crest of the Sierra Nevada. Coming from the west, this is one of the most easily accessed mountain regions between Kings Canyon and Yosemite National Parks. Much of the surrounding terrain is heavily wooded, and tall Kaiser Peak and its subordinate towers rise like a granite island, offering refuge to hikers looking for an alpine destination. Kaiser Ridge runs along the latitudinal axis of the wilderness. Most of the best terrain lies on the north side of the ridge. This area has experienced heavy glaciation. The large sheets of ice carved and scoured the peaks into rugged knobs that gaze down on sparkling lakes in rockbound bowls. This hike, to two of the prettiest lakes in the wilderness, explores the area on the north side of Kaiser Ridge, climbing easily through peaceful forests before leading to the higher terrain where it loops past the pair of lakes and a lush meadow, where views of the distant Ritter Range are inspiring.

From the trailhead the path heads downhill and immediately passes a sign marking the entrance to the Kaiser Wilderness. The trail makes a steady descent for 0.5 mile to Kaiser Creek. Cross the creek and proceed just a short distance before you reach an unmarked junction on the right. This trail leads to Sample Meadow, which lies to the north. Stay to the left and continue through the woods. The trail levels off after crossing the creek, gaining elevation slightly but at an almost imperceptible grade. In only 0.3 mile the trail crosses another creek. The first was the main branch of Kaiser Creek, which emerges from Kaiser Meadow. The second crossing is over the water that flows out of Lower Twin Lake and Round Meadow.

After crossing the creek, continue through the forest as the trail maintains its easy slope. The path skirts the edge of a large granite bluff as it heads south. After passing through the pleasant, sunny forest for 0.8 mile, the trail begins to steepen noticeably. Cross the creek one last time and begin a steep ascent up a wide gully. The steepness of the climb is mitigated by the presence of the creek, tumbling over boulders and cascading down smooth slabs of white rock. As you climb, the trail begins to emerge from the forest for the first time. Initially the trail crosses some sandy areas surrounded by brush, but eventually granite outcroppings become more common. At 2.2 miles from the trailhead, you arrive at a signed trail junction. The trail coming in from the south is the latter half of the loop section of this hike. In addition to the Twin Lakes, the trail climbs up to Potter Pass, where a few trails from the southern side of the wilderness converge. Many hikers who

Kaiser Peak is an imposing sight from the shores of Upper Twin Lake.

Though not as large as its nearby sibling, Lower Twin Lake is a scenic mountain jewel.

reach the Twin Lakes have taken these routes, which involve a lot more climbing and less water than the easy route from the northern boundary of the wilderness.

To begin the loop, stay right at the junction and hike west. The significant climbing essentially comes to an end once you reach the junction, but the rolling terrain means the trail undulates a lot. After passing along the north side of Round Meadow, you meet the trail coming from George Lake. Bear left and climb through a low, rocky gully. As you reach the top of the rise, you finally arrive at the edge of Upper Twin Lake. After the hike through the woods and the time on the trail spent negotiating the rolling terrain, there has been little indication of the awesome landscape you have entered until you reach the lake.

The large, glittering lake sits in a wide bowl. On the south and east sides, the lake is bounded first by a wide band of meadow and then by tall trees. Its western and northern shores are lined with large granite boulders and slabs. A rocky island rises from the water in the northwest corner of the lake. While this is nearly an ideal setting for the immediate lakeshore, it is the grand vista to the west that really makes Upper Twin Lake an incredible destination. A series of tall, crystalline towers rise almost 1,500 feet above the lake. Kaiser Peak, the highest point in the wilderness, is just out of sight, but the large bank of cliffs immediately south of it are the highest, most distant monolith you can see from here.

After exploring the area around the lake, it is time to resume hiking the loop. Follow the trail alongside to the south. The main path veers to the left and climbs above the water. A well-established path continues along the water's edge. If you miss the main trail and start to curve around the south shore of the lake, backtrack or take one of the use trails that head back east and connect to the main trail. Once you are heading away from Upper Twin Lake, climb easily over a low divide and drop down through the forest

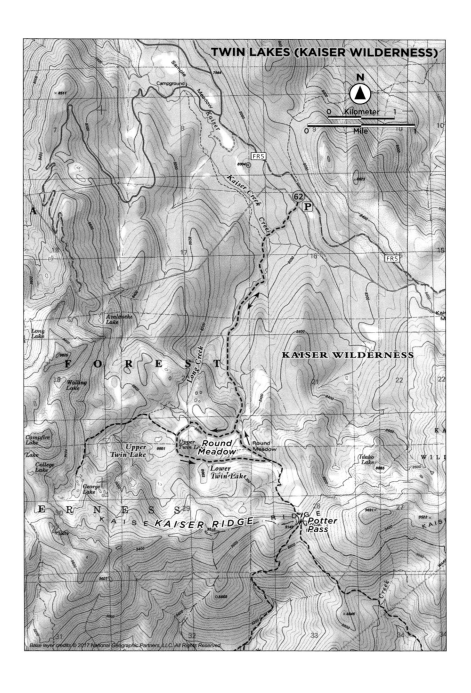

to Lower Twin Lake. It becomes readily apparent that these lakes are not really twins. Smaller than the upper lake, the lake is backed by a sheer granite headwall that, despite its scenic value, does not compare to the grand towers that rise behind Upper Twin Lake. Indeed, it is likely the similarity in their elevation that drew the equivalence between the lakes.

Moving on from the wildflower-ringed lake, the path continues east. The trail traverses the base of Kaiser Ridge as it passes above small Round Meadow. With little around the meadow obstructing your view to the north, you are treated to an awesome view of the Ritter Range rising 30 miles to the north. The dark, massive blocks of Ritter and Banner Peaks are an awesome reminder of just how epic the scale of the Sierra Nevada is. After passing the meadow, the trail descends into a gully where it meets the trail coming from Potter Pass. Turn left onto the trail and proceed downhill. The gully, initially dry, has numerous seeps; the water collects and begins gurgling alongside the trail. The path eventually levels off as you arrive at the edge of Round Meadow. It is a nice place to pause and enjoy the serene setting before crossing the creek and rejoining the trail leading up from the trailhead, completing the loop. From there, follow the trail back to the trailhead.

MILES AND DIRECTIONS

0.0 Start from the trailhead and head downhill.

0.5 Cross Kaiser Creek and stay left when the trail to Sample Meadow branches off to the right.

2.25 Stay right at the junction to begin the loop.

2.6 Bear left at the intersection with the George Lake Trail.

2.9 Arrive at Upper Twin Lake.

3.2 Reach Lower Twin Lake.

3.7 Turn left at the junction with the trail to Potter Pass.

4.1 Turn right at the end of the loop and head back to the trailhead.

6.3 Arrive back at the trailhead.

63. **DINKEY LAKES**

WHY GO?

This hike leads to the Dinkey Lakes, a cluster of alpine lakes on the western side of the Sierra Nevada. Large meadows and easy terrain capped by granite mountains make this a pleasant and scenic trip.

THE RUNDOWN

Start: Dinkey Lakes Trailhead
Distance: 7.1-mile lollipop
Hiking time: 3–4 hours or overnight
Difficulty: Moderately easy
Elevation gain: 810 feet
Season: Summer, fall
Trail surface: Packed dirt, rocky
Canine compatibility: Dogs permitted

Fees and permits: None
Land status: Dinkey Lakes Wilderness, Sierra National Forest
Trail contact: High Sierra Ranger District, 29688 Auberry Rd., Prather 93651; (559) 855-5355; www.fs.usda.gov/sierra
Other: Water is available in Dinkey Creek and numerous lakes.

FINDING THE TRAILHEAD

Note: Though not essential, a high-clearance vehicle is strongly encouraged for the drive to this trailhead.

From Fresno, drive east on CA 168 for 49 miles. Turn right onto Dinkey Creek Road. Drive 9.1 miles then turn left onto Rock Creek Road. This road is paved but there are numerous large potholes. Watch your speed carefully to avoid hitting them. Follow Rock Creek Road for 6 miles and turn right onto FR 9S10. This road was paved at one time but now is a bumpy road with sporadic sections of pavement. Drive this road for 4.5 miles and make a hard right-hand turn onto FR 9S62, which is signed for the Dinkey Lakes. Continue on this dirt road for 2.2 miles to the trailhead. The last section of this road is very rough. **Trailhead GPS:** 37°9'5.42"N / 119°6'14.38"W

WHAT TO SEE

The Dinkey Lakes Wilderness protects a cluster of tall peaks and alpine lakes that rise far to the west of the main crest of the Sierra Nevada. An island of granite high country in the midst of a vast sea of forest, this pocket wilderness is a haven for hikers looking for mountain beauty but not wanting to work too hard to get to and appreciate it. The obvious highlight of the area is the large collection of lakes that huddle around the tall Three Sisters, a long ridge crest that has three prominent points, and Dogtooth Peak, a spiked tower best viewed from Courtright Reservoir. There are nine lakes in the main group, and each has its own distinct character. This hike leads to four of the lakes, with an optional side trip to visit three more.

The hike through the Dinkey Lakes is one that rewards hikers with a lot of scenery for relatively little effort. The terrain here is gentle, and steep climbing is kept to a minimum.

The broad ridge of the Three Sisters rises above meadow-lined First Dinkey Lake.

The trail follows a lovely lollipop route along Dinkey Creek and loops to a succession of four beautiful lakes, each with its own perspective on the Three Sisters. The scenery is terrific and the trail pleasant. However, this is the only hike in this guidebook where high-clearance vehicles are recommended to reach the trailhead. While many do make the drive in low-clearance vehicles, it can be a bottom-scraping adventure. If you do not have access to a high-clearance vehicle, consider taking the paved road all the way up to the Cliff Lake Trailhead at the Courtright Reservoir. From there you can hike about 4.0 miles into Cliff Lake and then over a pass into the Dinkey Lakes. It is a longer outing than beginning at the Dinkey Lakes Trailhead, but access to the trailhead is much, much easier.

The Dinkey Lakes Trailhead is located in a large intrusion of sedimentary rocks set in the midst of the granite that is ubiquitous throughout the Sierra Nevada. The rock at the parking area is different in both color and consistency but provides little warning of the fascinating geology you encounter as you begin the hike. Follow the trail as it descends toward Dinkey Creek. On your left you pass an incredible rock outcropping that has red and white lines warped into amazing wavy patterns. This is, on a very small scale, the same type of formation seen throughout the Eastern Sierra's Sherwin Range, especially in Convict Canyon. Pass the unusual rock and arrive on the bank of Dinkey Creek. Cross over the creek and follow the trail north. Waterfall junkies can follow the creek upstream a little to a nice waterfall.

Continuing on the main trail, you maintain a gentle grade through the woods just south of the creek. You soon cross back over the water and follow along its northern bank. After you cross the boundary of the Dinkey Lakes Wilderness, the terrain gets a little rockier as the path traverses some large slabs. In 1.2 miles you reach a junction with the trail to Mystery Lake. This is the end of the return leg of the loop. Stay left here and continue hiking east. The trail moves closer to Dinkey Creek again, and as you walk through the woods, you can spot scenic cascades. The small cataracts correspond to a steepening of the trail, which means you are nearing the end of the creek and arrival at First Dinkey Lake.

The initial indication of your arrival at First Dinkey Lake is a small complex of marshy meadows just off the trail. They mark the beginning of Dinkey Creek as it flows out of the meadows and begins its course toward the trailhead. Walk past these marshy areas and arrive at a trail junction, just above First Dinkey Lake. At the junction there is a popular campsite where you are likely to find backpackers. Stay right here and follow along the edge of the lake's beautiful grassy fringe. Large granite boulders dot the landscape, bringing some pleasant contrast to the green field. Adjacent to the grass fringe is large First Dinkey Lake. Beyond the lake rises the gray crest of the Three Sisters. Though each of the lakes in the Dinkey Lakes Wilderness has its unique charm, First Dinkey Lake is the most attractive. The combination of meadow, boulder, lake, and peak is inviting and seems perfectly proportioned for maximum scenic value.

Contour along the east shore of First Dinkey Lake, enjoying the lush meadow and clear lake as you go. As you near the end of the lake, the path dips back into the woods away from the water before arriving at a small creek at the very edge of the large meadow that lines the lake's eastern shore. This small stream maintains its flow through much of the year despite its very small watershed. Cross the little creek and continue through an area with stunted trees until you arrive at a junction, 3.25 miles from the trailhead. The path to the left is the 0.6-mile route that connects to Second Dinkey, Rock, and Island Lakes. These are the highest of the main lakes in the wilderness area. If you are looking for a longer hike or a less-traveled place to camp, taking the spur over to this area is a good option. To proceed with the loop, bear right.

Once you pass the junction, the route leads through some of the prettiest forests in the region. The trees are large and well spaced. A thick green mat covers the forest floor, and occasional granite boulders punctuate the scene. These elements all blend together to form an almost parklike setting. After about 0.4 mile you pass a spur that leads to South Lake and campsites on the edge of the lake. Stay on the main path, which crosses the outlet and swings around to another point on the edge of the lake. Like First Dinkey Lake, the Three Sisters hold a commanding position above the water, except here they are much closer and the view is more intimate. The three points cannot be seen in their entirety, but enough of the cliffs around them are visible that they still form an impressive backdrop.

Linger at South Lake a bit before resuming the hike. The trail leaves the shore and climbs over a low rise. This is the highest point on the hike. After a short descent, you reach the edge of Swede Lake. Similar in many respects to South Lake, it is another beautiful body of water set beneath gray cliffs. Also like South Lake, the trail alights briefly at the edge of the water before veering away again. It gives you a good opportunity to stop and rest and enjoy the view before pressing onward. After leaving Swede Lake behind, the trail makes a steep, rocky descent on a heavily forested slope.

At the base of the steep grade, the trail splits at a patch of meadow. Both options lead to the same location, though the trail on the right travels through more meadows, while the one on the left spends more time on the shore of Mystery Lake, the final destination on the loop. Both trails reconvene at the west end of the lake. Unlike the previous pools, this lake is situated on the side of the Three Sisters, and you cannot see much more of the mountain than a high shoulder. Nonetheless, the lake, which also has a good view of a nice granite dome, is very pretty. With a couple of small rocky islands and a rock-lined shore, it is a good swimming lake. When you are ready to depart, follow the trail west and head down one final slope, crossing over Mystery Lakes small outlet creek about halfway down. When you reach the bottom, you must also cross Dinkey Creek. Pick up the trail on the other side, turn left, and follow the path back to the trailhead.

Garden-like forests of lodgepole pine are found along the path to South and Swede Lakes.

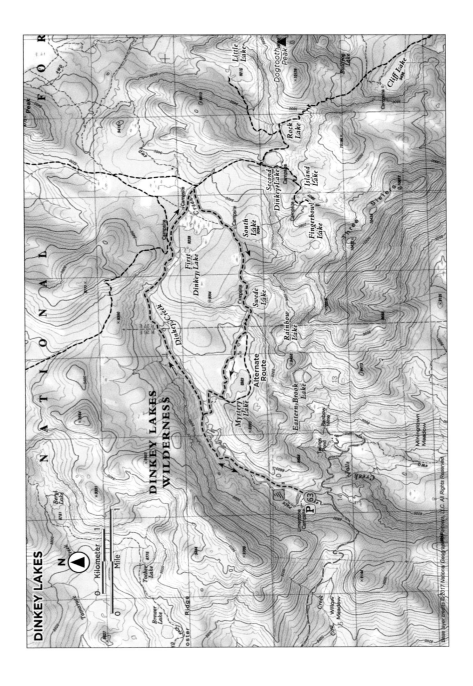

DINKEY LAKES

N

0 Kilometer 1

0 Mile 1

DINKEY LAKES WILDERNESS

NATIONAL FOREST

Base layer graphic ©2017 National Geographic Partners, LLC. All Rights Reserved.

South Lake is located near the base of the Three Sisters.

MILES AND DIRECTIONS

0.0 Start from the Dinkey Lakes Trailhead, passing the warped sedimentary rocks.

1.2 Stay left at the junction with the Mystery Lake Trail to begin the loop.

2.8 Arrive at First Dinkey Lake. Stay right at the junction and follow the trail along the shore.

3.25 At the junction with the trail to Second Dinkey Lake, stay right to continue to South Lake.

3.9 Reach South Lake.

4.5 Arrive at Swede Lake.

5.5 Pass Mystery Lake.

5.9 Turn left onto the Dinkey Creek Trail.

7.1 Arrive back at the trailhead.

64. REDWOOD MOUNTAIN LOOP

WHY GO?

This unique hike leads through the largest grove of giant sequoias in the world. The hike passes through the trees on top of Redwood Mountain then loops back to the trailhead through the lush canyon of Redwood Creek.

THE RUNDOWN

Start: Sugarbowl Trail from Redwood Saddle
Distance: 6.5-mile loop
Hiking time: About 4 hours
Difficulty: Moderate
Elevation gain: 1,430 feet
Season: Spring, summer, fall
Trail surface: Packed dirt, rocky
Canine compatibility: Dogs not permitted

Fees and permits: Entrance fee
Land status: Kings Canyon National Park
Trail contact: 47050 Generals Highway, Three Rivers 93271; (559) 565-3341; www.nps.gov/seki
Other: Water is available in Redwood Creek.

FINDING THE TRAILHEAD

From Fresno, drive east on CA 180 for 57.7 miles. Turn right onto CA 198/Generals Highway and continue for 3.5 miles. Turn into a dirt pullout across the highway from the road signed for Hume Lake. A dirt road with a sign stating "Entering Kings Canyon National Park" leads down into Redwood Canyon. Follow this road for 1.7 miles to the trailhead. **Trailhead GPS:** 36°42'26.81"N / 118°55'15.24"W

WHAT TO SEE

The giant sequoias are one of the chief attractions of Sequoia National Park as well as the General Grant Grove section of Kings Canyon National Park. These heavily trafficked areas showcase these incredible trees, highlighting their great age and monumental size. The sequoias deserve their renown, as they are the largest trees on Earth and are an important link to the Sierra Nevada's past. The trees thrive at elevations around 5,000 and 7,000 feet, which tends to be where the most precipitation falls in the Sierra Nevada. Though isolated trees can be found, they generally grow in groves, making spectacular, almost cathedral-like forests where the canopy is high overhead and the great trunks of the trees are akin to the columns holding up the huge structure. Like the forests of their cousins, the coast redwood, the groves of giant sequoias tend to have a hushed, peaceful atmosphere about them. Of course this may not always be the case at the famous groves of the national parks. If this is off-putting, and you want to see the colossal trees in a wilderness setting, the hike on Redwood Mountain is ideal.

Towering sequoias line the trail through
the Redwood Mountain Grove.

The journey over Redwood Mountain travels through the largest grove of giant sequoias in the world. Not only is this a superlative collection of big trees, but the grove also contains the tallest known giant sequoia as well as the Roosevelt and Hart Trees, which are both in the top twenty-five trees in terms of volume. The massive, towering trees line the trail for almost the entire hike, some standing in isolation, while others are clustered together in large groups. Hikers on this journey have the opportunity to observe the giants in a wild setting, unhindered by the development that is found in other great groves in the national parks. Complementing the exposure to the breathtaking forest, the hike also features good views of the granite dome of Big Bald, a nearby peak that is a popular hiking destination. You also have the opportunity to hike through the redwoods while traveling alongside beautiful Redwood Creek, which flows south to the Kaweah River.

The hike begins on Redwood Saddle, where you are surrounded by many giants. Two trails originate here. The Redwood Canyon and Hart Tree Trails descend into Redwood Creek's deep canyon. The Redwood Canyon Trail is the return leg of this hike. Take the Sugarbowl Trail, which climbs up a short slope. You then begin a long, rolling traverse of the Redwood Mountain. The path mostly stays on the east side of the long ridge, passing numerous giant sequoias that are often joined by firs and large sugar pines. Some of these trees are extremely large in their own right, though they still pale in comparison to the gargantuan redwoods.

Be sure to touch a sequoia alongside the trail and feel its smooth bark. Some of the giant trees can grow bark over a foot thick, which helps make the trees resistant to fire. Indeed, fire is a critical part of the sequoia's ecology, keeping the competing species clear of the trees and aiding in the cones' opening so that the seeds can be dispersed. As you hike along the top of Redwood Mountain, note that many of the trees have been singed by fire. After decades of fire suppression, the National Park Service now follows a program of proscribed burns in redwood groves.

As you continue across the top of the mountain, there are a few breaks in the forest where views open up to the southeast. From here you can peer down into Redwood Canyon below. Above the east side of the canyon, note the large granite dome of Big Bald, a popular hiking destination with a fantastic view. In the southeast the high peaks of the Great Western Divide line the distant horizon. Where the clearings occur on Redwood Mountain, you are likely to find rocks composed of marine sediment along the trail. These areas are more inhospitable to the redwoods, and other trees have taken root here.

After hiking through the Redwood Mountain Grove for 1.9 miles, you pass one last clearing with a great view as the trail travels just beneath the highest point on Redwood Mountain before encountering a final collection of sequoias. Here the trail starts to descend into Redwood Canyon. The descent lasts 2.6 miles, and you pass through a predominantly mixed conifer forest clinging to the steep slopes. Occasional clearings offer more glimpses of Big Bald as the trail makes a few meandering switchbacks down the side of the canyon.

An open spot on the trail reveals a dense cluster of round-topped giant sequoias.

When you reach the bottom, you arrive at a junction. The trail to the right leads quickly to the Fallen Giant, a massive tree that, as its name applies, is no longer standing. The trail continues, climbing up to the enormous Hart Tree, one of the largest trees in the world. From there the trail traverses the east side of Redwood Canyon, ultimately rejoining the Redwood Canyon Trail near the trailhead. This is a great option for hikers who want more sequoias or a longer hike. It adds about 4.0 miles to the hike. The more moderate option is to simply hike up the canyon, following along beautiful Redwood Creek.

In some ways the Redwood Canyon Trail is the prettier option. It may not have singularly large trees like the Fallen Giant and the Hart Tree, but it does not lack for giant sequoias that are still eye-poppingly massive. On top of that, the trail follows near Redwood Creek almost the entire way. It's not always close to the creek, but you can usually hear it if you cannot see it. The forest bottom is covered with ferns and other low vegetation. After hiking through the beautiful and peaceful forest for a while, you near the canyon headwall and start to climb more earnestly. The trail coming from the Hart Tree soon rejoins the Redwood Canyon Trail, and in short order you are deposited back at the trailhead, completing the loop. Giant sequoias still line the saddle, bidding an awesome farewell to hikers who have enjoyed sharing the forest with the magnificent giants.

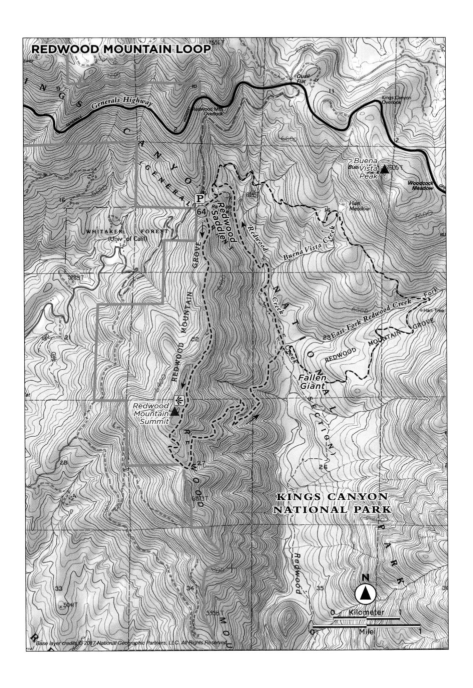

REDWOOD MOUNTAIN LOOP

Generals Highway

Quail Flat

Kings Canyon Overlook

Redwood Mtn. Overlook

Buena Vista Peak

Woodcock Meadow

Hart Meadow

P

64

Redwood Saddle

WHITAKER FOREST
(Univ. of Calif.)

Buena Vista Creek

East Fork Redwood Creek

Hart Tree

REDWOOD MOUNTAIN GROVE

Fallen Giant

Redwood Mountain Summit

KINGS CANYON
NATIONAL PARK

N

0   Kilometer   1

0   Mile   1

The granite dome of Big Baldy is visible from many places on Redwood Mountain.

MILES AND DIRECTIONS

0.0   Start the hike by heading right on the Sugarbowl Trail.

1.9   Near the top of Redwood Mountain, begin the descent into Redwood Canyon.

4.5   Arrive at the bottom of the canyon, where there is a junction with the Hart Tree Trail. Stay left and continue hiking on the Redwood Canyon Trail.

6.1   Stay left when the Hart Tree Trail rejoins the Redwood Canyon Trail.

6.5   Arrive back at the trailhead.

65. **WEAVER LAKE**

WHY GO?

This pretty hike leads to Weaver Lake in the Jennie Lakes Wilderness, where you will find a lovely lake backed by high granite cliffs.

THE RUNDOWN

Start: Fox Meadow Trailhead on unsigned FR 14S16
Distance: 4.2 miles out and back
Hiking time: 2 hours
Difficulty: Easy
Elevation gain: 820 feet
Season: Late spring, summer, fall
Trail surface: Packed dirt, rocky, sandy
Canine compatibility: Dogs permitted

Fees and permits: None
Land status: Jennie Lakes Wilderness, Sequoia National Forest
Trail contact: Hume Lake Ranger District, 35860 East Kings Canyon Rd., Dunlap 93621; (559) 338-2251; www.fs.usda.gov/main/sequoia
Other: Water is available at Weaver Lake.

FINDING THE TRAILHEAD

On the Generals Highway, 9.5 miles south of the Grant Grove and 18 miles north of the Lodgepole Visitor Center, turn north onto FR 14S11, which is signed for Big Meadows. Follow this paved road for 5.4 miles, passing the Big Meadows Campground and crossing over Big Meadows Creek. Take the first right after crossing the bridge onto unmarked FR 14S16. Follow the bumpy dirt road for 1.4 miles, staying straight when two roads branch off at 0.4 mile. *Note:* The last 0.3 mile before the Fox Meadow Trailhead is very rough. **Trailhead GPS:** 36°42'39.28"N / 118°49'1.07"W

WHAT TO SEE

The Jennie Lakes Wilderness is a small pocket of land tucked between the General Grant Grove section of Kings Canyon National Park and the southwest corner of the main body of Kings Canyon, with Sequoia National Park lying directly to the south. It is part, albeit a small one, of the large unbroken block of wilderness that stretches from Yosemite to the South Sierra Wilderness. The wilderness covers a low shoulder of the Kings–Kaweah Divide that extends beyond the boundary of the national park. In Sequoia National Park, the divide is a land of mighty peaks and dotted with dozens of alpine lakes. By the time the divide reaches the area protected by the Jennie Lakes Wilderness, the terrain is much more subdued, with the big mountains replaced by gentle, rolling granite bluffs. Only a few peaks and lakes remain to hint at what lies farther south. Yet in spite of the difference in the topography, the Jennie Lakes area is classic Sierra Nevada.

Weaver Creek is a lively presence on the trail to Weaver Lake.

The terrain may be gentle in comparison with the high divide that rises to the east, but it is still a beautiful and accessible area. The wilderness is covered with extensive forests that are punctuated by significant granite areas. The highest areas in the heart of the wilderness are the highlands occupied by Weaver and Jennie Lakes, the only notable bodies of water in the area. Indeed, these are the last two in a long series of lakes that occupied glacial basins in the Kings-Kaweah Divide. Just beyond the east boundary of the wilderness, the lakes in the divide get larger and more numerous. Weaver Lake is the most easily accessed, and the hike to the glittering alpine jewel is a great introduction to the beautiful scenery this area has to offer. The hike is moderately steep, but its short length makes it a fairly easy hike.

From the Fox Meadow Trailhead, hike south and immediately cross a creek that flows from a spring higher up in the gully. Follow alongside the little creek through dense forest canopy before reaching a junction with the trail climbing up from Big Meadow. (**Option:** If you want a longer hike, or don't want to drive the last section of the rough road, the Big Meadow Trailhead is a good option. It is 1.5 miles from the Fox Meadow Trailhead and climbs 640 feet, but it is a pleasant addition to this short hike.)

Turn left onto the trail, and after a very brief bit of level hiking, the path begins to climb again, promptly reaching a saddle at the headwaters of Stony Creek, which flows south toward the Generals Highway. Leave the saddle and begin climbing higher over

Fox Meadow. About 0.7 mile from the trailhead, you reach the spring-fed creek that waters the meadow. The trail splits near the edge of the water. One route climbs to the south, heading toward Poop Out Pass and Jennie Lake. Stay left, cross the creek, and continue climbing. The path enters an open area where there are no trees along the trail. This gives you an opportunity to observe the surrounding area, including some granite domes on the far side of Fox Meadow.

As you turn east from the open area, you enter a wooded section. Steady climbing leads you to the border of the Jennie Lakes Wilderness and, just beyond it, another spring-fed creek. Cross it and continue through the woods. The trail turns north, passes through a large field of boulders, and then turns east once more. Soon after the boulders, the trail reaches Weaver Creek, the largest creek on the trail. Early in summer it can have a strong flow, so use caution as you cross it. Once on the other side of the creek, you hike a little farther through the woods before arriving at another trail junction. The path to the left continues east and leads to large Boulder Creek, which flows out of Jennie Lake. This

The exfoliating granite face of Shell Mountain looms above Weaver Lake.

creek is a significant tributary of the Kings River to the north. Stay right at this trail. You will soon turn to the south and make the short, final climb up to Weaver Lake.

The scenic lake is a classic Sierra Nevada lake. Blue waters are pierced by occasional granite boulders. The shore is ringed with patches of trees and more boulders. Above the water is the exfoliating north face of Shell Mountain, one the few named mountains in the Jennie Lakes Wilderness. There are numerous campsites around the lake, but the area can get heavily impacted, and Weaver Lake should be treated more as a hiking destination than one for backpacking. Enjoy the beautiful lake and the smooth, rocky cliffs until it is time to retrace your steps to the trailhead.

MILES AND DIRECTIONS

0.0 Start at the Fox Meadow Trailhead.

0.2 Turn left at the junction with the trail coming from Big Meadow.

0.7 Stay left at the intersection with the trail to Poop Out Pass.

1.8 Turn right to take the spur trail to Weaver Lake.

2.1 Arrive at Weaver Lake. Return to the trailhead the way you came.

4.2 Arrive back at the trailhead.

66. **MIST FALLS**

WHY GO?

The spectacular hike from Road's End to Mist Falls in Kings Canyon National Park leads along the magnificent Kings River as it surges through the canyon beneath sheer granite cliffs soaring thousands of feet overhead. The hike ends at powerful Mist Falls, where the river hurtles over a ledge and crashes onto the rocks below.

THE RUNDOWN

Start: Permit station at Road's End
Distance: 8.0 miles out and back
(*Option:* 8.8-mile reverse lollipop)
Hiking time: About 4 hours
Difficulty: Moderately easy
Elevation gain: 820 feet
Season: Spring, summer, fall; best in late spring and early summer when the waterfall is at its fullest
Trail surface: Packed dirt, rocky, rock slabs

Canine compatibility: Dogs not permitted
Fees and permits: Entrance fee
Land status: Kings Canyon National Park
Trail contact: 47050 Generals Highway, Three Rivers 93271; (559) 565-3341; www.nps.gov/seki
Other: Water is available at the trailhead and from the Kings River.

FINDING THE TRAILHEAD

From Fresno, drive east on CA 180 for 90 miles to Roads End in Kings Canyon National Park. At 17.5 miles from Fresno turn left to continue on CA 180. Shortly after passing through the Big Stump entrance station, stay straight at the junction with CA 198/Generals Highway and continue the rest of the way to Road's End. **Trailhead GPS:** 36°47'40.95"N / 118°34'57.89"W

WHAT TO SEE

The powerful South Fork of the Kings River travels through a tremendously deep canyon, one of the most remarkable features in the vast Sierra Nevada. The canyon, scoured by glaciers and boasting exceedingly tall walls of stark granite, is often considered a rival of Yosemite Valley farther north. Though it lacks the distinctive domes and proliferation of mighty waterfalls, it does share the great walls of granite, awesome river, and incredible scenery. However, even though Kings Canyon does not have giant waterfalls, it is not lacking in massive waterfalls altogether. Energetic Mist Falls is the highlight among the cataracts in the canyon. The Kings River charges through the narrow valley and, upon hitting a sheer ledge, plunges headlong onto the rocks below. It is not a tall waterfall, but it is immensely compelling. Of course the waterfall is only part of the attraction of this classic Sierra hike. The canyon itself is a star feature, cutting deeply into the tall peaks of the High Sierra. Indeed, when those mountains are still covered in snow early in the year, this is a magical, mighty trail.

The hike begins at the permit station at Road's End. Head east on the wide, dusty trail and promptly cross a small wooden bridge over Copper Creek. Continue past the creek and enter wide-open areas where many trees have fallen. This area was once the site of the mining community of Kanawyers. Here you get good views of the canyon's awesome cliffs. On the far side of the clearings, the trail swings close to the Kings River for the first time on the hike. The water is a refreshing sight after passing through the dry woods. Shortly after meeting up with the river, the trail pulls especially close to a bend in the river. Follow some use trails over to the edge for a fantastic vista of the racing water and the tall cliffs. Keen eyes will spot the double-pointed head of the Sphinx, a large granite monolith that is best viewed from the end of the trail.

As you again head east, the path passes through another clearing before reentering a more heavily forested area. The sound of the water recedes a bit as the trail momentarily veers away from the river. The trees are mostly well spaced along the trail, and the forest floor is covered with ferns. Large boulders scattered around add a lot of interest to the area. As you near the river again, you arrive at a fork in the trail. To the right a bridge

The towering cliffs of Kings Canyon are a spectacular complement to the Kings River.

Mist Falls

crosses over the Kings River just downstream with the confluence with Bubbs Creek. The bridge is the route to take for the optional loop on this hike. For now, as the sign indicates, stay to the left to reach Mist Falls.

Once you pass the fork, the trail, level up to this point, begins to climb a little bit. The grade is not steep, and progress is still quick. The trail now maintains a course that essentially parallels the Kings River for the rest of the hike. As you climb, you catch glimpses of the river and the canyon's tall cliffs through the trees. Despite the slight increase in the steepness of the trail, the river maintains its fairly level, albeit swift, flow. At times the trail drops down near the riverbank and you can observe a few rapids. Note that by and large the river has not changed its character too much since you first met it near Kanawyers. The canyon is narrower and the floor not as wide or level; the river is swift flowing but does not have a very precipitous course. About 1.0 mile from the bridge, things begin to change. The grade of the trail changes noticeably, and you begin to climb at a steady clip. The river experiences a similar shift and becomes a torrent as it pours over and between boulders, racing down the increasingly steep canyon. At one point the trail comes right alongside the river as it roars down a large cascade. It is an impressive sight, and you haven't even reached Mist Falls yet!

Shortly after you see the first big rapid, the trail climbs up onto some granite slabs just as the river slams through an even steeper and larger cascade. Colossal boulders and

An iconic view of the distant Sphinx from the top of Mist Falls.

parts of the large granite slab have pushed together and forced the river through a steep channel. As if that were not impressive enough, you get your first really good view of the canyon from these slabs. Sheer cliffs soar high above you on both sides of the canyon, climbing unrelentingly toward the sky. To the south you are treated to what is perhaps the most iconic vista of this part of Kings Canyon National Park. The steep cliffs of the river canyon frame the towering, expansive wall that rises above the south side of Kings Canyon. Atop the smooth, glacier-polished wall sits the large pinnacle of the Sphinx. It is an unforgettable view.

Fortunately, since this is an out-and-back hike, you will have the opportunity to enjoy this view again. This being the case, press onward up the trail. Only 0.4 mile ahead, you finally reach a sign that marks your arrival at Mist Falls. The sign is largely unnecessary, since the waterfall announces itself marvelously. Mist Falls is not a high waterfall; it is an immensely powerful one, though. The entire fury of the Kings River cascades steeply down a long, smooth slab of granite before hurtling over the edge of a short freefall. In spring and early summer, when the river is a raging deluge, a misty maelstrom swirls around the falls. There is a good view of the falls just off the trail, and paths lead from there down to a wide spot in the river's channel where you can get close to the waterfall. It is a marvelous spectacle. If you want a bit different perspective, continue up the trail for 0.2 mile. As the trail rounds a bend in the midst of some oaks, it reaches a clearing

where you can look down on the top of Mist Falls as it begins its steep drop. From here you get an even better perspective on the iconic vista of the south end of the canyon and the great wall of the Sphinx, complemented by the thunderous river.

Eventually you will have to return to the trailhead. From Mist Falls follow the trail back 2.1 miles to the bridge that crosses over the Kings River. From here you have two choices. You can either follow the trail back the way you came or you can hike on the Kanawyers Loop Trail. This latter option adds no elevation gain to the hike, but it is 0.7 mile longer. It is, however, extremely scenic and much less busy than the main route. If you wish to go this way, cross the river on the bridge. Note that this is an old Bailey bridge, designed during World War II as a rapidly assembled, prefabricated truss bridge that could be built to various lengths quickly. The bridge has two sections that meet on a large rock in the middle of the river. From there the trail follows Bubbs Creek before it branches off the Bubbs Creek Trail. It heads west through a mix of forest and open areas. At times the trail is close to the river; at other times it veers inland. After 2.4 miles you cross a bridge over the river. From there it is only 0.3 mile back to the trailhead at Road's End.

MILES AND DIRECTIONS

0.0 Start at the Road's End Trailhead.

1.9 Stay left at a fork by a bridge over the Kings River.

3.26 Cross granite slabs with a great view of the Sphinx.

3.75 Reach Mist Falls.

4.0 At the top of the falls, enjoy the view of the canyon before turning around.

6.1 Arrive back at the junction at the bridge. Return the way you came. (***Option:*** Take the Kanawyers Loop for an 8.8-mile lollipop hike.)

8.0 Arrive back at the trailhead.

67. **TOKOPAH VALLEY**

WHY GO?

This easy hike in Sequoia National Park has all the elements of a great Sierra Nevada hike, including a large waterfall, towering cliffs, a swift river, and cool forests.

THE RUNDOWN

Start: Parking area in the middle of Lodgepole Campground
Distance: 4.2 miles out and back
Hiking time: 2–3 hours
Difficulty: Easy
Elevation gain: 580 feet
Season: Late spring, summer, fall
Trail surface: Packed dirt, rocky, duff

Canine compatibility: Dogs not permitted
Fees and permits: Entrance fee
Land status: Sequoia National Park
Trail contact: 47050 Generals Highway, Three Rivers 93271; (559) 565-3341; www.nps.gov/seki
Other: Water is available at the trailhead and from the Kaweah River.

FINDING THE TRAILHEAD

From Fresno, drive east on CA 180 for 57.7 miles. Turn right onto CA 198/Generals Highway and continue for 24.5 miles. Turn left onto Lodgepole Road and follow it 0.6 mile to the large day use parking area. **Trailhead GPS:** 36°36'17.56"N / 118°43'29.72"

WHAT TO SEE

The headwaters of the Marble Fork of the Kaweah River drain a significant portion of the west end of the Kings-Kaweah Divide. Several lakes in high cirques all contribute to the formation of the river, which then flows into the glaciated mountain paradise of Tokopah Valley. The passage of the river from the upper basins down into the main valley is one of the great natural pageants of western Sequoia National Park. Here the Kaweah River leaps off the polished precipice and cascades 1,200 feet down the headwall of Tokopah Valley. The stunning waterfall is the tallest in Sequoia, but it is only a part of the awesome scenery of the valley. In addition to the falls, the sheer cliffs, and the towering walls, the fang-like spike of the Watchtower adds to the grandeur of the setting. Few places in this part of the Sierra offer this much spectacle for such minimal effort.

The hike through Tokopah Valley is one of the premier hikes in Sequoia National Park. Visitors hungry for waterfalls, granite cliffs, and wild rivers will be satisfied by what they find in this incredible valley. The hike is also among the easiest in the area, meaning the beauty is available to nearly everyone. Though the trail can get busy at times, it remains a not-to-be-missed trip. The spectacle of Tokopah Falls crashing down the headwall of

The trail passes the Marble Fork of the Kaweah River as it surges over granite slabs.

the valley, the unyielding cliffs, and the Watchtower guarding the entrance to the upper canyon are an unforgettable sight.

The hike begins in the large parking area in the middle of the Lodgepole Campground. From there, walk along the road as it parallels the Kaweah River. Turn left onto the bridge where the road crosses over to the campsites on the north side. Just across the bridge is the official trailhead. Begin hiking on the easy trail, with the river to your left. The path continues parallel to the Kaweah River. On the far side of the swift-moving water you can see campsites in the farthest reaches of the extensive Lodgepole Campground. Just after the very last of the campsites, the route passes the river as it pours over a very attractive set of cascades. Long granite slabs protrude into the river, forcing the water to twist and turn as it finds the path of least resistance through the rocky intrusion. The slabs also provide a good opportunity to scramble out toward the base of the cascades.

After the cascades, the trail enters a heavily wooded area but continues following the river. The sound of the water remains constant, but there are fewer chances to see it because of the trees. However, if you cast your gaze upward when the trees part, you will note that the lower valley's wooded slopes are beginning to be replaced by sheer granite walls. Most notably, the Watchtower is coming into view. This awesome crag continues to change its appearance as your perspective changes. It finally assumes its most recognizable form when you arrive at the upper valley and the forest canopy no longer obstructs the view. Soon, however, the river catches your attention again, as the path has pulled close to it. When you draw near, note that the water has separated into several channels and forms many different courses through another series of granite slabs. These are not tall cascades, but the maze of water through the trees and over rock is a refreshing sight.

After 1.5 miles, the trail crosses a bridge over Horse Creek, which flows off the north side of the valley. Beyond the creek, the trail finally emerges from under the forest canopy and you get your first unfiltered view of the upper part of Tokopah Valley. It is an inspiring sight. In spring and early summer, Tokopah Falls is a raging ribbon of whitewater tumbling from one large cascade to the next as it crashes down to the floor of the valley. It can be heard from quite a distance away. The trail continues its gentle climb up toward the base of the falls and soon crosses a large talus slope. The path winds between, around, and over enormous boulders. Numerous opportunities to scramble on and explore the rocks await. A great view of the falls and cliffs that surround it is found right after the trail has passed between some particularly large boulders, about halfway across the talus slope. From there the path enters an area of low, riparian brush and finishes the climb all the way to the base of Tokopah Falls. Here there is an

The Watchtower is a prominent landmark above Tokopah Valley.

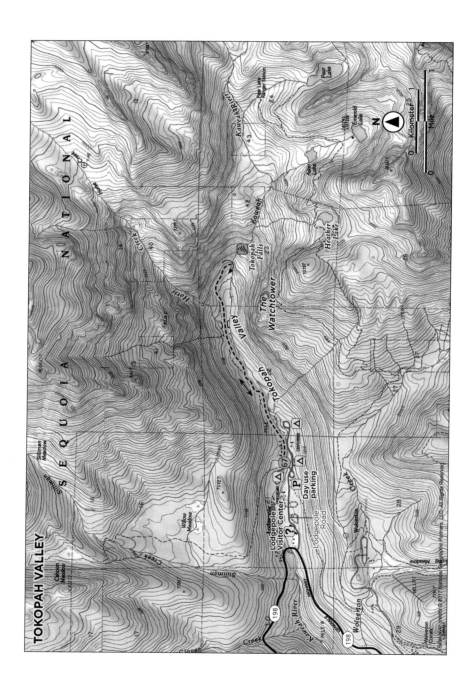

TOKOPAH VALLEY

Tokopah Falls thunders down the cliffs at the head of Tokopah Valley.

observation area where you can watch the Kaweah River make one final, massive leap off the valley's headwall and crash onto the rocks at its base. Like so many other famous waterfalls in the Sierra Nevada, later in the year the falls can be reduced to a trickle; but when they are flowing strongly they are tremendous. When you have had your fill, follow the trail back to the trailhead.

MILES AND DIRECTIONS

0.0 Start at the day use parking area by the Lodgepole Campground.

0.1 Cross the bridge and reach the official trailhead.

0.6 Pass a nice cascade on the Kaweah River.

1.5 Cross Horse Creek.

2.1 Reach the base of Tokopah Falls. Return the way you came.

4.2 Arrive back at the day use parking area.

68. **WHITE CHIEF BASIN**

WHY GO?

Exploring some of the high country in the remote Mineral King part of Sequoia National Park, this hike climbs steeply out of the Mineral King Valley into White Chief Basin, where beautifully unusual geology reigns.

THE RUNDOWN

Start: Eagle Lake Trailhead at the end of Mineral King Road
Distance: 5.8 miles out and back
Hiking time: 3–4 hours
Difficulty: Moderate
Elevation gain: 1,640 feet
Season: Summer, fall
Trail surface: Packed dirt, rocky

Canine compatibility: Dogs not permitted
Fees and permits: Entrance fee
Land status: Sequoia National Park
Trail contact: 47050 Generals Highway, Three Rivers 93271; (559) 565-3341; www.nps.gov/seki
Other: Water is available at the trailhead.

FINDING THE TRAILHEAD

Beginning in Visalia, drive east on CA 198 for 32 miles to the town of Three Rivers. Turn right onto Mineral King Road. Continue on this winding, twisting road for 25 miles to its end at the Eagle Lake Trailhead. The road is paved most of the way but there are a few sections when it becomes a well-maintained gravel road. At the very end of the drive, the road forks. Bear right, cross over the Kaweah River, and arrive at the trailhead. **Trailhead GPS:** 36°26'53.76"N / 118°35'43.18"W

WHAT TO SEE

The Mineral King Valley is one of the most geologically diverse parts of the Sierra Nevada. The granite typical of the great stretch of mountains from Yosemite to the regions south of Sequoia National Park is interrupted here by a large band of sedimentary rocks of marine origin, as well as metavolcanic rock. The unusual geology caught the attention of nineteenth-century miners, and the area had numerous claims and prospects. The focal point of activity was on the upper slopes of the deep valley of the East Fork of the Kaweah River, which cut into the sedimentary intrusion. The name "Mineral King" was given to the valley in the hopes that the mines would be extremely productive. However, little was ever extracted here, and the mines were eventually abandoned. In the 1960s a ski resort was proposed for the area, but preservationists won out, and in 1978 the land was instead transferred to Sequoia National Park. This was the most recent addition to California's oldest national park.

This hike travels through the Mineral King Valley, climbing into its upper elevations and venturing into lonely White Chief Basin. There are several beautiful lakes in cirques high above the valley, meaning lake-less White Chief Basin is often overlooked by hikers in search of more notable destinations. Despite not having a lake, the basin is an extremely scenic high-elevation setting with meadows, creeks, and even a small waterfall. The remnants of the White Chief Mine are also an interesting feature. Views of tall mountains and the unusual geology make it a good option for hikers looking to experience Mineral King while avoiding the more popular destinations.

Begin the hike at the trailhead at the end of the road. At the trailhead, a few vacation cabins surround the parking area. As you set out, the trail passes a tiny cabin as you first leave the trailhead. The East Fork of the Kaweah River flows just below to the left. Be sure to head over to the river and look down the length of the valley to the south. The classic view of Vandever Mountain and Tulare Peak is a great send-off for the hike as you prepare to hike closer to these high peaks. Head back up to the trail, which immediately begins to climb.

The hike is short, but it is unrelenting in its climb until you reach White Chief Basin. As you climb, your perspective on the valley changes and new peaks become visible. In many ways the peaks around the valley appear similar to the mountains in the Colorado Rockies, especially those of the San Juan Mountains. The warped, multicolored strata and deeply eroded peaks are reminiscent of those great mountains. Yet while the perspective on the peaks may change, the river far below remains constant. The East Fork of the Kaweah River starts high up in Farewell Canyon. It then flows swiftly through the deep valley as more tributaries cascade down the steep walls. The first part of the hike

On the far side of the canyon, Crystal Creek cascades out of the Crystal Lake basin.

Colorful mountains on the far side of the canyon are a dramatic sight while climbing to White Chief Basin.

offers good views of this spectacle. The peaks that surround the valley render a striking backdrop.

Cross a creek about 0.25 mile from the trailhead. High above is Tufa Falls, though it is not visible from the trail. This creek's substantial volume of water bursts from the rocky cliff several hundred feet above the trail. Past Tufa Creek, the path continues to climb at a steep grade. The route generally passes through forest, but the valley walls are steep, which means there are still filtered views to the east. The most noteworthy feature along this section of trail is the opportunity to watch Crystal Creek make a long series of cascades as it falls nearly 1,500 feet toward the Kaweah River. As you follow the line of cascades with your eye, note that just before the creek reaches the river, it is crossed by a trail. This is the path that leads to both the Franklin Lakes and Farewell Gap. The gap is on the southern border of Sequoia National Park and is the primary trail that leads from the southwestern part of the park into the Golden Trout Wilderness and the vast Kern River watershed.

The trail climbs for 0.6 mile beyond Tufa Creek before it crosses another creek flowing through a steep channel. This is the outlet creek from Eagle Lake. It does not have as much water in it as the first creek, but Eagle Creek has sinkholes where the water disappears underground only to reemerge downstream. The rock in Mineral King is so permeable that it is likely that the first creek is picking up water from another subterranean source to feed it. Only 0.25 mile past Eagle Creek, you arrive at the only trail junction on this hike. The trail branches off to the right and climbs steeply up the side of the canyon to the Eagle Lake basin. This lake, located in a gorgeous granite bowl, is one of the more popular hiking destinations in Mineral King.

To get to White Chief Basin, stay straight and continue the long traverse up the side of the valley. The grade steepens noticeably after the junction. This is the hardest part of the hike. As you climb, look to the southeast and watch Franklin Creek descend its own series of cascades. Finally, after climbing for 0.6 mile past the junction with the Eagle Lake Trail, you hear the sound of the creek flowing out of White Chief Basin. Your approach leads over open, rocky terrain before leveling off above the creek. The view across the valley is immense. A massive, unnamed 11,000-foot peak with multicolored strata seems close enough to reach out and touch. Heavily eroded Mineral Peak is just to the north, and between them you can catch glimpses of the granite needles of Sawtooth Peak and Needham Mountain. The view is fleeting, however, as the trail follows the creek around a bend and soon reaches a crossing that marks your entrance into White Chief Basin.

Don't be too concerned if the creek is dry when you arrive. Like the rest of Mineral King, the rock around White Chief Basin is very permeable, and even when it is dry at the crossing, there is typically water flowing upstream. When the volume is lower late in the season, it will hit sinks and disappear underground. Cross the creek and hike deeper into the basin. The bottom of the basin is a large grassy meadow strewn with logs from trees that fell long ago. The white and red walls are striking contrasts to the gray granite of which most of the Sierra Nevada is composed. Looking far to the south, you can see that the higher terrain of the upper basin is indeed more typical of the Sierra, but the trail does not climb that far. Instead the path climbs through the lower basin for another 0.9 mile before coming to an end at a rocky headwall.

As you hike toward the end of the lower basin, views of pointy Vandever Mountain and flat-topped White Chief Peak are excellent. As you near the headwall, the creek will typically be flowing, even if the lower section was dry. Watch for water flowing from the porous rock feeding into the stream. The trail finally ends on a grassy hill at the base of the rugged headwall. On the west side of the basin, look for the opening of White Chief Mine sitting just above a pile of tailings. A use trail leads from the end of the path across the creek and up to the mine. It was constructed at great expense in the nineteenth century, but little profit was made from it. A small waterfall flows down the face of the headwall, adding to the area's peaceful ambience. After enjoying the quiet location, follow the trail back to the trailhead.

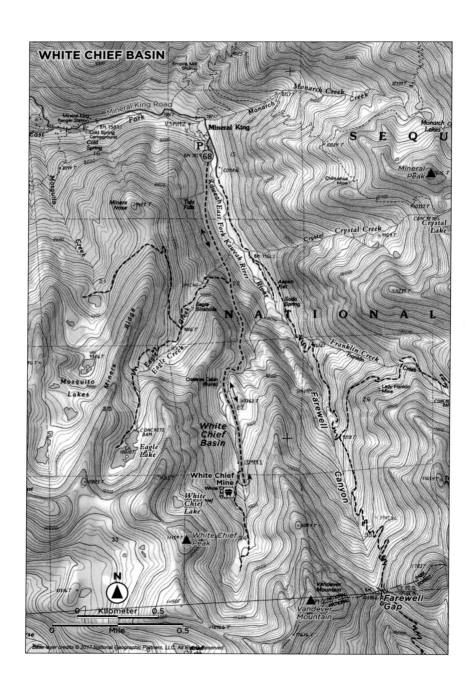

The complex geology of the Mineral King area is evident in White Chief Basin.

MILES AND DIRECTIONS

0.0 Start at the Eagle Lake Trailhead.

0.25 Cross a creek below unseen Tufa Falls.

1.1 Stay straight at the junction with the Eagle Lake Trail.

2.0 Cross a creek and enter White Chief Basin.

2.9 Reach the end of the trail at the end of the lower section of White Chief Basin. Follow the trail back to the trailhead.

5.8 Arrive back at the trailhead.

A nameless peak exhibits dramatic geology high above Convict Canyon.

EASTERN SIERRA

TO SAY THE EASTERN SIERRA is grand is to understate the scale of the range. For nearly 150 miles, the long, vertical escarpment of the Sierra Nevada rises anywhere from 5,000 to 10,000 feet in a sawtooth-like palisade of spectacularly jagged peaks. Nowhere else is the immensity and magnificence of the Sierra on more evident display than as you drive US 395. It culminates in the south at Mount Whitney, the tallest peak in the lower forty-eight states, where the mountains form a sheer granite bulwark nearly 2 miles high. It is a profoundly awesome sight.

Beyond the staggering wall of cliffs is the legendary High Sierra, that part of the Sierra Nevada that has a consistent series of peaks that exceed 12,000, 13,000, and even 14,000 feet. It can be roughly defined as the high country that lies between the northern boundary of Yosemite and the southern boundary of Sequoia National Park and the John Muir Wilderness. Some also include the adjacent Golden Trout Wilderness in this definition.

Trails in this region can be notoriously steep or have sustained climbs that are unrelenting from beginning to end. Fortunately there are significant exceptions to this rule, and there are great options for enjoying the alpine splendor without having to work too hard.

The Eastern Sierra can be roughly divided into three regions. The northern region is the Hoover Wilderness, which wraps around the northeastern corner of Yosemite. These mountains are composed of a mix of metamorphic and sedimentary marine rocks and granite. Several long, deep canyons cut into the escarpment and are surrounded by peaks that range from 11,000 to 12,000 feet. The second region comprises the mountains around the Mammoth Lakes. The Long Valley Caldera dominates this region, and volcanic activity is responsible for a number of the physical features. Two notable subranges of the Sierra Nevada are found here. West of Mammoth Lakes is the Ritter Range, crowned by prominent Mount Ritter and Banner Peak. These exceptional mountains are protected in the Ansel Adams Wilderness. To the south of Mammoth Lakes is the fantastically chaotic geology of the Sherwin Range. Here layers of seemingly unrelated rocks were welded together and polished by passing glaciers. It is part of the John Muir Wilderness. The third region of the Eastern Sierra is the long rampart of cliffs that extends south, towering above the Owens Valley. This area has many trails that cut into the particularly steep canyons climbing swiftly up to the Sierra Crest. It is all contained in the John Muir Wilderness.

Access to all the trails in the Eastern Sierra is along US 395. From the south this highway can be reached from southern California, southern Nevada, and from the southern Central Valley by crossing over Tehachapi Pass. From the north, CA 120 cutting through Yosemite is a good way to reach the Eastern Sierra, as are the trans-Sierra highways of the Central Sierra. US 395 can also be accessed through the Lake Tahoe region and then traveling through Nevada before reentering California.

69. GREEN CREEK BASIN

WHY GO?

This long hike enters a large canyon cutting into the Eastern Sierra. Drained by Green Creek, several lakes are scattered around a remote basin beset by rugged, metamorphic peaks.

THE RUNDOWN

Start: Trailhead on Green Creek Road
Distance: 12.5 miles out and back to Hoover Lakes (*Option:* moderate 8.2 miles out and back to East Lake)
Hiking time: 6–7 hours or overnight
Difficulty: Moderately strenuous
Elevation gain: 1,820 feet
Season: Summer, fall
Trail surface: Packed dirt, rocky
Canine compatibility: Dogs permitted

Fees and permits: None
Land status: Hoover Wilderness, Humboldt-Toiyabe National Forest
Trail contact: Bridgeport Ranger District, HC62, Box 1000, Bridgeport 93517; (760) 932-7070; www.fs.usda .gov/main/htnf
Other: Water is available from numerous creeks and lakes.

FINDING THE TRAILHEAD

Beginning in Bridgeport at the intersection of US 395 and CA 182, drive south on US 395 for 4.3 miles. Turn right onto Green Creek Road. Drive on this good dirt road for 3.5 miles and then make a sharp right turn to continue on Green Creek Road. Follow the road for 5.7 more miles to the trailhead. **Trailhead GPS:** 38°6'43.90"N / 119°16'31.73"W

WHAT TO SEE

The Eastern Sierra is cut by several large, glacier-carved canyons. The creeks draining these canyons begin at the Sierra Crest and flow eastward, discharging into the Great Basin. Green Creek flows through one of the northernmost of these large mountain troughs. The west end of the canyon opens up into a massive basin where there are ten named lakes, several unnamed tarns, and a splendid array of rugged peaks. The basin cuts through bands of sedimentary and metavolcanic rocks. The varied composition of the mountains around Green Creek Basin gives the area a visually distinct appearance. Protected as part of the Hoover Wilderness, these mountains and lakes are a magnificent mountain playground. This hike climbs up the canyon and pierces deep into the large basin, visiting six of the ten alpine lakes. Stunning scenery, good wildflower displays, and bright fall color combine to make this a very memorable journey into the backcountry in the uppermost section of the Eastern Sierra.

Unnamed towers rise above Green Lake.

From the trailhead, begin hiking west. The trail passes through a forest where the vegetation from drier climates mixes with those of the wetter, higher elevation. In particular, aspens and junipers mix with ponderosa and lodgepole pines. The mixing of these zones is typical in the Eastern Sierra, where the mountains drop precipitously into the desert. The path initially swings away from Green Creek and closer to the northern wall of the canyon in order to bypass some private inholdings near the trailhead. After 0.6 mile the path merges with a dirt road that runs alongside Green Creek. Follow the road for 0.3 mile, pass the last inholding, and begin hiking a singletrack trail after the road ends.

After the trail narrows you pass the boundary of the Hoover Wilderness and climb a series of closely stacked switchbacks. Once you reach the top of the switchbacks, you begin a long, steady climb up the canyon. Green Creek is usually audible and at times visible from the trail. The forest alternates from wooded conifer forests to more open terrain. Fall color along this section of the trail is great. After 2.6 miles the trail crosses a rocky bench. Though there have been some views of the canyon up until now, this is the first chance to get a real sense of the scale of Green Creek's basin. The most notable landmarks are to the south, where the white granite crags of Kavanaugh Ridge are superseded by the towering red bulk of Dunderberg Peak. This mountain is a prominent landmark when you are driving on US 395.

Just past the rocky bench, the trail splits. The path to the right climbs steeply up to West Lake, a large lake set on a high, cliff-bound bench. Stay to the left, after which you will soon have to cross the West Fork of Green Creek. Continue just a few yards up the trail and spot the spur on the right that leads over to the edge of Green Lake, 3.0 miles from the trailhead. Green Lake is the second-largest lakes in the Green Creek basin. The clear water sparkles beneath a large peak that towers nearly 1,700 feet above the lake. A large, vertical whitewater cascade pours down the flank of the peak. The source of this creek is West Lake, which is tucked into a hidden basin. Green Lake has an extensive shoreline, perfect for exploring, and this makes a good spot to turn around for a shorter day hike. However, East Lake, the largest in the basin, is only a short distance away and makes a more satisfying conclusion to a short hike despite Green Lake's beauty.

To reach East Lake, return to the trail and follow it south. The route quickly begins to climb up a steep slope. Soon switchbacks resume and one swings you over to the creek, which you then cross. On the far side of the creek, you make one long switchback before crossing the creek yet again. A series of short switchbacks commence and gain elevation rapidly. As the slope grows gentler, the switchbacks come to an end and you pass through a wide, shallow gully before arriving at East Lake.

East Lake is the largest and most spectacular lake in Green Creek's basin. The sapphire water covers an expansive area at the foot of a series of sedimentary peaks. From this vantage, Gabbro Peak looms closest to the trail, but it is the dark turrets of the Page Peaks, near the center of the lake, that are most impressive. A little farther south the bulky mass of Epidote Peak makes its presence known on the horizon. The sound of cascades falling to the water is audible from the edge of East Lake.

Once you reach East Lake, the trail levels off for the first time on the hike. Though it does still continue to gain elevation, the slight grade is almost imperceptible. Follow along the east shore of the lake before cutting inland a little bit and passing between some rockbound tarns. The path soon pulls alongside the lake again. From here you gain a different perspective on Epidote and the Page Peaks. These large towers of metamorphosed

Epidote and Camiaca Peaks are visible above the southern end of East Lake.

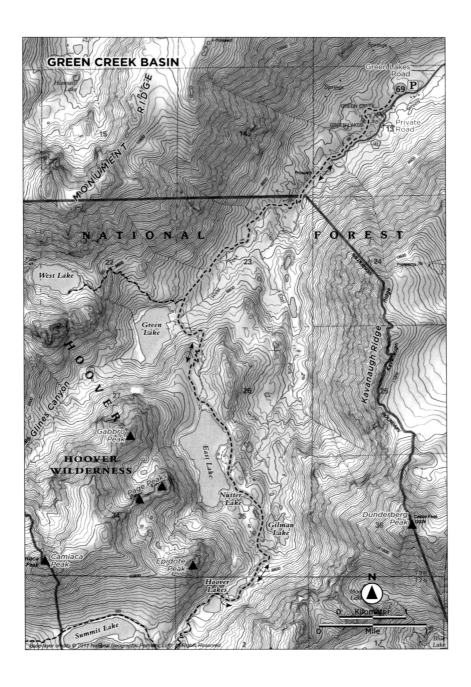

marine sediment rise dramatically above East Lake. A large basin occupies the space between them. A pretty cascade flows out of the basin and falls noisily into East Lake.

After traveling along East Lake for 0.8 mile, the trail veers away from the lake completely. Almost immediately you arrive at small Nutter Lake, the smallest named lake in the Green Creek basin. Small it may be, but it is definitely scenic. The south end of the lake is a great place from which to observe the Page Peaks and Gabbro Peak, framed in the foreground by a large, bright red rock. Continue past Nutter Lake and then traverse a steep slope high above Gilman Lake. From here you can see the massive scree field that flows off the west side of towering Dunderberg Peak into the water.

As you pass above Gilman Lake, you enter a small bowl occupied by a little pond. Climb out of the depression and reach the banks of the East Fork of Green Creek. Cross the creek and climb up a short, steep grade before the trail levels off amid rocky terrain. From here follow the path to the edge of the first of the two Hoover Lakes. This pair of lakes is among the prettiest in the basin. Fringed with both scree and verdant meadows, their blue waters contrast beautifully against the green grass, gray rocks, and red cliffs. Follow the trail out to the isthmus that separates the two lakes. If you are day hiking, this makes a good place to stop, about 6.3 miles from the trailhead. From here you can relax and enjoy the view of the rugged mountains all around you. It is a multicolored artist's palette of alpine glory. If you desire, you can press on to Summit Lake, at the boundary with Yosemite, or turn around and follow the trail back to the trailhead.

MILES AND DIRECTIONS

0.0 Start from the Green Creek Trailhead.

0.6 The trail merges onto a dirt road.

0.9 The road ends and a singletrack trail continues to the west.

3.0 Shortly after passing the long spur to West Lake, the trail arrives at Green Lake.

4.1 Arrive at East Lake, (*Option:* For the shorter hike to East Lake, turn around here.)

4.25 Reach the north shore of East Lake.

5.0 Leave East Lake and just moments later arrive at small Nutter Lake.

6.25 Stop and relax at the Hoover Lakes. You can continue to Summit Lake from here or turn around and head back to the trailhead.

12.5 Arrive back at the trailhead.

70. **LUNDY CANYON**

WHY GO?

Lundy Canyon offers hikers the opportunity to observe epic beaver dams in a spectacular alpine canyon loaded with waterfalls, wildflowers, and terrific fall color.

THE RUNDOWN

Start: Lundy Canyon Trailhead
Distance: 4.0 miles out and back
Hiking time: 2–3 hours
Difficulty: Easy
Elevation gain: 550 feet
Season: Summer, fall
Trail surface: Packed dirt, rocky
Canine compatibility: Dogs permitted

Fees and permits: None
Land status: Hoover Wilderness, Inyo National Forest
Trail contact: Mono Lake Ranger District, PO Box 429, Lee Vining 93541; (760) 647-3044; www.fs.usda .gov/main/inyo
Other: Water is available from Mill Creek.

FINDING THE TRAILHEAD

From Lee Vining, drive north on US 395 for 6.5 miles. Turn left onto Lundy Lake Road. Follow this road for 6.4 miles to the trailhead. Lundy Lake Road is initially paved but becomes a good dirt road after 5 miles. **Trailhead GPS:** 38°1'20.70"N / 119°15'42.91"W

WHAT TO SEE

Near Mono Lake, the high escarpment of the Eastern Sierra is cut by a series of long, glacier-carved canyons. Of these, Lundy Canyon is among the most beautiful. This canyon has almost everything hikers could look for in an easy walk through a splendid mountain setting. Like the rest of the Hoover Wilderness, the geology is complex and the granite that dominates so much of the Sierra Nevada has been intruded by bands of metavolcanic rocks and marine sediment. This manifests itself in the color and composition of the canyon walls, where the cliffs are red and russet in addition to the gray-and-white granite one might expect to find here. Within the canyon, it is a paradise for hikers. An easy walk through aspen groves leads past beaver ponds and waterfalls. Wildflowers line the trail in summer, while in autumn the aspens astound with their showy colors. It is a tremendous payoff for the minimal effort expended.

From the trailhead the hike sets off to the west, heading deeper into Lundy Canyon. The trail climbs gently through a beautiful aspen forest. In fall this section of the trail nearly glows as the light bounces off the gold, shimmering leaves. In 0.3 mile an obvious spur trail bears left off the main path. Follow this down to the edge of what appears to be a lake at first glance. Follow the trail a few steps farther and it is revealed to be a massive beaver pond—an impressively large beaver dam. Early in summer, the lake is so full the water pours over the top of the dam and makes a short but vibrant waterfall. Despite the force of the rushing water, the dam has maintained its integrity and continues to impound Mill Creek. Later in the season the water does not flow over the top of the dam but passes through some internal spillway. The water can be heard pouring through but remains unseen within the tangle of logs and sticks until it emerges as a creek from the base of the dam. As though the spectacle of the large dam weren't enough, the upper canyon looms regally above the pond. At the far end of the pond is Lower Lundy Canyon Falls, where Mill Creek plunges off a cliff in twin channels. It does not get too much better than this.

Eventually it will be time to hike beyond the beaver pond. When you are ready, return to the main path and turn left. The trail climbs out of the aspens and up onto a rocky bench. Hike across the bench to the west. There are plenty of good views of the canyon from here, but as you near the west end, a faint spur branches left and leads to a ledge with a particularly good view of Lower Lundy Canyon Falls. The trail eventually climbs off the rocky bench and then enters a lush riparian area. Cross over the large creek flowing down from Burro Lake, which is hidden away in an inaccessible cirque high on the north side of the canyon.

On the north side of the creek that comes from Burro Lake, you arrive at another beaver pond. If it were not for the colossal pond at the beginning of the hike, this would seem like a pretty significant impoundment. Numerous snags jut up from the water, having been drowned by the pond. Even though it is unlikely that you'll spot a beaver, it is an unusual opportunity to be able to get so close to their industrious handiwork. Follow the trail around the west side of the pond and then begin climbing up a steep slope that levels off when it reaches Mill Creek. It runs parallel to the large creek for some distance before finally crossing.

Fall color in Lundy Canyon reflects in the waters of a large, beaver-dam created pond.

Lundy Canyon's Mill Creek surges over a series of large cataracts.

When you are on the south side of Mill Creek, you enter a lovely, parklike aspen grove. As you pass through the peaceful forest, watch for the remnants of a nineteenth-century log miner's cabin. The trail then enters a marshy area that can get muddy in the first part of summer. Thankfully it quickly reenters the forest cover, leaving the mud behind. Here the narrow track follows alongside a pretty stream that flows swiftly just a couple of feet from the trail. You finally emerge from the aspen grove and veer away from the stream. The terrain gets rockier now, and after crossing a small stream, you climb over a talus slope before arriving at the base of Middle Lundy Canyon Falls.

As you approach the falls, a spur trail leads down to their base, which is surrounded by lush grass. The falls actually consist of several tiers, each about 20 feet or more high. The west end of the canyon, crowned by the distinctively rounded peak, is a dramatic backdrop to the waterfall. You can follow the spur down to the base of the falls and enjoy the thunderous roar as you relax alongside the fast-moving water. On the main trail, the route wraps around the south side of the creek, where it splits. The main trail continues to veer away from the creek, while another well-established spur trail climbs next to the creek. Follow this path alongside the cataracts, of which there are three primary tiers. The uppermost is the prettiest, with the crags of the north rim of Lundy Canyon visible above it.

The path adjacent the falls rejoins the main trail as it climbs higher into the canyon. Here Upper Lundy Canyon Falls, the largest of the three main falls in Lundy Canyon, waits. This falls is tucked into a narrow amphitheater and is best viewed from the trail that climbs alongside it. This section of the hike used to be part of an epic trip that traveled through the canyon and climbed an old nineteenth-century miner's trail that switchbacked up a scree-filled gully to the stunning Twenty Lakes Basin. The upper section of the switchbacks, which was built into solid rock rather than on the scree, had superb views

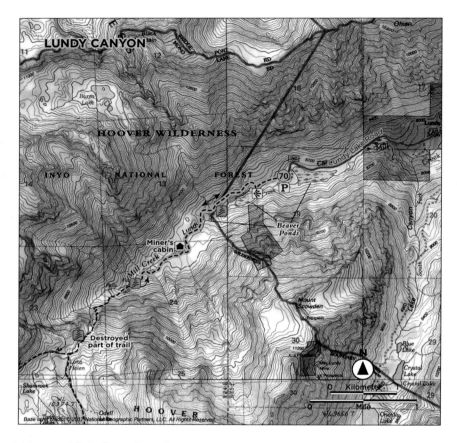

of this waterfall. Sadly, in the early 2000s, a rockslide obliterated a few hundred feet of the switchbacks. Though some hearty adventurers still scramble up the scree, it is no longer realistic for most hikers. Consequently, the Middle Falls makes the best destination for a reasonable hike. Having enjoyed the falls, follow the trail back to the trailhead.

MILES AND DIRECTIONS

- **0.0** Start from the Lundy Canyon Trailhead.
- **0.3** Bear left onto a short spur that leads to a large beaver dam and a great view.
- **0.9** Cross the creek coming from nearby Burro Lake.
- **1.25** Cross Mill Creek.
- **2.0** Arrive at Middle Lundy Canyon Falls. Return the way you came.
- **4.0** Arrive back at the trailhead.

71. DEVILS POSTPILE/ RAINBOW FALLS

WHY GO?

The walk to Devils Postpile leads hikers along the beautiful San Joaquin River to a fascinating collection of basalt columns. Continuing past the Postpile leads to awesome Rainbow Falls, one of the finest waterfalls in the Sierra Nevada.

THE RUNDOWN

Start: Trailhead at Devils Postpile parking area

Distance: 5.0 miles out and back to Rainbow Falls (*Option:* easy 0.8 mile out and back to Devils Postpile)

Hiking time: 2–3 hours

Difficulty: Easy

Elevation gain: 560 feet at Rainbow Falls

Season: Summer, fall

Trail surface: Packed dirt, rocky

Canine compatibility: Leashed dogs permitted

Fees and permits: Per person bus fare or per vehicle entrance fee

Land status: Devils Postpile National Monument

Trail contact: PO Box 3999, Mammoth Lakes 93546; (760) 934-2289; www.nps.gov/depo

Other: Hikers must use a mandatory shuttle bus to access trailheads during operating hours from mid-June to the Wednesday after Labor Day. At these times the road from the entrance station to Agnew Meadows is closed to cars. Cars can drive the road between 7 p.m. and 7 a.m. or if they are registered in the valley's resorts or campgrounds. Water is available at the trailhead.

FINDING THE TRAILHEAD

From the junction of Highway 395 and CA 203, drive west on CA 203 through the town of Mammoth Lakes to Minaret Road. Turn right onto Minaret Road and follow it 4 miles to the Mammoth Mountain Ski Resort. When the shuttle bus is operating, you must park here and purchase a bus ticket. The shuttle departs from here. When the shuttle is not in operation, continue past the resort for 1.3 miles to the entrance station. From here drive down the steep, narrow paved road for 6.7 miles. Turn right at the entrance to Devils Postpile National Monument. The parking area is located 0.1 mile down the road. **Trailhead GPS:** 37°37'47.32"N / 119°5'4.85"W

WHAT TO SEE

With its strikingly geometric shapes, the Devils Postpile is one of the more unusual and beautiful formations in the eastern Sierra Nevada. Composed of columnar basalt, the Post-pile is testimony to extensive volcanic activity that has taken place around the Long Valley Caldera. An active volcanic area, the caldera includes the volcano Mammoth Mountain, the

Inyo Craters, Hot Creek, lava flows, glass flows, and even geothermal power plants. Yet the Devils Postpile is the most famous bit of evidence that the fiery forces beneath the surface have shaped the world we see. As if the unusual sight of the ordered rows of basalt columns standing above the San Joaquin River was not enough of an attraction, the South Fork of the San Joaquin River adds much beauty to this hike. It winds gently around meadows and flows swiftly through a volcanic gorge before surging over awesome Rainbow Falls.

The hike begins at the large parking area for Devils Postpile National Monument. A small cabin at the start of the trail functions as a visitor center. The wide path leaves the trailhead and heads south. It immediately crosses a small meadow. At the far end a short spur provides access to the river. The trail then enters the woods and, after a short stretch, reaches a fork. The trail branching off to the right leads to a bridge across the San Joaquin. This bridge connects to the John Muir and Pacific Crest Trails, which run parallel to the west side of the river in the Ansel Adams Wilderness.

Stay left at the fork and proceed down the trail a little farther. Here the trail splits again. To the left are stairs that descend to the base of Devils Postpile. The option to the right is an even grade with a rail and allows wheelchairs to reach the formation's base. Also note the trail joining the main path on the left. This is a loop up to the top of the Postpile. Once at the bottom, you are presented with a unique sight. A large jumble of thick hexagonal basalt blocks lie piled up against the base of a cliff. The blocks, broken chucks of the columns that make up the Postpile, seem to form a paradox of chaos and symmetry as the polygonal lines of the blocks are stacked in a haphazard manner. Above them rises the columned rampart of the basalt pinnacles. It is hard to imagine that rock formed in such an ordered, precise form.

The columnar basalt beauty of the Devils Postpile

Rainbow Falls

Following the trail along the bottom, there are numerous vantage points from which to observe the Postpile, each with its own unique perspective. To do the loop, hike past the Devils Postpile and climb up a steep hill. As the path levels off, a signed spur splits off to the left. Follow it up to the base of a secondary cliff of columnar basalt. The path then loops around the back side of the formation and arrives at the precipice, where you can gaze down on hikers appreciating the unique sight. Be sure to walk out onto the hexagonal rocks. They are polished smooth, evidence that a glacier once passed by here. An interpretive display notes that hexagonal patterns are actually pretty common in the natural world. Continue on the loop trail as it heads downhill, back to the top of the stairs and wheelchair ramp.

To get to Rainbow Falls from the Devils Postpile, head south and climb back up the hill; stay right at the junction with the loop trail that leads to the top. The path gets considerably rougher after the Postpile and is no longer maintained for wheelchair access. About 0.8 mile from the trailhead, stay right at a fork with a trail that leads to Reds Meadow and then cross small Reds Creek and enter a burned area. The dusty path soon reenters the forest and, 1.3 miles from the trailhead, intersects the Pacific Crest and John Muir Trails. The trail comes in from the right and then heads west, crossing the trail to Rainbow Falls and a bridge over the San Joaquin. Hikers who want to extend the trip a little can use this route while returning from Rainbow Falls to form a loop. This option crosses back over the river at the bridge just upstream from Devils Postpile.

South of the junction with the long trails, the route continues south. At 2.0 miles, after passing another trail from Reds Meadow, cross another small creek. Nearly 0.3 mile farther turn right at a four-way junction, where a third option to Reds Meadow joins the trail to Rainbow Falls in another burned area. Here the path turns west, pulling closer to the

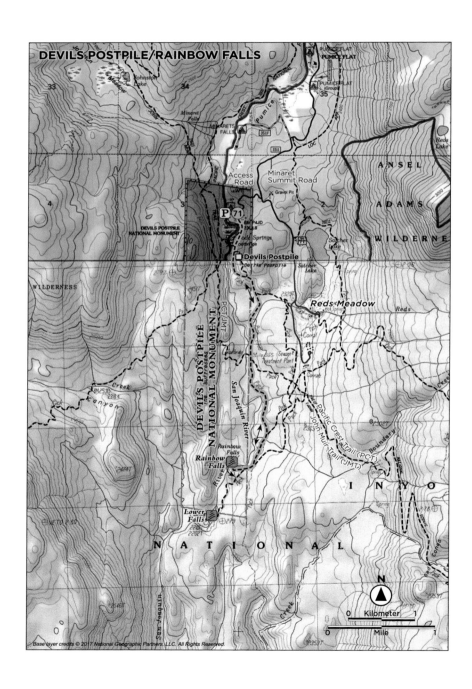

Lower Falls

San Joaquin River. The roar of the water is soon evident. The path becomes much more engineered, as the well-built trail descends stone steps to a series of vantage points where you can observe the marvelous spectacle of Rainbow Falls. Here the river plunges over a lip of dense, erosion-resistant rock and falls powerfully 101 feet to the rocks below. Its lines are reminiscent of Vernal Falls in Yosemite. Though it lacks the height and volume of that famed waterfall, Rainbow Falls more than holds its own among the panoply of great waterfalls in the Sierra Nevada. Stairs built onto the side of the canyon's cliff lead down to the river, and it is possible to walk close to the falls and enjoy the rainbows and spray. It is a beautiful and refreshing experience on a summer day. If you want more waterfalls, follow the trail 0.6 mile farther to the less-dramatic but still scenic Lower Falls. Otherwise, when you have had your fill of Rainbow Falls, follow the route back to the trailhead.

MILES AND DIRECTIONS

0.0 Start from the trailhead and head south toward the Devils Postpile.

0.4 View the unusual Devils Postpile. (**Option:** Turn around here for the shorter hike to Devils Postpile.) Continue south toward Rainbow Falls.

0.8 Stay right at a junction with a trail leading to Reds Meadow.

1.3 Continue straight at the intersection with the Pacific Crest and John Muir Trails.

2.0 Stay on main trail and pass another trail leading to Reds Meadow.

2.3 Turn right at a four-way junction and go to Rainbow Falls.

2.5 Arrive at Rainbow Falls. Follow the route back to the trailhead.

5.0 Arrive back at the trailhead.

72. **THOUSAND ISLAND LAKE**

WHY GO?

This trip, usually done as an overnighter, can also be a very long, epic day hike. It requires endurance, good fitness, and a hunger to see some of the most majestic mountains in the American West. This incredible journey includes glacier views, waterfalls, rivers, two massive lakes, and a host of smaller alpine lakes, as well as more mountain grandeur than you can shake a stick at.

THE RUNDOWN

Start: Agnew Meadows Trailhead
Distance: 17.0-mile lollipop (*Option:* moderate 7.0 miles out and back to Shadow Lake)
Hiking time: 10 hours or overnight
Difficulty: Very strenuous
Elevation gain: 2,700 feet
Season: Summer, fall
Trail surface: Packed dirt, rocky, rock slabs, duff
Canine compatibility: Dogs permitted
Fees and permits: Per person bus fare or per vehicle entrance fee
Land status: Ansel Adams Wilderness, Inyo National Forest
Trail contact: Mammoth Ranger District, PO Box 148 2500, Highway 203, Mammoth Lakes 93546; (760) 924-5500; www.fs.usda.gov/main/inyo
Other: Hikers must use a mandatory shuttle bus to access trailheads during operating hours from mid-June to the Wednesday after Labor Day. At these times the road from the entrance station to Agnew Meadows is closed to cars. Cars can drive the road between 7 p.m. and 7 a.m. or if they are registered in the valley's resorts or campgrounds. Water is available in the San Joaquin River, Shadow Creek, and numerous lakes.

FINDING THE TRAILHEAD

From the junction of US 395 and CA 203, drive west on CA 203 through the town of Mammoth Lakes to Minaret Road. Turn right onto Minaret Road and follow it 4 miles to the Mammoth Mountain Ski Resort. When the shuttle bus is operating, you must park here and purchase a bus ticket. The shuttle departs from here. When the shuttle is not in operation, continue past the resort for 1.3 miles to the entrance station. From here, drive down the steep, narrow paved road for 2.7 miles to the signed turn for Agnew Meadows. Follow the access road to the trailhead parking area. **Trailhead GPS:** 37°40'54.49"N / 119°5'10.29"W

WHAT TO SEE

The great naturalist John Muir once wrote that Mount Ritter was "the noblest and most ornate" of the mountains in the Sierra Nevada. This may very well be the case. The Ritter

Range, the large alpine region on the southeast side of Yosemite, contains some of the grandest and most awe-inspiring mountain landscapes in the Sierra Nevada. The massive, free-standing towers of Mount Ritter and Banner Peak, the highest points in the Ritter Range, rule over a domain of ragged crags, glaciated expanses, tall mountain crests, and deep river valleys. In some ways the scale of the land is hard to fathom. It is not until you arrive at the edge of Thousand Island Lake, one of the most astonishing lakes in the Sierra, that you can really grasp how monumental the area is. Of course this caliber of scenery does not come easily. The landscape is so vast and the geography so rugged that a long, demanding hike is necessary to really experience the essence of the Ritter Range.

The beauty of this area is such that it was initially seen as worthy of inclusion in Yosemite National Park. The majority of the Ritter Range, as well as nearby Devils Postpile, was within the park's original 1890 boundary. When the park's border was realigned in 1906, the region around Mount Ritter and Banner Peak was stripped from the park. While Yosemite may have lost what likely would have become an iconic part of the park, the area's removal does make a certain amount of sense. The realignment of the borders followed the crest of the Sierra, confining the park to the watersheds of the Merced and Tuolumne Rivers. The Ritter Range is wholly a part of the San Joaquin watershed and an area once removed from the park's main administrative centers. Geologically, the Ritter Range is distinct from Yosemite as well. Yosemite, much like the rest of the Sierra, is predominantly composed of granite. The Ritter Range, on the other hand, is centered on a large island of metavolcanic rocks. Its different composition gives the area a unique appearance.

The hike through the Ritter Range is challenging not only for its steep climbing but also for its distance. At 17 miles, it is a challenging amount of trail to tackle in one day. If you want a taste of these excellent mountains but are willing to forgo the entire experience, consider a shorter day hike from Agnew Meadows to Shadow Lake. You still get excellent views of Ritter and Banner from the lake, as well as a good perspective on some of the Minarets. The lake itself is lovely, and you get to experience the exhilarating section of trail between the San Joaquin River and Shadow Lake. This option is about 7.0 miles and has roughly 1,000 feet of elevation gain over the course of the whole hike. If you plan on hiking the entire trip, be sure to get an early start, preferably predawn. This will give you plenty of time to finish the hike, and you can drive down to the Agnew Meadows Trailhead. As an added bonus, you will have good morning light on Ritter and Banner when you arrive at Thousand Island Lake.

From the Agnew Meadows Trailhead, the River Trail sets out to the west, skirting the edge of Agnew Meadows. The meadow sits in a small bowl and is watered by numerous springs that flow down the steep slope of long San Joaquin Mountain. The water collects in the small bowl and flows through a gap as it cascades down to the Middle Fork of the San Joaquin River. The trail passes through the gap, crossing the creek on a log bridge. After crossing, follow the trail as it makes a gentle, descending traverse along the flank of the lower canyon. At points you can see the river flowing down below. After hiking for 1.3 miles, you reach the bottom of the descent and begin to climb almost imperceptibly. This is the beginning of the long climb along the river all the way to Thousand Island Lake. Most of the elevation gain on this hike takes place on this section of the trail. Fortunately, the grade is gentle throughout.

After you begin the very gentle climb, you pass pretty Olaine Lake, which lies 1.9 miles from the trailhead. From the edge of the lake, the rugged cliffs of the San Joaquin River's canyon can be seen without obstruction. Early in the morning as the sun is rising, it is a lovely, peaceful setting. However, much hiking remains, and you must press on. Shortly after leaving Olaine Lake you arrive at the first of many trail junctions on this hike. The wide path splits off to the left and leads up a spectacular section of trail that takes you to Shadow Lake. This is the return section of the large loop that constitutes the majority of the hike. Stay right at the junction and keep hiking deeper into the canyon. As you go, look up to the west, and note the large creek that comes from the gap in the cliffs and tumbles down toward the river in a series of cascades. You will see more of these cascades as you finish the loop.

Past the intersection with the route to Shadow Lake, the River Trail makes a couple of switchbacks up the side of a steep part of the canyon. Once you have surmounted the zigzagging trail, you continue to run parallel to the river. Soon the canyon widens a little bit and you pass a few pleasant campsites before arriving at a lovely little meadow. From the trail you can see the river meander gracefully through the grass. As you leave the meadow, the trail once again enters a dense forest. Despite having hiked only 4.0 miles of a 17-mile hike, this is essentially the last time the trail passes through a really sustained forest canopy. The forest cover lasts for about 0.5 mile, after which you pass through some open terrain and then arrive at a junction with a narrow trail heading up to the Badger Lakes. Stay left and begin to climb a series of very tight switchbacks.

At the first switchback, watch for an obvious use trail straying to the west, toward the river. Follow this path for just a few steps and arrive at the edge of a short cliff, where you can look down at the San Joaquin as it pours over a small waterfall into a perfectly proportioned pool. Head back to the River Trail and continue climbing up the switchbacks. After you reach the top of the switchbacks, you enter the upper section of the valley, where the forest is thinner, the terrain is rockier, and the cliffs are closer together. This beautiful section of trail hints at the scenery that lies just ahead. Pass through another band of trees before emerging onto the first really open, rocky terrain of the hike. As you walk across the slabs, the river flows just below you on the left.

Continue through the upper valley, climbing steadily as you go. As you approach the valley's headwall, the Pacific Crest Trail comes in from the right and merges with the River Trail, 6.1 miles from Agnew Meadows. After the two trails have combined, follow the path up through an increasingly narrow chute between cliffs. At the top of this narrow section, the trail finally levels off for the first time. It makes a sudden turn to the west and heads toward an area of rolling, heavily glaciated terrain. The path makes an easy trek through this area, passing small lakes and creeks before, rather suddenly, you catch sight of the solitary towers of Mount Ritter and Banner Peak. Just a short distance later, 7.1 miles from Agnew Meadows, you suddenly emerge at the edge of Thousand Island Lake and one of the great spectacles of the Sierra Nevada is revealed.

From where you stand at the edge of the water, gigantic Thousand Island Lake extends westward. Its namesake islands are scattered throughout the lake, giving it a unique, broken appearance. Towering above the lake are the great towers of Ritter and Banner. From this perspective, these twin giants seem to merge into one gargantuan monolith. In truth,

Mount Ritter and Banner Peak are a lofty presence above Garnet Lake and the nearby Minarets.

the highest point you can see from here is the summit of Banner Peak, which is 207 feet shorter than its neighbor, Mount Ritter. The summit of Ritter is obscured from this perspective, but a significant amount of the mountain is still visible from here. Banner, which is closer, is graced with two glaciers clinging to its flanks. The icy sheets add to the immensity of what stands before you. Just north of these stunning peaks is another large block of cliffs that climb upward toward the summit of Mount Davis. These cliffs alone would be a prime attraction, but in conjunction with the glory of Ritter and Banner, they are indeed a sublime vision.

After pausing at Thousand Island Lake for a long stretch to enjoy the view, it is time to continue the hike. When you arrived at the edge of the lake, you intersected the John Muir Trail. Turn left onto this fabled trail and cross the outlet of Thousand Island Lake on a small bridge. Leaving the lake, you cross large slabs of rock. Like all the territory around Thousand Island Lake, it is obvious that glaciers have heavily scoured these mountains. The polished metavolcanic rock is littered with countless erratics. As you pass through this open, rocky country, the trail climbs briefly before you reach Emerald Lake. Skirt the edge of the lake as you head south. When the path leaves the lakeshore, be sure to look back at the great view to the north, where you can spot the barren, brown mountains of the Koip Crest, which forms part of the southern boundary of Yosemite.

The trail maintains a level grade as you leave Emerald Lake and quickly arrive at Ruby Lake. Both lakes would be considered worthy destinations on their own, but here amid the giants of the Ritter Range, they are nearly overshadowed. As you pass Ruby Lake, the trail begins to climb again. A few quick switchbacks bring you to the 10,050-foot pass between Thousand Island and Garnet Lakes. This is the highest point on the hike. A great panorama greets you on the pass, including your first view of the excellent spires of the Minarets. After pausing a moment to enjoy the sight, you make your winding descent to Garnet Lake, reaching the lakeshore 9.25 miles from the trailhead.

Nearly as large as massive Thousand Island Lake, Garnet Lake fills a classic U-shaped glacial valley at the foot of Banner Peak. It is easy to imagine the glacier that still clutches to the upper slopes of the mountain being a great river of ice flowing off the summit and through the wide valley. Today's glacier is only a remnant of its former self, and the lake remains in the valley. Like its neighbor to the north, it is a staggering vision of alpine perfection.

When you reach the lake, follow the trail as it winds along a narrow bench between high cliffs and the water. You soon reach a bridge that spans the lake's outlet. As the water leaves the lake, it pours over a small outlet. Across the bridge a trail sets off to the east, where you can see the mountains on the east side of the San Joaquin River's valley through a gap in the rocks. This trail is a rugged route that descends back to the River Trail. It is steep and requires some rock scrambling and is not recommended. It is much easier and prettier to continue on the John Muir Trail for a while longer before returning to the River Trail.

Continue to contour around the lake. As you walk along the southern shore, you are treated to more breathtaking views of Ritter and Banner. Having moved south from

Mammoth Mountain rises above the South Fork of the San Joaquin River's canyon.

Thousand Island Lake, you can now clearly see Ritter's summit from the trail. Soon the easy hiking ends as the path begins to climb up the side of the walls of the Garnet Lake valley. As you get higher above the lake, note the horizontally aligned strata that form the buttes on the north side of the lake. The trail then moves directly up toward the top of the valley wall by climbing a series of tightly stacked switchbacks. When you reach the top, turn around and bid farewell to Garnet Lake and the high country around Ritter and Banner. As you turn back to the south, a new mountain pageant, filled with a fresh set of awesome crags and peaks, begins to unfold. Closest to the trail is the rugged crest of Volcanic Ridge. To the west are the awe-inspiring Minarets, second only to Ritter and Banner in majesty. Farther to the south you can see the Mammoth Lakes Basin, the peaks that line large Duck Lake, towering Red Slate Mountain, and the crags of the Silver Divide.

From the pass above Garnet Lake, you begin the long, steady descent back to the San Joaquin River. The views are good for a while, but you eventually enter a heavily wooded area, the first in several miles. After 2.0 miles of losing elevation, you reach the banks of vigorous Shadow Creek. This creek begins high in the Minarets, proceeds into fantastic Ediza Lake, and then makes a swift-flowing journey down to Shadow Lake. When the John Muir Trail meets the creek, you intersect the trail that leads up to Ediza Lake. Turn left to continue on the John Muir Trail.

The route follows alongside Shadow Creek as it surges from one pretty cascade to another. As you cross the rocky country, look to the east, where you can just make out Shadow Lake in the trees. Past the lake, look through a gap in the cliffs and spot the multicolored strata of San Joaquin Mountain. Incredibly, this solitary mountain is the final crest of the Sierra Nevada, the only obstacle that prevents the nascent San Joaquin from flowing into the Great Basin rather than the Pacific Ocean. After following Shadow

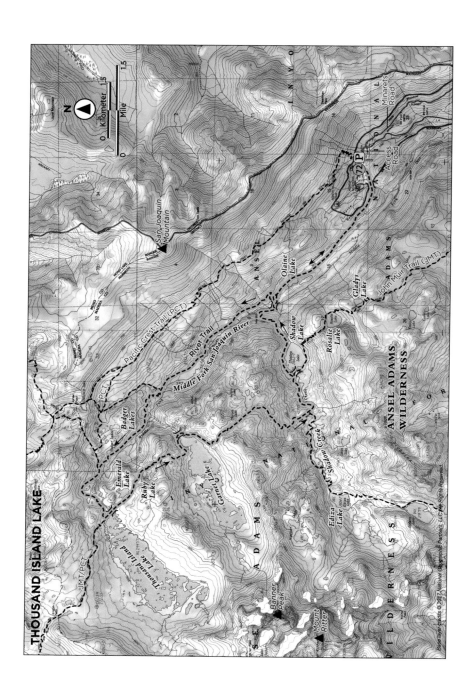

THOUSAND ISLAND LAKE

Creek for 0.6 mile, you reach a junction next to a bridge over the fast-moving water. For the 5.5 miles since leaving Thousand Island Lake, you have been following the John Muir Trail. Now it turns right and crosses the bridge. Instead, stay left and follow the new trail along the north shore of Shadow Lake. When you reach the lake's outlet, walk over to the water and turn back to the west for one final view of Ritter and Banner. When you are ready to complete the loop, return to the main trail and proceed along Shadow Creek as it flows out of Shadow Lake.

This is one of the most spectacular sections of the hike. As Shadow Creek leaves the lake, it enters a narrow gorge and crashes down a series of cascades on its way to the San Joaquin River below. At the same time, the trail traverses the steep cliff on a narrow ledge. The path winds around the contours of the sheer rock. As you get farther away from the creek, your view of the cascades improves. It is an awesome way to say goodbye to the amazing high country explored on this hike. As you descend past marvelously gnarled junipers, you are treated to one last great view. Looking south down the length of the San Joaquin River's canyon, you can see Mammoth Mountain, the volcano that sits on the rim of the Long Valley Caldera, rising against the horizon. From here the trail makes a broad switchback down the lower flanks of the mountain before reaching the river. Cross the bridge and merge onto the River Trail, just up the trail from Olaine Lake. From there follow the trail back to the trailhead.

MILES AND DIRECTIONS

0.0 Start hiking on the River Trail at Agnew Meadows.

2.25 Stay right at the junction with the Shadow Creek Trail. (*Option:* Turn left here and climb for 1.25 miles to Shadow Lake. Turn around there and return to Agnew Meadows for a 7-mile out-and-back hike.)

4.6 Bear left at the junction with the trail to Badger Lakes.

6.1 The River Trail is joined by the Pacific Crest Trail.

7.1 Reach Thousand Island Lake. Turn left on the John Muir Trail.

9.5 Arrive at the Garnet Lake outlet.

12.4 At Shadow Creek, the John Muir Trail is joined by the trail to Ediza Lake. Stay left, continuing on the John Muir Trail.

13.6 At Shadow Lake, bear left onto the Shadow Creek Trail.

14.75 Turn right onto the River Trail to retrace your steps to the trailhead.

17.0 Arrive back at the trailhead.

73. DUCK LAKE PASS

WHY GO?

This hike to a pass over the Sierra Crest features sweeping panoramas of the High Sierra and passes four alpine lakes in a wide mountain valley. From the pass you can look down at massive Duck Lake, one of the largest backcountry lakes in the Sierra Nevada.

THE RUNDOWN

Start: Duck Pass Trailhead
Distance: 7,8 miles out and back
(**Option:** The hike can be extended by 2 miles by continuing to either Pika Lake or the Duck Lake outlet.)
Hiking time: 4–5 hours
Difficulty: Strenuous
Elevation gain: 1,620 feet
Season: Summer, fall
Trail surface: Packed dirt, rocky, rock slabs

Canine compatibility: Dogs permitted
Fees and permits: None
Land status: John Muir Wilderness, Inyo National Forest
Trail contact: Mammoth Ranger District, 2510 Highway 203, Mammoth Lakes 93546; (760) 924-5500; www.fs.usda.gov/main/inyo
Other: Water is available in numerous lakes.

FINDING THE TRAILHEAD

From the junction of US 395 and CA 203, drive west on CA 203 through the town of Mammoth Lakes to the intersection with Minarets Road. Stay straight at the intersection, where CA 203 becomes Lake Mary Road. Follow this road for 2.5 miles and turn left onto Around Lake Mary Road, signed for the Coldwater Campground. Continue for 0.6 mile and turn left into the entrance to the Coldwater Campground. Drive through the camping area for 0.7 mile. At the far end of the campground loop, pass the Emerald Lake Trailhead parking lot and park in the Duck Pass parking area. **Trailhead GPS:** 37°35'27.89"N / 118°59'20.65"W

WHAT TO SEE

Duck Pass, which crosses a low point in the Sierra Crest just south of the Mammoth Lakes Basin, is one of the easiest routes into the High Sierra backcountry. From the paved roads of the Mammoth Lakes Basin, it is a convenient hike over the pass and into the vast backcountry of the northern John Muir Wilderness. While the splendid mountains beyond the pass are generally the domain of extended backpacking trips, the pass itself and the lakes that surround it make fantastic hikes on their own. On the way to the pass, the trail passes four diverse and beautiful lakes set in a gorgeous mountain valley. Beyond the pass is spectacular Duck Lake, an enormous deep blue jewel in a wide, craggy basin. From Duck Pass itself are incredible vistas far to the north toward Yosemite and south to the Silver Divide.

To begin the hike, be sure you are at the Duck Pass Trailhead. Another trailhead, to Emerald Lake, is nearby in the same large parking lot, and it is possible to confuse them. Having ascertained you are at the right place, hit the trail and follow it up a moderate grade into the shady forest. The path follows a ravine as it climbs to the south. Cross the boundary into the John Muir Wilderness and begin a succession of switchbacks. As the trail straightens out, it enters the wide valley drained by Mammoth Creek. Catch a glimpse of Arrowhead Lake below the trail before you arrive at the spur trail that drops down to the lakeshore, about 1.0 mile from the trailhead. If you only want a short hike, this is a good option; otherwise, continue hiking on the main trail.

Past the spur the trail continues to climb as it leads you up a series of benches on the west side of the valley. As you climb, the trees grow sparse in some areas, and you begin to get good views of the valley. After climbing gently for 0.6 mile past the spur to Arrowhead Lake, you reach the north end of Skelton Lake. Much of the lake's shore, especially on the east side, is bound by rocky knolls that fall away directly into the water. However, some sections where the water is easily accessible, including some areas right along the trail, have grassy shores and are idyllic spots to take a break and enjoy the peaceful setting. Across Skelton Lake the eastern wall of the valley rises abruptly and culminates in a massive knob of dark red rock. Two narrow bands of white rock run across the face of the knob, giving it a striking appearance.

From Skelton Lake, continue hiking south as the trail maintains a steady grade. The trees persist along the path, only breaking for occasional views. The path continues south and then switchbacks up a short hill. Drop down the other side and arrive at shallow Barney Lake. The green water lies at the foot of some massive scree fields that seem to

The rugged mountains of the John Muir Wilderness are seen on the far side of Skelton Lake.

Besides Barney Lake, nearby Mammoth Mountain and much of the Ansel Adams Wilderness can be seen from the pass.

flow off the rim of the valley headwall. The lake has a distinctive shape, resulting from the presence of two peninsulas sticking out into the water. Where the trail first comes near the lake, there are numerous fallen trees. Pass by the snags and drop down to the lake's outlet. The lively stream, the first section of newly birthed Mammoth Creek, leaps out of the lake and swiftly flows into nearby Red Lake. The lake is barely larger than some of the small tarns that dot the end of the valley, but since it is on Mammoth Creek, it does not grow stagnant like other bodies of water that are similar in size. A faint path leads along the creek over to the tiny lake.

Cross the outlet on a small bridge and walk through the rocky terrain on the other side, passing a small pond in a rocky bowl on your left. A quick comparison of the water in this pool with that of Red Lake quickly makes it apparent why Red Lake is considered a lake despite its diminutive stature. After passing the pond the trail briefly turns sandy before veering away from the lake and climbing up onto the bedrock. This marks the beginning of the climb up to the top of Duck Pass. Looking up you can make out the trail as it climbs up a series of ledges and switchbacks leading to the low point in the crest. The climb is not notably steep, but the grade is steady. Steel yourself, and know that soon you will be on the top of the Sierra Crest.

The wide, rocky path first switchbacks up a ridge protruding northward from the crest. After 0.3 mile the trail subtly moves off the ridge onto the actual headwall of the canyon. The climb is circuitous as it at times follows ledges on the cliff while at other times makes short switchbacks up rocky gullies. Finally, near the top there is a wide bench where you can walk off the trail quite a ways and get an incredible view to the north. The entire headwaters valley of Mammoth Creek lies at your feet. You can see Barney, Red, and Skelton Lakes glittering amid the valley's forested floor. Looming beyond the

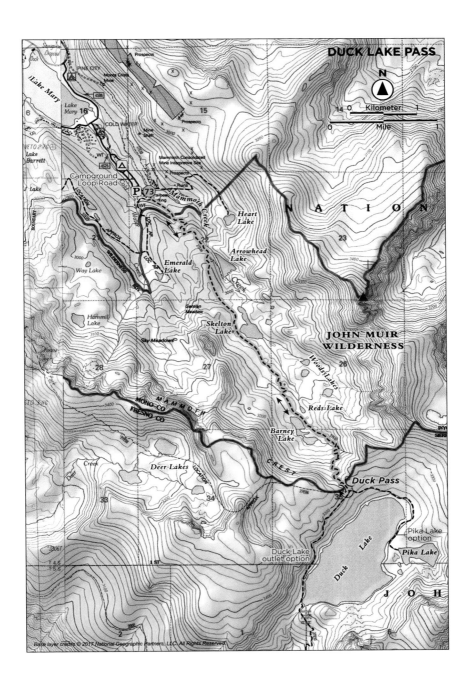

N

Kilometer

Mile

valley is the hulking mound of Mammoth Mountain. The tall volcano looks as though it was somehow transplanted from the Cascade Range far to the north. Beyond the region's namesake mountain, the section of the Sierra Crest that forms the southern boundary of Yosemite offers a climactic horizon. Prominent peaks including Donahue and Blacktop Peaks, the Koip Crest, and even distant Mount Dana, the second-highest peak in Yosemite, can all be observed unaided. It is a crowning vista of the Mammoth Lakes area, but it is not the final view.

Press on just a little farther until you arrive at Duck Pass proper. You are now sitting atop the crest of the Sierra Nevada. Tall pinnacles loom to the south, rising above the deep blue water of immense Duck Lake. Beyond the spires lining the western end of the lake, the awesome peaks of the High Sierra's Silver Divide make an alluring horizon. These alpine sirens beckon hikers to come and admire them. To do so, head downhill a little from the pass and arrive at a fork. The path to the left travels down to the water, wraps around the lake's east shore, and leads to Pika Lake, which is hidden from view by a low, rocky dike. The path to the right leads to the Pacific Crest Trail as it travels the Fish Creek drainage toward the Middle Fork of the San Joaquin. This route leads down to the lake's outlet, which is also a possible option for extending the hike. Both options are about 2.0 miles out and back to their respective destinations and are great extensions of the hike. Whichever you choose, enjoy the view of the gigantic blue lake and the crags that surround it from the pass before following the trail back to the trailhead in the Mammoth Lakes Basin.

MILES AND DIRECTIONS

0.0 Start from the Duck Pass Trailhead and hike south.

1.0 Pass the spur leading down to Arrowhead Lake.

1.8 Skelton Lake lies just east of the trail.

2.7 Arrive at Barney Lake.

3.0 Begin the final climb up to Duck Pass.

3.9 Reach the top of Duck Pass. (***Option:*** To add 2 miles, continue on to Duck Lake or Pika Lake.) Turn around and follow the route back to the trailhead.

7.8 Arrive back at the trailhead.

74. CONVICT CANYON

WHY GO?

This hike leads past breathtaking Convict Lake and ventures into amazing Convict Canyon, where soaring cliffs, painted with amazing warped strata, tower above the creek. The hike ends at gorgeous Mildred Lake, surrounded by incredible alpine scenery.

THE RUNDOWN

Start: Convict Lake day use area
Distance: 10.2 miles out and back to Mildred Lake. (**Option:** easy 3-mile loop around Convict Lake.)
Hiking time: 5–6 hours
Difficulty: Strenuous
Elevation gain: 2,220 feet
Season: Summer, fall
Trail surface: Packed dirt, rocky, rock slabs, gravel
Canine compatibility: Dogs permitted

Fees and permits: None
Land status: John Muir Wilderness, Inyo National Forest
Trail contact: Mammoth Ranger District, 2510 Highway 203, Mammoth Lakes 93546; (760) 924-5500; www.fs.usda.gov/main/inyo
Other: Water is available at the trailhead and in Convict Creek and Mildred Lake.

FINDING THE TRAILHEAD

From the junction of US 395 and CA 203 at Mammoth Lakes, drive south on US 395 for 4.5 miles. Turn right onto Convict Lake Road and continue for 2.2 miles until the road splits at the edge of Convict Lake. Turn left and follow the paved road 0.5 mile to the trailhead. **Trailhead GPS:** 37°35'20.78"N / 118°51'15.90"W

WHAT TO SEE

The Sherwin Range occupies a compact corner of the High Sierra in the John Muir Wilderness, just south of the community of Mammoth Lakes. The range is not well known on its own, but some of its constituent parts, chief among them Convict Lake, are among the most famous destinations in the Eastern Sierra. The Sherwins are recognized as a subrange of the Sierra Nevada not because they stand distinct from the surrounding mountains but because their geology is so radically different from anywhere else. Visually they are a range apart, looking like nothing else in Northern California. Here the mountains are stratified with radically contrasting rock types smashed up against one another, their different colors creating a massive kaleidoscope on the face of the mountains. The best place to observe the staggering scale of the Sherwin Range is by hiking through Convict Canyon. This is easily one of the most unusual and magnificent corners of the Sierra Nevada. This hike boasts some of the most superlative scenery imaginable. From

Convict Lake, to the great buckled strata of the canyon, to the intensely blue water of Mildred Lake and the final centerpiece of Red Slate Mountain, this trail is one great spectacle after another.

The hike begins at the day use area next to Convict Lake. Before setting out, be sure to walk out to the rocky beach and take in the mind-blowing scene from the edge of the water. Transcendent Laurel Mountain and its attendant Sevehah Cliff present a sensational vista that is matched by few other sites in Northern California. The lofty peak soars more than 4,000 feet above the large lake in a sheer cliff of fantastically twisted rock. With a few exceptions elsewhere in the Sherwin Range, it is unlike any other mountain in the Sierra.

From the day use area, follow the trail around the lake, enjoying the awesome sight of Laurel Mountain almost the entire time. Convict Lake is popular with anglers, and their boats are often seen on the water. Well-built paths lead down from the trail to the shoreline, providing good fishing access. The path wraps around the lake's western shore and descends to the water's level. The area at the western end of the lake is filled with cottonwoods. The ground is covered with a dense grassy carpet and cut by several channels of Convict Creek. A long boardwalk has been constructed to provide easy crossing of the numerous channels, which can flood the area in spring and turn the ground marshy in summer. In fall, cottonwoods glow yellow, combining with the lush grass and the elevated trail to make this a seemingly magic forest. After crossing the boardwalk for 0.25 mile, the trail returns to dry ground and continues just a little farther before arriving at a junction. Hikers looking to make the 3.0-mile loop around Convict Lake turn right here and follow the trail back around to the trailhead. To continue to Convict Canyon, turn left at the junction and begin climbing.

Spectacular Laurel Mountain reflects in Convict Lake.

After passing through the lush forest on the west end of Convict Lake, the high-desert terrain of the initial part of the climb can come as a bit of a shock. Junipers, sagebrush, and mountain mahogany dominate this area. At times it is hard to take note of the surroundings because of the overwhelming presence of Laurel Mountain and stark-white Sevehah Cliff. The trail heads directly toward the cliff, which looms higher and higher as you pass under its watchful gaze. After crossing the boundary of the John Muir Wilderness, the trail begins a long traverse along the base of the cliffs. Convict Creek becomes audible as you enter the mouth of the canyon.

After entering the canyon, the trail levels out a little and you travel alongside Convict Creek as it flows through a small, wide valley near the mouth of the canyon. The valley is filled with more cottonwoods. Though the Sevehah Cliff is no longer easily visible in its entirety once you enter this part of the canyon, peaks and cliffs come into view. On the north side of the canyon, great cliffs topped by turrets of white rock are streaked with rust-colored strata. On the south side is an even more striking sight. A single, nearly perfectly symmetrical triangular peak thrusts upward from the rim of the canyon. Closer inspection shows this is composed of multiple strata that have been uplifted violently. One series of layers, interspersed red on white, buckled, leaving a stunning and unique pattern on the cliff.

Leaving the small valley, the trail climbs a series of switchbacks before straightening out again. The canyon is much narrower now, the slopes descending steeply all the way to Convict Creek, which flows through a V-shaped channel at the canyon bottom. The tall, triangular peak continues to dominate the horizon, showing off its awesomely warped strata. Soon the canyon narrows to such a degree that the creek pours through a rocky notch and cascades down a small waterfall. At the little cataract, the trail climbs up to the rocky notch, passing alongside the top of the falls, and then ends on a rocky bench at the site of a former bridge crossing, 3.75 miles from the beginning of the hike.

At the old bridge site, the large creek flowing out of Lake Genevieve cascades down an exceedingly narrow channel. Where it joins Convict Creek, there are large concrete piers, the remnants of past bridges that once crossed to the other side of the canyon. Over the years the creek has defied being spanned and has repeatedly washed out any efforts to rebuild a bridge. Today the forest service seems resigned to not having a bridge and no longer attempts to construct new ones. This means that a crossing on logs or rocks is necessary. Early in summer this can be problematic, since these creeks can swell dramatically and make crossing very dangerous. If conditions are good to continue on to the other side of the river, it is recommended that you first cross Lake Genevieve's creek and then Convict Creek. Each creek is smaller on its own. Once they have combined forces, the volume of water can make getting to the other side a challenge in any season.

Once you have reached the south side of the creek, follow a use trail along the creek. Not only did the creek wash out the bridge, it washed out the trail on the south side altogether. A new path has been established by hikers, and it is not difficult to follow. After running parallel to the creek for about 100 feet, the new route turns south and climbs steeply up a small gully's rocky rim. The quick climb leads up to the old trail, now well above the creek and free from potential flooding damage.

Back on the main path, press onward, climbing steadily deeper into the canyon. The north side of the canyon begins to exhibit incredible patterns on large rock extrusions similar to the great buckled strata seen earlier on the triangular peak. The first really showy set is a massive dark rock cut countless times by thin ribbons of white rock. It is a beautiful geologic

Mildred Lake boasts beautiful views of Red Slate Mountain and other peaks of the Sherwin Range.

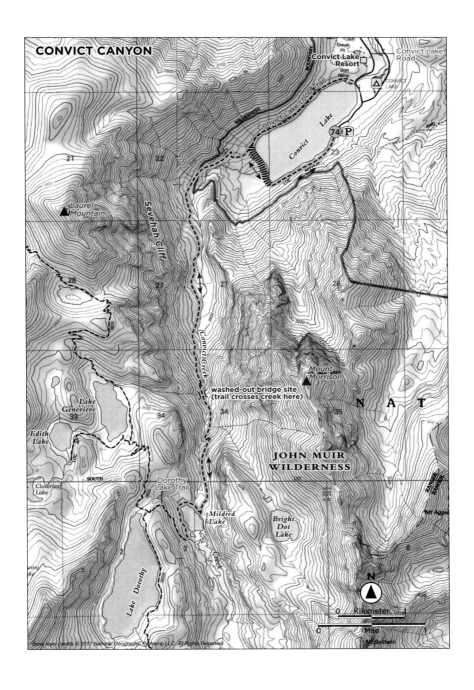

CONVICT CANYON

display. This is followed by a few switchbacks that bring the trail into the narrowest part of the canyon. No longer lined by steeply sloping walls, Convict Creek now charges through a sheer-walled gorge. Make your way through the gorge on the narrow trail built onto a long ledge. Here you come to the most impressive display of the showy strata waves on the north side of the canyon. Dozens of layers of white rock form giant wave patterns on the rust-colored cliff. The whole pattern is a couple hundred feet high, and it is humbling to think about the magnitude of the forces that broke and warped these mountains.

As you cross the ledge, Convict Creek cascades over several small but scenic cataracts as you gain the last bit of elevation before reaching a level area, where the canyon widens out. Note that the cliffs on the south side of the trail are no longer the rust-red color that has been consistent through most of the hike. Now the sheer cliffs are a slate-gray color, indicative of a major shift in composition. As you follow the trail across the gently rolling terrain, a new vista unfolds in the distance. The far end of the canyon culminates in a series of rugged cliffs that lead up to the remarkable summit of tall Red Slate Mountain, the highest peak in the Sherwin Range.

After following the easy section of trail onto some rocky bluffs, the path splits right above the deep blue waters of Mildred Lake. The path to the left follows the shoreline and then travels beyond the lake into the extensive meadow that stretches from the lake to the base of Red Slate Mountain. While this is a good option, instead stay to the right and descend to the lake's level. You soon cross a small bridge over the lake's outlet and then reach the easternmost part of Lake Mildred. Here you have an incredible view of Red Slate Mountain and the amazingly diverse sections of the Sherwin Range that surround it. Above the lake, a small waterfall, part of the creek that flows out of massive Lake Dorothy, nosily tumbles down a cliff. You can continue still farther and follow the trail on the lake's south side. Here you get an unbelievable view of the gray cliffs towering above the lake. The bright rock is a stark contrast to the red cliffs that surround you. They almost seem to have a flowing pattern, as though they were pouring down a ledge and then froze. From here the trail to Dorothy Lake lies just ahead. You can also venture out into the vast meadow that lies west of Lake Mildred. It is possible to loop around the lake, but that requires a ford across the creek. Whichever option you choose, retrace your steps when it is time to leave.

MILES AND DIRECTIONS

0.0 Start by heading down to the day use beach to get a great view of Convict Lake and Laurel Mountain. Then pick up the trail as it heads around the lake.

1.1 At the junction with the Convict Canyon Trail, turn left to hike into the canyon. (**Option**: Turn right to make the short loop around the lake.)

3.75 Arrive at the washed-out bridge site and cross both the creek flowing from Lake Genevieve and Convict Creek.

5.1 Reach the north shore of Mildred Lake. Return the way you came.

10.2 Arrive back at the trailhead.

75. LITTLE LAKES VALLEY

WHY GO?

The easy hike through the Little Lakes Valley is a stunningly beautiful journey through an alpine valley filled with meadows, lively creeks, and lakes amid a panoply of High Sierra peaks.

THE RUNDOWN

Start: Mosquito Flat Trailhead
Distance: 6.6 miles out and back
Hiking time: 3–4hours
Difficulty: Easy
Elevation gain: 556 feet
Season: Summer, fall
Trail surface: Packed dirt, rocky
Canine compatibility: Dogs permitted

Fees and permits: None
Land status: John Muir Wilderness, Inyo National Forest
Trail contact: White Mountain Ranger District, 798 North Main St., Bishop 93514; (760) 873-2500; www.fs.usda.gov/main/inyo
Other: Water is available in numerous lakes.

FINDING THE TRAILHEAD

 From Tom's Place on US 395, 15 miles south of Mammoth Lakes or 24.5 miles north of Bishop, drive south on Rock Creek Road for 10.3 miles to the road's end at the Mosquito Flat Trailhead. **Trailhead GPS:** 37°26'6.64"N / 118°44'49.96"W

WHAT TO SEE

Few hikes can match the exemplary scenery of Little Lakes Valley, a mountain paradise at the far end of Rock Creek Canyon. Surrounded by an abundance of monumental peaks that exceed 13,000 feet, the trail passes six named lakes and numerous tarns. Several streams, flowing from remote cirques hidden away in the cliffs above, cross the trail. Their swift vigor beautifully contrasts the serene beauty of the tranquil lakes. Yet despite these superlative features, the sum is greater than its parts. All the best attributes of the Little Lakes Valley fit together to create a nearly perfect alpine landscape. Normally you would expect such mountain splendor to demand a difficult climb or a long hike. In the Little Lakes Valley, neither is required. The trail is short, the climbing is minimal, and the landscape stunning from the very first step. If there is a drawback to this hike, it is that too many others have taken notice of the Little Lakes Valley, and the trail can get relatively busy at times. Don't let this be a deterrent to enjoying the hike. Skip the weekend or get an early start to avoid the majority of other hikers and imbibe deeply from this superb hike.

The hike starts at the Mosquito Flat Trailhead, where Rock Creek races through a small meadow. When the trail heads south, it follows alongside the creek, climbing up a

A swift-flowing creek enters lovely Heart Lake beneath the watchful gaze of Bear Creek Spire and other High Sierra peaks.

gentle rise. Looking up at Mount Starr, directly above the trail on the right, it is surprising to note that this is the Sierra Crest and that the rain and snow that falls on the other side of the mountain flows into the San Joaquin River and then all the way into San Francisco Bay. You quickly reach a junction with the trail to Ruby Lake and Mono Pass. Stay left here and continue to the south.

You soon pass small Mack Lake on the left. A few small snowmelt streams cross the trail before you climb over a gentle rise and then drop down to a junction with a spur trail on the left. Take this path and head out to Marsh Lake, the first of the truly great lakes of the valley. The south end of the lake is bound by a grassy thicket, contributing to the marshy name. Climb up on a rocky knob at the outlet of the lake for the first really grand vista of the hike. At the head of the valley, you see the giants that populate the Sierra Crest. Though not all are named, seven of the peaks along the end of the valley exceed 13,000 feet. At 13,726 feet, the tallest is Bear Creek Spire, the highest peak visible on the left, just to the right of a shorter, pyramidal peak.

From Marsh Lake, return to the trail and turn left. As you cross a small stream, you enter the demesne of meadow-lined Heart Lake. As you pull near the lake, you cross over the large creek that comes from Ruby Lake just as it flows into true-to-its-name Heart Lake. Bear Creek Spire and the V-shaped notch of Morgan Pass are visible beyond the lake. The trail curves around the south side of the lake, climbs up onto a granite bench, and then pulls alongside Box Lake. The water lies well below the trail in a deep granite trough. Continue on, following along above the water until you leave the lake behind. Here you cross Rock Creek for the first time. Climb gently before arriving at the outlet of Long Lake and one of the most exalted trail vistas in the Sierra Nevada.

The great peaks that crown Little Lakes Valley all gaze down on the clear water, which, when the wind is calm, presents a glorious reflection. Bear Creek Spire, as well as Mounts Dade and Abbot, all preside majestically over their wild domain. Note the intricate bands of crystalline rock marbling that streak the cliffs below the summits. Pause and consider the beauty and the harshness of the forces that created it before continuing. The trail skirts the east side of the lake on a rocky ledge and then proceeds alongside the grassy lakeshore. Look back to the northwest to spot the ragged face of Mount Starr.

About 0.7 mile past Long Lake's outlet, you arrive at the spur trail that leads up to Chickenfoot Lake. Though you can continue up the canyon to the Gem Lakes, Morgan Pass, and the Morgan Lakes, this lake marks a good place to stop. Climb easily up the spur and arrive at the inlet of Chickenfoot Lake. The large lake lies at the foot of the steep cliffs and talus slope of Mount Morgan. It has an extensive shoreline that includes a few coves, so there is plenty of area to explore. The prettiest spot though is in the meadow

Craggy Mount Starr reflects in the waters of Long Lake.

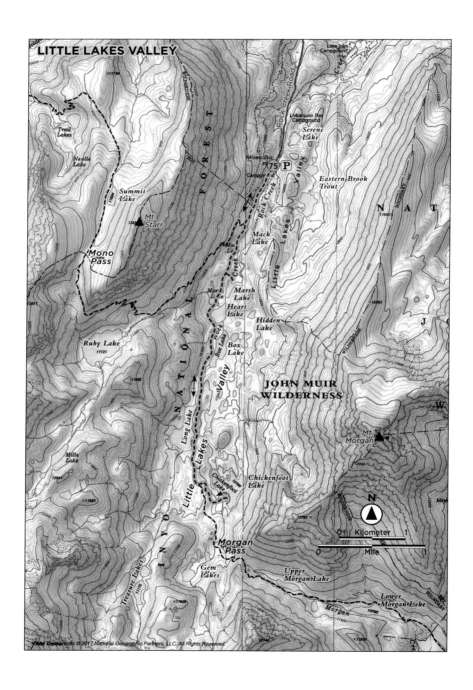

LITTLE LAKES VALLEY

The Sierra crest looms above meadows that lie adjacent to Chickenfoot Lake.

just south of the lake. The large creek flowing from the Gem Lakes flows like a clear ribbon through the lush grass. In addition to all the tall peaks at the end of the valley, there are also good views up to Mount Morrison and to the west toward Mount Mills and a palisade of granite spires. It is glorious. When the time comes to return to the trailhead, follow the trail the way you came.

MILES AND DIRECTIONS

0.0 Start at the Mosquito Flat Trailhead and hike south.

0.5 Stay left at the junction with the trail to Ruby Lake and Mono Pass.

0.9 Take the spur to Marsh Lake.

1.4 Arrive at Heart Lake.

1.8 Pass by Box Lake.

2.3 Reach the outlet of Long Lake.

3.0 Turn left onto the spur that climbs to Chickenfoot Lake.

3.3 Reach the inlet to Chickenfoot Lake. Turn around here.

6.6 Arrive back at the trailhead.

76. SABRINA BASIN

WHY GO?

This stunning hike enters a magnificent High Sierra basin where 13,000-foot spear-tip peaks soar above numerous spectacular tree-line lakes. A shorter option leads to gorgeous Blue Lake, while a longer, demanding hike travels all the way to an alpine paradise at Hungry Packer Lake.

THE RUNDOWN

Start: Parking spot at the trailhead or the pullout on CA 168 (add 1.2 miles round-trip)
Distance: 13.0 miles out and back to Hungry Packer Lake. (**Option:** moderately strenuous 5.6 miles out and back to Blue Lake)
Hiking time: 4–8 hours or overnight
Difficulty: Strenuous
Elevation gain: 1,320 feet (Blue Lake); 2,000 feet (Hungry Packer Lake)
Season: Summer, fall
Trail surface: Packed dirt, rocky, duff
Canine compatibility: Dogs permitted

Fees and permits: None
Land status: John Muir Wilderness, Inyo National Forest
Trail contact: White Mountain Ranger District, 798 North Main St., Bishop 93514; (760) 873-2500; www.fs.usda.gov/main/inyo
Other: There are a few day-use parking areas at the trailhead. Parking here, which requires an early start, shortens the hike by 0.6 mile (1.2 miles round-trip). Water is available in creeks and numerous lakes.

FINDING THE TRAILHEAD

 From Bishop on US 395, drive west on CA 168 for 18 miles to the wide pullout just prior to the right turn signed for North Lake. The wide pullout is the official parking area for the hike.

The trailhead, from which mileages were reckoned in this guide, actually lies 0.6 mile up the road, and it is necessary to walk along the road to reach the beginning of the trail. Just after the right-hand turn for North Lake, the road is lined with wide margins where it is permissible to park. Getting a spot at the west end of these margins shortens the walk to the trailhead to only 0.3 mile. The margins end at an entrance to the Sabrina Lake Campground, which coincides with the end of CA 168. From here, narrow Sabrina Lake Road continues to the day use area at Sabrina Lake, passing the Sabrina Basin Trailhead. A few parking spaces are scattered around the trailhead. An early start can increase your chances of claiming one of these spots, which will save you 1.2 miles of hiking distance. **Trailhead GPS:** 37°12'48.82"N / 118°36'36.36"W

WHAT TO SEE

Sabrina Basin, at the head of the Middle Fork of Bishop Creek, is a classic High Sierra wonderland. Hemmed in by a collection of breathtaking peaks, it boasts dozens of lakes, expanses of lush meadow, and a significant amount of open terrain at the tree line. Most of the lakes in this area are remarkable, but two in particular stand out as notably fantastic. Blue Lake, at the head of an awesome canyon, has a classic alpine horizon filled with tall, rugged mountains, perfectly proportioned and arranged. Hungry Packer Lake is a large lake with a giant, steeple-like tower soaring above it and a powerful sense of awe infusing the area. Unlike many other basins in the Eastern Sierra, Sabrina Basin does not have a pass leading over the range's crest into Kings Canyon National Park. Though it is a popular destination in and of itself, there is less traffic on the trail, since fewer people are passing through to reach other areas deeper in the Sierra Nevada. Those who do come to Sabrina Basin are blessed to be immersed in such a tremendous place.

If you parked in the pullout on CA 168, walk up the road 0.6 mile to the trailhead. If you were fortunate enough to get one of the precious day use spots at the beginning of the trail, you will be able to set out immediately. The path passes through a small stand of aspens, switchbacking up the south wall of the canyon. It straightens out, passes the

Early morning on the trail along Lake Sabrina

dam that forms Lake Sabrina, and begins the long traverse above the lake. The view to the south of the pointed peaks of the Sierra Crest looming high above Lake Sabrina's headwall beckons hikers to press on toward higher regions. Both this section of trail and the rest of the slopes above the lake have excellent fall color, making this part of the hike a delight in the fall.

Aside from the aspens, much of the slope along the water is covered in high-desert vegetation, including sagebrush and juniper. After following above the lakeshore for 1.0 mile, the trail begins to climb steeply. The grade will not abate until you reach Blue Lake, 1.75 miles away. About 0.2 mile later the trail to George Lake branches off and climbs to the left. Stay right and continue climbing. Soon you cross George Lake's outlet creek, which has steady flow all summer. The trail then begins a long sequence of short switchbacks up the wall above Sabrina Lake. Cross a second, smaller stream between switchbacks, then keep climbing.

As you near the top of a ridge, the trees clear and the rocky terrain opens up. A few more switchbacks lead to some rock slabs where there is an incredible view. From this overlook you can gaze down on Lake Sabrina. In the distance, far across the Owens Valley, lie the White Mountains, the tallest mountain range in the Great Basin. Even more

Mt. Emerson, the red Paiute Crags, and Lake Sabrina are a dramatic foreground to the distant White Mountains.

Lofty Mount Thompson crowns the High Sierra splendor around Blue Lake.

dramatic are the crags rising high above the north side of Lake Sabrina: tall Mount Emerson and the red Paiute Crags, a chaotic jumble of spires that contrast against the gray granite. Immediately below the trail you can see Bishop Creek spilling over a pretty waterfall.

This vista marks your parting with Lake Sabrina, a constant sight for the entire hike up to this point. Fortunately it means you are nearing Blue Lake and the gorgeous high country of Sabrina Basin. From the overlook the path rounds a bend and enters a small canyon. At the head of the canyon are a number of tight switchbacks built onto piles of rock. Climb to the top and get one more look at Mount Emerson and the Paiute Crags, and then walk the short distance to a large creek flowing out of Blue Lake. Cross the creek and then scramble up some rocks on the left to get a good view of the lake.

Blue Lake is situated at the end of a canyon on the south side of Sabrina Basin. Though tall cliffs rise out of the east side of the lake, it is the view down the canyon that is most captivating. The High Sierra paradise that lies at the end of the canyon is crowned by Mount Thompson and a series of majestic, shard-like 13,000-foot peaks cutting against the sky. The view from the lake imparts a sense of vastness and colossal scale. Blue Lake and its surroundings are worth the hike on their own, and they make a marvelous day hike. You could scramble and enjoy the area all day before heading back down to Lake Sabrina.

If you plan on continuing to Hungry Packer Lake, follow the trail as it curves to the south and crosses onto some granite slabs right above the water. These afford the best view of the lake and its backdrop. However, the view can be distracting, and it is easy to miss a sharp right turn as the trail climbs through a cleft in the rocks. Continuing forward on the use trail leads to a great view at the end of the slabs, but stay sharp to follow the trail off the slab and then descend to a trail junction. Going left here takes you to Donkey Lake; stay right and follow the trail to the northwest.

For the next 1.25 miles, the path maintains a fairly level grade as it makes a sweeping traverse of the north end of the divide that separates the Middle Fork of Bishop Creek from the canyon draining into Blue Lake. You first cross a ledge along a cliff and then turn west and pass the tiny Emerald Lakes, which are really just glorified ponds. Continue past them and you eventually round a bend and drop down to the edge of Dingleberry Lake. This lake is quite pretty, but it does not compare to the spectacle of Blue Lake.

As you leave the lake, the trail splits into a stock route on the left and a hiker route on the right. Follow this path and drop down to the creek flowing into Dingleberry Lake. The water is wide and shallow as it flows past rocky walls. Cross on well-arranged boulders and then continue to the south. You soon enter a lovely garden-like meadow. Small streams flow through grassy channels as you walk through this delicate area. You can hear, and at times see, Bishop Creek racing down the rocky terrain to your right. Climb a short rise and then arrive at the junction with the trail to Midnight Lake. Stay left here.

Past the junction you drop down and cross the outlet creek from Midnight Lake. Climbing briefly, quickly come to a vantage where you can look down on Topsy Turvy Lake. Filling a wide depression, the lake is bound by large boulders. The trail turns south, and after a short climb you enter the prodigious basin at the headwaters of the Middle Fork of Bishop Creek. The area is a sweeping plain of rolling granite and large slabs. Ringing the area are numerous 12,000- and 13,000-foot peaks. Bishop Creek pours over small cascades and races through channels as it passes from one small pool to the next. The largest and deepest of these pools is small Sailor Lake. It certainly is among the loveliest spots in this grand area.

From Sailor Lake, press on a little farther, climbing up a short rise before you finally arrive at Hungry Packer Lake. This staggering lake is set in an incredibly narrow, sheer-walled cirque. At the south end of the lake, a massive spire thrusts upward into the heavens. Behind it, above a palisade of stark granite walls, is the pinnacle summit of Mount Haeckel. The whole edifice overshadows the sapphire lake like a monumental stone citadel, holding a commanding position above its domain. A trail wraps around the west side of the lake, where the bowl widens out a bit. Stop and enjoy the sight; scramble on the rocks and bask in the glory of one of the great destinations of the High Sierra. Eventually you must follow the trail back to the trailhead.

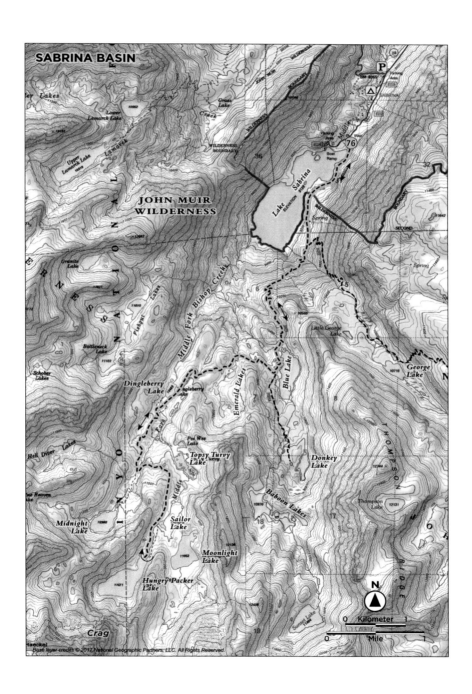

Awesome towers and vertical cliffs surround Hungry Packer Lake.

MILES AND DIRECTIONS

Note: Mileage is calculated from trailhead, not parking areas. Round-trip distance from the farthest parking area could be as much as 1.2 miles.

0.0 Start the trail by a small pullout on Sabrina Lake Road.

1.3 Stay right at the junction with the Lake George Trail.

2.8 Arrive at Blue Lake. (**Option:** Turn around here for a 5.6-mile out-and-back hike.)

3.25 Turn right at the junction with the Donkey Lake Trail.

3.75 Pass the small Emerald Lakes.

4.4 Reach Dingleberry Lake.

5.3 Stay left at the junction with the Midnight Lake Trail.

6.1 Pass Sailor Lake.

6.5 Arrive at Hungry Packer Lake. Return the way you came.

13.0 Arrive back at the trailhead.

77. CLOUDRIPPER LOOP

WHY GO?
A pleasant hike through cool mountain forests leads to a stunning High Sierra loop that connects six lakes under the watchful gaze of the mighty Cloudripper.

THE RUNDOWN

Start: Trailhead at the end of South Lake Road
Distance: 6.7-mile lollipop
Hiking time: 3–4 hours
Difficulty: Moderate
Elevation gain: 1,550 feet
Season: Summer, fall
Trail surface: Packed dirt, rocky
Canine compatibility: Dogs permitted

Fees and permits: None
Land status: John Muir Wilderness, Inyo National Forest
Trail contact: White Mountain Ranger District, 798 North Main St., Bishop 93514; (760) 873-2500; www.fs.usda.gov/main/inyo
Other: Water is available in numerous lakes.

FINDING THE TRAILHEAD

From Bishop on US 395, drive west on CA 168 for 15 miles. Turn left onto South Lake Road and follow it 7.1 miles to the trailhead at the road's end. **Trailhead GPS:** 37°10'9.36"N / 118°33'56.58"W

WHAT TO SEE
The name Cloudripper alone inspires visions of talon-like towers thrusting upward into the clouds, cutting them in two as they pass overhead. In truth, this is not far from reality. The Cloudripper is the highest summit in the imposing Inconsolable Range, one of the numerous subsections of the High Sierra. This range is adjacent to the mighty Palisades, a cluster of 14,000-foot glacier-clad crags just to the south. While the name Inconsolable may sound ominous, the trails at the foot of the range are a hiker's paradise, filled with joyous creeks and shimmering lakes. Rather than casting a gloomy pall over the area, the Inconsolables, through their awe-inspiring ruggedness, make you glad you are alive and able to witness their sublime beauty. The best way to do this is to hike the loop that passes along the base of the Cloudripper. Along the way you will pass six beautiful lakes, each with its unique perspective on the Inconsolable Range, as well as the main expanse of the Sierra Crest, a seemingly ceaseless maze of amazing mountains.

From the large trailhead, the trail heads south, immediately crossing a few small streams. A quick descent leads past a large rocky knob on the right until you near the edge of a ledge and can look out over South Lake. Like its near neighbor, Lake Sabrina, South Lake impounds one of the forks of Bishop Creek. From here the trail makes a climbing

Towering Mount Goode complements the peaceful beauty of Long Lake.

traverse across the slopes above South Lake, passing through aspens that offer a golden glow to this area in fall. As you climb, watch for views of pyramidal Hurd Peak jutting upward above the forest, separate from the rest of the ascendant Sierra Crest visible from South Lake.

In 0.3 mile the trail enters a gully where you say good-bye to the aspens. Cross a stream and make a short climb up to the boundary of the John Muir Wilderness. A little farther on, the trail levels off and arrives at a fork. The path to the right heads to the Treasure Lakes. Go left here, toward Bishop Pass. Most of the hikers on this path are heading there, to cross over into astonishing Dusy Basin in Kings Canyon National Park. If the trail is busy, the traffic will come to an end when you reach the loop section, and you are not likely to see many people.

After the junction, the trail climbs gently through airy forest. As you gain elevation, you pass a few small patches of meadow on your right. These provide just enough distraction that this forested section of the hike does not become monotonous. Pass a spur leading to the Marie Louise Lakes, then immediately afterward cross a small stream. Begin a series of short switchbacks and climb up a steep slope. When the forest opens, look west to spot small, tree-lined Hurd Lake. You continue climbing up the moderate grade until the trail straightens out and you pass into a gully. Near its end you arrive at another fork in the trail. This marks the beginning of the loop section of the hike.

Stay right at the loop and quickly pass a small pond surrounded by meadow. Just a few more steps brings you to the edge of Long Lake, where the grandeur of this sensational mountain landscape is first revealed. Long Lake, which extends south from here for more than 0.6 mile, is lined by lush grass, rocky terrain, and stunted trees. Above this is a wondrous collection of lofty granite peaks where glaciers cling to polished cliffs. The highest and most notable is the thumb-like summit of Mount Goode. It is pure mountain glory. Pause and enjoy this dazzling scene before resuming the hike. Once you have reached Long Lake, the trail follows along its east side. Undulating over rocky knobs and passing little coves, you easily cover a very satisfying section of trail.

Hike next to the lake for 0.5 mile until a small sign marks your arrival at the trail leading up to Ruwau Lake. Leave the Bishop Pass Trail and begin climbing up stairs made of cut wooden logs. It's obvious from the condition of this narrow path that the route to Ruwau Lake does not receive anywhere near the same level of traffic as the one to Bishop Pass. This trail is steep and rocky, but fortunately it does not last long. The climb levels off as you pass a small pocket of meadow and then are deposited on the edge of large, round Ruwau Lake. For the first time on the hike, you get your first good views of the dizzying crags of the Inconsolable Range.

The dark crags of the Cloudripper are an unforgettable sight when hiking past Lower Chocolate Lake.

Follow the path along the willow-choked west side of Ruwau Lake. When you have just about pulled even with a small, rocky island that is home to a few trees, the trail veers left and begins climbing up the steep slope. Like the climb to Ruwau Lake, the trail is narrow and sees little use. Nonetheless, the path is obvious and not hard to follow. As you gain elevation, the stunted trees part and you get incredible views of Mount Goode and the other peaks in the Bishop Pass area. Once again, the climb is short and it does not take too long to arrive at the top of the pass, which is just over 11,300 feet.

Here you finally meet the Cloudripper face-to-face. From the pass a parade of dusky spires march inexorably up to the summit of this august mountain. Even at the great height the trail has reached, the top of the Cloudripper still stands more than 2,000 feet above. However, the great bulk of the mountain seems close enough to touch. Not many trails as moderate as this one offer such intimate exposure to a mountain of this height and stature.

From the pass it is time to begin the return to the Bishop Pass Trail and complete the loop. However, the best section lies ahead. Chocolate Peak, around which the trail loops, lies just to the west. The trail is faint on the pass, but it is not hard to pick up if you stay close to the base of the peak. Cairns usually mark the route, which winds through some boulders and then begins a steep descent to Upper Chocolate Lake. The lake, lying in a large basin at the

The end of the loop features great views of Bull Lake and the high peaks of Thompson Ridge.

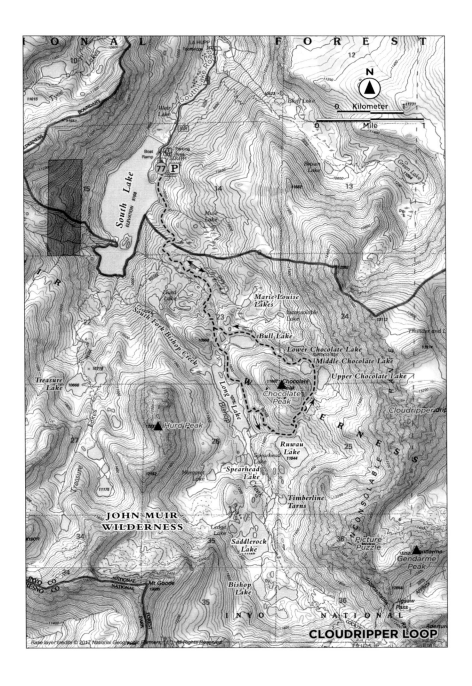

CLOUDRIPPER LOOP

foot of the Cloudripper's massive cliffs, is visible as you scramble down the gravelly track. Use caution as you follow this rough trail. Once you reach the bottom, follow along the edge of the lake to its outlet, where once again you are treated to a great view of the Cloudripper.

Cross Upper Chocolate Lake's outlet and proceed down the trail through a dense riparian area to Middle Chocolate Lake. Here, for the first time, you see the reason for the chocolate moniker. The cliffs on the south side of the lake are a dark red sedimentary intrusion into the typically granite area. The ruddy rock seems out of place in these surroundings. As the path wraps around the west end of Middle Chocolate Lake, you get an opportunity to inspect the deep-red rock more closely. The path then descends a short, rocky slope and crosses the creek at the bottom of a lovely little waterfall. Be sure not to turn right on the path that heads west before crossing the creek. This leads to a good overlook above Lower Chocolate Lake, but the route dead-ends there. Once you have crossed the creek, follow the path over large piles of red talus that has broken loose from the flanks of Chocolate Peak. Descend again to the edge of the lower lake, where there is another magnificent view of the Cloudripper and the ramparts of the Inconsolable Range.

As you leave Lower Chocolate Lake, the creek flows through a narrow gully. The trail follows the water down the steep, rocky channel. As you climb down, there is a fantastic view of Bull Lake below you. Above the lake is the stark expanse of the west side of the South Fork of Bishop Creek's large basin. These mountains are capped by Thompson Peak and the long crest of Thompson Ridge. Reach the lake and follow along its shoreline. The path arcs around to the west end of the lake; just as the path is about to depart the lake, follow a faint track back to the water's edge. Here, amid a grassy lakeshore, is a lovely sandy beach with a perfect view of the Cloudripper and the dark brown summit of Chocolate Peak. It is one of the finest scenes on a hike filled with exceptional scenery. Enjoy it and then walk the short distance back to the junction with the Bishop Pass Trail. From there, retrace the route back to the trailhead.

MILES AND DIRECTIONS

0.0 Start from the trailhead and hike south.

0.8 Bear left at the junction with the Treasure Lakes Trail.

1.7 Stay right at the junction with the Bull Lake/Chocolate Lakes Trail.

2.0 Arrive at Long Lake.

2.5 Turn left onto the trail to Ruwau Lake.

2.9 Arrive at Ruwau Lake.

3.4 Reach the top of the pass between Ruwau and Upper Chocolate Lakes.

3.8 Pass the outlet of Upper Chocolate Lake.

4.6 Arrive at Bull Lake.

5.0 Rejoin the Bishop Pass Trail. Turn right and head back to the trailhead.

6.7 Arrive back at the trailhead.

78. KEARSARGE PASS

WHY GO?

Though it requires a long, steady climb, the hike to Kearsarge Pass passes through an excellent High Sierra basin filled with beautiful lakes. The panorama from the pass is monumental.

THE RUNDOWN

Start: Onion Valley Trailhead
Distance: 9.0 miles out and back to Kearsarge Pass (*Option:* moderate 4.2 miles out and back to Gilbert Lake)
Hiking time: 4-5 hours
Difficulty: Strenuous
Elevation gain: 2,621 feet (Kearsarge Pass)
Season: Summer, fall
Trail surface: Packed dirt, rocky

Canine compatibility: Dogs permitted
Fees and permits: None
Land status: John Muir Wilderness, Inyo National Forest
Trail contact: White Mountain Ranger District, 798 North Main St., Bishop 93514; (760) 873-2500; www .fs.usda.gov/main/inyo
Other: Water is available in numerous lakes.

FINDING THE TRAILHEAD

 From the town of Independence on US 395, drive west on Market Street. In 0.2 mile it becomes Onion Valley Road. Follow the road for 12.4 miles to its end at the Onion Valley Trailhead. **Trailhead GPS:** 36°46'21.04"N / 118°20'28.46"W

WHAT TO SEE

The trail to Kearsarge Pass is one of the primary routes backpackers use to access the remote backcountry of Kings Canyon National Park. The trip is not particularly long, but it maintains a steady grade from the very beginning, climbing relentlessly to the crest of the Sierra Nevada. The journey passes a chain of gorgeous alpine lakes and offers a constantly changing perspective on a collection of extremely rugged mountains. From the top of the pass, visitors are treated to an unfathomably grand panorama of the Sierra Crest and the High Sierra interior of Kings Canyon National Park. Though the trip to the pass is demanding, it is also unforgettable. Hikers looking for a shorter journey would do well to hike up to exquisite Gilbert Lake, which boasts a mighty view of its own. Whichever option you hike, the trip promises tremendous scenery and a lifetime of grand memories.

From the Onion Valley Trailhead, begin hiking to the west. After a very short distance the trail switchbacks to the right and begins the long, unrelenting climb to Kearsarge Pass. Amazingly, despite all the twists and turns of this route, the grade is remarkably even, hardly varying at all over the course of 4.5 miles. At first the trail makes a sweeping traverse to the north. As you climb you can see the ragged cliffs of Kearsarge Peak high overhead. When you arrive at the first switchback, a trail branches off and continues straight to the north. This path leads to Golden Trout Lake, hidden in a high basin below the Sierra Crest. The lake may not be visible, but a nice waterfall on the lake's outlet creek can be seen ahead, tumbling down a high bench below Kearsarge Peak.

The main trail reorients back to the south and makes another long traverse. About 0.7 mile from the trailhead you cross the boundary into the John Muir Wilderness, and the switchbacks start to stack closer together. Watch for the red-barked foxtail pine growing along the trail. Onion Valley is near the northern limit of these handsome trees' range. They grow abundantly in the Southern Sierra, particularly in the Golden Trout Wilderness. They also have a disjunct range far to the north in the Klamath Mountains.

As you climb the switchbacks, the trail nears the creek cascading down the steep slope. After several switchbacks that inched closer to the creek, the path finally comes close enough that you can easily access the cold water. However, the trail turns away again and continues climbing. At 1.4 miles from the trailhead, the trail comes over a rise and you arrive at small Little Pothole Lake. The lake itself is not particularly impressive, but its location is superb. The lake is tucked into a small bowl with steep cliffs above it on two sides, each cliff complemented by a large cascade pouring into the lake. The water flowing down the south side comes from the Matlock Lake Basin; the western cliff is graced by the creek flowing out of the main basin below Kearsarge Pass. For the first time, you catch a glimpse of the summit of formidable University Peak, a mountain that will be a constant presence on the remainder of the hike. A large rock slab above the east shore of

University Peak reflects in the still water of Gilbert Lake.

Pothole Lake fills a rocky basin just below the Sierra Crest near Kearsarge Pass.

the lake offers a good spot to pause and enjoy the view. When it is time to go on, head back to the trail and resume climbing.

The trail continues to switchback above Little Pothole Lake for 0.5 mile before it levels off a little bit. Here the path cuts across a large boulder field. The route leads through a trough in the rocks, where the boulders seem rearranged so that there is a nice, level-bottomed path to follow. On the far side of the rocky area, the trail swings close to the creek and levels off. Though brief, this is the only sustained level section on the entire hike. Just a few steps along the creek bring you to the shore of Gilbert Lake. From the edge of this small lake, you are treated to a spectacular view of the mountains that form the rugged walls of the basin. Splendid University Peak is the highest point on the basin's rim, and it makes a striking impression when viewed from Gilbert Lake. It looks as though the glacier that carved it receded only yesterday and that its freshly scoured pinnacles, spires, and crevices—of which there are many—have only just been revealed to the world. To the west, another daunting series of peaks advance skyward. Particularly noteworthy is the pyramid-shaped peak on the right. Kearsarge Pass lies just north of this peak, and it is prominently visible from the pass, rising above Big Pothole Lake.

Continue on the level path past Gilbert Lake. Just beyond its western shore a trail branches off to the left. This leads south to the Matlock Lake Basin, located at the foot of University Peak. For hikers not interested in climbing all the way to Kearsarge Pass, this is a good option for an exceptional destination beyond Gilbert Lake. Just a short walk from Gilbert Lake is Flower Lake. Though pretty, it is not quite as spectacular as Gilbert Lake, since it is deeper in the rocky bowl, where the lower walls preclude some of the view of the surrounding mountains.

From Flower Lake the trail begins yet another set of switchbacks. The steady climb now takes you up the northern flank of the large basin. As you ascend the broad switchbacks, the forest begins to grow sparser. The elevation is beginning to have an effect on the trees, and you begin to near the elevation near the tree line where trees become stunted. Soon the path straightens out and makes a long push to the west, entering a small valley at the foot of a tall cliff. Below you, on the bottom of this small valley, is a tiny spring-fed pond. A narrow band of riparian vegetation extends from the boulder- and meadow-bound pond, showing the thin line this small amount of water flows in this increasingly harsh environment.

After cutting across the base of the cliff, the trail reaches a ledge where you can look down directly below the trail and observe Heart Lake. Though it looks inviting as it fills an impressive rocky depression, the lake is not easily accessed from the trail. Above the ledge, the trail begins another series of short, very tightly stacked switchbacks. Here the trail climbs a succession of rocky benches, ascending the last few hundred feet before rounding a lip and entering the awesome upper basin below Kearsarge Pass.

For the first time on the hike, you can see the pass itself, as well as the trail making the final leg of the journey up to the Sierra Crest. To get there, follow the trail as it angles to the northwest. It eventually swings back to the east, continues a little farther, and then switchbacks to the west again. As you make a long traverse along the flanks of the upper basin, Big Pothole Lake finally comes into view. The big lake is contained in a large crater that has no outlet. The east side is hemmed in by a high talus dike. The south and west sides are bounded by a fantastically fractured granite wall, with cracks and crevices radiating out in all directions. The fractured cliffs culminate in a tall peak that narrows to

The vast, wild interior of Kings Canyon National Park is a dramatic sight from Kearsarge Pass.

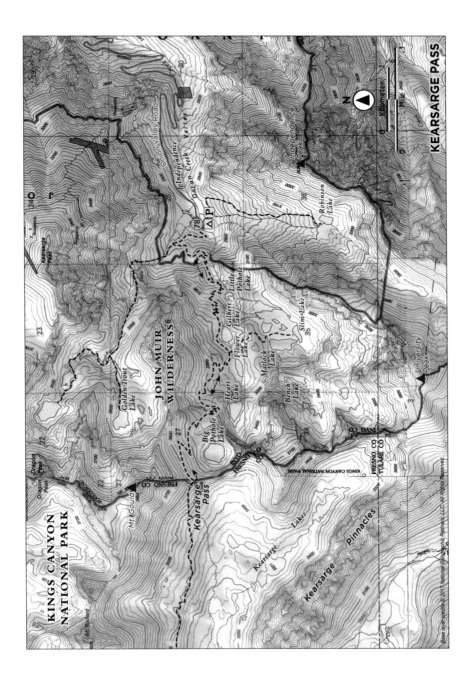

a single, slender finger of rock thrusting upward against the sky. This is the north side of the pyramid-shaped peak observed from the shores of Gilbert Lake.

As you continue to gain elevation on the steady grade, the trail once again turns back east and presses forward. The trees are short and very sparse in the upper basin and offer only very occasional bits of shade. Thankfully you can see the pass and know that you are not far from your destination. Make one final switchback, turning west, and with your goal in sight, make the final push up to the Sierra Crest. Finally, 4.5 miles from the trailhead in Onion Valley, you reach Kearsarge Pass.

When you reach the pass, you are greeted with an utterly transcendent view of the High Sierra. Looking back to the east, at the territory you just passed through, you now get an elevated perspective on the Onion Valley area and its attendant peaks. In the distance the desert peaks of the massive Inyo Mountains can be seen through the gap in the mountains occupied by Onion Valley. Looking north along the line of the Sierra Crest, Big Pothole Lake, the fractured cliffs above it, and a line of rugged peaks lead to stately University Peak.

To the west, however, is truly the highlight of this vantage point atop the Sierra Nevada. Below the pass lies the vast wilderness backcountry of Kings Canyon National Park. Here is the heart of one of the most greatest and most fabled mountain range in America. It is also among the largest unbroken wildlands remaining in the lower forty-eight states. Directly below Kearsarge Pass is a broad valley covered in a patchwork of stunted trees, meadows, and granite terrain. Above the west side of the valley looms a bank of tall, dark towers, the forbidding Kearsarge Pinnacles. At the foot of the pinnacles are the five Kearsarge Lakes. Farther down the valley is large Bullfrog Lake. Above it is the rounded, reddish mound of Mount Bago. Between this peak and the Kearsarge Pinnacles is a gap through which you can discern a deep canyon. This deep trough belongs to Bubbs Creek, which flows west to its confluence with the Kings River near Kanawyers and Mist Falls, nearly 10 miles and a world away. Crowning this sublime vision is the apogee of the Great Western Divide, including its highpoint, Mount Brewer, as well as South Guard, North Guard, Mount Farquhar, and Cross Mountain. It is a superb meeting of earth and heavens. At long last, after sitting atop the pass and soaking in this incredible view, you must abandon the post and return to the trailhead.

MILES AND DIRECTIONS

0.0 Start from the Onion Valley Trailhead and begin climbing promptly.

1.4 Pass Little Pothole Lake

2.1 Reach the edge of Gilbert Lake. (*Option:* Turn around here for the shorter 4.2-mile option.)

2.4 Pass the trail leading to Matlock Lake.

3.6 Enter the upper basin.

4.5 Reach Kearsarge Pass. Return the way you came.

9.0 Arrive back at the trailhead.

79. COTTONWOOD LAKES

WHY GO?

This memorable hike leads to the southernmost major lake basin in the High Sierra and the John Muir Wilderness. Large forests of attractive foxtail pine line the trail that leads to extensive alpine meadows and numerous lakes, all within the gaze of 14,000-foot Mount Langley.

THE RUNDOWN

Start: Horseshoe Meadow Trailhead
Distance: 10.7 miles out and back
Hiking time: 5–7 hours
Difficulty: Moderate
Elevation gain: 1,100 feet
Season: Summer, fall
Trail surface: Packed dirt, rocky, duff
Canine compatibility: Dogs permitted
Fees and permits: None

Land status: John Muir Wilderness, Inyo National Forest
Trail contact: Mount Whitney Ranger District, 640 South Main St., Lone Pine 93545; (760) 876-6200; www.fs.usda.gov/main/inyo
Other: Water is available at the trailhead, in Cottonwood Creek, and in the Cottonwood Lakes.

FINDING THE TRAILHEAD

From Lone Pine on US 395, drive west on Whitney Portal Road for 3.1 miles. Turn right onto Horseshoe Meadow Road and proceed on this steep, winding paved road for 19.2 miles. Turn right onto the signed road for the Horseshoe Meadow Campground and the trailhead. **Trailhead GPS:** 36°27'11.38"N / 118°10'12.19"W

WHAT TO SEE

The Cottonwood Lakes are among the last major lake basins of the High Sierra. They occupy the very southernmost corner of the John Muir Wilderness's long finger that extends south from Mammoth Lakes to the Golden Trout Wilderness. This large collection of lakes is nestled beneath the high cliffs of Mount Langley, the Sierra Nevada's southernmost 14,000-foot peak. When you hike here, you may sense that you are hiking at the edge of something massive and final. This may come from the perception that the Cottonwood Lakes are near the end of the High Sierra or that the gentler terrain near the trailhead is how things appear as you move south toward the southern end of the Sierra Nevada. Whatever you perceive, the one inescapable fact is that the hike to the Cottonwood Lakes is a gorgeous journey.

In many ways the Cottonwood Lakes have more in common with the adjacent Golden Trout Wilderness and the southern reaches of the Sierra Nevada. One of the most notable similarities is the presence of foxtail pine, a tree found in small pockets of the Eastern Sierra but in much greater numbers in the Golden Trout Wilderness (as well as in the Klamath Mountains in far northwest California). The terrain is more subdued as well, with the more open, rolling topography of the Kern Plateau replacing the towering peaks and great canyons of the High Sierra. The hike to the Cottonwood Lakes encapsulates the transition from High Sierra to Kern Plateau. The trip begins in the Golden Trout Wilderness, travels easily through great stands of foxtail pine, and then climbs up to the high alpine basin of the Cottonwood Lakes, where Mount Langley and Cirque Peak welcome hikers into the splendor of the John Muir Wilderness.

The hike begins at the Horseshoe Meadow Trailhead. Though the hike does not pass Horseshoe Meadow, it is worth noting that this nearby feature is in keeping with the pattern found throughout the Golden Trout Wilderness. Similar meadows, situated in low, flat-bottomed valleys, are scattered all over the east side of the Kern Plateau. The path strikes out to the west, passing through open stands of lodgepole and foxtail pine. You promptly reach a large sign welcoming you into the Golden Trout Wilderness before the trail swings to the north and drops down into the wide valley drained by Cottonwood Creek. The trail cuts through the sandy terrain as it descends the side of the valley. In about 1.4 miles from the trailhead, the path nears the South Fork of Cottonwood Creek. This creek originates in the South Fork Lakes, which are located at the base of tall Cirque Peak in a basin adjacent to the Cottonwood Lakes. The trail crosses the creek on a log bridge and then continues to the north.

The sounds of the creek fade as you hike north through the forest, leaving the creek on its journey down to the dry bed of Owens Lake. However, the route soon pulls near the main fork of Cottonwood Creek. This branch, larger than the South Fork, empties the Cottonwood Lakes' basin. The route climbs a little, but it is not taxing, and you can

Cirque Peak and 1st Cottonwood Lake mark the southern end of the John Muir Wilderness.

Numerous tarns are scattered around the meadow beneath Mount Langley, the southernmost 14er in the Sierra Nevada.

make steady progress through this vast forest. Fortunately, the presence of Cottonwood Creek is refreshing, even if you are not hiking directly adjacent to it. It is always audible and breaks the monotony that can set in during this part of the hike. At 2.2 miles the trail pulls close to the creek. On the far side there is a complex of small meadows, where some rugged crags rise above the creek's valley.

Beyond the small meadows, the trail continues. Watch for more grassy breaks in the forest ahead. Note the narrow ribbon of fence line that subtly cordons off this section of the forest. This is part of Golden Trout Camp, which is operated by the Golden Trout Wilderness School. At 2.8 miles you pass a sign that marks the passage from the Golden Trout into the John Muir Wilderness. Take heart, knowing you are nearing the Cottonwood Lakes. Shortly after the wilderness boundary, you arrive at a log bridge that spans Cottonwood Creek. As you cross the water, watch for small golden trout darting through the water. The Cottonwood Lakes are not part of the original home of these fish (the official freshwater fish of California), but they were transplanted there early and the lakes were used as a reserve for the fish. The fish have thrived in Cottonwood Creek's watershed and are often visible as you cross the bridge.

Once you cross the creek, the trail begins to climb at a steeper grade, though it is still easy going. To the left you can see another meadow that is well watered by Cottonwood Creek. The sound of the racing water is welcome as you head up the hill. At 0.5 mile from the creek crossing, you arrive at a fork. Going left here continues along Cottonwood Creek and ultimately leads to Cottonwood Lake No. 1 and the South Fork Lakes. Instead, stay to the right and begin the steep climb out of Cottonwood Creek's valley. The climb is fairly steep but does not last too long. A little effort finally brings you over a lip and to the edge of an expansive meadow, where an awesome vista is revealed.

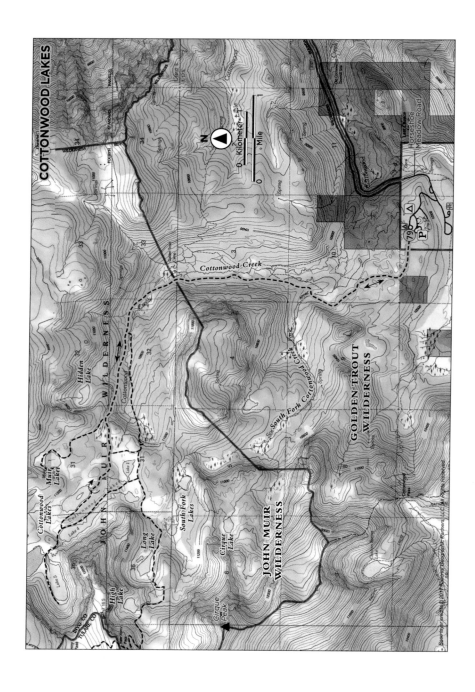

When you arrive at the edge of the meadow, you get your first taste of the stunning view of Mount Langley crowning the bank of cliffs that line the north end of the Cottonwood Lakes Basin. The cliffs, composed of glaciated white granite, are classic High Sierra scenery. Mount Langley, the rounded summit just above the cliffs, is not only the southernmost 14,000-foot peak in the Sierra Nevada but also in the entire United States. The grand sight is good reward for the climb, but it is not the end of the hike. When you first arrive at the meadow, another trail leaves to the right. This is the path to Muir Lake. Skip this route, stay left, and continue west. The trail passes just above the meadow. While Mount Langley grabs your attention immediately, don't neglect Cirque Peak. This is one of the final major peaks of the High Sierra and is impressive in its own right.

Near the end of the meadow, a spur branches off to the left and heads toward Cottonwood Lake No. 1, which you can see just off the trail. Press on past the lake, pass through one last band of forest, and then arrive at another meadow. Small streams can be heard flowing through deep channels in the lush grass. Mount Langley gazes down as the trail skirts the edge of the meadows. The trail turns to the north, where you arrive at a series of small lakes and ponds. When the wind is still, the ponds provide good reflections of the towering mountain and crags. This is roughly in the center of the Cottonwood Lakes Basin and makes a good jumping-off point for exploring the other lakes, all of which lie close by. Each has its own distinct personality, and all are beautiful. If you simply want to stop here and enjoy the grand view of Mount Langley, there are plenty of grassy spots and large rocks to sit on. Whatever you decide, when it is time to depart, bid farewell to the High Sierra and return the way you came.

MILES AND DIRECTIONS

0.0   Start from the Horseshoe Meadow Trailhead.

1.4   Cross the South Fork of Cottonwood Creek.

2.8   Enter the John Muir Wilderness.

3.1   Cross Cottonwood Creek.

3.6   Stay right at a trail junction and begin climbing steeply.

4.5   Arrive at the edge of the meadows that cover the Cottonwood Lakes Basin.

5.35 Reach the center of the Cottonwood Lakes Basin. Numerous lakes await exploration from this point. To return, follow the route back to the trailhead.

10.7 Arrive back at the trailhead.

80. ALABAMA HILLS

WHY GO?

This trip is an adventure in hunting natural rock arches hidden in the rocky hinterland of the Alabama Hills. Off-trail exploration is encouraged among the rocks, where there are excellent views of the Sierra Nevada.

THE RUNDOWN

Start: See individual hikes.
Distance: 0.7-mile loop (Mobius Arch); 0.3 mile out and back (Eye of Alabama); 1.3 miles out and back (Whitney Portal Arch)
Hiking time: Variable
Difficulty: Easy
Elevation gain: Minimal
Season: Year-round
Trail surface: Packed dirt, rocky, rock slabs, sand, cross-country

Canine compatibility: Dogs permitted
Fees and permits: None
Land status: Alabama Hills Recreation Lands, Bureau of Land Management
Trail contact: Bishop Field Office, 351 Pacu Ln., Suite 100, Bishop 93514; (760) 872-5000; www.blm.gov
Other: No water is available.

Trailhead GPS: Varied—see individual hikes.

WHAT TO SEE

Making your way south through the Sierra Nevada, you travel through a world of soaring alpine mountains. As you reach the southern section of the range, the great deserts of Southern California make their presence felt. This is especially true at the foot of the mountains, where the mighty eastern palisade of the Sierra plunges steeply to the flat floor of the Owens Valley. At the southern end of the valley, two great desert environments, the Great Basin and the Mojave Deserts, meet. The arid environment prevails in the interior of the valley, strikingly different from the land of ice and rock in the mountains above. Perhaps the best place in Northern California to experience the desert is in the Alabama Hills beneath the watchful gaze of Mount Whitney, the tallest peak in the coterminous United States. Here the great mountain range of Northern California is still a powerful presence, but the desert also makes its influence felt.

Anyone who has made the drive from Lone Pine to Whitney Portal or Horseshoe Meadow is familiar with the Alabama Hills. Lying just west of Lone Pine's downtown area, the Alabama Hills are a surreal landscape of heavily weathered brown granite domes, slabs, pinnacles, and boulders. The majestic eastern escarpment of the Sierra Nevada towering regally above the russet-colored rocks is both an iconic and unforgettable vista.

Even those who have not visited the Alabama Hills will likely still recognize them from some of the more than 400 movies that have been filmed here. For almost one hundred years, Hollywood productions have been using the Alabama Hills and the magnificent backdrop of the Sierra Nevada as a film setting. From John Wayne and Clint Eastwood Westerns to science-fiction movies such as *Star Trek* and *Iron Man*, the spectacular setting of the Alabama Hills has been used to imbue the films with a powerful visual flair.

The Alabama Hills are not just a scenic location. They are also a fascinating geologic area. Most notably, the hills have an incredible number of naturally occurring stone arches. Hundreds have been documented in the wilderness of rocks in the interior of the Alabama Hills. Worn into the rock by wind and the expansion and contraction of ice, the process is ongoing; new arches are being formed as old ones weather away.

Exploring the Alabama Hills is a classic Eastern Sierra rite. There are not many established trails here. Nonetheless, the open terrain and low rocks are perfect for exploration. Indeed, venturing into the craggy expanse is one of the chief delights of this area, and hikers are encouraged to get out and explore. Arches make a good reason to roam this area, but the ruggedly beautiful hills and the awe-inspiring views of the Sierra are reason enough in themselves. This description provides directions to three arches, each with varying degrees of developed access trails. The final description merely leads to a jumping-off point where the backcountry has an unusually high concentration of arches waiting to be discovered. Despite the beauty and adventure that awaits, be cautious in the hills. Rattlesnakes call this area home, and cacti, especially cholla, are common throughout the rocks and desert expanses.

MOBIUS ARCH

Named for its appearance, similar to the one-sided plane known as a Möbius strip, this is the most famous arch in the Alabama Hills and the only one accessed by a regularly maintained trail. The arch is well known for its perfect framing of Mount Whitney.

FINDING THE TRAILHEAD

From Lone Pine on US 395, drive west on Whitney Portal Road for 2.7 miles. Turn right onto Movie Flat Road. Proceed down this dirt road for 1.6 miles. When the road reaches a T, veer right and look for the large parking area on the north side of the road.

The Hike

The hike to the Mobius Arch is a loop that has two separate starting points at the same trailhead. Begin at the western path and drop down into a dry wash. Three trails split here. The two on the right both go to the Mobius Arch. The other is a long trail through the desert. The middle trail is the most direct. Follow this trail for 0.2 mile until it turns east. Pass a large rocky area on your right containing the small but awesome Lathe Arch before dropping down and finding the Mobius Arch above you on the right. There are numerous ways to scramble up to the arch and wonder at the awesome view visible through it.

Mount Whitney framed by the Mobius Arch in the Alabama Hills

When you are ready to continue, follow the trail past the arch. Consider venturing into the area to the north, where there are more arches hidden among the rocks. The trail drops down into another dry wash before continuing east. As the path bends south, the views of the Inyo Mountains rising above the east side of the Owens Valley are dramatic. Not far from the Mobius Arch, the trail splits. The route to the left leads to an alternative trailhead. Stay right and follow the trail through a narrow gap in the rock. Watch for little hollows that have formed in the rock, as well as some tunnels that kids can crawl through. Above this section of trail is the Heart Arch, but it is best viewed at the end of the hike, when the perspective has shifted enough to make it actually look like a heart. The trail then descends some well-built stone steps into the dry wash crossed at the beginning of the loop and then climbs back up to the trailhead. Be sure to look back and observe the Heart Arch from here.

THE EYE OF ALABAMA
Visible from the Mobius Arch loop, the Eye of Alabama is one of the few large arches that can be seen from Movie Flat Road. The short hike to the arch takes you close to the large, impressive collection of crags in the northeastern corner of the Alabama Hills.

The Whitney Portal Arch points the way to the unparalleld beauty of the Sierra Nevada.

rocky terrain a little easier. When you get to the top, climb behind the arch for a stunning view of the finest mountains in the world.

EAST MOVIE FLAT ARCH AREA

There are no established trails in this area, but there is an incredible collection of arches. These are easy to find for anyone willing to scramble through the crags of the Alabama Hills. This rewarding endeavor is really the heart of what the Alabama Hills offer: the chance to get out on your own, to explore, to guess, and to discover, all while gazing up at the mighty Sierra Nevada.

FINDING THE TRAILHEAD

From Lone Pine on US 395, drive west on Whitney Portal Road for 2.7 miles. Turn right onto Movie Flat Road. Proceed down this dirt road for 0.2 mile and turn right onto a dirt road. Follow the dirt road, part of a web of dirt roads, north to the base of the rocks. The arches are hidden in the interior of these rocks, with many easily accessible to the northeast.

LOCAL TRAIL FINDER

	GREAT VIEWS	MEADOWS/WILDFLOWERS	PEAK BAGGERS	LAKES	RIVERS AND CREEKS	WATERFALLS	CANYONS	REMARKABLE TREES	INTERESTING GEOLOGY	HISTORY BUFFS	BACKPACKERS	KIDS	HIKEABLE OFFSEASON
SOUTH COAST RANGE													
1. Ewoldsen Trail/McWay Falls	•				•	•		•					•
2. Pfeiffer Falls						•		•				•	•
3. Andrew Molera State Park	•	•						•	•				•
4. Pinnacles	•								•				•
5. Big Basin					•	•		•			•		•
6. Sunol Regional Wilderness		•			•				•			•	•
7. Mount Diablo Grand Loop	•		•						•				•
NORTH COAST RANGE													
8. Alamere Falls				•		•			•				•
9. Sonoma Coast	•		•					•	•				•
10. Palisades (Napa Valley)	•								•	•			•
11. Snow Mountain	•		•								•		
12. Russian Gulch					•	•	•	•				•	•
13. Lost Coast									•	•	•		
14. James Irvine Trail/Fern Canyon					•		•	•	•				
15. Boy Scout Tree					•	•		•				•	•
KLAMATH MOUNTAINS													
16. Devil's Punchbowl	•			•				•			•		
17. North Yolla Bolly Mountains	•	•	•	•							•		

	GREAT VIEWS	MEADOWS/WILDFLOWERS	PEAK BAGGERS	LAKES	RIVERS AND CREEKS	WATERFALLS	CANYONS	REMARKABLE TREES	INTERESTING GEOLOGY	HISTORY BUFFS	BACKPACKERS	KIDS	HIKEABLE OFFSEASON
KLAMATH MOUNTAINS—CONTINUED													
18. Canyon Creek	•	•		•	•	•	•			•	•		
19. Bear Lakes	•			•	•						•		
20. Gulck Lakes Loop				•	•						•		
21. Taylor and Hogan Lakes	•			•							•	•	
22. Shackleford Basin	•	•		•	•						•		
23. Mount Eddy	•	•	•	•	•				•	•	•		
24. Heart Lake	•			•									
CASCADE RANGE													
25. South Gate Meadow	•	•				•			•				
26. McCloud River Falls					•	•	•					•	•
27. Lava Beds									•	•		•	•
28. Pine Creek Basin/Patterson Lake	•	•		•					•		•		
29. Susan River					•		•		•	•		•	•
30. Thousand Lakes Wilderness	•		•	•					•		•		
31. Lassen Peak	•		•						•				
32. Warner Valley		•				•			•	•		•	
33. Butte Lake-Snag Lake Loop				•					•		•		
34. Caribou Wilderness				•							•	•	
SACRAMENTO VALLEY													
35. Iron Canyon	•				•		•			•		•	•
36. Orland Buttes	•	•	•						•			•	•

	GREAT VIEWS	MEADOWS/WILDFLOWERS	PEAK BAGGERS	LAKES	RIVERS AND CREEKS	WATERFALLS	CANYONS	REMARKABLE TREES	INTERESTING GEOLOGY	HISTORY BUFFS	BACKPACKERS	KIDS	HIKEABLE OFFSEASON
NORTHERN SIERRA													
37. Independence Trail/Jones Hole Loop					•		•			•		•	•
38. Feather Falls						•	•						•
39. Bucks Lake Wilderness	•			•							•		
40. Frazier Falls						•						•	
41. Lakes Basin	•			•	•								
42. Sierra Buttes	•		•	•						•			
43. Glacier Lake	•			•							•		
44. Five Lakes Basin				•							•		
45. Rubicon Trail				•					•	•			
46. Twin Lakes (Desolation Wilderness)	•	•		•	•	•					•		
47. Desolation Valley	•	•		•							•		
CENTRAL SIERRA													
48. Meiss Meadow/Showers Lake	•	•		•	•				•		•		
49. Round Top Loop	•	•		•	•								
50. Wheeler Lake				•							•		
51. Noble Lake	•	•		•					•		•		
52. Sword Lake				•					•		•		
53. Burst Rock and Lake Valley	•	•		•						•	•		
54. Blue Canyon	•	•		•	•		•		•				
55. Sardine Falls		•				•	•					•	
56. Leavitt Meadow Loop	•	•		•	•						•		

	GREAT VIEWS	MEADOWS/WILDFLOWERS	PEAK BAGGERS	LAKES	RIVERS AND CREEKS	WATERFALLS	CANYONS	REMARKABLE TREES	INTERESTING GEOLOGY	HISTORY BUFFS	BACKPACKERS	KIDS	HIKEABLE OFFSEASON
WESTERN SIERRA													
57. Hetch Hetchy						•				•	•	•	
58. Panorama Trail	•				•	•	•		•				
59. Tuolumne River to Glen Aulin	•	•			•	•	•				•		
60. Gaylor Lakes	•			•						•			
61. San Joaquin River Gorge		•			•						•		•
62. Twin Lakes (Kaiser Wilderness)		•		•	•						•	•	
63. Dinkey Lakes	•	•		•	•						•		
64. Redwood Mountain Loop								•					
65. Weaver Lake				•	•						•	•	
66. Mist Falls	•				•	•	•					•	
67. Tokopah Valley	•				•	•	•					•	
68. White Chief Basin	•	•			•				•		•		
EASTERN SIERRA													
69. Green Creek Basin	•			•	•						•		
70. Lundy Canyon	•	•			•	•	•				•	•	
71. Devil's Postpile/Rainbow Falls					•	•			•			•	
72. Thousand Island Lake	•			•	•	•	•		•		•		
73. Duck Lake Pass	•			•							•		
74. Convict Canyon	•				•	•		•	•		•		
75. Little Lakes Valley	•	•		•	•						•		
76. Sabrina Basin	•			•	•						•		
77. Cloudripper Loop	•			•							•		
78. Kearsarge Pass	•			•		•	•	•	•		•		
79. Cottonwood Lakes	•	•		•	•				•		•		
80. Alabama Hills	•								•	•		•	•

HIKE INDEX

FINDING THE TRAILHEAD

From Lone Pine on US 395, drive west on Whitney Portal Road for 2.7 miles. Turn right onto Movie Flat Road. Proceed down this dirt road for 2.3 miles to a small pullout on the right, big enough for 1 or 2 cars.

The Hike

From the pullout on the side of Movie Flat Road, follow the old dirt road up the steep slope. The road is blocked off to prevent motor vehicles from using it. After climbing for about 150 yards, veer right, walking past some rocks placed to line the old road. Look for a well-established use trail that crosses the sandy terrain and then climbs over a granite rib. From the rib, cross a gully where the path splits. Both options lead to the arch, but the one to the right is more direct. Stay right and skirt the bottom of a large outcropping. Follow the path as it turns uphill and climb a little ways. On your left, watch for a cleft in the rock with a rocky ramp climbing into it. If you are comfortable with rock scrambling, make the easy climb up the ramp. From there you can look through the Eye of Alabama. It does not neatly frame other landmarks in the area but, true to its name, does have an ocular shape.

WHITNEY PORTAL ARCH

This awesome arch is located at the western end of the Alabama Hills and affords an incredible view of Mount Whitney and the rest of the escarpment of the Eastern Sierra. Sunrise from this spot is phenomenal.

FINDING THE TRAILHEAD

From Lone Pine on US 395, drive west on Whitney Portal Road for 5.2 miles. Turn right onto a short dirt road that immediately arrives at a parking area next to a fence. If you pass Olivas Ranch Road, you have gone too far.

The Hike

From the parking area alongside Whitney Portal Road, follow the fence line to a crossing over Lone Pine Creek. Once a lush riparian zone, a fire has turned the creek channel into a collection of ghostly snags. Scramble down to the creek and hop across before climbing back up the other side. From there a well-established trail heads off to the northwest. Unfortunately, this is not the route to the arch. Continue for only 100 yards or so before bearing right and going cross-country toward the main block of the Alabama Hills on the right. When you reach a dry wash, turn left and follow it to the northwest. Be sure not to cross the wash, since the terrain is much easier to negotiate on the south side. Continue for 0.2 mile until you see a large, fist-shaped crag at the base of the Alabama Hills on the opposite side of the wash, rising out of the channel. Head down into the dry gully and pass the crag. From there, scramble out of the wash and continue along the base of the rocks to the east. Watch for a use trail that gets more obvious as you continue toward an amphitheater in the rock. Once you find it, you can follow the narrow path up into the amphitheater toward the arch. The arch is visible from the trail, making navigation of the

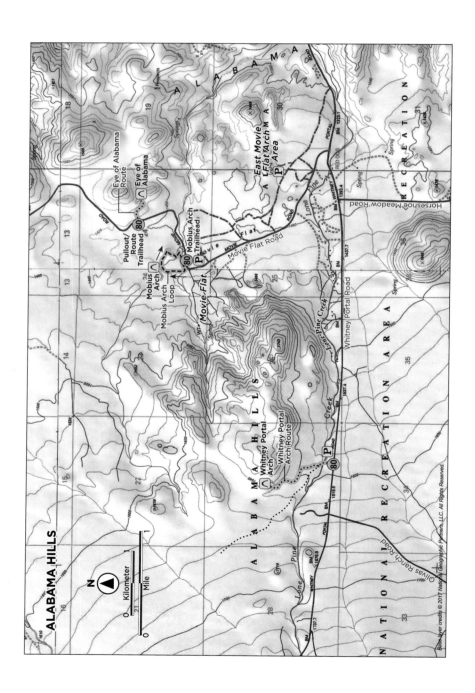